...p of England in Queen ...s time, showing county ...es and principal towns, ...n in 1590 by the Dutch ...her Jodocus Hondius. In ...s are depicted an English ... and noblewoman and ...to-do London citizens. ...der decorations represent some of the varied activities for which the age was noted: warfare and literature, farming and commerce, ocean-voyaging and music.

Elizabethan England

ELIZABETHAN ENGLAND
was edited and designed by
The Reader's Digest Association Limited,
London

Editor
Michael Worth Davison, MA
Art Editor
Gay Burdett

First edition
Copyright © 1982
The Reader's Digest Association Limited,
Berkeley Square House, Berkeley Square,
London W1X 6AB
Reprinted with amendments 1993

Copyright © 1982
Reader's Digest Association
Far East Limited
Philippines Copyright © 1982
Reader's Digest Association
Far East Limited

Printed in Great Britain

Reader's Digest

LIFE IN BRITAIN

Elizabethan England

LIFE IN AN AGE OF ADVENTURE

Alison Plowden

PUBLISHED BY
THE READER'S DIGEST ASSOCIATION LIMITED
LONDON · NEW YORK · MONTREAL · SYDNEY · CAPE TOWN

Contents

Foreword

BY A. L. ROWSE

I T IS AN HONOUR TO COMMEND THE WORK OF AN EXCELLENT AND DISCERNING scholar who bears an Elizabethan name, descendant of a famous lawyer in that age, one of the Founder's kin of All Souls College, Oxford. In her depiction of social life Alison Plowden has an advantage over male historians in her instinct for the kind of detail that brings the age vividly before us. I did not know, for instance, that at Elizabeth I's accession the landing of crimson silk at the port of London was held up until the Queen had taken her pick for the coronation; or that 'cloth of gold', of which her shining new litter was made, was material woven of yellow silk one way and gold thread the other. It is the detail that is important and brings things home to us, not sociological theorising; sociology is one thing, social history another.

It is the keynote, and the quality, of this book that it brings back to us what it was like to have lived in that age, to which the most successful of women rulers has bequeathed her name. We are given a very fair, balanced and dependable picture of Elizabethan life, from that scintillating Renaissance Court downwards through the various grades of society and outwards across the land. Town and country, schools and universities; trade and labour in the fields; housing, fairs and customs, folk ways of all kinds; music and dancing; health, medicine and science, or what passed for such; navigation, overseas exploration; religion and popular beliefs: all these are here – facets of that inspiriting time when a small people of only five million began to make such a mark in history. 'We are a people such as mend upon the world,' wrote William Shakespeare: they were on their way up through the virtues of individual initiative, energy released and rewarded, guided and inspired by a very keen and incisive intelligence at the top. The Queen herself constantly appealed to the motive of renown – leaving a name to be remembered for what one achieved.

It is difficult to describe briefly all that the age owed to that memorable woman, to define precisely what her contribution was. Everyone had to agree at the time on the remarkable success of her rule, her political sense amounting to genius at her job – her most eloquent admirer was her grand opponent, Pope Sixtus V himself. A worldly woman, she was in touch with so many sides of life illustrated in this book – not only politics, her chief concern and duty, but society. Though not a very religious woman, she had a good conscience, upright and moral, attentive to the interests of religion, trying to achieve consensus and make it work. She set good standards at her Court; in fact she was more like a Mistress of Newnham – her education was Cambridge-inspired – than the modern media, films and plays, are apt to suggest.

Elizabeth I loved theatre – and we owe the Shakespearean stage in part to her protection. The more puritan sourpusses of the City, and increasingly the town corporations, would have suppressed the theatre if they could – and, after the monarchy was defeated in the Civil War, they eventually did. She loved music and dancing, ceremony and the arts, and the progresses around the countryside depicted here, which enabled her to keep in touch with real life and see for herself how things were getting on.

So the adulation she received from the poets and painters was genuine: her personality was an inspiration to them as to her people at large. Some male historians – the great J. A. Froude among them – have failed to appreciate this: they thought that all the success was due to the men around her, shrewd and hardworking as they were. William and Robert Cecil, the great Lord Burghley and his son, Sir Nicholas Bacon and Sir Francis Walsingham, themselves knew better.

It is a great advantage, and a help to bringing it all alive, to have appropriate and telling illustrations to interpret them for us. I have always been keen on the visual approach to history, and often enough been disappointed in the lack of visual sense and sensibility in academic historians. Not so here – and of course historians of genius such as Macaulay, Carlyle, Froude and Trevelyan have all had it. Macaulay used to take a notebook to the places that came into his history and describe them as they lay under his eye. Here the gazetteer provides a useful guide to enable readers to seek out Tudor buildings still with us, and help them to re-create the age by seeing some of the places referred to in the body of the book.

A. L. Rowse

CHAPTER ONE

A Queen is crowned

AMID STATE CEREMONY AND PUBLIC REJOICING
A 25-YEAR-OLD GIRL INHERITS THE THRONE, TO FACE THE PROBLEMS
OF A BANKRUPT AND DIVIDED NATION

Symbols of power, and a token of marriage to England
*In sumptuous robes (left) Elizabeth made her triumphant Recognition Procession through the streets of London on
the eve of her coronation. On her wedding ring finger she wears the coronation ring, the
token of her symbolic marriage to all her husbands, 'the good people of England'. This ring never left her
finger until a few weeks before her death, when it was found to be growing into the
flesh and had to be cut away. The coronation portrait was the model for numerous charter and manuscript
illuminations (above), which were intended not as likenesses of the
Queen but as stylised representations of a goddess-like personage, invested with the symbols of royal power.*

O peerless sovereign Queen,
        Behold what this thy town
Hath thee presented with,
        At thy first entrance here . . .
. . . God thee preserve we pray,
        And wish thee ever well.   Anon

*T*he Queen and the Privy Council, in consultation with John Dee – mathematician, astrologer and, some said, wizard – had settled on Sunday, January 15, 1559 as being the most auspicious day for her coronation. It was always good policy to get a new monarch crowned and anointed as soon as possible after the accession, but at the same time it meant that the royal officials responsible for the preparations had to work fast, and the moment the date had been fixed the various departments under the Lord Steward, the Lord Chamberlain and the Treasurer of the Household moved into action.

Everyone connected with the Court, from the Queen herself down to Will Somers the jester, Joan Hilton the laundress and William Toothe the royal fishmonger had to be fitted out with new clothes, and an order went down from the Privy Council to the customs officers at the Port of London to stop the landing of all crimson-coloured silk until the Queen had taken her pick 'for the furniture of her coronation'. Meanwhile, the officials of the Wardrobe were hurrying round the warehouses of the City merchants buying all the rich materials they could find, and Sir Richard Sackville the Under-Treasurer paid out nearly £4,000 to William Chelsham, mercer, for cloth of gold, cloth of silver, crimson cloth of gold, velvet and satin.

Other items on the shopping list included 672 oz. of gold and silver spangles for trimming the guards' coats, and 700 yds of blue cloth to make a carpet from Westminster Hall to the choir door of the Abbey (the bill for that came to £145). New tabards were needed for 17 trumpeters, and the gorgeous coats of the Kings of Arms and their attendant heralds and pursuivants cost £255. Even a shillingsworth of cottonwool 'to dry up the oil after the Queen's anointing' was carefully entered in Sir Richard Sackville's accounts.

No expense was being spared to make this a truly splendid occasion. The great Officers of State were to have crimson velvet gowns, with crimson satin for the Privy Councillors. The 18 henchmen riding in the royal procession would be wearing cloth of gold, with red, white and yellow ostrich plumes in their helmets; while the ladies attending on the Queen were each given 16 yds of velvet for a gown and 2 yds of plain cloth of gold for turning up their sleeves. A magnificent new litter, covered with yellow cloth of gold (material woven of yellow silk one way and gold thread the other) and lined with white satin, was being made for the Queen, and the Surveyor of Works had ordered supplies of

The young Elizabeth
Elizabeth Tudor was 13¼ years old when Henry VIII died. This portrait, possibly marking her fourteenth birthday, shows the studious young lady whose 'maiden shamefastness' was commended by the sober Protestant clergymen who frequented her brother Edward's Court.

The Great Seal
Used to authenticate state documents, the Great Seal was kept in the custody of the Lord Chancellor, or Lord Keeper of the Great Seal. He was the highest judicial functionary of the realm, and was also said to be the keeper of the monarch's conscience.

timber from Windsor and the New Forest for the extra seating which would be needed for the congregation in the Abbey. London hummed with activity as an army of craftsmen and craftswomen – carpenters, scene-painters, tailors, seamstresses, embroiderers, skinners, upholsterers and harness-makers – worked day and night to get everything ready.

The ceremonial of a coronation in Tudor times was divided into four parts, spread over several days. First, the new sovereign had to take formal possession of the Tower of London – the principal fortress of the realm. Then came the great Recognition Procession back through the City streets to the Palace of Westminster; this was a deliberate piece of showmanship, designed to impress the populace with the power and grandeur of the monarchy and to give as many people as possible an opportunity of seeing their new monarch. The third stage was the coronation ceremony itself, and the festivities ended with an elaborate, medieval-style banquet in Westminster Hall.

London's royal route
The Recognition Procession which preceded the coronation of a Tudor monarch started from the Tower of London, then passed over Tower Hill to Cornhill, via Fenchurch Street, along Cheapside to St Paul's, down Ludgate Hill into Fleet Street and on to Temple Bar. Here Elizabeth left the City boundary, passed the church of St Clement Danes on its island site (on the right in this map drawn in 1593) and continued

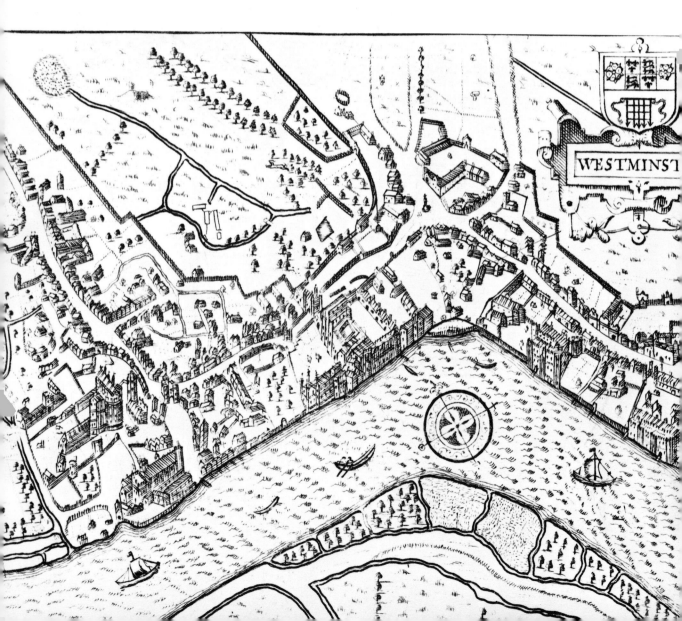

along the Strand to Charing Cross. Here the royal procession turned left through the Holbein Gate and King's Gate into King Street (modern Whitehall) and past Whitehall Palace. At last the Queen reached the Palace of Westminster, clustered around its great Abbey (extreme left). Between the Abbey and the river are Westminster Hall, the home of the law courts, and St Stephen's Chapel, where Parliament met. Across the river are Lambeth marshes.

Queen Elizabeth came to the Tower on Thursday, January 12. She travelled by river from Whitehall in the royal barge, surrounded by her Court and escorted by the Lord Mayor and Aldermen, with representatives of all the 'crafts', or livery companies, of the City of London in barges decorated with streamers and banners emblazoned with their arms. The noise of artillery being shot off from the mercers' barge mingled with the melody made by numerous bands of musicians; an Italian observer was reminded of the scene at Venice on Ascension Day, when the Doge and Signory go out to celebrate their city's mystic marriage with the sea.

In triumph through the City

The 'march' through London took place two days later. At about 2 p.m. the procession, headed by the lesser officials of the household, began to emerge from the gates of the Tower of London and make its ponderous way over Tower Hill towards Fenchurch Street, while the guns of the fortress crashed in salute. After the Gentlemen Ushers came the Aldermen of London, and then the chaplains and clerks. Next followed the legal profession and the judges in their scarlet and ermine walking two by two. Then came the knights and barons, the nobility and the bishops – the lords temporal and spiritual, all in their proper order. After them walked the great officers of the government and the household, followed by Garter King of Arms, the Lord Mayor, the Lord Treasurer, Lord Keeper of the Great Seal, and the Secretaries of State.

At last, behind all these imposing and important personages in their velvet and satin, their crimson and scarlet and blue, their furs and jewels and chains of office, came the Queen herself, riding aloft in her golden palanquin carried by two horses, with a canopy of crimson velvet held over her and flanked by the footmen and equerries and the Gentlemen Pensioners with their halberds. Immediately behind the Queen came her Master of the Horse, leading the royal palfrey, and then the ladies of honour, some on horseback and some in open chariots, while the yeoman of the guard and mounted attendants brought up the rear.

It was a cold January day, with flurries of snow in the air and muddy underfoot, but no discomforts of cold or wet feet could dampen the enthusiasm of the Londoners as they waited to greet their Queen. 'At her entering the City,' says a contemporary account, 'she was of the people received marvellous entirely, as appeared by the assemblies, prayers, wishes, welcoming cries, tender words, and all other signs, which argued a wonderful earnest love of most obedient subjects towards their sovereign. And on the other side, her grace by holding up her hands, and merry countenance to such as stood far off, and most tender and gentle language to those that stood nigh unto her grace, did declare herself no less thankfully to receive her people's good will, than they lovingly offered it unto her. To all that wished her grace well, she gave hearty thanks; and to such as bade God save her grace, she said again God save them all, and thanked them with all her heart.'

In the difficult and often dangerous days of the previous reign, Elizabeth

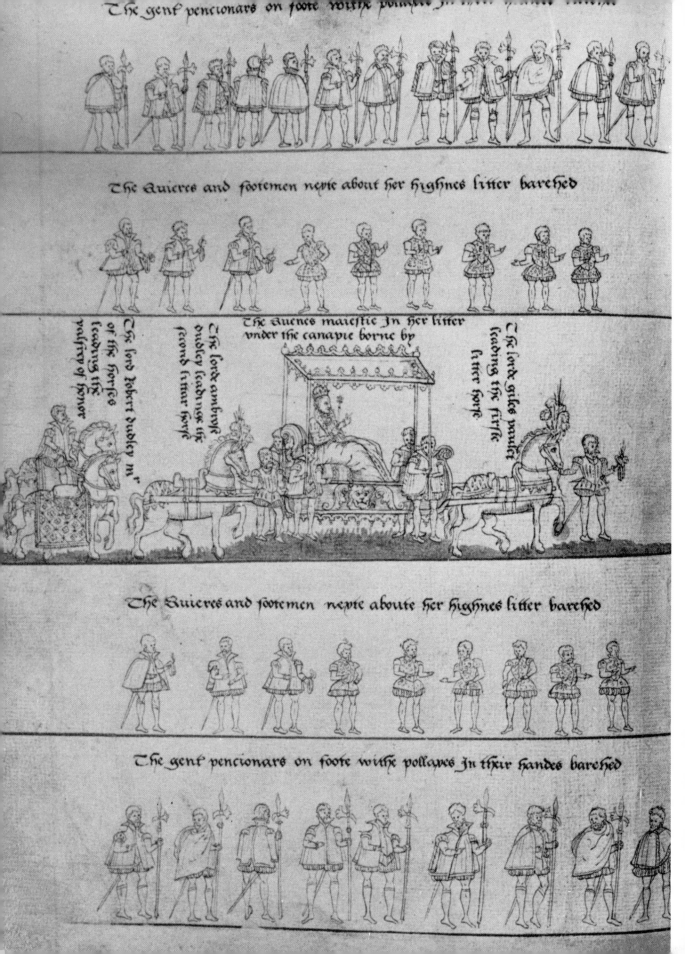

The gent pencionars on foote withe pollaxes in their handes barehed

The Squieres and footemen nexte about her highnes litter barehed

The Squenes maiestie In her litter under the canapie borne by

The lord Robert Dudley mr of the horsses leading the palfrey of honor

The lorde ambrye Dudley leading the second litter horse

The lorde giles pawlet leading the firste litter horse

The Squieres and footemen nexte aboute her highnes litter barehed

The gent pencionars on foote withe pollaxes In their handes barehed

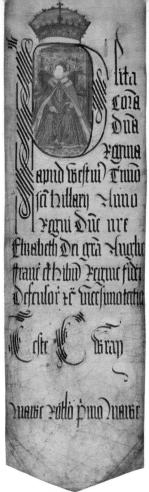

Royal judge
In this extract from the plea roll of the Court of Queen's Bench for the Hilary Term of 1581, Elizabeth's portrait is the illumination of the initial letter.

Borne in state
The design for the Recognition Procession (left) shows the Queen in her litter, carried between two horses. The first is led by Lord Giles Paulet, the second by Ambrose Dudley, later Earl of Warwick. Behind rides Lord Robert Dudley, Master of the Horse, leading the palfrey of honour. Four knights carry the canopy over the Queen, and she is surrounded by squires and footmen, bareheaded, as well as by the Gentlemen Pensioners, her official bodyguard, carrying their poleaxes, or halberds.

Tudor had drawn her greatest strength from the steadfast support of the people of London, and so owed them a debt of gratitude she was eager to repay. The citizens, for their part, were determined to give 'their' Elizabeth a welcome worthy of this auspicious occasion. The streets along the processional route had been swept and gravelled and decorated with streamers and banners. Hangings of cloth of gold and silver and brightly coloured silks fluttered from the windows of every house; and from Fenchurch Street to Cornhill the members of the various City companies lined the way, standing in railed-off enclosures, wearing their best clothes, their rich furs and the hoods of their liveries. From Fenchurch to Temple Bar there were tableaux and pageants, presentations and loyal addresses in Latin and English. Bells pealed, musicians played and everywhere the crowds cheered in ecstasy as they caught their first glimpse of the slim, red-headed young woman in her sumptuous robes, made from 23 yds of gold and silver tissue.

'Welcome – as much as tongue can tell'

All along the route, the dialogue between Queen and people continued. At Fenchurch, the chroniclers relate, a 'fair child' in costly apparel welcomed her in the name of the City:

Welcome again O Queen,
As much as tongue can tell,
Welcome to joyous tongues,
And hearts that will not shrink.

The Queen stopped and called for quiet, and as she listened the bystanders noticed 'a marvellous change' in her expression, as the child's words 'either touched her person or the people's tongues and hearts'.

At the upper end of Gracechurch Street were a triumphal arch and a tableau arranged in three tiers representing the Queen's ancestry and the union of York and Lancaster. In Cornhill, a child representing the Queen sat in the seat of worthy governance, while the figures of Pure Religion, Love of Subjects, Wisdom and Justice trod underfoot Superstition, Rebellion, Folly and Bribery. As she approached each of these set-pieces, Elizabeth ordered her litter to be halted while she asked for their meanings to be explained to her, and listened attentively to the painstakingly rehearsed speeches of the youthful actors. And everywhere she had an appropriate word of thanks and appreciation.

In Cheapside, the principal shopping street of Elizabethan London, which was especially gay with banners and noisy with fanfares of trumpets, the Recorder of the City was waiting to present the Queen with an embroidered purse of crimson satin containing 1,000 gold marks. Her reply – one of the earliest examples of her matchless gift for winning hearts and minds – was greeted with special delight. 'Whereas your request is that I should continue your good lady and Queen,' she told the Recorder, Ranulph Cholmeley, 'be ye assured that I will be as good unto you as ever Queen was to her people. No will in me can lack, neither do I trust shall there lack any power. And persuade

yourselves, that for the safety and quietness of you all, I will not spare if need be to spend my blood.'

No incident was too small for the Queen's comment and attention. 'About the nether end of Cornhill' some spoilsport pointed out an old man who turned his head away and wept, but Elizabeth was not dismayed: 'I warrant you it is for gladness,' she exclaimed. 'How many nosegays did her Grace receive at poor women's hands?' demanded the author of the commemorative pamphlet which was on sale within a fortnight of the event. 'How oftentimes stayed she her chariot when she saw any simple body offer to speak to her Grace?' And it was noticed that she had kept a branch of rosemary, given to her with a supplication by a poor woman at the Fleet Bridge, on the floor of her vehicle all the way to Westminster.

The head of the procession, tramping rather wearily now along the Strand to Charing Cross and Whitehall, was nearing its destination; but outside St Dunstan's Church, where the charity children of Christ's Hospital were drawn up, the Queen, seeing a child waiting to recite, had once more brought her chariot to a halt. At Temple Bar, a choir sang a farewell, and the City, which had turned itself into a stage for one of the happiest dramas of its long history, parted reluctantly with its golden girl 'with no less shouting and crying of the people' than at her entrance. And so, as the winter dusk closed in, borne along on a great warm emotional wavecrest of love and joy, England's Elizabeth came home to Westminster by torchlight.

Coronation in a candle-lit Abbey

After the hugely successful popular triumph of the Saturday, Coronation Day itself was something of an anticlimax. There was another grand procession from Westminster Hall to the Abbey Church of St Peter. The Queen, robed in crimson velvet, with an ermine cape and a cap of crimson velvet embroidered with pearls and Venice gold, walked between the Earls of Pembroke and Shrewsbury. Her train was carried by her cousin Margaret, Countess of Lennox, while the Barons of the Cinque Ports held a canopy over her head. As she passed, the watching crowds broke through the barriers to scramble for pieces of the blue carpet she had walked on, nearly knocking the unfortunate Lady Lennox off her feet.

Inside the crowded Abbey, aglow with candles and reeking with the smell of hot wax, incense and unwashed humanity, the Queen was brought to a Chair of Estate in the middle of the church, facing the High Altar. Here, according to ancient custom, she was proclaimed to the four corners of the building and then acclaimed by the congregation with such a cacophony of shouting, pealing bells, organ music, fifes, trumpets and rolling drums that it seemed to one spectator 'as if the world were come to an end'.

The main items of the ceremony – the administration of the oath, the consecration, the anointing, the crowning and the homage – were performed as they had been performed over the previous 500 years, and very much as they were performed at the coronation of Queen Elizabeth II 400 years later.

The Queen when young
This portrait of the young Queen was painted in days before the romantic, neo-classical, neo-medieval cult of Gloriana had gathered momentum. Elizabeth here is thought to be about 30, which would place the portrait in the early 1560s, around the time when the Scottish envoy Sir James Melville had several personal interviews with her. He remarked on her 'golden coloured hair', more reddish than yellow, which 'curled in appearance naturally'. In later years, the Queen took to wearing a wig. A few weeks before her death, when she received a new Venetian ambassador, she wore hair 'of a light colour never made by nature', but the story that she went bald in her thirties is certainly untrue.

There was, however, one important difference from modern practice. As a result of the brief reaction of Queen Mary Tudor's reign, England at the beginning of 1559 was still officially a Roman Catholic country. It had, in fact, been quite difficult to find a bishop willing to crown a Queen well known to favour the cause of Protestantism. Oglethorpe of Carlisle had finally agreed to officiate, but the service was conducted for the most part in Latin, and at the Mass which followed the crowning the Host was elevated according to the Roman rite. The Queen, though, did not take the sacrament and was careful to dissociate herself from this part of the proceedings in the Abbey by retiring to a screened pew.

It was half-way through the afternoon by the time the religious ceremony came to an end and the Queen, robed now in a surcoat and mantle of purple velvet and invested with all the insignia of royalty, emerged from the Abbey to return to Westminster Hall. She had a smile and a greeting for everyone and appeared to be in the highest spirits – so much so that, in the opinion of a censorious Italian diplomat, 'she exceeded the bounds of gravity and decorum'.

At the great banquet which followed, everything, in the words of Holinshed's *Chronicle*, was 'ordered in such royal manner as to such a regal and most solemn feast appertained'. Sir Edward Dymoke, in his capacity of Queen's Champion, rode into Westminster Hall in full armour, mounted upon a magnificent charger arrayed in cloth of gold, flung down his gauntlet and offered to fight anyone that 'should deny her to be the righteous and lawful queen of this realm'. Needless to say, no one accepted his challenge, but the Queen, following the custom, drank to Sir Edward from a gold cup and then sent it to him for his fee. The Lord Mayor of London also got a gold cup. At last, at 1 a.m., the banquet which had been celebrated 'with all royal ceremonies

Notorious mother

In her lifetime Anne Boleyn was the most notorious woman in Europe. To the Catholic powers she was the 'concubine' for whom Henry VIII separated England from the Church of Rome. To the people of England she was 'that goggle-eyed whore Nan Bullen'. In later years, when her daughter Elizabeth had become Queen, she was rehabilitated as a wronged and virtuous Protestant heroine – but her daughter was never heard to mention her name.

Revered father

In his 38 year reign Henry VIII (top left) became a national father-figure, often cruel, yet inspiring genuine loyalty and affection. His daughter Elizabeth revered his memory. 'She prides herself on her father and glories in him,' remarked the Venetian ambassador after meeting her early in her reign.

and high solemnities, due and in like cases accustomed, took end with great joy and contentation to all the beholders'.

Any outsider privileged to watch the ostentatious parade of regal pomp and circumstance surrounding the coronation might have been surprised to learn that the Treasury was empty, that there was a huge foreign debt and that the financier Sir Thomas Gresham was already in Antwerp negotiating a further loan on his country's virtually non-existent credit. But although she was to acquire a reputation for parsimony, Elizabeth, like her father and grandfather before her, knew when it paid to put on a splendid show. 'In pompous ceremonies a secret of government doth much consist,' was an accepted piece of 16th-century political wisdom.

The legacy of Elizabeth's Tudor ancestors

The first two Tudor kings had done much to build up the power and prestige of the monarchy. By putting an end to that bitter and complicated royal family feud known as the Wars of the Roses, Henry VII earned the gratitude of the great majority of Englishmen; and at his death he left the realm prosperous and peaceful, the crown stronger and richer than it had been for generations. His son, that bulky bejewelled figure whose overwhelming personality has impressed itself so strongly on the national folk memory, broke with Rome, repudiated the Pope and assumed the title of Supreme Head of the Church in England. This unprecedented and revolutionary act, abolishing the clergy's age-old freedom from secular control, gave the English monarchy an extra dimension of authority which no other Christian king had ever aspired to. By his 'nationalisation' of church property, Henry also enriched the monarchy to a degree undreamt of by his predecessors – although he contrived to squander most of the spoils of his Reformation on personal extravagance and a series of expensive and unprofitable military adventures.

A wide variety of adjectives – from patriotic, wise and courageous, to tyrannical, sadistic and paranoid – have been applied to Henry VIII. Certainly as a husband and father he left much to be desired, his egotism was often preposterous and he could be mercilessly cruel. On the other hand, he provided strong leadership (and deserved his traditional title of Father of the English Navy); while to most of his subjects, who saw only the glittering façade, he seemed to embody the very essence of the kingly ideal, offering them a deeply satisfying focus for their growing sense of national pride.

When Henry VIII died his throne passed peacefully to his son and heir, but unfortunately the heir was a child of nine. King Edward VI, everyone agreed, was a bright, promising little boy, but his minority meant that for six uneasy years of recession, rising prices and internal dissension, control passed into the hands of a succession of greedy factions.

Henry VIII's Reformation had jettisoned the Pope and given the people their first English Bible, but his church retained nearly all the basic tenets of Roman Catholicism. As long as he lived, the old king kept a tight rein on the more radical reformers, but after his death the new men began to assert themselves.

Henry VIII's Seal
Always round in shape, the Great Seal showed the monarch 'in majesty', crowned and enthroned and flanked by the royal arms. On the other side Henry VIII is seen on horseback. The Privy Seal, by contrast, was the sovereign's personal seal or emblem, and was used for more private documents or those of lesser importance. It was kept in the charge of the Lord Privy Seal. Not every state document was signed by the monarch personally. A number of routine warrants were embossed with an outline facsimile of the royal autograph, then inked in by the Clerk of the Dry Stamp.

Old familiar rites and ceremonies were swept away, the clergy were allowed to marry, and the Prayer Book of 1552 completed the process of transforming the Latin Mass into an Anglican communion or commemorative service. This was going too far and too fast for the more conservative sections of the community, and religious dissatisfactions, combined with growing economic distress, produced several outbreaks of popular discontent in rural areas.

In 1553 Edward died of tuberculosis at the age of 16, whereupon the English people were visited by that old recurring sickness, a disputed succession. Owing to the Tudor inability to sire healthy sons, the royal house had been reduced to a handful of women and girls; the rightful heiress – Henry's elder daughter Mary – was a delicate, ageing spinster, and the way seemed clear for the strong men to take over. However, the *coup d'état* engineered by the current strong man, John Dudley Duke of Northumberland, and aimed at excluding King Henry's daughters in favour of his teenage great-niece Lady Jane Grey (who also happened to be Northumberland's daughter-in-law), collapsed in ruins; and Mary Tudor, the first English Queen regnant since the far-off days of the Empress Matilda, came into her inheritance.

Mary, daughter of Henry VIII and his first wife, the ill-used Spanish princess Catherine of Aragon, was an embittered, unhappy woman of 37 and a devout

King at the age of nine
Henry VIII had been unlucky in his efforts to beget a male heir, so the birth of Prince Edward in October 1537 was greeted by a nationwide outburst of relief and rejoicing. Edward was nine years old when he had to step into his father's shoes, a small, solemn, blond boy of above average intelligence. He is here seen presenting the charter for Christ's Hospital in 1552. Homeless boys and girls who were cared for in the foundation line up and pay homage to their young benefactor.

Roman Catholic, who naturally saw the defeat of her enemies as a direct result of divine intervention – and as a divine command to lead her people back into the arms of Holy Mother Church. But the queen, who had spent most of her adult life in rural retirement surrounded by her Catholic friends, had quite failed to realise how strongly a nationalistic form of Protestantism had taken root in London and the south-east.

Mary also totally misunderstood the real feelings which lay behind the popular support her cause had received. The people were sick of the rule of John Dudley and his like and wanted to see the true royal line maintained; but while the bulk of the population would probably have been content to return to the form of Anglo-Catholicism evolved by Henry VIII, very few were prepared willingly to return to the Pope's authority — or 'the tyranny of the Bishop of Rome', as the more advanced Protestants put it. The result was a period of religious persecution which earned the queen her unenviable nickname of 'Bloody Mary', and sowed the seeds of an implacable fear and hatred of Rome.

When Mary tried to turn back the clock

Serious heresy-hunting began in February 1555 and continued spasmodically over the next three years, during which time some 300 people, including 60 women, were burned at the stake. Although the so-called Marian persecution was not, by contemporary European standards, an especially harsh campaign, it remains an unhappy episode in our history; and although it was confined very largely to London and the south-east, it cast a shadow of gloom and disgust over the whole country. Apart from Archbishop Thomas Cranmer and a handful of other Protestant bishops, the vast majority of the victims were humble people – poor widows, journeymen and apprentices, agricultural labourers, weavers, clothworkers, artisans and tradesmen – who died in agony in their local market-place for the sake of what they believed to be God's truth. Higher-placed Protestants either conformed sufficiently to keep out of trouble, or else took themselves and their consciences abroad to Lutheran Germany or Calvinist Switzerland more or less unhindered by the authorities.

If Queen Mary's religious policy proved a grim and personally disastrous failure, so too did her intensely unpopular marriage to Prince Philip of Spain. The English people were convinced that this would lead to their enslavement by a horde of Spaniards, all armed to the teeth and ready to ravish their wives and daughters and despoil them of their goods and lands. Many otherwise quite sensible people allowed themselves to be carried away by a rising tide of panic and prejudice. Early in 1554 this had erupted into one of the century's most serious revolts against the authority of the Crown, when Thomas Wyatt and his Kentishmen came close to gaining control of the capital.

Mary possessed all the stubborn courage of the Tudors, but none of their political genius or personal magnetism. A 'good' woman, of rigid moral principles, a simple, painfully honest woman, narrow in outlook and limited in experience, she was hopelessly out of her depth in the complicated, un-principled world of high politics and could only do what she believed to be

A royal line-up
Queen Elizabeth, two of her predecessors and her successor, James I, are depicted on these carved ivory knife handles, part of a set of 14 knives dated 1607 and bearing the figures of English monarchs from Henry I onwards. Between the bearded Henry VIII and his daughter Elizabeth is the youthful figure of the boy king Edward VI.

right, with predictably fatal consequences. Under her inept and unlucky rule the country steadily declined, with a sullen, rebellious people and a rapidly worsening economic situation. This was depressing enough, but when, as opponents of the Spanish marriage had always prophesied, England was drawn into Spain's perennial quarrel with France and in January 1558 lost the town of Calais, last outpost of her once great continental empire, national humiliation was added to national discontent.

Mary did not long survive this final disaster, dying later that year at the age of 42, probably of cancer of the womb. There was little or no pretence at public mourning. As news of the queen's death spread through London, the citizens rang the church bells and, according to a contemporary account, 'at night did make bonfires and set tables in the streets, and did eat and drink and make merry for the new Queen Elizabeth'.

A comely Princess with red-gold hair

The new Queen Elizabeth, who succeeded to her half-sister's throne on November 17, 1558, had just passed her twenty-fifth birthday. She was never, even as a girl, considered strictly beautiful by dispassionate observers, although a Venetian envoy who saw her in her twentieth year described her face and figure as 'very handsome' and commented on the regal dignity of her bearing. Another Venetian, who wrote a detailed report on the Princess when she was 23, thought her 'comely rather than handsome' but mentioned her fine eyes and beautiful hands, which she took care to display; her incredibly long beringed white fingers are prominently featured in so many portraits.

Described as 'indifferent tall, slender and straight', Elizabeth seems to have been about average height for a woman of her time – perhaps 5 ft 3 in or 5 ft 4 in. Her eyes were probably grey, and she had the Tudor red-gold hair – 'more reddish than yellow' remembered a Scottish envoy, Sir James Melville – with some natural curl, at least in her twenties. She was always very pale, her skin having that clear, almost transparent pallor which often goes with red hair. Her spare, wiry figure and high-nosed profile may not have measured up to any accepted standard of feminine beauty; and as she grew older she became thin to the point of emaciation, her teeth decayed and she took to hiding her greying hair under a series of elaborate red wigs. But in her prime Elizabeth must have been a striking-looking woman, graceful, stylish and supremely elegant.

Elizabeth had inherited Henry VIII's colouring, together with his autocratic temper, and always liked to be told that she resembled her father. As a physical type, however, she took after her grandfather, Henry VII, and was soon to demonstrate that she had also inherited her grandfather's well-known 'politic wisdom in governance'. She had been a clever child and, thanks largely to the influence of her last step-mother, Katherine Parr, had received an excellent education. When she was 16 her tutor, Roger Ascham, reported proudly that 'her mind has no womanly weakness, her perseverance is equal to that of a man, and her memory long keeps what it quickly picks up'. The Venetian

Queen for nine days
The tragedy of Lady Jane Grey, and her only crime, was her royal blood. A great-niece of Henry VIII, she was proclaimed queen by the Duke of Northumberland after the death of Edward VI. Precisely nine days later, the forces rallying to Mary Tudor had defeated the attempted coup. In February 1554, Jane was beheaded on Tower Green. She was still only 16 years old.

'The most unhappy lady'

Mary Tudor, the only surviving child of Henry VIII's first marriage to the Spanish princess Catharine of Aragon, was 17 when her half-sister Elizabeth was born. Mary had suffered bitterly as a result of her parents' divorce. She was bastardised, disinherited and forced to yield precedence to the baby Elizabeth, and the humiliations inflicted on her during her adolescent years wrecked her health and her disposition. She became, as she put it, 'the most unhappy lady in Christendom'. Her short reign was politically disastrous, and the religious persecution resulting from her efforts to bring England back to the Roman Church earned her the nickname of 'Bloody Mary'. Her marriage to Philip of Spain brought her little personal happiness, and her last years were further clouded by disappointment and a corroding jealousy of Elizabeth which she took no trouble to conceal.

ambassador, writing in 1557, commented respectfully on Elizabeth's wonderful intellect and understanding.

The Queen's abilities as a linguist were considerable. Latin, still the universal language of culture and diplomacy, came as naturally to her as breathing, and she had 'no slight knowledge' of Greek. Her French and Italian were fluent, and she could speak some Spanish. In the midst of all her other preoccupations, she kept up a lifelong habit of devoting some part of nearly every day to study, and in the 1560s Roger Ascham believed she was reading more Greek every day than many churchmen read Latin in a whole week. Towards the end of her reign she was still capable of squashing a brash foreign envoy in vigorous, vituperative off-the-cuff Latin, and a few weeks before her death she was chatting in Italian to a new Venetian ambassador.

No one who ever had anything to do with Queen Elizabeth doubted the quality of her trained and formidable intelligence. More important, no one

The Queen's Champion
The Dymoke family had held the hereditary office of Champion of England since the coronation of Richard II in 1377. It was the Champion's duty to ride on a charger, fully armed, into Westminster Hall during the coronation banquet, fling down his gauntlet and challenge to mortal combat anyone who denied the newly crowned monarch's right to the throne. By Elizabethan times this had become a purely ceremonial gesture, but the tradition was still maintained.

Elizabeth in Parliament
In the 45 years of her reign, Elizabeth summoned only 13 Parliaments (facing page), which were in session altogether for less than two and a half years. The Queen would tolerate no parliamentary interference in affairs of state, and scolded members for meddling in matters 'beyond the reach of a subject's brain to mention'. Thanks to the mystique of monarchy and to the Queen's own personality, confrontation never developed into head-on collision.

could doubt that she was a born ruler and a born politician – shrewd, cautious and subtle. This was just as well, for few English monarchs had to meet a more severe test in their first few months on the throne.

A succinct list of the most pressing problems facing the new administration drawn up by one government official gives some idea of the task before her. 'The Queen poor, the realm exhausted, the nobility poor and decayed. Want of good captains and soldiers. The people out of order. Justice not executed. All things dear. Excess in meat, drink and apparel. Divisions among ourselves. Wars with France and Scotland . . . Steadfast enmity but no steadfast friendship abroad.'

At home, the religious question overshadowed everything else. In an age when religion played such a vital part in daily life, and religious differences roused the sort of passions now more commonly associated with rival political ideologies, this particular nettle had to be grasped without delay. Elizabeth's first Parliament met on January 25, 1559, and by Easter had hammered out a settlement which finally separated England from Rome and established the Church of England as we know it today.

There is some evidence that the new Anglican Church leaned further towards Protestantism than the Queen would have liked. She always disapproved strongly of married clergy, and in her own chapels she continued to indulge her moderately High Church taste for ritual and ceremonial. But, unlike her sister, she was no zealot. She could not, of course, allow her Roman Catholic subjects to practise their religion in public. In the 16th-century context, when religion and politics were, for all practical purposes, one and the same thing, toleration would have posed too great a threat to the unity and security of the state for any ruler to contemplate. At the same time, Elizabeth never attempted to 'make windows into men's souls'. As long as people obeyed the law and attended their parish church on Sunday, she would not inquire too closely into their private beliefs and practices.

Courtships that served political ends

In foreign affairs, the religious power struggle was to dominate the rest of the century. In the spring of 1559 it looked very much as if the two Roman Catholic super-powers of France and Spain were only waiting to settle their differences before proceeding to dismember Protestant England between them. All over Europe, in fact, bets were being laid that the new Queen of England would not keep her rickety throne for six months. But the new Queen of England had learned some useful lessons in the art of survival during her precarious girlhood – lessons of self-reliance, self-command, discretion and duplicity – and before six months were up she had proved herself second to none in the closely related art of international diplomacy.

In an age when so many alliances were sealed by royal marriages, Elizabeth's single status was a priceless asset, and her inner resolve to stay single did not for a moment prevent her from zestfully exploiting all the advantages attached to being 'the best match in her parish'. She was to go on exploiting them for the

The Chancellors Seat.

next 20 years, allowing her numerous suitors just enough encouragement to keep them hopeful (and friendly) for just as long as they served her purpose. Queen Elizabeth's famous 'courtships' figure largely in the diplomatic correspondence of the period, but while she undoubtedly enjoyed being the centre of attraction, the courtships themselves were essentially political exercises.

To her own friends and admirers – her councillors, her parliaments and people – the Queen's unwomanly refusal to fulfil her natural role of wife and mother caused a good deal of disquiet, and her frequently expressed aversion to the holy estate of matrimony seemed both incomprehensible and more than a little shocking. As she herself remarked: 'There is a strong idea in the world that a woman cannot live unless she is married, or at all events that if she refrains from marriage she does so for some bad reason.'

It has been suggested that Elizabeth's determination to refrain from marriage was either caused by some mysterious physical disability, or else was rooted in childhood traumas. There is no contemporary evidence at all that she suffered from any congenital physical defect – her doctors believed her to be quite capable of childbearing – and the second theory can only be a matter of conjecture. Possibly the real reason why Elizabeth never married was the most obvious one. She was first and foremost a woman devoted to her role as monarch, and seems from the beginning to have made up her mind that, in her case, marriage and a career would not mix. In her world, a wife, however exalted her position, was regarded as being subject to her husband by divine law. Nor could the Queen's husband have remained a political cipher. He would have expected, and been expected, to take an active share in the government of the country, and the Queen had no intention of sharing her throne with anyone. As the blunt Scottish envoy Sir James Melville claims he once said to her: 'Madam, I know your stately stomach. You think if you were married, you would be but Queen of England; and now you are King and Queen both. You may not endure a commander.'

A monarch wedded only to her people

If the Queen refused to take a conventional husband, she considered herself to be symbolically married. Very early in the reign she told a parliamentary delegation which had come to urge her to choose a consort, 'I have already joined myself in marriage to an husband, namely, the Kingdom of England'; and taking the coronation ring from her finger she flourished it under their noses. No doubt at the time the sober members of the House of Commons regarded this as another rather tiresome piece of coyness on the part of their sovereign lady, but Elizabeth's claim to be married to her kingdom was no mere flight of fancy. 'She is very much wedded to the people and thinks as they do,' wrote the Spanish ambassador, and the 45 year love affair between Elizabeth and her people was to become one of the wonders of the age.

For Elizabeth this relationship was a matter of vital importance – there was no way in which she could have ruled a tough, vigorous, quarrelsome, independent nation by force – and from the very beginning she set out to gain

Descent from a Trojan king
In its early days the Tudor dynasty was sensitive about its pedigree, and Henry VII appointed a commission to inquire into the matter. The commission knew what was expected of it and drew up the king's 'perfect genelogie' from the ancient Kings of Briton and Princes of Wales, of which this is a section. The Tudors, the commissioners declared solemnly, could prove lineal descent from Brute the Trojan, mythical first King of the Britons who was reputed to have given his name to the land. All ambitious Elizabethans were interested in genealogy, and many rising or newly ennobled families, such as the Cecils, went to considerable expense to demonstrate the antiquity of their origins.

and keep the goodwill of all her good people. As she wisely observed, 'if they did not rest assured of some special love toward them, they would not readily yield me such good obedience'.

In the constant assurance of her 'special love' for her people lay the secret of the Queen's seemingly miraculous ability to gain obedience. In speech after speech throughout her reign she emphasised the point, telling Parliament over and over again that, although they might have many greater princes to rule over them, they would never have one that loved them better. And in her last speech of all, she told the Commons: 'This I count the glory of my crown, that I have reigned with your loves.'

It was certainly a glorious achievement, but it was not won by words alone (though the thrifty Queen made good use of words). In her tireless pursuit of the goodwill of all her 'husbands', she jolted on royal progresses over countless miles of atrocious roads in order to show herself to as many people as possible, listened to countless loyal addresses, sat patiently through countless amateur pageants and tedious Latin plays and orations, always smiling, always gracious, always appreciative of the efforts made to entertain her.

'In her progress,' wrote a near-contemporary biographer, 'she was most easy to be approached. Private persons and magistrates, men and women, country people and children came joyfully and without any fear to wait upon her and see her. Her ears were then open to the complaints of the afflicted and of those that had been any way injured. She would not suffer the meanest of her people to be shut out from the places where she resided, but the greatest and the least were then in a manner levelled. She took with her own hand, and read with the greatest goodness the petitions of the meanest rustics. And she

A royal notice to quit
This warrant, dated January 1598, signed by the Queen and endorsed by Lords Burghley and Buckhurst and by the Earls of Essex and Nottingham, orders the merchants of the Hanse Towns to leave the country. The Hanseatic Towns were a league of north German ports which had for many years held the monopoly of trade with the Baltic and dominated the North Sea routes. By the 1590s, this monopoly was being challenged by English merchant venturers. The Hanse depot stood on the site now occupied by Cannon Street Station.

would frequently assure them that she would take a particular care of their affairs, and she would ever be as good as her word. She was never seen angry with the most unseasonable or uncourtly approach. She was never offended with the most impudent or importunate petitioner. Nor was there anything in the whole course of her reign that more won the hearts of the people than this her wonderful facility and condescension, and the sweetness and pleasantness with which she entertained all that came to her.'

'If ever any person had either the gift or the style to win the hearts of people, it was this Queen' – the point is made again and again by everyone who knew her. 'Stay thy cart, good fellow,' cried a sturdy citizen to the royal coachman on one such occasion, 'stay thy cart, that I may speak to the Queen,' and Elizabeth laughed 'as she had been tickled' and gave him her hand to kiss.

In 1572, when she was staying at Warwick Castle, a firework display was put on for her amusement, but unfortunately it got rather out of hand and 'fire-balles and squibbes' fell into the town. One house was burned to the ground and its occupants, a man and wife asleep in bed, were only rescued 'with much ado'. Next morning, says the contemporary account, 'it pleased her Majesty to have the poor old man and woman that had their house burnt, brought unto her; whom so brought her Majesty comforted very much'. A collection was taken up among the courtiers, and with her Grace's bounty, £25 'given towards their losses that had taken hurt'.

Ways that won the hearts of her people

The following summer the Queen was in Kent, and spent four days at the ancient sea-port of Sandwich, where the wives of the local dignitaries had provided a banquet of 160 dishes laid out in the school-house on a table 28 ft long. Elizabeth was 'very merry', paying her hosts the compliment of eating without any assay – that is, without the preliminary ceremony of tasting, which was normally performed as a precaution against poison – and later asked for some of the dishes to be carried to her lodging.

A year or so later, at Norwich, Master Lambert, the local schoolmaster, was waiting to make a Latin oration to the Queen. 'Her Majesty drew near unto him, and, thinking him fearful, said graciously unto him, "Be not afraid".' Thus encouraged, he launched bravely into his speech and Elizabeth called to the French ambassadors, who were with her, and several of the English lords and 'willed them to hearken'. She herself listened attentively to the end, and then told Master Lambert it was the best speech she had ever heard and gave him her hand to kiss. When the time came for her to leave, she thanked the Mayor and Aldermen 'for the great cheer they had made her'. She knighted the Mayor, 'and so departing, said "I have laid up in my breast such good will, as I shall never forget Norwich"'; and proceeding onward, did shake her riding-rod and said "Farewell Norwich", with the water standing in her eyes'.

Gestures like these, and many more, endeared the Queen for ever to the towns she visited; while people like the old couple at Warwick, the councillors' wives at Sandwich and the schoolmaster from Norwich, who would probably

The moon goddess queen
The romantic cult of Elizabeth as the moon goddess Cynthia recurs constantly in the poetry, Court pageantry and portraiture of the last decade of the reign. This miniature by Nicholas Hilliard shows Elizabeth as Queen of Love and Beauty, with the crescent moon of Cynthia in her hair.

Gloves for royal fingers
The Queen was proud of her beautiful hands, and liked to display them. A German visitor who watched her going by in procession to church noticed that 'her hands were small and her fingers long'. He saw her pulling off her glove and giving her right hand, 'sparkling with rings and jewels', to be kissed.

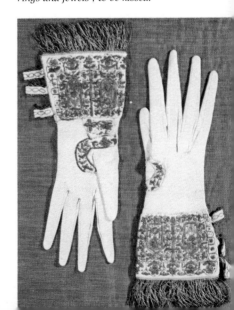

never see her again, remained her slaves for life. 'Her speech did win all affections,' wrote her godson, John Harington, 'and her subjects did try to show all love to her commands; for she would say her state did require her to command what she knew her people would willingly do from their own love to her. Here did she show her wisdom fully . . . for who would withhold a show of love and obedience, when their sovereign said it was their own choice and not her compulsion?' Although, he added, 'she could put forth such alterations, when obedience was lacking, as left no doubt whose daughter she was!'

Certainly, the Queen's temper was by no means uniformly sunny. Elizabeth in a rage could be heard several rooms away filling the air with good round oaths and, when 'vehemently transported with anger', was not above throwing things, or boxing the ears of the nearest maid of honour. 'When she smiled,' remembered Harington, who frankly adored her, 'it was a pure sunshine that every one did choose to bask in; but anon came a storm from a sudden gathering of clouds, and the thunder fell, in wondrous manner, on all alike.' But the Queen's tension-relieving outbursts were always confined to the domestic atmosphere of Court and council chamber.

Worshipped by friends, respected by enemies

From across the centuries one can only marvel at the force which emanated from this incredible woman, isolated in a world of men, who never accepted her sex as an infirmity but used it deliberately and sometimes ruthlessly as a weapon in her lifelong battle to avoid male domination; who, it was said, 'did fish for men's souls, and had so sweet a bait that no one could escape her network'. At the same time, Elizabeth could undoubtedly be a most infuriating female, both to serve under and to negotiate with – 'a daughter of the devil' complained one exasperated ambassador – and she frequently drove her parliaments and her sensible male advisers to near despair by her maddeningly devious, capricious and apparently wilful feminine ways.

Elizabeth became in her lifetime the object of a personality cult unprecedented among a plain-spoken, individualistic people seldom given to hero-worship, and gained the respect, sometimes even the admiration of her enemies. 'She certainly is a great Queen,' exclaimed Pope Sixtus V, 'and were she only a Catholic, she would be our dearly beloved. Just look how well she governs! She is only a woman, only mistress of half an island and yet she makes herself feared by Spain, by France, by all.'

Elizabeth's genius, her magic, defy definition or explanation, and those of her contemporaries who knew her best admitted that they never really fathomed her. Perhaps Robert Cecil came nearest the mark when he said of the Queen that she was 'more than a man, and (in troth) sometimes less than a woman'. The only thing that can be said of her with certainty is that she loved England and England's people with a deep, abiding, selfless love. She understood and identified with her people as no other English ruler has ever done, and through her inspiration, her insight and her guidance she made possible the achievements of the age which bears her name.

Queen of peace and purity
In Sir Philip Sidney's pastoral romance Arcadia *Elizabeth appears as Helen, Queen of Corinth, a strong-minded ruler who has brought peace to her people, although other countries were 'full of wars'. She is beautiful and pure. A courtly knight clad in golden armour rides as her champion in the lists, taking for his device the ermine, symbol of purity. This Ermine Portrait of the Queen, dated 1585, is probably intended to show Elizabeth as Sidney's Helen, attired in her colours of black and white, with an ermine on her sleeve and the additional symbols of Justice and Peace in the shape of olive branch and sword. As usual, the exquisite, long-fingered hands of which Elizabeth was proud are prominently displayed.*

Queen of Scots

A CATHOLIC RIVAL TO ELIZABETH WHO FLED TO ENGLAND
BUT FOUND ONLY DEATH

A medallion portrait of Mary Stuart

Mary Stuart became Queen of Scotland when she was a baby and died at the hands of Queen Elizabeth's executioner 44 years later. Some Catholics regarded her as the rightful Queen of England. To the Protestants she was not only a papist but also an adultress who had connived at her husband's murder. When she took refuge in England from the Scots who had deposed her, she presented her cousin Elizabeth with a cruel dilemma. How deeply Mary was involved in the plots to put her on the English throne is a matter of debate. But in the crisis climate of the 1580s England could not tolerate a rival queen.

Execution relics
Mary bequeathed the golden rosary, crucifix and prayer book she carried at her execution to the wife of Philip Howard, Earl of Arundel. The relics remain in the possession of the Howards.

Fateful letters
In a silver casket identical to this were said to have been found incriminating letters written by Mary to her lover, Bothwell. The letters disappeared in 1584.

The scene of the crime
A contemporary sketch shows the scene at Kirk o' Fields, near Edinburgh, where Mary's second husband, Lord Darnley, was murdered in February 1567. The house is a heap of rubble, the bodies of Darnley and his servant lie at top right, and below Darnley's body is carried away and buried. At top left Darnley's infant son James calls from his cradle for vengeance.

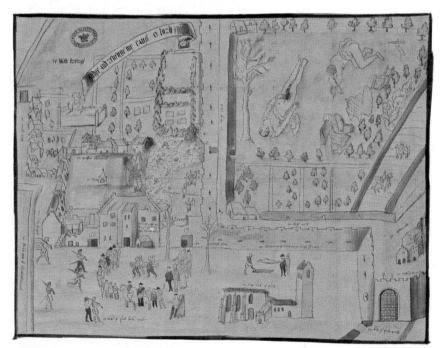

A third husband for Mary

James Hepburn, Earl of Bothwell, a divorced man of unsavoury reputation, became the third husband of Mary, seen (right) in a portrait painted during her captivity in England. The marriage took place according to the rites of the Protestant Church barely three months after the murder of Darnley.

Death in the castle

Mary, Queen of Scots was beheaded on a wooden stage specially erected in the Great Hall of Fotheringhay Castle on February 8, 1587, before a carefully selected audience.

Mementos for a maid

Mary gave these jewels and fan to one of her Maids of Honour during the last hours before her execution. The locket bears a tiny miniature of the queen.

Honour for a queen – and virgin goddess

*All the glamour and glitter of the Elizabethan Court surrounds the Queen, resplendent in
her favourite white and silver, as she is carried in procession by her courtiers. Gentlemen Pensioners line the route,
Garter Knights lead the way, and ladies of honour in ruffs and farthingales
follow their mistress. The painting was probably commissioned by the Earl of Worcester,
Master of the Horse, who stands in the middle foreground.*

CHAPTER TWO

Life at Court

AMBITIOUS YOUTHS
FILL THE QUEEN'S PALACES WITH
BUSTLE AND COLOUR,
WHILE COUNTRY-HOUSE OWNERS
VIE FOR THE
FAVOUR OF A ROYAL VISIT

The Court of England, which is necessarily
holden always where the prince lieth, is in these days one
of the most renowned and magnificent courts
that are to be found in Europe.
            William Harrison *Description of England*

A**S** well as being the seat of government and focus of political life,
the Elizabethan Court was the acknowledged centre of English culture, elegance and high society. It was the place where reputations were made and the
greatest prizes won; it was the magnet which attracted the best brains and the
best people; the honeypot which drew ambitious young men hoping to catch
the eye of a wealthy patron, and ambitious young women hoping to catch a
husband.

The Court could also be a dangerous place for the unwary, a disappointing
and expensive place for the unlucky. 'I have spent my time, my fortune, and
almost my honesty, to buy false hope, false friends, and shallow praise,'
lamented John Harington, after he had only narrowly escaped being dragged
down in the Earl of Essex's disgrace towards the end of Elizabeth's reign. The
poet Edmund Spenser had to wait many weary years for even a limited amount
of recognition, while others, without the right kind of influence, never achieved
it at all, so that it became fashionable to denigrate the flattery, the falseness,
the envy, intrigue and corruption of a courtier's life.

Fashionable, that is, among the disillusioned. Given the opportunity, very
few Elizabethans were strong-minded enough to resist the temptation to show
themselves off at Court, false and corrupt or not. In any case, everyone who
wanted to cut a dash in the world, everyone with a grievance to air, a career to
advance or a favour to seek sooner or later had to come where power was
centred and favours were granted. Sooner or later, everyone who was anyone
in Elizabethan England paid a visit to Court, and the galleries and antechambers of the Queen's palaces were always thronged with jostling crowds of
sightseers, petitioners and hangers-on.

The Court, in London, meant Westminster or Whitehall – then, as now, the
nerve centre of officialdom. The old royal apartments in the Palace of Westminster, home of the monarchy from time immemorial, had been severely
damaged by fire early in Henry VIII's reign. After the death of Cardinal Wolsey
in 1530 Henry quietly appropriated York Place, the Cardinal Archbishop's
sumptuous London house, which stood on the river-bank about a quarter of a
mile downstream from Westminster, at the point where today Horse Guards
Avenue joins the Embankment.

Henry re-christened his new domain Whyte Hall, and at once embarked on
major extensions and improvements. He acquired another valuable piece of
property in the large tract of open land lying to the west of the road from

Privileged envoys
*The Queen spent a good deal of
her working day in the Privy
Chamber, where she saw her
councillors and secretaries, gave
private audiences and ate her
meals. Unlike the Presence
Chamber, which was open to
all who were entitled to appear
at Court, access to the Privy
Chamber was carefully
controlled, making it the
Queen's private office and
sitting-room where she could
relax with her friends. In this*

painting she is seen receiving the respects of two kneeling Dutch ambassadors. A select group of courtiers, including the Earl of Leicester and the Lord Admiral, look on and three Maids of Honour sit on a cushion on the floor.

Charing Cross to St Margaret's Church, where he laid out tennis courts, cock-pits, bowling alleys and a tilt-yard (the site of Horse Guards Parade), and built two magnificent gateways – the so-called Holbein Gate, almost opposite the Horse Guards, and King's Gate, slightly to the north of Downing Street. These gateways, or bridges, connected the two halves of the Palace complex and spanned King Street, the public thoroughfare following the line of modern Whitehall and running through the middle of the royal enclave which had now become the sovereign's London headquarters. It was in a turret room at Whitehall that Henry was secretly married to Anne Boleyn, his second wife and mother of Elizabeth, and it was at Whitehall that he died 14 years later.

During this time the Palace had spread until it occupied roughly the area bounded today by Charing Cross and Northumberland Avenue on the north, the River Thames (then much wider and shallower) on the east, Westminster Hall and the Abbey on the south, and St James's and the Green Park (which

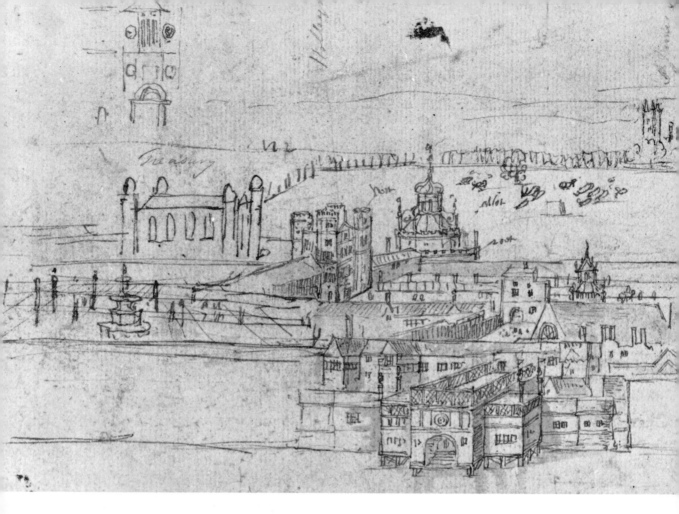

were royal hunting grounds) on the west. Although described as 'a regal mansion', it was really more of a village than a palace – a complicated rabbit warren of galleries, halls, living quarters, chapels, presence chambers, storehouses, kitchens, cellars, stables, courtyards, gardens and orchards, and still bisected by a public right of way. The Tudor monarchs knew better than to try to exclude the Londoners from any part of their town, although Henry did ban funeral processions.

Apart from being the largest royal palace in Europe – with its surrounding gardens and grounds it covered 23 acres – Whitehall was much admired for the number and length of its galleries, its princely furnishings, tapestries and pictures. Paul Hentzner, a German lawyer who visited England in the 1590s, was particularly impressed by the library, which was well-stocked with Greek, Latin, Italian and French books, bound in red velvet 'with clasps of gold and silver', and some with pearls and precious stones set in their bindings. Other treasures mentioned by Hentzner included 'two little silver cabinets of exquisite work' in which the Queen kept her paper and which she used as writing boxes; the Queen's bed, 'ingeniously composed of woods of different colours, with quilts of silk, velvet, gold, silver and embroidery'; and 'a little chest, ornamented all over with pearls' where she kept her bracelets and earrings.

Whitehall was Elizabeth's principal palace, though not necessarily her favourite one. The Court normally went into residence there around the

Steps to the river

The Court had its own landing stage beside the River Thames at Whitehall Stairs, and from here the Queen and her attendants embarked on frequent river journeys, especially to the palaces of Greenwich and Richmond. This sketch made by Anthony van Wyngaerde about 1555 shows also some of the other buildings of Whitehall Palace, including the Holbein Gate and, in the background, the cockpit with the tilt-yard beyond it. Westminster lies to the far left.

beginning of November, ready for the Accession Day Tilts, held on the 17th of the month to celebrate the anniversary of the Queen's accession to the throne. This display of jousting or tilting – in which pairs of armoured knights on horseback charged one another at full gallop down either side of a parallel barrier, with the object of shattering the opponent's lance – became more and more elaborate and ostentatious as the reign went on.

The knights, who were drawn from the younger and more athletic members of the Court, would enter the arena in a variety of outlandish and expensive disguises, some riding in chariots drawn by strange beasts or by men, from which they would vault in full armour on to their chargers. Others, less confident of their horsemanship, arrived already mounted. There were Black Knights, Wandering Knights, Melancholy Knights, a Blind Knight from the Americas whose sight miraculously returned in the Queen's presence, Unknown Knights, Arthurian Knights and even a Clownish Knight, all attended by retinues of servants, squires and lance bearers dressed up as wild men, as Indian princes, sailors or shepherds according to the chosen theme.

Pageantry to open the social season

The Accession Day Tilts were an important event in the social calendar, and by the second half of the 1580s they had taken on something of the character of a Royal Command Performance – a romantic, neo-medieval pantomime with music, speeches, pageants and tableaux all carefully devised as tributes to the Queen in her role of Gloriana. Courtier vied with courtier to put on the most impressive show and offer the most ingeniously turned compliment to Her Majesty on what had become, in effect, her official birthday, when 'fair England's knights' donned their archaic panoply and played out the game of chivalry, in the words of the poet George Peele,

In honour of their mistress' holiday
A gracious sport, fitting that golden time.
The day, the birth-day of our happiness,
The blooming time, the spring of England's peace.

The Accession Day festivities marked the beginning of the winter season. This was the time when all the leading figures of Elizabethan society were in town, keeping state and entertaining their friends; a time when the Queen could often be glimpsed riding through the streets in her coach on her way to dine at one or other of the great London houses, or coming home again by torchlight; a time, too, when the tradesmen and shopkeepers of the City hoped to do their most profitable business.

The Court was usually at Whitehall for Christmas, the revels lasting until Twelfth Night. There would be a full programme of dancing, feasting, masques and plays, with the various theatrical companies being invited to perform before the Queen. On New Year's Day it was customary for members of the Court to offer gifts to the sovereign according to their wealth and station. These varied from purses of gold or items of jewellery from senior nobles and

Champion of the Tilt
Dressed for the Accession Day Tilts, George Clifford, 3rd Earl of Cumberland, wears Elizabeth's jewelled glove in his plumed hat. The portrait is by Nicholas Hilliard.

Een Grave oft Lord
van den Parlemente

Een Lord van
der ordre zoo sy
ghecleedt
gaen op St
Joeris dach

Een
ridder
oft Ligentie

officers of the state, to an embroidered petticoat, gloves or 'a pair of sleeves' in fine cambric from individual ladies of the Bedchamber, 'a fair pye of quynces' from the Serjeant of the Pastry, a chessboard made of marchpane – a type of marzipan – from the Master Cook and boxes of sweets and crystallised fruits from the Clerk of the Spicery. In return, the donors received a piece of plate from the Jewel House, again graded in value according to their position in the hierarchy.

The Queen remained at Whitehall for the Parliamentary session. This was by no means an annual event – there were 13 sessions in a reign of 45 years – but it normally took place in the winter or early spring. Large assemblies were never encouraged during the summer, when the risk of plague and other infections was at its height.

By river to a palace by the Thames

When Parliament was not sitting, the middle or end of January saw the Court on the move either to Richmond or Greenwich, the two Thames-side palaces most easily reached from the centre. Winter was not a time for travelling on roads knee-deep in mud or made treacherous by frost, but the river provided a convenient and comfortable highway – one of the reasons why so many palaces were built on its banks.

The palace at Greenwich, Elizabeth's birth-place, which stood on the site now occupied by the Royal Naval College, dated from the mid-15th century and was known as Placentia, or the Manor of Pleasaunce. In Tudor times it was a large, luxurious and well-used residence, built round three quadrangles lying along the river front, and the scene of many royal extravaganzas. It was a place for river carnivals and regattas, hunting in the park and military parades and field days on nearby Blackheath.

Greenwich was also, reputedly, the place where Walter Raleigh once sacrificed an expensive cloak so that the Queen could walk dryshod over a patch of mud. Rather more reliably, a German visitor, Lupold von Wedel, describes the scene at Greenwich at Christmas, 1584 with Elizabeth in relaxed mood seated on a cushion watching the dancing, and summoning a stream of people to come and kneel beside her for a chat. According to von Wedel, 'she talked and jested most amiably with them, and pointing with her finger at the face of one Master, or Captain, Raleigh, told him that there was a smut on it. She offered to wipe it off with her handkerchief, but he anticipating her, removed it himself'.

Richmond, at the other end of the tideway, was another popular resort of the Elizabethan Court. There had been a royal manor at Shene, or Sheen – an old English word meaning 'beauty spot' – for generations, but Henry VII had built a handsome new palace there of brick and stone in the latest architectural style. Renamed Richmond, to commemorate the earldom of Richmond in Yorkshire conferred on Edmund Tudor, progenitor of the dynasty, the new palace boasted 'many windows full lightsome and commodious' and the modern convenience of piped water, drawn from local springs and stored in a cistern beneath an elaborate ornamental fountain in the inner courtyard.

Robes of state

Two peers of the realm, perhaps on their way to Parliament, are attended by a Gentleman Pensioner carrying his halberd, a combination of spear and axe. The peer on the left is dressed in Parliament robes; the one on the right wears the insignia of the Order of the Garter. The Gentlemen Pensioners, formed in 1509, acted as the sovereign's personal bodyguard and survive today as the Honourable Corps of Gentlemen at Arms. In Elizabethan times the Pensioners consisted of a hand-picked group of 40 stalwart young members of the nobility and gentry, and there was great competition to be admitted to their select ranks.

Later in Elizabeth's reign it also boasted the curiosity of a water closet, designed by the Queen's godson, which actually flushed.

Apart from its plumbing, Richmond was famous for its turrets, its 'singing' weather vanes, melodious on a windy day, and for the beauty of its gardens and pleasure grounds. It must have been a charming spot, and the Queen grew particularly fond of it.

With the coming of spring and better travelling weather, the Court had a choice of several other royal residences within easy reach of London. There was Eltham on its hilltop south of the Thames, much frequented by the earlier Tudors. By Elizabeth's day, though, it had become little more than a hunting lodge and presently fell into disuse. More favoured by the Queen – indeed, it was said to be the place she liked best of all – was Nonsuch in Surrey, which lay on the fringes of modern Ewell. This was a fantasy palace of turrets and cupolas, gilded domes, mock battlements and florid icing-sugar rococo built by Henry VIII to impress visitors, especially the French. Nonsuch, too, was renowned for its gardens, and Elizabeth probably liked it more for its surroundings than for its resemblance to an over-decorated wedding cake. Also in Surrey, near Weybridge, was Oatlands, another hunting lodge and summer palace, and near that again Hampton Court, most famous of the riverside palaces and the only one to have survived.

A 'family' of 1,500 constantly on the move

Hampton Court, like Whitehall, was a legacy from Cardinal Wolsey and greatly admired by foreign visitors for its size and magnificence and for the treasures it contained. The tapestries, worked in gold and silver and silk, were said to be so lifelike 'that one might take the people and plants for real'. Elizabeth, though, made less use of Hampton Court than her father and sister had done. The fact that she very nearly died there of smallpox in 1562 may well have given her a superstitious dislike of the place.

Windsor, too, does not seem to have been one of her favourites, although the Court went there for the Garter ceremonies on St George's Day during the early years of the reign, and usually spent some part of the autumn there. The Queen built a gallery where she could walk sheltered from the weather and spent quite a lot on repairs and modernisation, but the old castle was still cold, draughty and uncomfortable in comparison with the more up-to-date palaces.

Except in unexpected circumstances such as political crises or times of plague, the Court year followed a fairly regular pattern. After six weeks or so at Whitehall in the winter, the court moved out on the Richmond, Greenwich and Nonsuch circuit, with perhaps a visit to Windsor in April and sometimes to Whitehall again for the Royal Maundy. Then it returned to one or other of the riverside palaces. The routine was varied in some years by short journeys, or 'by-progresses', further afield. August and September were usually set aside for major progresses, and the autumn would be spent at Windsor, Oatlands, Hampton Court or Nonsuch.

Sound practical reasons kept the Court constantly on the move. The royal

Across the Thames
The River Thames was the main artery of Elizabethan London. Below London Bridge was the bustling activity of a growing port; above the bridge, splendid town houses built by the nobility lined the north bank as far as the Queen's Whitehall Palace. This view by Wenceslaus Hollar shows wherries, or light rowing boats, carrying passengers between the Whitehall side of the river and the south bank, near Lambeth. It shows Whitehall Stairs, Scotland Yard (so called because it was the traditional lodging for visiting kings of Scotland), the tower of St Martin's in the Fields (then

literally 'in the fields'), and Suffolk House, by Charing Cross. The Banqueting House which dominates the skyline at the centre of the picture was designed by Inigo Jones and completed in 1622. Despite the river flowing through their city, pure water was a rare commodity for most town dwellers, as rivers were often foul with sewage and public wells choked with rubbish. Some parts of London were served by leaden conduits bringing fresh water from springs on Hampstead Hill and other northern heights. Householders had to fetch their water from the public supply or pay the water carrier to bring it to their doors.

household numbered more than 1,500 people, not counting the swarms of gate-crashers who, despite periodic purges, formed a permanent feature of the below-stairs population. The palaces were always crowded and, with sanitary arrangements of the chamber pot, bucket or hole-in-the-ground variety, they soon became noticeably unhygienic; this was true even in places where it was possible to dispose of sewage in the river – another advantage of siting great houses on its banks. It was, therefore, obviously necessary to move on at frequent intervals, so that the rushes which still covered the floors of the great halls and communal eating-places and soon became foul with food refuse and excreta, could be shovelled up and carted away, together with the piles of stinking kitchen waste, and so that the whole palace could be swept, aired and allowed to 'sweeten'.

The other main reason for moving on was economic. It did not take long for the Court to eat the surrounding countryside bare, and the purveyors, buying up provisions for the household at a low fixed rate, were never the most popular of royal officials.

Three men who managed the royal household

The organisation of the elaborate, unwieldy travelling circus which was the Elizabethan Court was controlled by three main administrative departments under the Master of the Horse, the Lord Steward and the Lord Chamberlain. The Master of the Horse was responsible for keeping the Queen and her entourage supplied with transport, and for the buying, training, breeding and welfare of riding and coach horses, pack horses and mules, horses capable of dragging heavy wagons over impossible roads, and horses which could be trusted in crowds and processions. The Master of the Horse always rode at the Queen's bridle hand on state occasions, or else led the royal palfrey immediately behind her chariot.

For nearly 30 years the office of Master of the Horse was held by Robert Dudley, Earl of Leicester, a tall, handsome, flamboyant man and one of the most prominent figures at Court. Elizabeth described him as 'her brother and best friend', and although the rumours that they were lovers were almost certainly without foundation, his position as favourite made Leicester an important, powerful and much-hated man. He had a seat on the Privy Council and was a member of the charmed inner circle surrounding the Queen whom she honoured with pet names.

The Lord Steward's department was in charge of catering and house-keeping, the actual day to day work being done by the 'White Staves', so called from the white staff of office presented to them on their appointment. These functionaries formed the Board of Green Cloth, a body responsible for house-hold expenditure and generally keeping order within the precincts of the Court. The Kitchen, with its Clerks, Cooks and hordes of lesser menials, came under the superintendence of the Green Cloth, as did the Bake-house the Pantry, Cellar, Buttery, Spicery, Chandlery, Pastry, Confectionery, Larder, Scullery, Scalding-house, Poultry and Wood-yard. Each of these sub-divisions of the below-stairs establishment had its own carefully graded hierarchies of Serjeants, Clerks, Yeomen, Grooms, Pages and Children.

The Lord Chamberlain, a dignified and prestigious personage, was con-cerned with the smooth running of the machine above-stairs and the orderly carrying out of the intricate ritual surrounding the sovereign's every move. All those liable to come into personal contact with the Queen – the gentlemen ushers, the grooms of the chamber, the carvers, cupbearers, sewers (servers), pages and messengers – were under his supervision, and he himself was usually in close attendance on Her Majesty.

An important part of the Lord Chamberlain's duties was his overall re-sponsibility for Court entertainments. These were organised by the Office of the Revels, which arranged the programme of plays, masques and concerts presented during the Christmas holidays, on Candlemas Day, at Shrove-tide and other special occasions, such as weddings and state visits. Some were amateur efforts performed by law students from the Inns of Court, by the Children of the Chapel Royal, or the ladies and gentlemen of the Court; but the Master of the Revels also acted as a sort of impresario for the companies of professional players, calling on them to audition and rehearse their latest pieces, which, after a preview at Court, would be shown to the general public. Properties and costumes were often supplied by the Revels wardrobe, and the actors were paid by the Treasurer of the Chamber. (It is an entry in the Chamber accounts for the year 1595 that provides the first official record of the name of William Shakespeare.)

Merriment and mischief of the Maids of Honour

The Queen also had her ladies and gentlewomen of the Privy Chamber and Bedchamber and the famous Maids of Honour – a dozen or so young girls of good birth whose business was to make a decorative background for the Queen, walk with her in the Palace gardens, accompany her to prayers, play, sing and read to her, and to dance for her. Music and dancing were always

The Queen's 'she-wolf'
Elizabeth's cousin Lettice, the daughter of Catherine Carey and Francis Knollys, was the only one of her maternal relations whom the Queen cordially disliked. By her first marriage to Walter Devereux, Lettice became the mother of Robert, Earl of Essex. Widowed in 1576 she secretly married the Earl of Leicester, much to the fury of Elizabeth who persistently referred to her cousin as that 'she-wolf'. But Lettice survived both the Queen's displeasure and the Queen herself. She married twice more, and died in 1634 at the age of 92.

Elizabeth's favourite indoor recreations. She was a skilful and energetic performer herself, and a French diplomat, in London on a special mission towards the end of the 1590s, has left a vivid picture of the Queen watching her Maids of Honour dance with the critical eye of a ballet mistress, beating time with head and foot and calling out sharp rebukes when they missed a step.

The Maids of Honour were a lively group and used to 'frisk and hey about' in their dormitory at night, to the annoyance of their nearest neighbour, the Vice-Chamberlain, William Knollys. The Queen watched over their manners and morals as fiercely as any Victorian dowager, and any man, however highly placed, who ventured to take liberties with them soon felt the full weight of royal displeasure. But the girls still managed to find opportunities for getting into mischief. Bess Throckmorton and Elizabeth Vernon were both obliged to get married, and according to a court gossip Mary Fitton used shamelessly to tuck up her skirts, put on a large white cloak and march out 'as though she had been a man' to meet her lover.

Discipline was inevitably a problem in a community containing so many high-spirited young people; so many proud, touchy lordlings quick to resent any slight, real or imagined, on their honour; so much rivalry and jockeying for position in the endless striving to reach the top of the heap and stay there. In a male-dominated world, it was especially difficult for a single woman to maintain control, and only an exceptional woman could have succeeded in keeping her Court respected and respectable.

On the whole, Elizabeth succeeded remarkably well. Corruption, which was endemic in a system where everyone expected to pay for the privilege of a word in the right ear, remained a constant headache, but at least it was kept within the bounds of decency. There seems to have been very little drunkenness or disorderly behaviour – foreigners were always greatly impressed by the pre-

Greenwich Palace

Many important events in the Tudor family story took place at Greenwich. Henry VIII was born there in June 1491 and married his first wife, Catherine of Aragon, in the nearby Friars' Church. Both his daughters, Mary and Elizabeth, were born at Greenwich and christened in the Friars' Church. Greenwich was often used for the reception of ambassadors and state visitors. They were rowed downstream in the Greenwich barge, an eight-oared vessel with a red satin awning and a cabin. Nothing remains of the old palace, for in 1617 James I commissioned Inigo Jones to design a new house, seen in this painting of 1670, for his queen, Anne of Denmark.

vailing air of decorum – and scandals were few and far between. Very early in the reign it was noticed that the Queen gave her orders and had her way as absolutely as her father had done, and she ran the Court, as she ran the country, by an artful mixture of authoritarianism and blandishment.

In a sense it was all a gigantic confidence trick. The exaggerated deference and the pompous, time-consuming ceremonial of the Elizabethan Court were no mere charade to gratify the vanity of the Queen. On the contrary, they were carefully designed to enhance the authority and mystique of the Crown by presenting the monarch in a setting calculated to inspire the maximum awe and reverence. Nor were the jewels, the gold plate and costly dresses extravagance for its own sake. In a violent, yet intensely status-conscious age outward display was regarded as the visible symbol of power, and to economise on the magnificence would have been to run the risk of being despised.

An audience for the Sunday church parade

Sunday was the day for seeing the Queen in all her glory – the day when visitors were admitted to the galleries and Presence Chamber of the Palace to watch her going by in state to church. The German visitor Lupold von Wedel was at Hampton Court in October 1584 and recorded his impressions of the scene.

'Before the Queen marched her lifeguard, all chosen men, strong and tall . . . They bore gilt halberds, red coats faced with black velvet in front and on the

Riverside grandeur
Richmond Palace, built by Henry VII on the site of the old burned palace of Shene, was a favourite residence of the Elizabethan Court and possessed an unusually good fresh-water supply. Foreign visitors were much impressed by its modern comforts, its grandeur and by the fact that it contained eight kitchens. Covering ten acres of ground, the palace was surrounded by orchards and gardens which supplied fresh fruit – fine peaches, pears, apples and damsons – as well as salads, herbs and flowers for the other royal establishments.

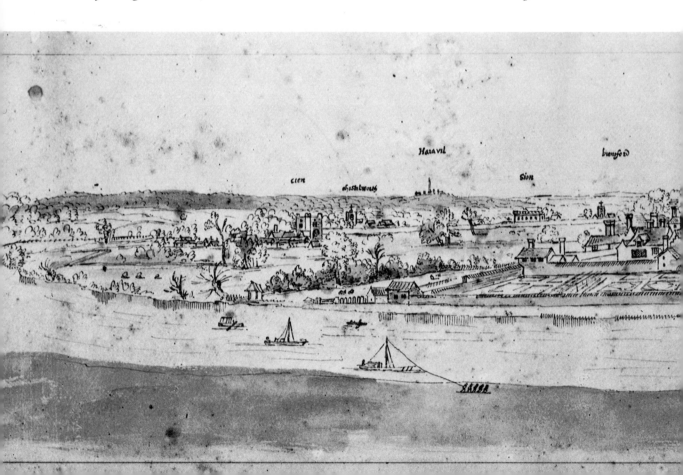

Royal nursery
Eltham Palace, in Kent, was extensively renovated and improved by Henry VII. The earlier Tudors used it as a nursery for the royal children, and Henry VIII and Anne Boleyn visited their daughter Elizabeth there when she was six months old.

back they wore the Queen's arms in silver gilt. Then came gentlemen of rank and of the council, two of them bearing a royal sceptre each, a third with the royal sword in a red velvet scabbard, embroidered with gold and set with precious stones and large pearls . . . The people standing on both sides fell on their knees, but she showed herself very gracious, and accepted with an humble mien letters of supplication from rich and poor.'

In 1598 the German lawyer Paul Hentzner was at Greenwich for the Sunday church parade and also saw the Queen and her ladies pass by on their way to the chapel, escorted by the great officers of state and a contingent of Gentlemen Pensioners – a hand-picked group of 40 stalwart members of the nobility and gentry who acted as the sovereign's personal bodyguard. Hentzner described the Queen as looking 'very majestic, her face oblong, fair but wrinkled, her eyes small, yet black and pleasant, her nose a little hooked, her lips narrow and her teeth black'. (All the English were inclined to have bad teeth, a defect which Hentzner believed was due to their passion for sweets.) Elizabeth was wearing a pair of very fine pearl earrings and a small crown on top of an obvious red wig. 'Her bosom was uncovered, as all the English ladies have it till they marry; and she had on a necklace of exceedingly fine jewels.' That particular Sunday she was dressed in white silk bordered with pearls the size of beans, and over it a mantle of black silk shot with silver threads. Hentzner remarked on the enormous respect with which the Queen was treated. 'Whoever speaks to her, it is kneeling; now and then she raises some

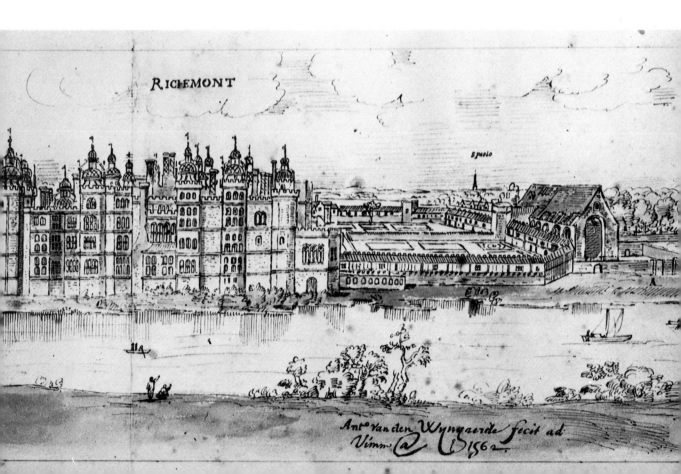

RICHEMONT

Ant° van den Wyngaerde fecit ad
Vimm 1562

with her hand . . . Wherever she turned her face, as she was going along, everybody fell down on their knees.'

While the Queen was in church, the visitors were able to watch the ceremonial laying of the royal dinner table – the various officials responsible for spreading the cloth and carrying the bread and salt kneeling and behaving with as much awe as if the Queen had been present. The meal itself, served on gilt plate, was brought in by the Yeomen of the Guard in their scarlet coats, while the hall rang with the braying of trumpets and rattle of kettle drums. The dishes were received by the Servers and laid out in order, while one of the ladies of the Privy Chamber, armed with a tasting knife, 'gave to each of the guards a mouthful to eat of the particular dish he had brought, for fear of any poison'. Then the Maids of Honour appeared, and 'with particular solemnity, lifted the meat off the table and conveyed it into the Queen's inner and more private chamber, where, after she had chosen for herself, the rest goes to the Ladies of the Court'.

The old custom by which everyone in a great household ate together in the hall was dying out, and it was only at Christmas or some other special occasion that Elizabeth dined in public. As a rule, Hentzner reported, 'the Queen dines and sups alone, with very few attendants; and it is very seldom that anybody, foreigner or native, is admitted at that time, and then only at the intercession of somebody in power'.

A morning walk, state papers at night

The plan of the royal apartments was much the same in all the palaces. Behind the Great Hall was a Guard, or Watching Chamber leading into the Presence Chamber. This was semi-public – that is, open to all who were entitled to appear at Court, and to visitors who could obtain a pass from the Lord Chamberlain. Within this again lay the Privy Chamber, where the Queen gave private audiences, saw her councillors and ate her meals. Beyond the Privy Chamber was her bedroom, surrounded by a labyrinth of smaller rooms and closets – the innermost part of the hive, where no strangers were ever admitted.

Elizabeth once described herself as not being 'a morning woman' and seldom appeared in public until the day was fairly well advanced, but she liked to slip out early for a brisk walk in the privy garden or private gallery, and was in the habit of lurking at her bedroom window to listen to the passers-by. Breakfast was not a formal meal, and the Queen would have it either in her bedroom or one of the adjoining withdrawing rooms. Usually it consisted of a manchet loaf – that is, white bread made from the finest wheat flour – and butter, a pottage, or thick broth, of boiled mutton, chine of beef, rabbit or chicken, with wine or beer to drink.

Dressing was a complicated business, though Elizabeth only wore the ornate, immensely heavy gowns shown in her portraits on state occasions. To be seen in 'princely apparel' was part of the job, but her private tastes were more austere and she usually stuck to a simple colour scheme of black, white and

A 'pearl' at Nonsuch
Henry VIII ordered the demolition of the village of Cuddington, near Ewell in Surrey, to make room for the Palace of Nonsuch – 'the very pearl of the realm', as it became known. An army of 520 workmen from all over the south of England toiled through the summer of 1538 to finish the building quickly, but the plans were so complicated and ambitious that the inner court was not ready for occupation until 1541, and the king did not live to see the outer court completed. Nonsuch, which was

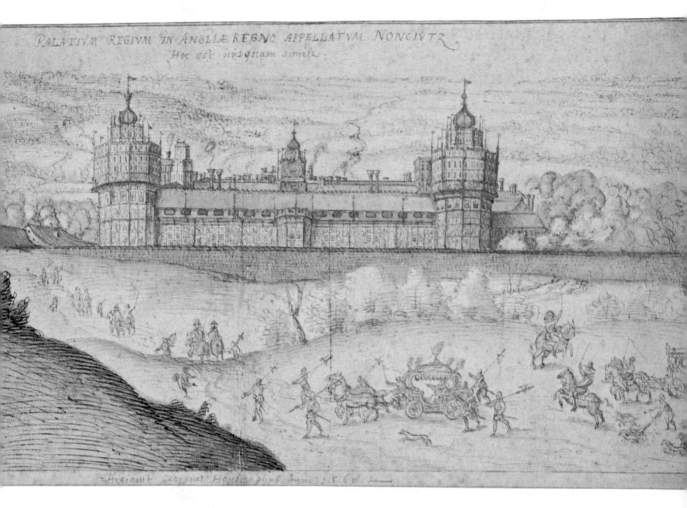

RALATIVM RIGIVM IN ANGLIÆ REGNO APPELLATVM NONCIVTZ
Hoc est nusquam simile.

intended to rival the chateaux of the French kings, stood in a park of 1,200 acres well-stocked with deer and was another special favourite of Queen Elizabeth's. Nothing now remains of this Tudor fantasy palace, although excavations have been carried out there and there is a small museum on the site.

silver. She used a cosmetic lotion compounded of white of egg, powdered egg-shell, alum, borax and poppy seeds mixed with water and beaten till frothy, and her favourite perfume was made from marjoram.

The Queen's day was a full one. 'Six or seven galliards (a quick, lively dance) of a morning, besides music and singing were her ordinary exercise,' wrote Edmund Bohun, a 17th-century biographer describing her life at Richmond. 'First in the morning she spent some time at her devotions, then she betook herself to the dispatch of her civil affairs, reading letters, ordering answers, considering what should be brought before the council and consulting with her ministers. When she had thus wearied herself, she would walk in a shady garden or pleasant gallery, without any other attendants than a few learned men; then she took coach and passed, in the sight of her people, to the neighbouring groves and fields, and sometimes would hunt and hawk.'

The main meal of the day was dinner at noon. Supper was at 5 o'clock and at 9 o'clock came the ceremony of Good Night, when all those entitled to Bouche of Court – that is, board and lodging – could draw a bedtime snack of bread and ale from the Buttery to the usher's cry of 'Have in for All Night!' After this, the

public rooms would be cleared by the Esquires of the Body responsible for internal security, the Watch prowled outside and everyone was supposed to be in bed. The Queen, who slept badly, would often be still wakeful and at work on her papers, and councillors and government officials were always liable to be suddenly called to a late-night conference.

For the Maids of Honour, the Gentlemen Pensioners, the Ladies of the Privy Chamber and anyone else whose business was to attend, guard or wait on the Queen personally, Court life inevitably entailed a good deal of hanging about. The men played tennis, fenced or practised their horsemanship, and quite a few had scholarly interests. Many of the older ladies also had a sound knowledge of Latin and Greek and would spend part of their day studying, making translations and reading the Bible. Others possessed special skills in needlework, in the distillation of perfumes and cordials, or the making of special sweetmeats and preserves which helped to keep them busy. The girls, some of whom were as young as 14 or 15 and still finishing their education, were supposed to use their free time for practising their music, sewing and serious reading. All the same, a good many hours were frittered away lounging about, gossiping, playing cards and gambling while the courtiers waited for their mistress to emerge from her inner fastness, ready to walk abroad, ride, hunt or be entertained with conversation, music and dancing.

The cost of maintaining one of the most renowned and magnificent courts of Europe was naturally high, and at the beginning of the reign amounted to about £40,000 a year. But inflation was a 16th-century problem too, and in 1601 the Queen, disturbed by the way her household expenses were rising, ordered Richard Browne, an official of the Green Cloth, to carry out a detailed comparison between the budget for one of the early years of the reign and 'one year's expenses now'. The result of this investigation showed an increase of £12,000 a year just for bread, wine, beer, wood and coal, wax and tallow lights and torches, some wages and other incidentals. Elizabeth, who suspected that much of this was due to waste and dishonesty, complained bitterly about the general laxity of the White Staves, swearing that she would cleanse her

Gateway to a palace
The imposing Great Gate-house in the west front of Hampton Court, reached by a bridge over a moat, is one part of Cardinal Wolsey's original palace that survives today. Originally, however, it was two storeys higher. Henry VIII added two wings, to create a façade nearly 400 ft long.

Gift for a king

Cardinal Wolsey began to build himself a new riverside mansion at Hampton in 1515. The handsome red-brick house, built round a series of court-yards, became the most ambitious piece of purely domestic architecture to be seen in England at that time and soon began to provoke envious comment among the cardinal's numerous enemies. In 1525 Wolsey felt it would be prudent to make Henry VIII a present of Hampton Court. The king rebuilt the Great Hall and added new kitchens, a tilt-yard, bowling alleys, and a covered tennis court which survives. The fabric of the palace suffered severely in the fire of 1986, but a comprehensive programme of repair and restoration has been completed.

Court of the abuses and extravagance currently being complained of in Parliament and elsewhere. However, as Browne recorded, before the necessary action could be taken, 'it pleased God to take Her Majesty to his mercy'.

Money, or the lack of it, was a perpetual nagging anxiety, especially during the last years of the Queen's life. Even when every source had been squeezed dry, her income never amounted to more than £300,000 a year, and out of this she not only had to pay for the Court but all the ordinary day-to-day expenses of government as well. Elizabeth has acquired a reputation for parsimony, but it was only her constant vigilance which kept the monarchy anything like solvent.

On summer tour – to 241 sleeping-places

One of the best-known features of Elizabethan Court life are the Queen's annual summer progresses. The Queen undoubtedly enjoyed her travels through the kingdom, which gave her a welcome change of scene and break from the daily grind of state business. They were not just pleasure trips, however, for they were undertaken, at least in part, to bring her into contact with the people and give her an opportunity to 'view the estate of the country'.

The itineraries of the progresses were worked out in advance by the Vice-Chamberlain's office, in close consultation with the Queen. The mayors of towns and the owners of suitable private houses would then be informed by letter carried by a royal courier. The next stage was a preliminary visit by the royal Harbinger who, among other things, would want to know about any cases of plague or infectious disease in the neighbourhood. A couple of ushers of the Bedchamber would inspect the accommodation and give advice to prospective hosts, while the road masters and equerries surveyed the route to be taken by the Queen and her entourage. This was only the beginning. A progress entailed an immense amount of hard work and detailed organisation; according to a contemporary estimate it took up to 400 carts and 2,400 pack-horses and mules to transport the Court and its belongings on a major progress, covering a distance of 10 or 12 miles a day.

In general, the progresses were confined to the south-east, East Anglia, the Home Counties and the Midlands. Although visits to York and Shrewsbury were discussed and even planned, Elizabeth never went further north than Lincolnshire or further west than Bristol, but within these limits she covered a lot of ground and actually slept in 241 different recorded places. This was no small achievement, considering the expense and the logistical problems involved in bringing the Queen to the people in suitably magnificent state.

The list of towns she visited in the 1560s includes Winchester, Colchester, Harwich, Ipswich, Hertford, Coventry, Stamford, Guildford and Southampton. She also paid extended visits to the Universities of Oxford and Cambridge, sitting through crowded programmes of sermons, Latin orations, learned disputations and plays.

During the visit to Oxford in 1566, while the Queen was watching a play in the hall at Christ Church part of the stage collapsed killing three undergraduates and injuring five others. Elizabeth was much concerned, and sent the Vice-Chancellor of the University and her own surgeon with orders to help the injured, and 'to have a care that they want nothing for their recovery'. But the show went on, and the actors performed their parts so well that 'the Queen laughed heartily thereat and gave the author of the play great thanks for his pains'.

The 1570s, the last full decade of peace, saw the longest and most ambitious progresses. In 1574 the Court visited Bristol and was entertained at Sudeley Castle, Longleat and Wilton. The following year came probably the most famous progress of them all, which took Elizabeth through the Midlands and culminated in the Princely Pleasures of Kenilworth. The Queen stayed for nearly three weeks with the Earl of Leicester at Kenilworth Castle, the War-

Garter procession
The solemnity of the annual procession of the Knights of the Garter in 1576 is portrayed in an engraving by the Court painter Marcus Gheeraerts the Elder. In the centre are the five principal officers of the Order – the Chancellor, the Bishop of Winchester, the Usher of the Black Rod, the Registrar (a post usually held by the Dean of Windsor) and Garter King of

Arms. On the far right is Emperor Maximilian II, one of the foreign Garter Knights, and on the far left are two gentlemen ushers. The Order of the Garter was instituted by Edward III in 1348. The dedication of this picture sets this particular St George's Day Garter Feast at Windsor, though in Elizabeth's time the occasion was more often celebrated at Greenwich or Whitehall.

wickshire estate she had bestowed on him 12 years before, and was treated to a non-stop programme of plays, masques, pageants, feasts, revels, hunts, bear-baiting and firework displays, presented against a backdrop of idyllic countryside through a succession of hot, still July days.

There were no long journeys during the 1580s, a time when international tension was at its height, but the custom was revived in the 1590s and the Queen visited Chichester, Portsmouth and Southampton in 1591, staying at Cowdray Park, Petworth and the Earl of Hertford's house at Elvetham in Hampshire. In 1592 she was in Gloucestershire again, returning by way of Oxford, and she continued to make shorter trips round the Home Counties almost to the end of her life. As late as 1600 plans for another long journey were under discussion, and when some of the older courtiers grumbled at the prospect (progresses could be quite uncomfortable affairs for those who no longer found it amusing to sleep in a tent) Elizabeth, who was then approaching her sixty-seventh birthday, snapped that the old could stay behind and the young and able go with her.

The high cost of entertaining a Queen

A great deal has been written about the financial burden that the summer progresses imposed on the Queen's hosts, but there is no evidence that anyone complained at the time. On the contrary, towns fought for the honour of a place on the royal itinerary, and as soon as the route had been settled the fortunate municipalities set about beautifying themselves for the occasion. Streets were cleaned, houses decorated and pageants rehearsed. The local dignitaries bought new clothes and learned welcoming speeches by heart. It was customary on these occasions to present the Queen with a piece of plate or some similar token of esteem. At Coventry in 1565, according to a contemporary account, 'the Recorder presented unto Her Majesty a purse, and in it about £100 in angels, which Her Grace accepting, was pleased to say to her Lords, "it was a good gift, £100 in gold; I have but few such gifts". To which the Mayor answered boldly, "if it please Your Grace, there is a great deal more in it". "What is that?" said she. "It is," said he, "the hearts of all your loving subjects." "We thank you, Mr. Mayor," said she; "it is a great deal more indeed".'

Since a royal visit meant a public holiday and a free show, with very often a free ration of wine or beer as well, the Queen was assured of an enthusiastic welcome from the townspeople, and the Spanish ambassador, who was with her on a progress in 1568, described a typical scene. 'She was received everywhere,' he wrote, 'with great acclamations and signs of joy, as is customary in this country; whereat she was extremely pleased and told me so, giving me to understand how beloved she was by her subjects and how highly she esteemed this, together with the fact that they were peaceful and contented, whilst her neighbours on all sides are in such trouble. She attributed it all to God's miraculous goodness. She ordered her carriage sometimes to be taken where the crowd seemed thickest and stood up and thanked the people.'

Elizabeth was always a satisfactory guest, taking care to be well briefed on local conditions, local sights and specialities, and missed no opportunity for a graceful compliment or gesture to the local community.

As far as her visits to private houses were concerned, the Queen had a perfect legal right to make use of any house belonging to one of her tenants-in-chief – all manors being held ultimately from the Crown – and in theory all the occupier had to do was vacate the premises, leaving the royal purveyors to provide food, fuel and even furniture for the Court. In practice, of course, no self-respecting gentleman would dream of behaving in such an inhospitable fashion. The expense and inconvenience of a royal visit was more than outweighed by the valuable prestige it conferred on the host, and the pleasure and excitement, not to mention the extra employment, it brought to a whole neighbourhood. Owners of stately homes competed for the privilege of entertaining Her Majesty in suitable style, and their chief anxiety was to receive sufficient notice of the event.

No one was under any obligation to ruin himself. Indeed, the Queen was said 'to mislike the superfluous expense of her subjects bestowed upon her in times of her progresses'. She never abused her subjects' hospitality, and if anyone spent more than he could afford in a desire to show off his status or curry

Pageants at Elvetham

An artificial lake with three islands was specially dug out in the gardens of Elvetham House in Hampshire as the setting for pageants enacted during the Queen's visit to the Earl of Hertford in 1591. Overlooking the lake was a large rustic pavilion. The outsides of the walls were decorated with green boughs and ripe hazel nuts, while the inside was hung with arras, the roof lined with ivy leaves and the floor strewn with rushes and sweet herbs.

Loyal Secretary
Sir Robert Cecil (far left), son of the great Lord Burghley, became Principal Secretary of State in 1596. Although handicapped by a deformed shoulder and constantly vilified by the Earl of Essex and his friends, Robert Cecil proved an able Secretary, supporting the Queen loyally through the last difficult years of her reign.

Devoted Chancellor
Of all the circle of able and good-looking men who surrounded Queen Elizabeth, only Christopher Hatton (left) was to remain single for her sake. As he once said, 'the Queen did fish for men's souls and had so sweet a bait that no one could escape her network'. All the same, Hatton prospered by his devotion. The Queen appointed him Lord Chancellor in 1587 and helped him to acquire a valuable London estate which, as Hatton Garden, still commemorates his name.

favour with his sovereign, then that was his own affair.

Accommodation was usually the biggest problem. Most of the royal entourage lived in tents brought along in the baggage train or else were boarded out in nearby towns and villages, but some hosts ran up temporary buildings – the Earl of Hertford built an encampment in his park and provided two extra kitchens and a special lodging for the cook. Others used the occasion as an excuse to enlarge and improve their properties, and these works appearing in the accounts could artificially inflate the actual cost of the visit. Provisions were bought up locally and most of the rank and file were fed at royal expense. Elizabeth herself was abstemious in matters of food and drink and usually brought her own wine and beer – nothing was so calculated to annoy her as to offer her too-strong beer – but the Court consumed alarming quantities of food. At Cowdray Park in 1591 the houseparty's Sunday breakfast alone accounted for three oxen and 140 geese, which gives some indication of the strain a progress could put on local resources.

Secretary, spy-master and trusted counsellors

Even on a progress the Queen was never really able to forget the cares of state for, not unlike a modern United States President, she carried the government with her wherever she went. She was always accompanied by some members of the Privy Council and nearly always by the Principal Secretary of State. The Secretary was the workhorse of the Elizabethan executive machine. He handled all the routine business of the Council and its relations with the Queen. He was also responsible for the day-to-day administration of foreign and domestic policy, defence, finance and internal security. There was, typically enough, no very precise definition of his powers, but William Cecil, the most famous holder of the office under Elizabeth, was the Queen's right-hand man, and their partnership lasted until his death.

Cecil's successor as Principal Secretary was Francis Walsingham, whose reputation as a spy-master has added a sinister flavour to his name. Closer inspection, though, reveals a conscientious, over-worked and under-staffed government official, frequently in poor health and much given to taking physic, who combined the functions of Home and Foreign Secretaries with those of head of MI5 and the Special Branch. It is on his performance in these latter capacities that Walsingham's notoriety depends; but in fact there were probably never more than about a dozen full-time agents on his pay-roll at any given moment. Reliable spies were scarce and expensive, and it was not until the early 1580s that Walsingham began to receive any regular budget for this side of his work. It started at a grudging £750 per annum and gradually rose to £2,000 by the crisis year of 1588. In the early days most of the cost of maintaining a secret service is said to have come from its founder's own pocket.

By the 1570s Elizabeth had gathered round her most of that coterie of trusted friends and advisers whose names are permanently linked with her own. First among them always was William Cecil, later Lord Burghley, a wise, patient and long-suffering statesman whom the Queen nicknamed her 'Spirit'. The Earl of Leicester, 'that great Lucifer' to his numerous enemies, was her 'Eyes'. Leicester, immensely capable, astute, sophisticated and a splendid ornament to the Court, was the constant companion of Elizabeth's off-duty hours, and although their peculiar relationship was often a stormy one, it too was broken only by death.

All the Queen's intimates had their nicknames. Christopher Hatton, the tall, good-looking young lawyer who came into favour towards the end of the 1560s, was her 'Lids', and later 'Mutton' or 'Bellwether'. Francis Walsing-

Master of the Horse
One of the most prominent figures at Court was Lord Robert Dudley, created Earl of Leicester in 1564. After the mysterious death of Dudley's first wife at Cumnor Place, near Oxford, in September 1559, many people feared that the Queen meant to marry her handsome Master of the Horse. But although she was undoubtedly very fond of him, Elizabeth was too wise to risk taking a husband whose elevation would have given rise to furious jealousy among his peers and caused acute offence to the majority of her subjects. Robert eventually married Lettice Knollys, but he remained one of the Queen's most trusted friends until his death in 1588.

Royal spymaster
Sir Francis Walsingham (far left) was the Queen's Private Secretary of State from 1573 until his death in 1590. An ardent Protestant, he founded the first English secret service to counteract the numerous Catholic plots directed against the Queen during the 1570s and 1580s. A contemporary illustration (left) shows Elizabeth steering The Royal Ship of Europe, with Walsingham, Burghley and Leicester as her crew.

Favoured cousin
The Queen always showed affection and favour to her maternal relations. Her first cousin Catherine Carey, daughter of her aunt Mary Boleyn, was appointed a gentlewoman of the Privy Chamber.

Pause in the hunt
Stag hunting was always the Court's favourite outdoor pastime, and as late as 1600 the Queen was reported to be 'excellently disposed to hunting, for every second day she is on horseback and continues the sport long'. This woodcut, from Turberville's Book of Hunting *published in 1575, shows the Queen and her courtiers enjoying an elaborate picnic during an interval in the chase. Wine flows freely – even the young pages in the foreground are having their share. Roasted poultry is distributed, musicians play, and the Queen receives the supplication of a kneeling attendant.*

ham, with his dark colouring, was 'Moor', and when Walter Raleigh, who 'spake broad Devonshire to his dying day', joined the circle, he was christened 'Water'. There were other friends, less well known – Nicholas Bacon, Francis and William Knollys, Thomas Heneage, and the Queen's cousin Henry Carey, Lord Hunsdon. In the last years of her life, the scene was dominated by the contrasting personalities of Robert Devereux, the dazzling but tragically unstable Earl of Essex, and old Burghley's son Robert Cecil, with his crooked back and cold, formidable intelligence.

Surrounded by all the brains and brilliance of a dazzling age, surrounded, too, by the intrigue and ruthless self-seeking of an age in which the prizes went to the strong and the fortunate and there was scant sympathy for failure, the Queen held her own without apparent difficulty. 'She ruled much by faction and parties,' remembered Robert Naunton in his *Fragmenta Regalia*, 'which she

Doomed adventurer

Sir Walter Raleigh was one of the most brilliant and glamorous figures of the age – soldier, seafarer, courtier, poet, scholar and explorer. Elizabeth admired his abilities and enjoyed his company – she made him Captain of her Guard – but did not consider him suitable material for government office. After the accession of James I, Raleigh was tried, convicted and condemned to death on a charge of treason, but was subsequently reprieved and imprisoned in the Tower, where he wrote his unfinished History of the World. *In 1616 he was released to lead a treasure-hunting expedition up the Orinoco River. This failed disastrously, and on his return he was executed under his former sentence.*

herself both made, upheld, and weakened, as her own great judgement advised.' No one, not even Leicester, was allowed to presume on his position. When the Earl once attempted to take a high hand with one of the royal servants, the Queen turned on him, rapping out 'her wonted oath'. 'God's death, my lord, I have wished you well, but my favour is not so locked up for you, that others shall not participate thereof . . . and if you think to rule here, I will take a course to see you forthcoming: I will have here but one mistress and no master.'

The Court was essentially an artificial world, where a man's career and livelihood could depend on maintaining friendly relations with the right people, but under Elizabeth it was never an entirely closed world. Of course it helped to have connections or a known name (the Elizabethan establishment was very much a family affair, almost all its leading members being related by blood or marriage or both), but it was still perfectly possible for a talented and presentable outsider to break in. Walter Raleigh, the son of a Devonshire squire, is one example, and so is Christopher Hatton, who first attracted the Queen's attention when dancing in a masque put on by the students of the Inner Temple.

'Know the Court,' wrote a veteran courtier, Walter Mildmay, to his son, 'but spend not thy life there, for Court is a very chargeable [expensive] place. I would rather wish thee to spend the greatest part of thy life in the country than to live in this glittering misery.' But the glamour of the Court continued to exercise a powerful fascination over eager and optimistic youth, which continued to dress up in its finest feathers and crowd into the Presence Chamber on every available opportunity.

A 17-year-old Welsh squire, later Lord Herbert of Cherbury, who joined the throng one day in 1600, recorded what *could* happen. 'As it was the manner of those times for all men to kneel down before the great Queen Elizabeth, I was likewise upon my knees in the Presence Chamber when she passed by to the Chapel at Whitehall. As soon as she saw me she stopped and, swearing her usual oath, demanded "Who is this?" Everybody there present looked upon me, until Sir James Croft, a pensioner, finding the Queen stayed, returned back and told who I was, and that I had married Sir William Herbert of St Julian's daughter.'

The influence of the Court spread outwards, too, and not only by means of the progresses. Great lords and their retinues returning to their country estates, even quite humble petitioners and place-seekers returning to their native towns, brought the latest political gossip, news of the latest fashions, of how the Queen's majesty had looked and smiled, so that those who never aspired to make the pilgrimage themselves could take a proprietorial interest and feel a vicarious pride in the doings of shining ones who dwelt in palaces.

Faithful to the state
William Cecil, Lord Burghley, was the greatest statesman of the Elizabethan era. Born in Lincolnshire in 1520, he began his career during the reign of Edward VI as private secretary to the Lord Protector Somerset. The young Princess Elizabeth asked him to act as surveyor of her landed property, at a salary of £20 a year. Three days after her accession she appointed Cecil her Principal Secretary, saying 'this judgement I have of you that you will not be corrupted by any manner of gift and that you will be faithful to the state – and that without respect of my private will you will give me that counsel which you think best'. Her judgement was not at fault. Cecil was created Baron Burghley in 1571 and became Lord High Treasurer in 1572. In this portrait he holds the Lord Treasurer's staff of office. In 1589 Burghley completed the building of Burghley House, near Stamford (left), which still stands today.

Colourful costumes

CLOTHES THAT SHOWED THE WEARER'S STATUS AND MIRRORED AN AGE OF SPLENDOUR

High fashion in Elizabethan times became more and more extravagant as the years went by. Men's and women's garments were padded and quilted, stiffened with whalebone or buckram, lavishly embroidered and slashed to show an even richer lining or shirt. Such clothing was extremely heavy, restricting and expensive, but in dress, as in everything else, it was essential to make a fine show. The ambitious young man intent on getting himself noticed at Court would often be wearing his entire fortune on his back.

This sort of fashion, of course, was for the upper classes. The so-called 'sumptuary laws' were intended to prevent anyone below a certain rank from wearing the more costly furs and fabrics. Ordinary middle-class and working-class people wore far simpler and more practical clothes, and even the very rich did not spend their lives in the sort of garments seen in their portraits. The Queen herself, when she was not on show, would relax in a comfortable loose gown called a nightgown – rather like a modern housecoat.

From frills to ruff
The gentleman in this miniature by Nicholas Hilliard displays the ruff in the early stages of its development – that is, as a frilled shirt collar. He also wears a slashed doublet and the jaunty, beret-like cap, usually feathered and bejewelled, which was popular with both sexes.

Finery for man and maid
In the peacock age of Elizabethan fashion, men's clothes frequently outshone women's. For his formal portrait (left) Richard Sackville, Earl of Dorset, wears a high starched collar, tight-waisted stiffened doublet, padded and embroidered breeches and blue silk stockings. One elegantly gloved hand rests on his helmet. For women, styles that became fashionable during the last years of Elizabeth's reign included the French wheel farthingale, with a skirt 'frounced' or gathered in folds, worn (far left) by Ann Vavasour, one of the Queen's Maids of Honour. Not all the maids lived up to their title. Ann Vavasour had a reputation for promiscuity and in 1581 gave birth to a son in the maiden's chamber at court. The Queen was said to be 'greatly grieved'.

A frame for the face
This ornate ruff is decorated with cut-work embroidery and edged with lace. The hair-style shows the fashion for frizzing and puffing out the hair and covering it with jewellery.

Winged beauty
Sleeves, as displayed by the young woman in this portrait of 1569 (right), were made separately from the bodice and tied or pinned together. The padded 'wings' concealed the join.

A 'Judgment' in silks
Biblical scenes were favourite embroidery subjects: a cushion cover at Hardwick Hall (below) depicts the Judgment of Solomon. The box (below, right) is richly embroidered in fine silk thread.

ÆTATIS·SVE 21

AN° DOMINY 1569

Scenes from a diplomat's life

A memorial portrait, or pictorial biography, of her husband was often commissioned
by an Elizabethan widow. The subject of this one is Sir Henry Unton, a soldier and diplomat, who died in 1596.
In a montage of scenes from his life he is depicted as a baby, as a student at Oxford, travelling in
Italy as a young man, soldiering in the Low Countries and finally brought to
his death-bed while on a diplomatic mission to France. His funeral procession wends its way home to his burial in
Faringdon parish church and his elaborate monument, which was destroyed during the Civil War,
appears in the bottom left-hand corner. The picture also shows glimpses of Unton's life as a well-to-do country gentleman
at home at Wadley in Berkshire. There is a banquet in progress and the
guests are being entertained by a masque, accompanied by a group of musicians seated round a table.

CHAPTER THREE

The seven ages of man

CUSTOM AND TRADITION GUIDE THE COURSE
OF FAMILY LIFE, WITH HALLOWED CEREMONIES TO MARK BIRTH,
MARRIAGE AND DEATH FOR RICH AND POOR ALIKE

All the world's a stage,
And all the men and women merely players:
They have their exits and their entrances;
And one man in his time plays many parts,
His acts being seven ages.

William Shakespeare *As You Like It*

*I*n every civilised society the birth of a baby is a cause for family rejoicing, and Tudor England was no exception to this rule. In royal or noble households a special room would be set aside and sumptuously furnished as a lying-in chamber, and in the late 15th century Lady Margaret Beaufort, mother of Henry VII, had laid down detailed instructions covering the preparations to be made 'against the deliverance of a queen'.

As soon as it had been decided where the birth was to take place, a suite of rooms was to be got ready and 'hanged with rich arras'. The lying-in chamber was to be completely hung with tapestry, except for one window 'so as she may have light when it pleaseth her'. The 'furniture appertaining to the Queen's bed' included a mattress stuffed with wool, a feather bed and a bolster of down. The sheets were to measure 4 yds broad by 5 yds long, and there must be two long and two square pillows stuffed with fine down. The counterpane should be of scarlet cloth, furred with ermine and trimmed with crimson velvet and rich cloth of gold. Luxury on this scale was confined to royalty and the greater nobility, but every household except the poorest could provide a feather pillow and some additional comforts for the woman in childbed.

At Court the great ladies of the realm gathered as of right to attend a royal birth, but in every walk of life a lying-in was a social occasion, when all the neighbourhood wives would assemble 'to make good cheer', and to support and encourage the woman in labour.

The party would be presided over by the midwife, an influential and respected member of the community. Indeed, of all the careers open to women in Elizabethan England, that of midwife was the most eagerly sought after. 'Many a good thing passes through the Midwife's hand,' wrote the playwright Ben Jonson, 'many a merry tale by her mouth, many a glad cup through her lips; she is a leader of wives, the lady of light hearts, and the queen of Gossips.' The social importance of the midwife was recognised by the Church, which required her to be licensed by the local bishop and to swear an oath not to use 'any kind of sorcery or incantations in the time of travail of any woman'. She was to be ready to assist the poor as well as the rich, and faithfully and diligently to exercise her office according to such cunning and knowledge as God had given her.

The midwife learned her craft mainly from other midwives and by experience. There were a few technical manuals available, which decreed that

Into the world
A woman in labour is attended by her female friends, while in the background a male astrologer studies the stars in order to cast a horoscope for the new-born child. In Elizabethan times childbirth was still regarded as an event at which only women could be in attendance. In royal circles women would be appointed to all the household offices usually held by men, and everything needful would be delivered to the outer door of the great chamber to be received by the women officers. When the male obstetrician or 'man-midwife' first began to make his appearance during the 17th and 18th centuries he met with considerable hostility and prejudice.

she should be cheerful, gentle, courteous, painstaking and physically strong. She should also be sober and chaste and, most important, discreet – 'not a blabber, or reporter of any thing she shall either hear or see in secret in the house or person of her she hath delivered'. Coming to more practical matters, the author of one of these manuals advised the midwife to keep her nails clean and well-pared, and to anoint her hands with butter or hogsgrease before commencing operations; she should not wear rings or bracelets while she was about her business.

It is highly unlikely, however, that the average midwife knew of the existence of any of these books. Most practising midwives, especially in country areas, were not far removed from the wise woman or white witch, placing their reliance on a well-tried stock of spells, charms and herbal recipes handed down through the generations. Many such women were skilful enough within their limits. They would usually be able to recognise the signs and perhaps even guess at the causes of complications, even if they were helpless to alleviate their patients' sufferings.

The oft-repeated pangs of childbirth

In an age lacking anaesthesia, antiseptics or antibiotics, childbirth was frequently an agonising and always a hazardous affair. No one pretended otherwise. But the woman in travail was expected to keep cheerful, to be patient and obedient, and to strive to help herself as much as she could, instead of wasting her strength crying and lamenting. She must call on God to send her a safe delivery, while at the same time remembering that it was plainly stated in the Scriptures that women shall bring forth in labour and pain.

The women of Elizabethan England accepted the situation stoically, facing the ordeal of childbirth upwards of a dozen times between their mid-teens and late thirties. Such physical servitude had been their lot from time immemorial – it was an inescapable fact of life and there was no point in making a fuss about it. If the mother survived – and, in spite of everything, she often did – then the focus of attention shifted to the baby, which would have been carefully washed and swaddled by the midwife and her assistants. All babies were breast-fed, though not always by their own mothers. It was generally accepted that mothers ought to undertake this duty themselves if at all possible. 'Wherefore as it is agreeing to nature, so it is also necessary and comely for the own mother to nurse the own child,' declared one writer on the subject. Women who shirked their responsibilities were accused of vanity, and fearing 'to change the form of their hard round paps' by breast-feeding.

However, wet nurses continued to be employed by the upper classes, by mothers unable to feed their own babies (many, of course, would be pregnant again within a matter of a few months), in cases where the mother had died in childbirth, and by city-dwellers who preferred to put their babies out to nurse, hoping they might stand a better chance of survival in clean country air. (Wet nurses were sometimes used to nourish the old and toothless as well as the young and toothless.)

The Cholmondeley sisters
All babies were swaddled and wrapped up like parcels to protect them from cold and draughts. The two proud mothers sitting side by side in bed with their infants have obviously taken every precaution. The name of the portraitist who was commissioned to paint this brightly coloured scene is unknown, but the women whose identical faces stare out of the

portrait are twin sisters named Cholmondeley. Their lives ran parallel courses to the extent that they were not only born on the same day, but also married on the same day and brought to childbed on the same day. The unusual double-portrait of the sisters and their babies was painted about 1600, and is typical of the formal, decorative style of portraiture which Queen Elizabeth herself is said to have favoured.

The choice of wet nurse, or foster mother, was an anxious business for conscientious parents. She must be healthy, clean in her person and habits and of unimpeachable character, for there was a widespread belief that the infant absorbed its nurse's morals, or lack of them, together with her milk. If the nurse was dissolute, unchaste or a drunkard, the child would take after her, and if there was a trace of blood in the milk, he might grow up to be a murderer.

The safeguard of an early christening

Baptism always took place as soon as possible, usually on the Sunday following the birth. Infant life was altogether too uncertain to admit of any unnecessary delay. The Church taught that an unchristened child would be excluded from the Kingdom of Heaven, and even if perhaps not everyone went along with this stark doctrine, a great many people did believe that such a child stood in grave danger of being bewitched or stolen by the fairies.

The baby was carried to church on a cushion, as expensive and elaborately embroidered as its parents could afford, and was brought home again wrapped in the 'chrisom' – originally a white linen cloth laid over it by the priest as a token of innocence, which developed into a christening robe. The chrisom was used until the mother had been 'churched', or purified, about a month later, and a baby which died during this period would be buried in it.

After the religious ceremony came the christening party, which varied in grandeur according to the social status of the family concerned. It was always a convivial occasion, when friends and relations gathered to congratulate the parents and admire the baby, just as they do today. It was also, as today, an occasion for present giving – godparents and friends offering a gilt cup, a porringer or a silver-mounted piece of coral with bells, used as a teething ring. Spoons bearing the figures of the 12 apostles on the handles were very popular as 'first' gifts – a wealthy godparent might rise to a whole set of apostle spoons – while poorer families hoped for useful presents of money or baby clothes from more prosperous kinsfolk.

Parents were not much in evidence at the baptismal ceremony. The mother, who was rarely in any condition to leave her bed, held court at home, and although fathers were urged to be present at church to hear the vows being made in their offspring's name, this was principally the godparents' occasion. The choice of sponsors would be a matter of much anxious thought in socially ambitious households, and an invitation to 'stand gossip', or godparent, was always taken seriously, as both an honour and a responsibility. The choice of names also received serious consideration. Devout parents might turn to the Bible for inspiration, and the more worldly minded to the classics; in the majority of cases, however, a child would be christened to compliment an influential godparent or relative. Henry, Edward, William, John, Richard and Robert were commonest for boys, and Mary, Elizabeth, Anne, Margaret and Katherine for girls.

Clothes that bound, and a diet of slops

Once it had been safely enrolled as a member of the Christian community, an Elizabethan baby spent the first precarious months of its life in a carved wooden cradle set on rockers and carefully shielded from fresh air and draughts, while mother or nurse rocked it with her foot and sang the old lullabies – 'Rock a-Bye Baby on the Tree-top' and 'Bye Baby Bunting, Daddy's Gone a-Hunting'.

The unfortunate infant would be smothered in clothes and coverings. At birth it was wrapped in swaddling bands (which were supposed to make the limbs grow straight) over a shirt, and always wore a biggin, or cap. Older babies also wore caps and layers of long petticoats covered with a bibbed apron. Boys and girls were dressed alike until about the age of five, when boys would be put into breeches.

Children were not fully weaned until their second year and even then continued to be fed largely on milk, or a pap made of bread and milk, gradually supplemented by poultry and other white meats. Rich food was considered unsuitable and when Elizabeth was three years old her nurse, Margaret Bryan, grumbled that the Steward of the Household wanted the lady Elizabeth to dine and sup every day at the grown-ups' table. 'It is not meet for a child of her age to keep such rule yet,' complained Lady Bryan. 'If she do, I dare not take it upon me to keep her Grace in health; for there she shall see divers meats, and fruits, and wine, which it would be hard for me to restrain her Grace from.'

Ill-fated orphan

As soon as they were out of baby clothes, children were dressed as miniature adults. However, Lady Arbella Stuart, aged 23 months, is depicted still clutching her doll. Arbella was the daughter of Charles Stuart, Earl of Lennox, and Lady Elizabeth Cavendish. Orphaned at an early age, she was brought up by her grandmother, Bess of Hardwick, who planned a brilliant future for her. However, Arbella's royal blood caused both Queen Elizabeth and James I to regard her with suspicion, and she died in the Tower in 1615.

Fruit, especially, was to be avoided, being regarded as a cause of 'the flux' – the diarrhoea or 'summer complaint' which killed so many young children.

The nursery child was brought up on all the old rhymes and jingles – 'This Little Pig Went to Market', 'Little Boy Blue', 'Baa Baa Black Sheep', 'Who Killed Cock Robin?' and many others equally familiar. It 'rode a-cock horse to Banbury Cross' on its mother's knee, learned that its toes were called Harry Whistle, Tommy Thistle, Harry Thible, Tommy Thible and Little Oker Bell, and its fingers Tom Thumbkin, Bess Bumpkin, Bill Winkin, Long Linkin and Little Dick. Too much baby talk was, however, held to be bad for children.

Most of the toys in upper and middle-class nurseries were imported from France or Holland. There were stiffly jointed wooden dolls with painted faces, toy ships and soldiers and drums, and children of both sexes rolled hoops and played ball. In poor homes, of course, the children had to make do with such unsophisticated playthings as could either be made at home or perhaps bought with great extravagance at a local fair or from a travelling packman.

In all classes of society these carefree days were all too brief. The Elizabethans had an immense respect for education, and writers of the numerous hand-books on the subject all agreed that it should begin as early as possible, though

At home with the Cobhams
Household pets are much in evidence in this domestic scene of Lord Cobham with his wife, sister and six children. The little girl on the far right is holding a monkey, one of the boys has a tame bird on his fist and a small dog is jumping up at the baby on the far left. The parrot picking its way among the fruit on the table must have been brought as a present by some seafaring friend. Lord Cobham held the office of Warden of the Cinque Ports.

Lessons in the Bible

The importance of religion in the home and of bringing children up in the fear of the Lord was stressed by the Elizabethan Church. Parents were constantly urged to remember their obligations in this respect. This pious family group, from a Book of Psalms of 1563, is receiving instruction from a conscientious father.

they also agreed that the transition between play and study should not be too abrupt. Children from caring, literate homes naturally got the best start. They would be taught to say their prayers from a very early age and would learn their letters from the 'criss-cross row' of a horn book, before progressing to simple sentences: 'Ah, it is so; he is my foe' and 'Boy, go thy way to the top of the hill where the big tree is' were the Elizabethan equivalents of 'The cat sat on the mat'. The next step would be little story books, moral tales like Aesop's *Fables* and, in devout households, the Bible. Such children would also learn the accepted rules of decorum and good manners. As they reached the age of discretion, they would be expected always to stand in the presence of their parents, to call them Sir and Madame, and kneel to ask a blessing when they met first in the morning and before going to bed at night.

Responsibility for providing primary education for the masses lay in the hands of the parish priest. In practice, both the quality and availability of instruction (which was, of course, chiefly religious instruction) varied from parish to parish, according to the zeal of individual incumbents, but in most towns and villages of any size someone was appointed to give the local children the rudiments of education. In Falmouth the children of the poor were taught by the bell-ringer, while in Launceston instruction was provided by an aged man chosen by the mayor.

Such education tended to be a rather hit-or-miss affair, and the children of the poor had other calls on their time, being expected to start earning their keep as soon as they were capable of simple fieldwork, or of helping their parents in the family trade or business. All the same, a surprising number do seem to have attended the parish school, at least for a year or two, and there was always the chance that the parson or squire or a craft guild would take an interest in a promising boy and help him to get to grammar school.

From horn book to grammar school

The grammar schools were the backbone of the Elizabethan educational system. Many of them were re-foundations of schools formerly attached to abbeys or monasteries. Others were endowed by the craft guilds, and others again had been founded by public-spirited individuals such as Andrew Judd, skinner, at Tonbridge, Peter Blundell, wool merchant, at Tiverton and Roger Chomeley, lawyer, at Highgate. Tuition was generally, though not always, free. In many cases an entry fee was fixed; in others, parents paid according to their means. Extras such as fires, candles and stationery had to be paid for; so did board and lodging when pupils lived in, unless, as at Jesus College, Rotherham, the endowment explicitly provided for 'six poor children' to be educated, boarded and lodged free of charge. Such phrases as 'poor scholars' or boys whose parents 'were poor and needy' which appear frequently in school statutes seldom applied to the labouring or very poor classes but rather to the children of tradesmen, skilled craftsmen, yeoman farmers, country squires and small landowners who made up the bulk of the grammar schools' intake.

The average age of entry was six or seven, and certain standards of literacy were required of intending pupils. At St Paul's the master was to see that applicants knew their catechism and could read and write. It was the same at the Merchant Taylors' School, and the re-foundation statutes of Canterbury Grammar School demanded that 'No one shall be admitted into the school who cannot read readily, or does not know by heart in the vernacular the Lord's Prayer, the Angelic Salutation, the Apostles' Creed and the Ten Commandments'. In practice, though, these standards were not always insisted on and the assistant master taught the youngest children, or 'pettys' as they were called, the basic essentials before they embarked on the school course proper. In some places a system of pupil teachers was instituted, with the older boys helping the usher. But the aim of the grammar schools was always to get on with their main business, the teaching of Latin grammar – hence their name.

Latin was taught as a living language, which indeed it was. A sound knowledge of Latin, both spoken and written, was indispensable for anyone contemplating a professional career, whether in the Church, the law, government service or medicine, or, for that matter, anyone who wished to be regarded as educated. The foundation of this knowledge in all schools was Lilly's *Latin Grammar*, written by the first High Master of St Paul's School, in the City of London. Boys also read Cicero, Ovid, Virgil and Horace, and were expected to produce Latin prose and verse in imitation of the classical authors.

Mastering the alphabet
The first step in the rigorous process of education was learning the alphabet from a horn book, which this child holds. On the table are an open book for the master's use, an inkstand and quill pen, made from the feathers of a goose, and the inevitable birch.

Horn book ABC
The horn book consisted of a sheet of paper mounted on a wooden tablet and protected by a thin sheet of transparent horn. On this horn book is inscribed the alphabet, preceded by a cross and known as the criss-cross row, followed by some simple elements of spelling and the Lord's Prayer.

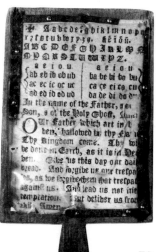

The study of Greek as a school subject spread only slowly, largely because of the shortage of Greek scholars competent to teach it, though this improved towards the end of the century. English was not yet regarded as a separate subject, and any knowledge of English grammar was picked up incidentally to the learning of Latin. Much the same applied to history and geography. Arithmetic was also a side issue little regarded by the majority of grammar schools – a subject, like calligraphy, taught on Saturday afternoons and half-holidays, which doubtless did not add to its popularity.

Latin and Greek from dawn to dusk

School hours were long. A typical day started at six o'clock in the morning, or seven in winter, and lasted till four or five in the afternoon with a two-hour break for the midday meal, usually from eleven to one o'clock, and holidays were shorter than today's. Although the drudgery of parsing and construing was occasionally relieved by the performance of a Greek or Latin play, and the better schools devoted a few hours a week to music, school life must on the whole have been unimaginably laborious. Discipline, enforced by the omni-present birch rod, was harsh and often brutal, despite the pleas of a few enlightened educationists like Roger Ascham. Small wonder that Shakespeare's schoolboy crept 'like snail unwillingly to school'.

The routine of the senior boys at Westminster, as remembered by one old pupil, sounds particularly gruelling. 'About a quarter of an hour after five in the morning,' he wrote 'we were called up by one of the monitors of the chamber, with a *Surgite* ('Rise!'), and after Latin prayers we went into the

St John's College
Lady Margaret Beaufort, the grandmother of Henry VIII, was a pious, serious-minded lady, well-known for her charitable works. She founded St John's College at Cambridge at a time when the prime function of the universities was to turn out an educated clergy.

Learning the hard way
The Elizabethans had a deep respect for learning, and education was regarded as a serious business. No one expected it to be pleasant, and the average small-town grammar school, attended by the sons of the local shop-keepers, skilled artisans and professional men, was likely to be a crowded, uncomfortable place with few amenities. Here at least three classes appear to be in progress, and the birch rod is evidently in constant use.

cloisters to wash, and thence in order two by two to the school, where we were to be by six o'clock at the farthest. Between six and eight we repeated our grammar parts – out of Lilly for Latin, out of Camden for the Greek, fourteen or fifteen being selected and called out to stand in a semi-circle before the master.

'From eight to nine there was a break, and then betwixt nine and eleven those exercises were made which had been enjoined us overnight (one day in prose, the next day in verse), which were selected by the master, some to be examined and punished, others to be commended and proposed to imitation. Which being done, we had the practise of *dictamina*, one of the fifth form being called out to translate some sentence of an unexpected author, extempore, into good Latin, and then one of the sixth and seventh form to translate the same, extempore also, into good Greek. Then the master himself expounded some parts of a Latin or Greek author . . . wherein we were to be practised.'

Between three and four there was another break, and from four to five the boys 'repeated a leaf or two out of some book of rhetorical figures or choice proverbs and sentences collected by the master', had more practice in *dictamina* and sometimes, by way of light relief, turned Latin or Greek verse into English verse. Then a theme was given to them 'whereon to make prose and verse, Latin and Greek, against the next morning'. After supper, in summer time, the seventh form would be called to the master's chamber 'and there instructed out of Hunter's *Cosmography*, and practised to describe and find out cities and countries in the maps'.

Westminster, of course, was one of the top schools, and this is probably an extreme example. The average small town grammar school, such as the one where William Shakespeare acquired his 'small Latin and less Greek', would not have expected such prodigies of its pupils, and the average small-town parent would have been content if his son learned to read, write 'a fair hand', keep simple accounts, and pick up a nodding acquaintance with the classics.

Modern languages did not figure in the grammar school curriculum. They were taught by conversational methods mainly by refugees from religious persecution abroad, who were either employed as visiting tutors, or else set up private schools in the capital – men like Claude Hollyband and Peter Erondell, who wrote some delightful little books of dialogue as teaching aids which make it clear that boys were still capable of being boys, despite a ten-hour day of Latin grammar.

Stratford Grammar School
Many Tudor grammar schools which bear the name of Edward VI or of Queen Elizabeth were refoundations of much older schools, previously attached to abbeys, cathedrals or collegiate churches. King Edward VI Grammar School at Stratford-upon-Avon, where William Shakespeare received his education, had existed since 1295 and was re-endowed in 1482 by one of the town guilds – craft or religious brotherhoods which played an important part in civic life.

Universities for the earnest – and the idle rich

Noblemen's sons continued for the most part to be educated at home, usually with a small group of carefully chosen companions, by tutors who would prepare them for university – which, of course, meant Oxford or Cambridge. Generally speaking, though, the grammar schools provided the fortunate few with the intellectual equipment for university entrance and some schools, such as Eton and Winchester, had close connections with certain colleges. The average age of first-year students was 15 or 16.

The 16th century saw the development of the college as a self-contained unit with its own tutorial system, and a decline in the number of lectures given in the university 'Schools'. It also saw a decline in the number of poor and serious students, and an increasing number of rich, idle undergraduates more interested in having a good time than in taking a good degree. Since the principal aim of the universities was still, in theory at least, to turn out an educated clergy, this led predictably to complaints that they were becoming overcrowded with great men's sons, whose fathers did not expect them to become preachers, and that it was now 'a hard matter for a poor man's child to come by a fellowship, though he be never so good a scholar'.

In fact, although the gentry were certainly sending their sons to university in increasing numbers, they were still in a minority, and the student population of some 3,000 represented a far wider social mix than it did in the 18th and 19th centuries. The Elizabethans regarded the provision of education, like almsgiving, as a Christian duty, and under the system of charitable endowments it was perfectly possible for the son of a tradesman or shopkeeper or yeoman farmer to get to the university – provided, of course, he had brains and determination and was not afraid of living hard.

The full Arts course, leading to a Master's degree, took seven years – like the seven-year apprenticeship to a craft – but a good many students were now going out of residence after their four-year Bachelor's course. Those who were up only to acquire a little social polish might not even finish the Bachelor's course, and the more practically minded middle-class students would often cut short their academic careers in order to spend a year or two at one of the Inns of Court. In an energetically litigious age, a working knowledge of the law was as necessary to a man of affairs as a knowledge of Latin.

Girls learn 'to look to house and family'

There was still no formal provision for the education of girls. The enthusiasm generated by scholars such as Juan Luis Vives, Erasmus and Sir Thomas More in the early years of the century which had led to the emergence of such learned ladies as Margaret Roper, the Cooke sisters, Lady Jane Grey and, indeed, Queen Elizabeth herself, had now largely died away. All the same, literacy among women in general was becoming more widespread. The numbers of cookery books, books on household management, needlework and related 'feminine interest' subjects, as well as books of advice and pious exhortation to wives published during the period indicate that there must have been a worthwhile market for them. The wives and daughters of country squires, merchants, traders, shopkeepers and small businessmen of every kind were finding it more and more useful to be able to write a letter, con a legal document and cast up accounts, while among the upper classes the standard of education was higher than at any time until the late Victorian era.

Girls as well as boys attended parish schools and the preparatory forms of some grammar schools, but the majority of girls continued to learn to read and write at home from parents, older brothers or governesses, and at the top of the social scale there would be tutors and visiting masters for music, dancing and

Humanist of St Paul's
John Colet became Dean of St Paul's Cathedral in 1505, and in 1508 he founded St Paul's School, endowing it from his private fortune. Colet was a leading member of the circle of scholars and intellectuals who helped to bring the New Learning to England in the early years of the 16th century. The 'humanists', as they were known, also included Erasmus of Rotterdam, Luis Vives the Spaniard and the Englishmen Thomas Linacre, William Grocin and Thomas More. All were deeply interested in education and worked to propagate their ideas for a wider and more liberal curriculum in schools and universities. Unfortunately, the high ideals of the reformers were often frustrated by harsh economic and political realities.

IO COLET DECA S PAVLI

ISTVC RECIDIT GLO
RIA CARNIS

A case for valuables

Business affairs often took the city merchant away from home on visits to other parts of the country. He usually went on horseback and was followed, if he was wealthy enough, by two or three baggage horses led by servants. A travelling chest such as this was used for transporting valuables and documents; in front are an inkpot and quill pen, and a silk purse.

French. Well brought-up girls were also trained in the complicated arts of housewifery. Every educationist, however advanced his views, was agreed on the necessity for this, and Richard Mulcaster, a strong advocate for book learning for young maidens, wrote: 'I . . . know it to be a principal commendation in a woman: to be able to govern and direct her household, to look to her house and family, to provide and keep necessaries . . . to know the force of her kitchen.' Girls' education, in short, was still firmly based on the assumptions that a woman's place was in the home and that a nice girl's only ambition should be to make an honourable marriage.

Marriages where love took second place

Shakespeare's lover, 'sighing like furnace, with a woful ballad made to his mistress' eyebrow', was a figure more often met with in romantic literature than in real life, for the Elizabethans regarded marriage – a solemn contract entered into for life and sanctified by the Church – as something far too serious and important to be based merely on carnal love. It was generally accepted that a father's first duty to his daughter was to provide her with a suitable husband, and many child betrothals or espousals were arranged as an insurance against an uncertain future.

The initial form of contract, known as *de futuro*, as the promises were made in the future tense, was not necessarily binding. It could, in fact, be little more than a conditional statement of intent to arrange a marriage at some future date. If the situation changed, some impediment was discovered, or the young people concerned objected, then the agreement could be terminated by mutual consent, much like a modern engagement, unless, of course, the couple had lived together. If all went well and the financial arrangements, dowry and marriage settlements had been satisfactorily agreed on, the next stage would be the *de praesenti* betrothal, with the vows exchanged in the present tense. 'I, N. do willingly promise to marry thee, N. if God will, and I live, whensoever our parents shall think good and meet; till which time, I take thee for my only betrothed wife, and thereto plight thee my troth.' This promise was sealed with a kiss and a handclasp and an exchange of rings.

A betrothal *in verbis de praesenti* was binding and indissoluble, and any attempt to marry someone else after entering into a *de praesenti* contract was illegal. Even after a marriage had been completed and blessed by the Church, it could still be invalidated and children bastardised if evidence of a previous *de praesenti* betrothal were produced. For this reason, a wise bride and her parents would insist on plenty of publicity. Secret, or clandestine marriages – that is, those without publication of the banns on three successive Sundays in the period between betrothal and the actual marriage ceremony – were frowned on by the Church and by society in general.

Although the great majority of marriages, certainly among the propertied classes, were 'arranged', the Church insisted on the 'full and free consent' of both parties as an essential pre-condition for entering the holy estate of matrimony, and all writers on the subject were agreed on this point. One authority described forced marriage as 'the extremest bondage there is', while the playwright Thomas Heywood stressed that such marriages were bound to be self-defeating. 'How often,' he inquired, 'have forced contracts been made to add land to land, not love to love? And to unite houses to houses, not hearts to hearts? which hath been the occasion that men have turned monsters, and women devils.'

Fulminations of this kind seem to indicate that forced marriages, though uncommon, were by no means unheard of. But even if the concept of romantic love had little place in the normal run of Elizabethan marriage plans, it was generally accepted that there should be 'liking' and a reasonable amount of compatibility between an engaged couple. In any case, sensible parents could see the force of Thomas Heywood's warning. An unhappy, discontented wife or husband could quickly poison not only the spouse's life but those of the in-laws as well. The quarrels of an unhappy, ill-assorted couple would inevitably react on their respective families, sides would be taken, and scandal and bad feeling quickly spread through the small, tightly knit community.

There were love matches, too, of course. No one had any objection to love, providing the price was right, and many youthful romances flourished with parental approval. Meanwhile, among the landless poor, couples followed the age-old rituals of courtship guided only by their biological urges.

On the whole, people married young. The legal age of consent was 12 for girls and 14 for boys, though this was generally felt to be rather too young and liable to result in 'dangerous births, diminution of stature, brevity of life, and such like'. The average age for girls seems to have been 14 to 16, and for boys 18 to 21, but this varied according to circumstances and social class, the agricultural labourer marrying younger than his middle-class contemporary.

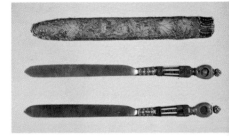

Knives for the bride

Elizabethans often carried their own knives when they dined out. This pair of knives with its decorated cloth case, given by a bridegroom to his wife-to-be on their wedding day, was a practical present as well as a token of love. Sheffield was already noted for the fine products of its cutlers.

The ardent wooer

The Elizabethans considered marriage as far too important a matter to be based on love alone, and most marriages among the propertied classes were 'arranged'. However, this did not stop people falling in love, and parents had no objection to a love match, providing the match was otherwise suitable. This courting couple do not seem averse to each other's company, but the young woman is showing a proper maidenly modesty.

Higher up the social scale, where important family alliances and the future of great estates might be at stake, the age tended to drop again, though here it was common practice for a very young couple to be separated after marriage, the bride returning to her parents while the groom finished his education.

The culmination of what could be quite prolonged preliminary negotiations was the religious ceremony insisted on by the Church. This completed and sanctified the union, and also conferred on the wife her dower right to one-third of her husband's property if she was left a widow. In the vast majority of cases, this ceremony took the form of a public church wedding, though it could be a private, even a secret, occasion. But it must be performed by an ordained priest and witnessed by at least two other persons.

The content and wording of the marriage service has changed very little since Elizabethan times: the last opportunity to disclose any impediment, the confirmation of the *de futuro* promises in the 'I will' of bride and groom, the

Banquet for a wedding
A marriage feast, with its promise of the hopeful beginning of a new generation, was always an occasion for rejoicing which often lasted for several days. Here the banquet has been spread at a long table, while the meat roasts, servants scurry about with dishes and some of

giving away of the bride, a repetition of the *de praesenti* vows, the ritual of putting the ring on the bride's finger, the joining of hands and the final, awesome pronouncement – 'those whom God hath joined together let no man put asunder'.

Weddings, like baptisms, usually took place on Sundays and were traditionally celebrated in the church porch. The service would be followed by a wedding sermon, in which the minister discoursed solemnly and at length on the responsibilities of the married state. It was the husband's duty to provide for his wife and children, to guard them from danger and want, to be faithful, generous and considerate. The wife must be a good homemaker, chaste, submissive and, God willing, fruitful. Husbands and wives must trust one another and be tolerant of each other's faults, remembering that they would be together till God did them part. Divorce in its modern sense was so rare as to be virtually unknown, and although a separation 'from bed and board' could be obtained through the Church courts in some cases of cruelty or adultery, the procedure was too complicated and expensive for ordinary people to contemplate.

A festive wedding and a public bedding

Once the knot had been tied, everyone was ready for the festive part of the proceedings, and the rest of the day (and very often several succeeding days) would be given up to merrymaking, beginning as the bridal procession made its way through the streets escorted by a cheerful band of musicians. The white wedding of satin, orange blossom and veil is, in fact, a comparatively recent innovation, dating from about the mid-18th century. An Elizabethan bride would simply wear her best dress trimmed with 'favours' of coloured ribbon, though she always appeared 'in her hair' – that is, with her hair hanging loose over her shoulders as a token of virginity – and would be garlanded with flowers and ears of corn. Everyone else was in their best clothes, and the home would have been swept and garnished for the occasion. There was music for dancing, and food and drink in as great an abundance as possible.

Many of the customs observed at weddings, such as the drinking from the bride cup, the distribution of the bride's cake, and the sprinkling of the newly wedded pair with grains of corn or broken pieces of oaten cake, had their origin in pagan fertility rites, and many of them survive in some form or other to this day. The young couple would be showered with gifts of money, plate and linen to help them set up house, but there was no 'going away', no honeymoon and precious little privacy, for the highspot of the jollity of every wedding feast was the public bedding of bride and groom.

It was the bridesmaids' duty to prepare the bride for bed, to throw her stocking and distribute her garters and the knots of ribbon from her gown (if these had not already been snatched in the general horseplay), before the groom arrived, surrounded by his friends. At grand weddings there might be a bishop or two on hand to bless the marriage bed, but in every case everyone still capable of standing up expected to come crowding into the nuptial

the assembled guests are already beginning to dance to the fiddlers' music. The scene of this panorama, painted by Joris Hofnägel in about 1569, is Bermondsey, still a country village on the banks of the Thames, and the Tower of London can be seen across the river in the background.

81

A jar for medicine

Medicines for the sick room were made up from a wide range of herbs and spices, and stored in glazed and decorated jars such as this. Apothecaries included ingredients such as gold leaf, quicksilver and even gunpowder in their potions, though more reliable drugs such as aloes and senna were coming into use.

By the death-bed

Death was a frequent and familiar visitor to the Elizabethan home, to be met as far as possible with dignity and without complaint. The Protestant denial of the doctrine of purgatory dealt a blow to the age-old belief that the dead could be helped by the prayers of the living. However, prayers were always said over the dying, while the family gathered round to receive the dying person's final blessing.

chamber to offer good wishes, encouragement and explicit advice. What sort of an ordeal this must have been for a shy girl or a nervous, inexperienced young man one can only speculate, but it was an inescapable initiation ceremony.

Among the well-to-do and lower middle classes, a wedding, marking the hopeful beginning of a new generation, was always a joyous occasion, especially if it represented a step up in the world – if, as quite often happened, the daughter of a yeoman farmer was marrying into the minor gentry, or a prosperous merchant had secured an aristocratic wife for his son. But among the really poor, if indeed they bothered with the formalities at all, marriage was likely to be no more than an incident in the harsh struggle for survival. Fear of poverty was ever-present, even for those possessing a trade or skill. A merchant could easily be ruined by some unlucky venture, the skilled craftsman incapacitated by illness or accident, and those without helpful kinsfolk could quickly find themselves looking into the pit of misfortune.

State relief and charity for the 'deserving poor'

Owing to a variety of complicated economic and social causes, the problem of the poor and their relief was acute throughout the 16th century. Elizabethan society recognised this and tried conscientiously to deal with it. William Harrison in his *Description of England*, written in the 1570s, explains that 'With us the poor is commonly divided into three sorts, so that some are poor by impotence, as the fatherless child, the aged, blind and lame, and the diseased person that is judged to be incurable; the second are poor by casualty, as the wounded soldier, the decayed householder, and the sick person visited with grievous and painful diseases; the third consisteth of thriftless poor, as the rioter that hath consumed all, the vagabond that will abide nowhere, but runneth up and down from place to place (as it were seeking work and finding none), and finally the rogue and the strumpet.'

In London provision for the poor was made in five institutions. There was St Bartholomew's Hospital for the sick, with 100 beds, one physician and three surgeons, Bethlehem (or Bedlam) for the insane, Christ's Hospital for the children, St Thomas's for the aged and infirm, with some 500 out-pensioners depending on it, and Bridewell, formerly a royal palace, as a house of correction and training for the thriftless poor.

Although London, with its greater resources, naturally led the way, other towns – notably Ipswich, Norwich, Cambridge, Lincoln, Reading, Bristol and York – were active and by no means unsuccessful in their efforts to get the beggars off the streets and either care for them in institutions or put them to useful work. In country districts the poor were the responsibility of the parish authorities, who coped as best they could according to their means.

The state possessed neither the resources nor the administrative machinery necessary to tackle poor relief on a national scale. Instead it had to be financed by local levies, supplemented by private philanthropy, and organised by the people on the spot, the justices, the churchwardens, mayors, constables and beadles. At the same time, the Privy Council offered advice, directives and temporary palliatives, such as the import of cheap foreign grain in times of scarcity. Legislation passed in the closing years of the Queen's reign codified the experience gained and experiments made at local level and, by imposing a compulsory poor rate, became the basis of the Poor Law up to modern times.

Justices of the Peace were empowered to appoint overseers for the poor in every parish, to collect the poor rate, and arrange for the binding of poor children as apprentices to learn a trade. Quarter-sessions were made responsible for the building of workhouses, which would shelter the aged and infirm and set the able-bodied to work. It was a long way from being a perfect system, but it was practical and sensible, and went a long way towards meeting the basic needs of the society it was designed to help.

In the midst of life
As every Elizabethan knew, death was no respecter of rank or wealth. Everyone might meet his or her end at any time (below), as they were frequently reminded by the preacher in church on Sunday, by the sudden fatal illness of friend or neighbour or by the quite usual sight of a corpse rotting on a wayside gallows.

Carrying the coffin
Like birth and marriage, death was surrounded by custom and ceremonial (below right). A baby that died within a month of baptism was buried in its christening robe; here the coffin of a young girl with her maiden garland is escorted by unmarried women. All except the poorest wished for a handsome funeral, and the wealthy often spent enormous sums on elaborate obsequies.

Faithful servant

A life-long virgin who served the Virgin Queen, Blanche Parry is said to have rocked the infant Elizabeth in her cradle. Blanche became a gentlewoman of the Privy Chamber, and the Queen made her Keeper of the Royal Books at Windsor. She remained with her mistress until her death, old and blind, in the 1590s. Her unusual monument in St Faith's Church, Bacton, Hereford and Worcester, bears witness to her lifetime of devotion, for it shows her kneeling beside a figure of the Queen as large as Blanche's.

The new laws were never intended to do more than provide a national minimum, for no one dreamed of expecting the state to take full responsibility for the problem. The medieval concept of voluntary charity as a cardinal Christian virtue was still far from dead, and voluntary charity continued to play a vital part in the relief of want. Bess of Hardwick endowed an almshouse at Derby for 'the perpetual relief of eight poor men and four poor women', and the Earl of Leicester founded a hospital at Warwick to shelter 12 poor men 'decayed by sickness or misfortune'. There were hundreds of similar institutions up and down the country. Indeed, there was hardly a town of any size which did not possess at least one almshouse or hospital for the 'impotent poor' and many, like Bristol and Hereford, had several. In country districts the local 'big house' could usually be relied on to do something constructive for the poor of the parish, and countless wills contained charitable bequests.

The emphasis was always on self-help, and benefactions were almost invariably restricted to the 'deserving poor' of the immediate neighbourhood. Vagrants or 'sturdy beggars' got little sympathy. The Elizabethans were down-to-earth, practical people, and not even the most charitably minded felt inclined to waste his money on the thriftless or on strangers who were the responsibility of their own kin.

On the most practical level of all, the family, the basic unit of society, was expected to look after its own unfortunates – the feeble-minded, the sick and the old. Shakespeare's 'lean and slipper'd pantaloon' could be assured of a place in the chimney corner of his son's or daughter's home, when at last he became 'sans teeth, sans eyes, sans taste, sans everything'.

An elaborate funeral and a lasting memorial

In spite of the numerous hazards to be encountered in daily life, a surprising number of the Queen's subjects did succeed in reaching the last of Shakespeare's seven ages of man. Those who survived their first five years were, after all, likely to be the fittest specimens of the race, and there were some notable examples of longevity. Old Lord Burghley died, still in harness, in his seventy-seventh year, the redoubtable Bess of Hardwick lived to be 87, the Marquis of Winchester and the Earl of Hertford survived well into their eighties, and Lettice Knollys, the Queen's cousin and mother of the Earl of Essex, into her nineties.

Generally speaking, though, the Biblical span of three score years and ten was as much or more than the average person could expect, and death was a familiar visitor in the Elizabethan home. Scarcely a parent escaped the grief of losing a child or children in infancy, and it was rare indeed for anyone to reach adulthood without having seen death at first hand. It came in many forms, from the public execution to the death of a respectable citizen expiring in his bed with the family kneeling to receive his blessing. Probably its most dreaded manifestation was an outbreak of plague, which could deprive the sufferer of the comfort of dying surrounded by his loved ones, and result in ignoble burial in a mass grave.

Children in stone

An Elizabethan canopied tomb in the 13th-century Church of St Nicholas in Montgomery, Powys, includes these figures of two of the children of Richard Herbert and his wife Magdalen. The Herberts' sons included the future Lord Herbert of Cherbury, George Herbert the poet, and the Royalist commander of Montgomery Castle during the Civil War. The Herbert family tomb was erected in 1600, and was probably designed by Walter Hancock of Much Wenlock.

Death, like birth and marriage, was an occasion for ceremonial. The departed would be prepared for burial by his or her nearest kin – no stranger would be entrusted with this final act of family piety – while the funeral was always as elaborate and dignified as the family could afford, with custom carefully observed. Just as a baby was shrouded in its christening robe, so a young girl would be accompanied to her last resting place by an escort of virgins and her 'maiden garland' hung up in the parish church.

Often the poor of the town would be hired as mourners to swell the crowd of family and friends, servants, tenants and retainers, and black mourning cloaks and hoods would be provided for them. At a nobleman's funeral, banners of the dead man's arms proclaiming his rank and dignities would be carried in the procession, and at the funeral of a royal personage, the officers of his household broke their staves of office and cast them into the grave.

A splendid memorial was considered almost as important as a splendid funeral, as the many which survive still testify, but life had to go on, and once all proper respect had been paid to the deceased a bereaved husband or wife would be expected to temper grief with Christian resignation. In fact, both widows and widowers frequently remarried within a matter of months without incurring censure from a society which recognised that in a harsh world men and women needed one another – for, as the marriage service put it, 'the mutual society, help and comfort that the one ought to have of the other'.

Crafts to adorn

IN SILVER AND GLASS, FURNITURE AND TILES, PATRONS DISPLAY THEIR TASTE AND THEIR STATUS

The Elizabethans were fond of show and of showing off. It was not an age of delicacy or restraint, and most people's taste ran to the ornate and the flamboyant. This was noticeable – especially towards the end of the period – in the heavy, bulbous style of furniture. Every available surface was carved with acanthus leaves, scrolls, rosettes, classical and mythological figures and anything else the craftsman could cram into his design, to satisfy the customer who would otherwise feel he was not getting his money's worth.

Silver and glassware were also extremely elaborate, and even quite modest households could display an impressive collection of silver and gilt plate. Silver was pouring in from the New World, while a large amount of church plate had been broken up and transferred to secular hands. Wherever the Queen went in the course of her 'progresses' she would be given a piece of plate; the tall covered cup was an especially popular presentation piece. Everyone who could afford to do so invested in silver spoons, cups, bowls, ewers, jugs, salts and candlesticks, while silver-gilt lids and handles were added even to ordinary pottery drinking-vessels.

Tudor 'finger-bowl'
In days when a good deal of food was still eaten with the fingers, it was polite to wash one's hands between courses. This aquamanile, or ewer, was used to pour water over sticky fingers.

Tiles in a chapel
Painted tiles (below left) decorate the chapel of The Vyne, a mansion near Basingstoke. Among Tudor roses, the upper right-hand tile shows the Duke of Urbino – home city of the Italian craftsman in whose Antwerp workshop the tiles were made.

Stool in oak
A joint stool – made by a joiner using joints but no nails – of carved oak was a familiar object in every home. Chairs were rare; most people sat on cushions on the floor, or on stools or benches.

Clockwork elegance

Pocket watches date from about 1504, with the invention of the mainspring. But the Elizabethan timepiece was distinguished more for ornateness than accuracy.

Chair in cedar

This elaborately carved cedarwood armchair, dated 1575, is obviously a rich man's possession: the crest on the back is that of the Fauconberg family.

For store or seat

A chest was used for storing linen, clothes or plate. Topped with a cushion it served as a seat. This chest (below right) is inlaid with holly and bog oak.

Courtier's cup

The Parr Pot, a covered cup of white-striped glass in silver-gilt mounts, belonged to the courtier Sir William Parr, the uncle of Katherine Parr.

A spur to charity

A silver-gilt vessel (left) bears the portrait of William Lambarde, Elizabeth's Keeper of the Rolls. Inscribed 'A proctour [protector] for the poore, remember them before thou die', it belongs to the Company of Drapers. The earthenware jug (right) has silver-gilt mounts.

Salt in splendour

The salt cellar occupied an important place on Tudor dinner tables. This Vivyan Salt, of silver-gilt with painted glass panels, dates from the late Elizabethan period. It stands 16 in. high, and is surmounted by a figure representing Justice.

'Thou art the flower of cities all'

By Elizabethan times London had spread well beyond the confines of its medieval walls.
The City, with its ancient gateways, was still the commercial and residential heart of the capital, but many wealthy
citizens had smart new houses in the suburbs. To the Scots poet William Dunbar, London was
'the flower of cities'. Outside the walls, however, shanty towns were springing up; while across the river in
Southwark, theatres, brothels and bull-baiting and bear-baiting rings flourished.
This bird's-eye view of 1572 appeared in a German atlas of European cities by Georg Braun and Frans Hogenberg.

STILLIAR.DS) Hansa, Gothica dictio, conuentum, vel congregationem sonans, multarum ciuitatum est confoederata Societas, tum ob præstita Regibus, ac Ducib. beneficia: tum ob securam terra maríque, mercaturæ tractationem, tum denique, ad tranquillam Rerumpub. pacem, &. ad modestam adolescentum institutionem conseruandam, instituta: plurimor. Regum, ac Principum, maximé Angliæ, Galliæ, Daniæ, ac Magnæ Moscouia, nec non Flandriæ, ac Brabantiæ Du cum priuilegijs, ac immunitatib. exornata fuit. Habet ea quatuor, Emporia, (untores quidam vocant, in quibus ciuitatum negotiatores resident, suasque mercatus exercent. Hor. alterum hic Londini, domestica oeconomia nitet, habens domum Gildehallã Teutonicã quã vulgo Stiliard, nucupat.

CHAPTER FOUR

The peopled streets

FROM DAWN TO DUSK, THE
CITY ECHOES WITH
THE CLATTER OF WORKSHOPS
AND CRIES OF TRADERS,
AND JOBLESS
BEGGARS JOSTLE GALLANTS
IN THEIR FINERY

More troublesome and tedious well I know
'Twill be into the peopled streets to go . . .
There squeaks a cart-wheel; here a tumbril rumbles;
Here scolds an old bawd; there a porter grumbles.
Here two tough car-men combat for the way;
There two for looks begin a coward fray.
Two swaggering knaves here brabble for a whore;
There brawls an ale-knight for his fat-grown score.   E. Guilpin *Skialetheia* (1598)

*O*ut of a population estimated at getting on for 5 million by the end of Elizabeth's reign, some four-fifths are generally reckoned to have been country-men, and most town dwellers dreamed of retiring to the country. It was the ambition of every prosperous townsman to be able to buy an estate and set up as a country gentleman. But even the most confirmed town dweller lived far closer to the earth than his modern counterpart. Elizabethan towns may have been noisy, insanitary places, but every house, even the humblest, had its patch of land, many were surrounded by orchards and gardens, and no town centre was more than an easy walk from open countryside.

In fact, apart from London which stood in a class of its own, there were scarcely more than half a dozen towns of any real consequence in the whole country. Manchester, an ancient market town, was growing, and doing well out of its rough woollens which were exported through the port of Chester. But it had not yet achieved the status of a borough, and nor had Leeds, another market town living by woollen cloth. Birmingham was also growing, and noisy with the anvils of its metal-workers, but it was still a manorial village governed by the lord of the manor, as was the little town of Sheffield, whose cutlers already had a name for knives and scythes.

Newcastle had an expanding and profitable trade sending coal to London by sea (hence the expression 'sea-coal'), but the largest and most important northern town was the venerable city of York, administrative capital of the region. In the Midlands, Ludlow and Shrewsbury were cloth and market towns. Coventry had a thread-making industry and Leicester, with a population of 3,000 or 4,000, relied on cattle and tanneries.

The bulk of England's wealth and trade was concentrated in the southern half of the country. After London, the second biggest and richest manufactur-ing town was Norwich, centre of the textile industry, with a population of about 17,000, while the flourishing port of Bristol ran it a close third. Exeter was also a thriving sea-port, with some 8,000 inhabitants, and the Elizabethan period saw the rise of Plymouth from insignificant fishing village to vital naval base guarding the mouth of the Channel.

The number of boroughs returning members to Parliament rose during the

Bridge below the Tower
Every visitor to Elizabethan London went to see the grim fortress-prison of the Tower. Equally, every tourist marvelled at London Bridge, which crossed the Thames from the fish market on the north bank to Southwark on the south, lined on both sides with the homes and shops of rich mercers and haberdashers. This picture, dated 1578, comes from the album of Emanuel van Meteren, an Antwerp merchant who lived in London for many years. It also shows St Saviour's Church, later Southwark Cathedral. The heights in the background presumably represent Shooters Hill, but the grassy mound and bale of hay in the foreground seem to be no more than an artistic flourish.

Queen's reign and the size of many towns increased with the growth of the population generally. But to foreign tourists and the Elizabethans themselves, 'town' meant London – the 'flower of cities all', as the Scottish poet William Dunbar described it. By contemporary standards London was huge, the biggest capital city in Europe and growing fast; the population, estimated at 90,000 in the early 1560s, had more than doubled by the end of the century. But it was still a coherent whole and not a shapeless wilderness, a real and recognisable town in which a man could live and raise a family, get to know his neighbours and feel a pride in his citizenship.

Great mansions by London's busy river

The heart and centre of Elizabethan London was the City, bounded by the river and by its ancient Roman and medieval walls; these followed a roughly semi-circular line from the Tower in the east via Aldgate, Bishopsgate, Moorgate, Cripplegate and Aldersgate (still with their battlemented towers and closed at nightfall) to Newgate and Ludgate, both used as prisons, in the west. But even before Elizabethan times the western limit of the City had spread beyond its fortified boundary and, then as now, Temple Bar marked the frontier where the Lord Mayor's jurisdiction ended.

Along the Strand, connecting London proper with the royal suburb of Westminster, lay a string of great mansions with gardens running down to the river. These houses, many of which are commemorated by modern street names, included Essex House, Arundel House, Somerset House (the only survivor today, though not in its Tudor form), the Savoy (once John of Gaunt's palace), Russell House (the Earl of Bedford's London residence), Worcester, Salisbury and Durham Houses; all combined to make this the most fashionable and exclusive quarter of the town. Beyond Westminster was the country, with

Homes with a view
Fine mansions with watergates to the river made the Strand an Elizabethan 'millionaires' row'. Durham House was used by the Queen to accommodate distinguished foreign visitors, and lent or leased to favoured courtiers. Sir Robert Cecil built Salisbury House as a town residence late in the reign and entertained the Queen to dinner there in 1602. Worcester House was owned by the Earl of Worcester who succeeded the Earl of Essex in the office of Master of the Horse.

the riverside villages of Chelsea, where Queen Elizabeth had spent some months of her girlhood and where the Lord Admiral had a house, Putney, Hammersmith and Chiswick, where the boys of Westminster School were evacuated in times of plague.

The Thames, then a crystal stream 'full of swans white as snow' according to a foreign visitor, played a vital part in the life of the capital and was alive with craft of every kind – wherries (the taxis of Elizabethan London) plying for hire, private barges, skiffs, lighters and sailing ships – for everyone, from the Queen downwards, used the river for convenience, pleasure and trade. Ferries operated from several places, for London Bridge, connecting the City with Southwark and the Dover Road, was still the only other means of crossing from north to south. This bridge, one of the sights of Europe, was an astonishing structure built on 20 arches of squared stone 60 ft high and lined on both sides with houses, shops and chapels, 'so that it seemeth more a continual street than a bridge'. There were towers with gates in them at either end, and a drawbridge which could be raised both for defence and to allow tall-masted vessels to pass upstream to the dock basin at Queenhithe. An additional point of interest was the display of shrivelled heads of those executed for high treason which were impaled on poles over the tower guarding the drawbridge – the Duke of Württemberg counted 34 of them on one occasion in 1592.

In Southwark and adjoining Bankside were the bull-baiting and bear-baiting rings, the brothels and theatres which gave the district an unsavoury reputation. Also on the south bank were no fewer than five prisons – the King's Bench, the Marshalsea, the White Lion, the Counter and the Clink – and, of course, the famous Tabard Inn, once the rendezvous of the Canterbury pilgrims.

Throughout the Elizabethan period the suburbs encroached steadily on the

The seat of government
Royal Westminster on its marshy riverbank, home of the monarchy from time immemorial, remained the administrative nerve centre of the realm. The House of Commons met in St Stephen's Chapel, the Parliament House; next to this was Westminster Hall, seat of the English law courts and all that survived of the ancient Palace. The Abbey Church of St Peter was already a national shrine where every English monarch was crowned and many monarchs lay buried.

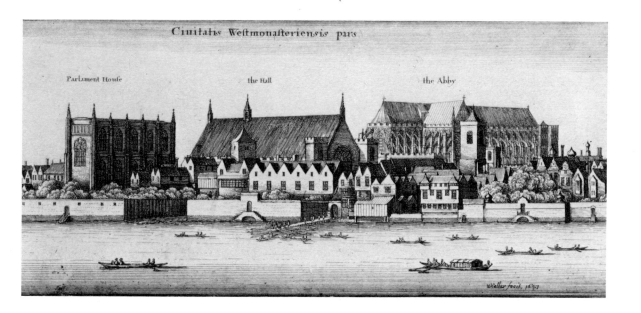

93

'Green belt' at the gates

In spite of its rapid growth London was still in many respects a 'country' town, with orchards, gardens and pasture land coming right up to its walls. Cattle were herded through the City streets to market, and dairymaids sold milk and butter. Moorfields, where laundresses laid out clothes to dry, Finsbury Fields and Spitalfields were pleasant open spaces to be enjoyed by the citizens for sport and exercise, and all within easy walking distance of their homes. The house marked 'The Papye', off Bishopsgate, was the home of Sir Francis Walsingham, the Queen's Principal Secretary of State.

THE SPITEL

surrounding countryside, despite government attempts to control development. John Stow, tailor, antiquarian and chronicler, deplored the eastward sprawl towards Wapping and Limehouse, and complained about the mean cottages and alleys which were springing up round Whitechapel church and common. Stow also recalled wistfully that when he was a boy it had been possible to walk from Cornhill to a farm near Aldgate and buy milk, three pints for a halfpenny in summer, and 'always hot from the kine'. But Islington, Clerkenwell, Hackney, Hoxton and Paddington were still country villages, the churches of St Giles and St Martin still stood in the fields, the Queen went hunting in Marylebone and Hyde Park, and it was said that the fairies danced on Bethnal Green.

John Stow, a Londoner born and bred and with the true historian's feeling for the past, might regret any change in the outlines of his beloved town, but visitors were unanimous in respectful admiration of London's size and obvious wealth. In 1599 Thomas Platter of Basle recorded that 'this city of London is so large and splendidly built, so populous and excellent in crafts and merchant citizens, and so prosperous, that it is not only the first in the whole realm of England, but is esteemed one of the most famous in all Christendom'.

Streets full of noise, bustle – and traffic jams

The first thing that must have struck most visitors, as they picked their way nervously through the narrow congested streets, trying to avoid being jostled into the open drain which ran down the middle of most of them, was the din: the clatter and hammering from a thousand workshops, the rumble and squeak of cart-wheels, the lowing of cattle being driven to market, the raucous cries of street vendors proclaiming their wares (anything from hot mutton pies to mouse-traps), and the constant noisy sales patter of shopkeepers standing in their doorways to lure the passer-by with their 'What do ye lack?'

The crowds, too, with their vigorous, free-and-easy ways, came as something of a shock to the newcomer. Pickpockets and cutpurses – so called because they cut off the purses that people carried attached to their belts – mingled with sober groups of merchants in long furred gowns on their way to do business at the new Royal Exchange, and with gaggles of smartly dressed housewives out shopping. Apprentices and maidservants, making an errand last as long as they could, joined in backchat with urchins hoping to earn a penny by holding some fine gentleman's horse. Foreign sailors and tourists stood gawping at the sights and were sworn at by a porter pushing a loaded barrow, while a Court gallant, resplendent in satin and velvet, shouldered his way unceremoniously through the throng. Gangs of boys from rival schools engaged in running battles, using their satchels as weapons, and the drivers of carts and drays exchanged insults and sometimes blows over a disputed right of way.

London already had its traffic problems. 'The number of cars, drays, carts, and coaches, more than hath been accustomed, the streets and lanes being straitened [narrow], must needs be dangerous, as daily experience proveth,'

Clothes for a gallant
*This Elizabethan gallant is
wearing Venetians, a form of
padded or quilted knee-breeches
which came into vogue during
the 1570s, a short-waisted
doublet with shoulder pads or
'wings', and the little flat beret-
like cap so characteristic
of the period.*

Ensuring a fair deal
*Merchants were strictly
supervised to make sure that
they gave accurate measure.
These bronze weights stamped
with a crowned 'EL', for Elizabeth, were kept at London's
Guildhall and used as the official
standard for testing all commercial weights in the city.*

wrote John Stow. 'I know that, by the good laws and customs of this city, shod
carts are forbidden to enter the same, except upon reasonable cause . . . also
that the fore horse of every carriage should be led by hand; but these good
orders are not observed.' To make matters worse, everyone wanted one of the
newfangled coaches recently introduced from Germany, 'for the world runs on
wheels with many whose parents were glad to go on foot'.

But there was no stopping the march of progress in 'the storehouse and mart
of all Europe', the magnet which attracted the trade of the civilised world.
'Most of the inhabitants,' wrote Thomas Platter, 'are employed in commerce.
They buy, sell and trade in all corners of the globe, for which purpose the water
serves them well, since ships from France, the Netherlands and Germany and
other countries land in this city, bringing goods with them and loading others
in exchange.' 'What can there be in any place under the heavens,' asked the
dramatist John Lyly, 'that is not in this noble city either to be bought or
borrowed?' And Fynes Morrison, author and seasoned European traveller,
thought he might lawfully say, setting all love of his country apart, that he had
never seen 'any such daily show, anything so sumptuous in any place in the
world' as in the goldsmiths' shops in London.

Ruling merchants and jobless vagrants

London, like most towns of any importance, was ruled by a merchant oli-
garchy. It was divided into 26 wards, each of which elected an Alderman who
held office for life. The Aldermen in turn chose one of their number annually to
be Lord Mayor, appointed the Recorder who was their legal adviser and
spokesman, and generally ran the City's affairs.

The Lord Mayor and Aldermen were all, of course, freemen of the City and,
as such, belonged to one or other of the Livery Companies – so-called because
the members wore their company's livery, or uniform, on state occasions.
These companies, which had evolved out of the medieval guilds, exercised an
immense and controlling influence over every aspect of commercial life. No
strangers were permitted to buy or sell in London, and no one might practise a
trade or craft except under the auspices of the appropriate guild or company.
The companies laid down and enforced strict standards of workmanship,
regulated markets and prices, settled the frequent 'demarcation' disputes
which arose, as for example, between the Merchant Taylors and the Clothworkers, dictated and supervised the working conditions of apprentices and
journeymen (those who had finished their apprenticeship but still worked for a
master), and dealt with admissions and recruitment.

The companies also acted as benefit societies for their members. They helped
widows and orphans, and those who had fallen on hard times. They maintained almshouses and schools, such as St Paul's and the Merchant Taylors',
sponsored promising scholars and sometimes provided funds to enable a likely
young man to set up in business.

Apart from the Merchant Taylors and the Clothworkers, the 12 'great'
Livery Companies included the Mercers, importers and wholesalers of silks and

luxury fabrics, and the Grocers, also importers and wholesalers of commodities like sugar, currants (for which the English with their passion for sweetmeats seemed to have an insatiable appetite) and spices, a necessity in days when pickling and salting were the principal means of preserving food. Then came the Drapers, the Fishmongers, the Goldsmiths, Skinners, Haberdashers, Salters, Ironmongers and Vintners. Among the lesser companies were the Cordwainers (manufacturers of fine leather goods), the Dyers, Plasterers and Stationers (or printers).

Although not first in precedence, the Goldsmiths were perhaps the wealthiest and most influential of the companies, acting as they did in the role of merchant bankers and financiers. Goldsmiths' Row, at the western end of Cheapside by Wood Street, was noted by John Stow as being 'the most beautiful frame of fair houses and shops that be within the walls of London'. The various trades and occupations tended to congregate together, as some City street names – Poultry, Skinners Lane, Ironmonger Lane, Milk and Bread Street – still testify, while the richest and most successful members of the business fraternity dwelt in princely style in tall, handsome timber-framed houses in the fashionable areas of Lothbury and Bishopsgate.

But behind the fine new houses and the sumptuous shops lurked squalid, rat-infested slums – rookeries where whole families crowded into one room of some old mansion, long abandoned by aristocratic owners migrating westwards to a smarter address. Laws forbidding multi-occupation unfortunately clashed with other laws which sought to prevent new building within a 3 mile radius of the City limits, but, in any case, neither the natural growth of London

Goods for market

Carts like these came rumbling into the City every morning from farms and small-holdings in the surrounding villages of East Ham, Hackney, Islington and others to meet the insatiable demand of the London market. The City streets, too, would be crowded with porters carrying goods in baskets on their backs or pushing loaded barrows.

'Buy the fair ballads!'
The ballad seller hawked his wares in city streets and at country fairs and markets. An increasingly literate public flocked to buy the latest ballads and broadsheets on topical, political, patriotic and romantic subjects.

'News, great news'
The town crier made public announcements of all kinds. He would give the date of forth-coming attractions such as a fair or a royal visit, ask for information about the whereabouts of missing property, warn the townspeople of danger, such as an epidemic or a river about to burst its banks, and promulgate any new government regulations.

nor the overcrowding and poverty which created the slums could be controlled by repressive legislation.

The urban poor formed a shifting, rootless population largely made up of dispossessed country dwellers who had drifted into town hoping for work, of discharged soldiers, masterless men, natural vagrants and misfits of both sexes, too illiterate and too insignificant to leave a mark on the record. Supporting themselves as best they could by petty crime, by begging, by casual labour or a mixture of all three, they lived from hand to mouth on the fringes of society, eating when they were lucky and all too often ending short, miserable lives on the gallows.

Early risers – and one who overslept

London's day began at about 5 a.m., as carts laden with produce from the outlying farms and villages started to rattle into town. The stall-holders in the open-air markets were among the earliest risers, and soon after them the street-vendors would be preparing to set out on their long day's round, with cries of 'Fine Seville oranges, fine lemons!' 'Ripe Cowcumbers, ripe!' or 'Cherry ripe, apples fine, medlars fine!', while a chimney sweep hopefully serenaded the neighbourhood housewives with his 'Sweep chimney sweep, mistress! With a hey derry sweep from the bottom to the top, sweep chimney sweep!' By 6 o'clock yawning apprentices were taking down the shutters and opening the mercers' and haberdashers' shops on London Bridge. The grocers' warehouses in Bucklersbury were getting ready for the day's business, as were the shoe-makers' workshops around St Martin's-le-Grand, and schoolboys with satchels of books on their backs, inkhorns and penknives hanging from their girdles, were already scampering through the streets on their way to one or other of the City's famous grammar schools.

Not everyone was so well organised. Claude Hollyband, in his *French Schoolmaster*, a little book of dialogues in French and English written in the 1570s, gives us a vivid picture of one young citizen who has overslept.

Francis, evidently the son of a prosperous tradesman, is woken by Margaret, the maidservant. 'Ho, Francis, rise and get you to school. You shall be beaten, for it is past seven.' Francis calls imperiously for his stockings, his garters and his shoes. 'Where is my doublet? . . . Give me that shoeing horn!' Margaret wants him to take a clean shirt, but when she tells him to wait while she airs it first by the fire he snatches his old one, disregarding her protests that his mother will chide her for letting him go to school without a clean shirt.

The young man scrambles hurriedly into his clothes, but has time to be fastidious about his washing water. 'I will have no river water, for it is troubled. Give me well or fountain water. Take the ewer and pour it upon my hands.' 'Can you not wash in the basin?' exclaims Margaret. 'Shall you have always a servant at your tail?' 'Wilt thou that I wash my mouth and face where I have washed my hands?' retorts Francis virtuously. 'Give me a towel, maiden. Now give me my breakfast, for I am ready. Make haste!'

Francis is a well-brought-up boy and, late though he is, he goes into the shop

Fortress and prison

The Tower of London, built after the Norman Conquest to keep Saxon London in subjection, still loomed menacingly over the Tudor city. It is here seen as the decoration on a plate, probably made in London to judge by its inscription in praise of Elizabeth, but in the style associated with Delft in the Netherlands. Even in Elizabethan times the prime function of the Tower was as a fortress, for whoever held the Tower held London, and whoever held London held the kingdom. It was best known, though, as a state prison. Elizabeth herself had spent some time there during her sister's reign, and the headless corpses of her mother and several of her close relatives lay buried in the chapel of St Peter ad Vincula, within its precincts. The Tower was also officially a royal palace, though seldom now used as such. It also housed the royal mint, the Crown Jewels, the ordnance and a menagerie for the rare animals presented to the sovereign – including, in Elizabeth's day, two lions, a wolf, a tiger and a porcupine. It had already become a popular tourist attraction, though visitors complained about the tips they were expected to give to the numerous officials.

to ask his father's blessing before leaving for school. 'Are you up?' says his parent. 'Is it time to rise at eight of the clock?' But he is sent off with instructions to invite the schoolmaster to dinner, which will save him from beating, and an admonition to learn well, so that he can repeat his lesson when he returns.

Another book, *The French Garden*, a companion volume to the *French Schoolmaster* and written by Hollyband's compatriot Peter Erondell, portrays another early-morning scene in a more aristocratic town household. The masterful Lady Ri-Mellaine, a character probably based on Erondell's patroness Lady Elizabeth Berkeley, has also overslept and is horrified to discover that it is half-past seven. 'O God!' she cries, 'I went to bed yesternight so timely, thinking to rise this morning at the farthest at six o'clock.' She scolds Prudence, the chamber-maid, for suffering her to sleep so long. 'Go to, go to, draw the window curtains. Call my Page, let him bring some wood to my chamber door. Make a fire quickly, that I may rise . . . Warm my smock and give it me . . . Will you keep me here all day? Where be all my things? Go fetch my clothes!'

An Elizabethan lady's toilet was a complicated affair. So many garments needed pinning, tying or lacing together that getting dressed was virtually impossible singlehanded. The universal undergarment was a smock or shift

A lady of fashion

This fashionable beauty, comb in hand, is Elizabeth Vernon, one of the Queen's Maids of Honour, who caused a scandal by becoming pregnant by the Earl of Southampton in 1598. She is wearing the pointed, low-waisted bodice characteristic of the later years of the reign, which would be stiffened with whalebone, pasteboard or canvas, and a richly embroidered kirtle over a Spanish farthingale. Her gown is also heavily embroidered, and a luxurious velvet cloak lined with ermine lies thrown over a stool. Her ruff and gauze veil hang waiting to be put on, and jewellery is scattered on her dressing-table.

which went on first, then stockings, usually knitted, silk for the wealthy and fashionable, and wool for the rest. Some very conservative or poor people still wore cloth stockings, more like gaiters, but in either case they were gartered just above or below the knee with lengths of ribbon.

Elizabethan women's dress was based on a separate skirt and bodice. The bodice or 'body', often referred to as 'a pair of bodies', was a corset-like affair reinforced by wooden or whalebone 'busks' which slipped into pockets in the lining. It could have a high neck and small stand-up collar, or a low square-cut neckline filled in with a partlet, or collar, which could be plain and gathered up round the neck in an embryo ruff, or embroidered and richly decorated according to the wearer's taste and means. The waist came to a point in front, and as time went by this became lower and more exaggerated, with a V-shaped opening filled in with a stomacher, stiffened with pasteboard or canvas and sometimes boned as well.

Clothes that relied on padding and starch

Skirts were nearly always worn over some kind of foundation. Commonest was the Spanish farthingale, similar in construction to a crinoline and giving a smooth, cone-shaped outline without folds. Nearly always, too, the skirt or kirtle (also sometimes confusingly called a petticoat) was split down the front in an inverted V, displaying a decorative panel known as the forepart attached to an underskirt. The other form of farthingale – the French or wheel type – consisted of a padded roll (commonly called a bum-roll) tied round the waist with tapes and holding the skirt out at right-angles before letting it fall in folds to the ground. This developed into an elaborate wheel-shaped structure made of wire or whalebone and tilted up at the back – an ugly fashion which must have been very uncomfortable to wear.

Sleeves were also separate, attached to the bodice with pins or ties, the join being hidden by 'wings'. The graceful hanging sleeves of early Tudor times had disappeared, and they were now generally stiffened or padded, like so much of the costume. A long gown was sometimes worn over the bodice and kirtle, either for warmth or show, and was either loose-bodied, hanging from the shoulders and open down the front, or close-bodied, fitted to the waist with a gathered skirt and fastened with ribbon ties or buttons and loops.

Ruffs, starched and crimped and so characteristic of the period, first became fashionable for men and women during the 1570s; starch was first introduced into England in 1564. They evolved out of the frilled shirt or chemise collar, and by about 1580 had become enormous, giving the familiar 'head on a platter' effect. A lot of well-dressed women, however, preferred an open or fan-shaped ruff supported by a wired frame, or a rebato, a shaped wired collar standing up round the back of the neck and pinned to a low-cut bodice.

Lady Ri-Mellaine, in Erondell's account, decided to wear a rebato edged with cut-work, a petticoat (or skirt) of wrought crimson velvet with silver fringe, a green silk bodice and an open gown of white satin laid on with buttons of pearl. Then came the question of headgear. When the maid had combed her hair

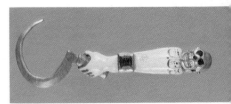

A scythe for the teeth
In an age before toothbrushes were known, a toothpick was the principal method of cleaning the teeth, supplemented sometimes by rubbing them with a piece of mallow root or linen. This toothpick in gold and porcelain bears the skull and scythe of Father Time.

Sweetening the air
Elizabethan women carried a pomander or scent bottle at their girdle – and frequently used it to counteract unpleasant odours in home and street. This ornate example, gold-enamelled and set with panels of precious stones, was found buried under the floor of a goldsmith's shop in Cheapside, London.

(and been scolded for pulling), her ladyship debated whether or not to wear her French hood with a border of rubies, but being assured that the weather was fine, made up her mind to go bare-headed except for a hair-cap or caul, which was rather like a hair-net and made of goldsmith's work or silk thread.

At last, after demanding some small pins for her cuffs, she is ready for her accessories – a pearl chain round her neck, a clean handkerchief, gloves, fan and, most important, her girdle, on which is hung a purse, a silver comfit box and a case containing such useful items as scissors, penknife and bodkin. Now fully equipped to face the world, Lady Ri-Mellaine sends the page off on an errand to invite two of her friends to dinner, instructs the maid to tidy her night-gear and 'dress the chamber', and finally sallies forth to make her presence felt about the house.

She summons her daughters and their governess, inspects their needlework and cross-questions them about their day's activities, visits the nursery to superintend the baby's bath and to kiss her 'little boykin', and descends on the schoolroom where her sons are working with their tutor. Pleased to find them hard at work on their lessons, she reads them a homily on paying attention and then decides to take them shopping with her, first making sure that they are wearing their clothes 'gentleman-like' and ordering a servant to brush their breeches.

Servants to attend to household chores

Other ladies around the town are also busy with their morning occupations. Every reasonably well-to-do household had a staff of men and maidservants, so the main job of the tradesman's and merchant's wife was to make sure that everyone else was working properly. As well as keeping an eye on the servants and caring for husband and children, there were the apprentices to be thought of. These lads lived with the family in their master's house during their seven-year indentures, and their moral and physical welfare was the responsibility of both master and mistress. It seems, though, that quite a number of housewives did not allow these duties to interfere unduly with their social lives – at least

A herbal fumigator
One means of quenching the bad smells caused by insanitary living conditions was to burn herbs over charcoal in a small portable stove. The device was introduced from Spain, and made by potters outside London's Moorgate.

Plates with a pattern
Food was eaten off trenchers, or wooden plates, which were sometimes decorated on their reverse sides. These small beechwood trenchers, used for sticky desserts, are painted with rhymes mocking marriage which featured in after-dinner games.

Away with the cobwebs

The commonest occupation for a girl who had to earn her own living was some form of domestic service. There was no stigma attached to being a servant, and although the work might be hard, the hours long and the wages small, a cheerful, willing and energetic maidservant was a valued member of the average middle-class household, sharing the ups and downs of her employers' lives. An intelligent girl would have the opportunity to learn useful domestic skills, and when she married could expect a generous wedding present from her master and mistress.

according to Emanuel Van Meteren, a Dutch merchant living in London during the 1580s.

Van Meteren, like most other foreigners, commented on the amount of freedom enjoyed by English married women. 'They are well-dressed, fond of taking it easy, and commonly leave the care of household matters and drudgery to their servants. They sit before their doors, decked out in fine clothes, in order to see and be seen by the passers-by . . . The rest of their time they employ in walking and riding, in playing at cards or otherwise, in visiting their friends and keeping company, conversing with their equals (whom they term gossips) and their neighbours, and making merry with them at child-births, christenings, churchings and funerals; and all this with the permission and knowledge of their husbands, as such is the custom.'

It was not only the ladies who took time off during the day. Claude Hollyband depicts his jovial shopkeeper setting out with a friend to watch a wedding procession and to listen to a sermon at Paul's Cross, the famous open-air pulpit in St Paul's churchyard. Here benches were provided for the audience, while

Metal on the anvil
In towns like Sheffield and Birmingham, English metal-workers were already beginning to gain an international reputation for skill and the quality of their wares. The work produced by the London goldsmiths' shops was famous. Shopkeeping was a man's business, and in London only a Freeman of one of the City companies was allowed to practise a trade or open a shop within its boundaries.

A stitch for a shoe
London and all the big towns were full of small workshops like this shoemaker's. Most of them were family concerns operated by the master, his wife and children and perhaps a couple of apprentices who all lived together over the shop.

Cloth by the yard
The draper and his assistants are measuring cloth with a yardstick. Drapers dealt principally in woollen cloth and the Drapers' Company, founded in 1364, was one of the 12 senior craft guilds.

grander folk listened from a gallery in the north wall of the cathedral. The good citizen and his gossip, having found seats near the preacher, amuse themselves by looking for well-known faces in the gallery and pick out my Lord of Bedford, a prominent member of the Privy Council, the Lord Admiral's wife and 'my Lady Treasurer', wife of the Lord Treasurer, Lord Burghley.

Round the City on a shopping expedition

Meanwhile, though, work *was* going on in countless workshops throughout the City, where tailors, printers and metalworkers, brewers, coopers, weavers and upholsterers, seamstresses, embroiderers and harness-makers plied their trades, most of them in their own homes. Down on the riverside wharves, cargoes of wool and grain, hides and salt, silks and spices, barrels of tar and casks of wine were being loaded and unloaded. In warehouses and cellars consignments of merchandise were being packed and unpacked, sorted and listed, while in the counting-houses accounts were being made up and letters written with quill pens and ink made of oakgall.

By mid-morning the crowds were congregating at the Royal Exchange in Cornhill, built by Sir Thomas Gresham as 'a public place for the meeting of merchants' and opened by the Queen in January 1571. The Exchange was another of the sights of London and favourably compared by foreigners with the great Bourse at Antwerp. The open quadrangle where the merchants met to do business was surrounded by a cloistered walk with shops and storehouses opening off it, but the best and most exclusive shops were to be found on the upper storey, and here we can follow Lady Ri-Mellaine and her friends as

Erondell describes them on their way to 'cheapen', or bargain.

Attracted by a pretty girl standing at the door of a draper's shop fluently praising her wares – 'Mistress, I will show you the fairest linen cloth in London' – they go in, and her ladyship proceeds to haggle expertly over some cambric. The assistant dares not show such a knowledgeable customer anything but the best, and asks 20 shillings an ell (a unit of measurement of 45 in.). Lady Ri-Mellaine offers 15 shillings and eventually they settle on 16 shillings, the shopkeeper protesting that she is losing money but hoping her ladyship will patronise her again. Her ladyship remarks tartly that, on the contrary, she is paying too much but buys half a dozen ells, resisting all offers of shirts, ruffs, handkerchers, nightcaps and edged lace.

She then calls for her coach to take her to Cheapside. Brightly painted signs – dragons, crowns, roses, mermaids, lions – swing over every shop door, and Lady Ri-Mellaine visits a goldsmith at the sign of the Green Dragon. Here she examines his selection of pearls and they have a highly technical conversation about the supposed magical properties or 'vertues' of the various precious stones – a discussion which her ladyship brings to an end by declaring that she will fortify herself with no other stone than 'the true corner stone, the lively rock, our Saviour Jesus Christ'. Then, tired out with so much trotting round the town, she orders the coachman to take her party home.

Barrels for beer
All liquids, from beer and drinking water to tar and imported wines, were stored in wooden casks or barrels. The cooper who made these vessels was therefore a skilled and important craftsman. If the barrel staves were of green or unseasoned wood, anything kept in them would quickly deteriorate and be wasted.

Balancing the books
Wealthy merchants kept large quantities of merchandise stored in warehouses on their premises. A wise businessman would hire watchmen to guard the goods from thieves. Here a merchant sits surrounded by bales which are being corded by his workmen, while he studies a ledger to calculate his profit.

Most people are now beginning to think about the midday meal. The schoolchildren have been sent home to dinner with a stern warning to be back in their places not a minute later than 1 o'clock, and the young men about town are making their way to an 'ordinary' – a tavern which offers a meal at a fixed price. Individual ordinaries had their own specialised clienteles, so that one might be a haunt of poets, writers and actors, another of lawyers or businessmen, yet another of fashionable society and wits.

At Paul's Cross the sermon has ended by this time, but the churchyard, centre of the book trade, is still thronged with passers-by and browsers at the numerous bookstalls. Inside the cathedral, along the middle aisle, is Paul's Walk, where sooner or later every kind of London character can be found. Here the knight, the dupe, the gallant, the upstart, the gentleman, and the captain rub shoulders with the pimp, the lawyer, the usurer, the citizen and the bankrupt, the scholar, the beggar, the ruffian, the Puritan and the cut-throat.

Paul's Walk was the place to show off new clothes, to meet one's friends and pick up the latest gossip, to look for a job among the advertisements posted on pillars, to hire a servant, to borrow money, to cadge a meal or a drink and, all too often, to have one's purse stolen. By noon, though, even Paul's Walk had become relatively deserted as the last of the strollers drifted off to eat. Those unfortunates left behind, unsuccessful in their quest for a loan or a free meal, were said 'to dine with Duke Humphrey' – the tomb of Humphrey, Duke of Gloucester, being a prominent feature of the central aisle.

Fingers before forks at the midday meal

No one was in danger of going hungry under the hospitable roof of the citizen of Claude Hollyband's account, who arrives home with his friend to be scolded by his wife for loitering. 'All is ready,' she tells him. 'The meat marreth. Where have you tarried so long?' The company gather round the table, which is probably literally a board supported on trestles. It will, however, be covered with a fine linen cloth, and each place set with a trencher or plate. In poor homes plates were still made of wood, or just a thick slice of bread, but in this house they are more likely to be of pewter or silver-plate. A napkin was also provided for each diner, and a spoon. Forks, introduced from Italy, were not yet in common use, but everybody had a knife, though often guests carried their own – a hang-over from the days when a man cut his meat with the dagger which hung at his belt. Anything which could not be eaten with a spoon was picked up in the fingers, so well-bred people washed their hands before and after eating, in a basin offered by a servant.

The housewife, bustling out of the kitchen where she has been supervising the dishing-up, calls the children to come and greet their father and his guests, telling the little boy to go quickly and say grace. 'Take your sister by the hand. Take off your cap and make curtsey.' The children eat at a separate table, where they are served by their own lackey with a good nourishing broth of stewed meat and vegetables thickened with oatmeal or barley, and everyone else sits down to eat. There will probably be only one or two chairs, reserved for

Shopping in Cheapside
Ordinary town dwellers did their day-to-day shopping in one of the many open street markets, such as the one shown in the reconstruction on pages 108–9. London's principal market was held in Cheapside, or West Cheap as it was sometimes called to distinguish it from East Cheap, also a market. The scene is a busy one, as men on horseback push their way through the crowds. Housewives (1) can be seen bargaining over stalls made from open carts (2). Pears, apples, cheese, eggs and fish are all on sale, heaped up together on the same stalls (3). Country dwellers brewed their own beer, but townspeople bought this staple of daily life from the barrel – or by the barrel (4). The surface of the street is plain earth beaten underfoot (5), dusty in summer, a miry mess in winter as people and horses ploughed their way through it. Performing bears (6) were a popular and familiar sight in the streets, and a bearward with his two bears can be seen on the right (7). With his wooden leg he is probably a war veteran, and has a set of bagpipes under one arm. Behind him, one of the tall timber-framed houses is propped up under repair showing the lath-and-plaster construction (8), while men work on the roof (9). Doorways give access to the garrets under the eaves (10). Washing was often done in

the master of the house or a specially honoured guest, and the others make do with stools. 'Sirs,' says the host, 'I pray you make good cheer, ye be welcome,' – and he orders the butler to broach the best wine in his cellar.

There is food in abundance – salt beef with mustard, a leg of mutton stuffed with garlic, capon boiled with leeks, a shoulder of veal, a turkey cock, roasted chickens and a venison pasty. The meal progresses cheerfully. 'An ounce of mirth is better than a pound of sorrow' declares the host, and when the wine runs out a servant is dispatched to fetch some more from the sign of The Rose at Temple Bar. The company has reached the dessert stage – roasted pears, apples, cold tarts, cake and cheese – when more guests arrive and are pressed to capon broth, pike with sauce and stewed carp. The host inquires why they are so late, and is told they have been at Court and have seen the Queen in her coach coming back from walking in the park. Someone remarks that the weather has turned very cold, and another servant is sent for wood and a bushel of coals to make a good fire. Another guest suggests some music, and the party seems set to go on for the rest of the afternoon.

In writing his *French Schoolmaster* dialogues, Claude Hollyband was chiefly concerned with improving his pupils' vocabularies, and probably the ordinary shopkeeper did not normally fare quite as sumptuously as this. But foreigners were always recording their astonishment at the amount of food Englishmen put away, and Londoners generally ate more butchers'/continued on page 110

these garrets, and the clothes strung across the street to dry (11). Colourful signs hang over every shop doorway, swinging and creaking in the wind (12). These signs served a useful purpose in days when many working people were illiterate, for a message or parcel could be sent to the sign of the Black Horse, or the Rose, or the Green Dragon in a certain street with some confidence that it would reach its destination. Later, hanging signs were forbidden, as they became so numerous as to be dangerous, often falling on the heads of passers-by.

continued from page 107/meat and enjoyed a greater variety of diet than country dwellers, having so many markets on their doorsteps. The poor, of course, had to make do with what they could get, living chiefly on coarse bread, cheese and sometimes a piece of bacon.

Across the river, in velvet and satin finery

Midday dinner was the most important meal of the day, and all reasonably prosperous people expected to take a couple of hours over it. For leisured townsfolk the afternoon was a time for digestion and perhaps some gentle exercise. Lady Ri-Mellaine and her guests went for a stroll in the orchard and garden, admiring the beauties of nature and gathering a bouquet of roses and gillyflowers, while the young gallants emerging from the ordinaries at about 2 o'clock might look for entertainment at one of the theatres on the South Bank, where performances began around three.

According to Thomas Platter, the visitor from Basle, the wherrymen would be waiting in great crowds, eager to catch a customer, 'for all are free to choose the ship they find most attractive and pleasing, while every boatman has the privilege of placing his ship to best advantage for people to step into'. Platter was much impressed by the wherries – light rowing boats mostly carrying two passengers and propelled by one or two pairs of oars. 'They are extremely pleasant to travel in,' he observed, adding that they were upholstered with embroidered cushions laid across the seats and that many of them had awnings to protect their passengers from rain or fierce sunshine.

Dinner at home
Chairs were a luxury in Elizabethan homes. Most families would possess no more than one, reserved for the master of the house or an honoured guest. At this family meal father and mother sit on stools, while the children eat standing up. The father, as was usual, keeps his hat on indoors. The family eat with spoons; forks were still rare.

A meal at the tavern

The city was full of taverns, known as 'ordinaries', which offered a meal at a fixed price. Most of them had their own specialised clienteles; Thomas Dekker, the playwright and pamphleteer, advised the would-be young man-about-town anxious to show himself off to inquire for an ordinary 'whither most of your courtly gallants do resort'.

A flotilla of wherries must have made a pretty sight, and the customers gathered at the water's edge were equally gay in their finery of brightly coloured velvet and satin, tight-waisted doublets slashed to show a contrasting lining and padded into the fashionable 'peascod belly', trunk-hose or breeches, also slashed and padded, and short cloaks swinging from the shoulders. Fashions for both men and women grew more and more exaggerated in the 1580s and 1590s as the Elizabethan period reached its high noon, and moralists fulminated over the prevailing extravagance and vanity of the times.

Such impractical and uncomfortable clothes were not, of course, for the ordinary working man or woman, whose everyday garb would be a rough shirt and breeches, or a plain coarse kirtle and apron, seldom removed and rarely washed. Hollyband's citizen would wear woollen hose and slop breeches (rather like plus-fours), a plain doublet, and a gown or cassock of sober brown or mulberry colour, modestly trimmed with velvet or fur. His wife might have a Spanish farthingale, but would wear wool or linen about the house; she would no doubt possess a velvet gown and a satin or taffeta kirtle to wear on special occasions. She would wear a linen cap indoors and a high-crowned hat of beaver or velvet, similar to a man's, when she went out. Imported foreign hats were becoming so popular that in 1571 an Act of Parliament was passed ordering every male over the age of six, with the exception of certain officials, to wear an English-made woollen cap on Sundays and holydays. This became known as the 'Statute Cap', and was not at all popular with the fashionable.

The upper echelons of the merchant class and their wives also dressed

soberly, but in cloth of the very best quality with plenty of fur trimming and gold ornaments. They could well afford the quality, the fur and the gold, for the merchant entrepreneurs of Elizabethan England were very rich men with fingers in a great many pies. Such a man was Thomas Myddelton of Tower Street, grocer, who began his career trading in sugar at Antwerp as a member of a London firm. Later he had his own 'sugarhouse' in Mincing Lane, and in 1588 he and his partners set up a depot in northern Germany at Stade on the Elbe. Their trade was by no means confined to groceries. They exported English kersey (woollen cloth) and fustian (cotton cloth), trading them for Italian silks and other mercers' wares which were sold to retailers not only in London, but as far afield as Bristol and Edinburgh.

By the early 1590s Myddelton, like many other members of the mercantile community, had become a regular investor in the lucrative business of commerce raiding on Spanish shipping. He and his partners took a third share in a vessel which captured a valuable cargo of sugar and cotton, and prize goods such as calicoes, silks, pepper and spices continued to figure largely in his ledger accounts. Always on the lookout for new openings, he took a share in a copper-smelting works at Neath in South Wales, and later tried his hand at farming, taking a lease of pasture and meadow land in Lincolnshire.

Men like Thomas Myddelton formed the élite of the business world. But there were plenty of smaller operators, equally tough, vigorous and alert – all of them ready to seize any opportunity for making money in the thrusting, self-confident dynamic society which was Elizabethan England.

At dusk, back to supper at the fireside

As the London afternoon wore on, shops and counting-houses all over the City continued to be busy with the routine of buying and selling, craftsmen toiled on at their benches and traffic thronged the streets until dusk. At 5 o'clock the schoolchildren were released from their long day's drudgery over Latin verbs, with orders not to go 'playing the fools by the streets' and to be sure to rehearse after supper the lessons they would recite in the morning. In winter they carried lanterns to light the way as they scurried home to supper, homework and bed, but in summer the temptation to loiter was a strong one, for there was always the chance of seeing a bit of fun. There might be a hue and cry after some thief, the fugitive dodging and weaving through the crowds as he sought sanctuary in the slum quarter known as Alsatia around Blackfriars. They might encounter an outlandish-looking party of foreigners returning to their inn after a day's sightseeing – there was already a well-established tourist circuit, taking in the Tower, with its sinister reputation, its famous Armoury and menagerie of wild beasts, St Paul's, the Royal Exchange, and Westminster Abbey with its royal tombs. London boys had a bad reputation for shouting insults at foreigners and pelting them with snowballs or other missiles, and the grammar schoolchildren would have had no inhibitions about joining in. They might see some City dignitary in his coach escorted by liveried footmen making his stately way to supper at one of the noblemen's mansions in the Strand; or,

Two ways across the Thames
The roadway on London Bridge, hemmed in by shops and houses, was narrow and constricted, and the fashionably dressed party in the foreground of this picture are making the crossing instead in a wherry propelled by two oarsmen. Passing under London Bridge in a boat was a hazardous proceeding. Each of the piers supporting its 20 arches of squared stone was

encased by a massive boat-shaped 'starling', or island, which restricted the flow of the river and turned the water into a mill race. When the tide was flooding there could be a difference of as much as 5 ft in the level of the water on either side. People travelling up or downstream usually preferred to get out and walk, re-embarking on the other side of the bridge.

best of all, they might be lucky enough to catch a glimpse of the Queen herself.

One young Londoner, Godfrey Goodman, later to become Bishop of Gloucester, always remembered how, at 5 o'clock on a dark December evening in the year 1588, someone came rushing into his lodgings in the Strand by St Clement's Church with the exciting news that the Queen was holding a Council at nearby Somerset House. 'If you will see the Queen, you must come quickly' he was told. 'Then we all ran, when the court gates were set open, and no man hindered us from coming in. There we stayed an hour and a half, and the yard was full, there being a great number of torches, when the Queen came out in great state. Then we cried "God save your Majesty!" And the Queen turned to us and said "God bless you all, my good people." Then we cried again, "God save your Majesty!" And the Queen said again to us, "Ye may well have a greater prince, but ye shall never have a more loving prince." And so the Queen and the crowd there, looking upon one another awhile, her Majesty departed. This wrought such an impression upon us, for shows and pageants are best seen by torch-light, that all the way long we did nothing but talk of what an admirable Queen she was, and how we would all adventure our lives in her service.'

Supper in most town households was at 6 o'clock and was generally a lighter meal than the midday dinner, but it was a poor man indeed who supped off only one dish. After supper on light summer evenings, whole families might be seen taking the air in one or other of the pleasant open spaces which still lay on their doorsteps, while groups of apprentices kicked a football about and generally let off steam after a long day in the shop. But every decent citizen was indoors by his own fireside by dusk. The day ended with evening prayers, often followed by father reading aloud and 'expounding' a passage of Scripture to his assembled household, and by 9 o'clock everybody would be in bed.

Outside, a few late revellers were leaving the taverns to make their way home through the darkened streets. London's street lighting was still a matter of private enterprise. Every householder was supposed to hang a lantern outside his door at dusk, but a single candle flickering behind a pane of smoke-blackened horn did little to illuminate the dark corners where a footpad or cut-throat might be lurking, and prudent people whose business or pleasure took them out at night hired a servant or link-boy with a torch to escort them home. The supply of water also depended on private enterprise. Over the centuries, various public-spirited individuals had provided conduits to bring 'sweet water' from springs on high ground north of London; this was carried round the City by water-carriers, for sale to those householders who could afford the service and had no wells of their own. Others carried their buckets to the pump, or managed without.

Those who did not have to get up early to go to work could spend their evenings dancing, playing cards, backgammon and other games, and it was nearly eleven before Lady Ri-Mellaine went to bed. Her daughters' governess had been busy seeing that everything was properly prepared. 'Now maidens, is all my lady's night gear ready? Take out of the way this pewter candlestick . . .

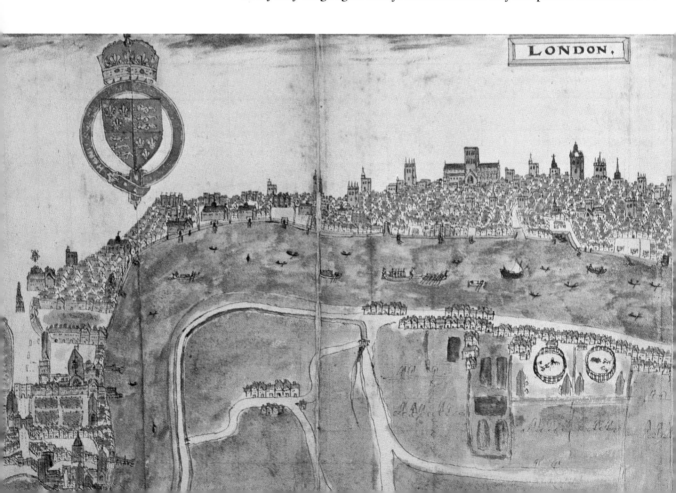

LONDON,

make ready the silver candlesticks with the wax candles, for you know that she cannot endure the smell of tallow . . . Where is the warming pan, that it be not to seek when she cometh . . . See that the chamber pot be under the bed.' Her ladyship appeared, remarking that it was very late, but adding complacently that 'we will sleep the longer tomorrow for amends'.

She then demands to be undressed. 'Go to, take off my clothes . . . help me to put off my gown, pull off my shoes, give me my pantoffles [slippers] and my nightgown, for fear I catch cold . . . Do not pull of my hosen yet until I be ready to go to bed, but warm my bed well . . . Let everybody kneel down. Let us say evening prayers.' The children ask for and receive a blessing, and wish their mother 'good night and good rest'. 'God give you good night and wholesome rest, Madame' chorus the maids, and are dismissed graciously with a 'God be with you'.

By midnight London lies silent, the streets deserted. The citizens and their wives sleep peacefully behind their bed curtains, even the poor and outcast have found some shelter in the rookeries around Blackfriars and on the South Bank, and only the Watch is abroad with his lantern, his dog and his staff and bell, giving his comforting hourly cry.

Twelve of the clock, look well to your locks,
Your fire and your light, and God give you good night.

Capital on a teeming river
This panoramic view of the early Elizabethan London skyline (below left) is decorated with church towers and spires, and dominated by the high tower and long nave of Old St Paul's, which lost its steeple in a violent thunderstorm in June 1561. Always prominent in any view of 16th-century London is the river, the main artery of trade and transport. Trading vessels sailed up past the Tower of London to the Pool; above London Bridge the river was crowded with smaller vessels carrying passengers about their daily business or across to the theatres and animal-baiting rings of the South Bank.

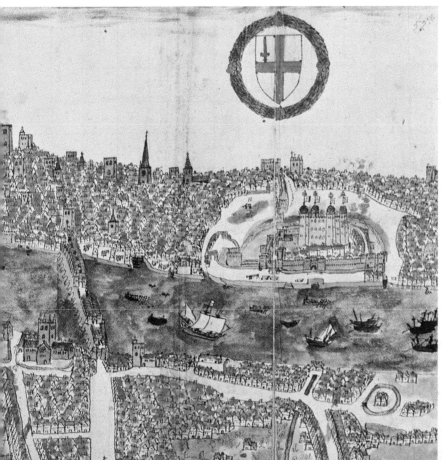

'Past one o'clock' . . .
In Tudor London the only law enforcement lay in the hands of the parish constables, or the Watch employed by the parish. This individual, carrying a lantern, a staff and a bell and accompanied by his dog, patrolled the streets at night, calling the hours and keeping a look-out for anyone abroad without good reason.

The underworld

TRICKSTERS AND THIEVES DEFY THE THREAT OF HANGING TO PREY ON THE UNWARY 'CONEY'

Despite the savagery of the penal code, a well-organised and defiant underworld flourished beneath the surface of Elizabethan society. The criminal classes used a private language or thieves' cant, remnants of which survived into the 19th century; the art of parting the unwary from his money was known as 'coney-catching'.

At the head of the criminal hierarchy were the 'rufflers', swaggering in tawdry finery, who lorded it over lesser thieves. These included horse thieves, known as 'priggers of pransers', and 'anglers' who used a long pole to pilfer clothes from windows or washing lines. Apart from pickpockets, cutpurses and highway robbers, there were hordes of professional beggars and confidence tricksters. 'Whipjacks' pretended to be discharged sailors, while 'drummerers' feigned dumbness. 'Demanders for glimmer' said they had lost their goods by fire, and 'moonmen' asked leave to sleep in a farmer's barn and then stole his poultry. A contemporary authority lists no fewer than 23 different categories of thieves and swindlers. No less dangerous were the women – the 'doxies' or 'kinchin morts' who lured the victim up a dark alley where he would be robbed of his money, valuables and even clothes.

Rich man, beggar man
This drawing shows two categories of professional beggar – the 'upright man' who pretended to be a proud gentleman down on his luck, and the 'counterfeit crank' who made himself froth at the mouth and feign epilepsy.

Hearing the evidence
However harsh the ultimate sentence, an accused man could be sure of a reasonably fair trial. Kneeling here before a magistrate is Jasper Coningham, a figure in a 16th-century ballad who 'denied God' – a serious offence. A clerk is setting down the charge and evidence.

A public warning

A book published in 1592 and 'done by a Justice of Peace of great authoritie', offered advice to the public on how to recognise and avoid the unwelcome attentions of the 'coney-catchers', or various forms of thief.

Contract to kill

A contemporary drawing shows the murder of Thomas Arden, a customs officer of Feversham in Kent, by two professional ruffians, Blackwill and Shakebag, hired by Arden's wife and her lover, a tailor named Mosbie. This celebrated murder case of about 1550 was the basis of Arden of Feversham, published in 1592, the first domestic tragedy in English drama.

A public whipping

To be whipped through the streets was a common punishment for the vagabond or 'sturdy beggar' – or, in fact, anybody found wandering without visible means of support. As always, the gallows looms in the background.

The pleasures of the chase

*The Elizabethan countryman's passionate addiction to all kinds of field sports was well
known throughout Europe, as was the excellence of English sporting dogs. Large stretches of countryside were the
private hunting grounds of the Queen and her nobles. Fishing, shooting
and boar-hunting are all depicted on this elaborately embroidered border of a table cover worked in many coloured silks.
Even the sportsman's country apparel reflects the colourful fashions of the age.*

CHAPTER FIVE

Country ways and country days

NINE OUT OF TEN
ENGLISHMEN LIVE BY THE
LAND; NEW FARMING
METHODS RAISE
YIELDS, BUT UNREMITTING
TOIL REMAINS
THE COUNTRYMAN'S LOT

Who can live in heart so glad
As the merry country lad?
Who upon a fair green balk
May at pleasure sit and walk,
And amid the azure skies
See the morning sun arise,
While he hears in every spring
How the birds so chirp and sing.

Nicholas Breton (1542–1626)

*I*f it were possible to go back in time and see the English countryside as it was 400 years ago, the first thing which would strike a 20th-century observer would be its wildness and emptiness. Many thousands of acres were still covered by dense woodlands, such as the Forest of Dean, Cranborne Chase, the Sussex Weald, Epping Forest, the Forest of Arden, Sherwood Forest and Cannock Chase. The Midlands and the northern moors lay unscarred by the blight of the Industrial Revolution, most of Lancashire was still morass or 'moss', and in the remoter parts of Wales and the Lake District the wolf was not yet finally extinct.

In the east, the Great Fen, which stretched for nearly 70 miles from Cambridge to Lincoln and from King's Lynn to Peterborough, was still undrained. This was a region apart, where the inhabitants, 'people of brutish, uncivilised tempers' according to the historian and topographer William Camden, lived out their strange, amphibious lives much as they had done in the days of Hereward the Wake: 'Usually walking aloft upon a sort of stilts, they all keep to the business of grazing, fishing and fowling.'

Something else which would certainly surprise the modern eye would be the absence of that familiar tidy patchwork of fields and hedgerows and drystone walls which has come to be regarded as an essential feature of the English country scene. Elizabethan England was still largely farmed on the old medieval open-field system, with the land divided into half-acre strips separated by narrow unploughed paths known as balks, while everyone's cattle grazed together on a communal pasture. This sort of country was called champaign or 'champion', as distinct from those areas where the land was beginning to be enclosed and farmed 'in several' – that is, where landowners and tenants had separated their holdings from the common fields, fencing them in and cultivating them individually, either themselves or with hired labour. Generally speaking the Midlands were still mostly 'champion', as were Dorset, Wiltshire, Hampshire, Berkshire and East Anglia, but Kent, Essex and other parts of the south-east had adopted the newer system.

The crops grown varied with the character of the soil and climate, but rye, the basis of most people's bread, was the prevailing cereal crop, supplemented

Palace in the countryside
Elegant, symmetrical and restrained in its splendour, Longleat in Wiltshire is a beautiful example of the brief influence of High Renaissance architecture on Tudor building. Longleat was begun by Sir John Thynne in 1554; in 1575 the Queen stayed there, though the building was still very likely without its top storey. The architect was Robert Smythson, and the master mason and his men built the shell of the house

for an average wage of sevenpence a day. The master carpenter was responsible for the interior, working in conjunction with the plasterers – often artists in their own right – who created the marvellous moulded ceilings and elaborate friezes.

by oats and barley. The best wheat was said to grow at Heston, now the site of Heathrow Airport but then according to the map-maker John Norden 'a most fertile place of wheat . . . accounted the purest in many shires'. The flour for Queen Elizabeth's own white bread came from Heston, and in his *Description of Middlesex*, John Norden waxed lyrical in his praises of the 'Purevale' (present-day Perivale) as it appeared from the top of Harrow Hill at harvest time, when 'a man may behold the fields round about so sweetly to address themselves to the sickle and scythe, with such abundance of all kind of grain, that the husbandman which waiteth for the fruits of his labours cannot but clap his hands for joy to see this vale so to laugh and sing'.

Kent, then as now, was the Garden of England, Herefordshire and Devon were also renowned for their orchards and the Vale of Evesham was the granary of all the country round about. Less familiar crops were saffron, much used for medicinal and culinary purposes, and flax and hemp which were

Bess of Hardwick

Elizabeth Talbot, Countess of Shrewsbury, better known as Bess of Hardwick, was probably the richest and most powerful woman in the country after the Queen. Without any initial advantages of birth, influence or fortune she carved out a brilliant business career in an age when competition for power and position was fierce and unremitting. She made four advantageous marriages, was a buyer and seller of land, a financier, farmer and merchant in lead, coal and timber. She also founded a family and dabbled in politics.

widely grown for clothing. English beef was already famous, though the cattle would have looked small and scraggy to modern eyes. English sheep, on whose backs grew so much of the nation's wealth, wandered in huge flocks over the northern moors, the Cotswolds, the South Downs, Romney Marsh and the rich pasture lands of the other southern counties.

Houses that reflect the more prosperous times

Elizabethan literature is full of idyllic-sounding descriptions of country folk and the joys of the simple life:

O God! methinks it were a happy life,
To be no better than a homely swain . . .

The reality was often a good deal harsher than the anonymous poet would have us believe, but at the same time there is no doubt that the standard of living of many countrymen rose during the Queen's reign. Farmers benefited by the rising prices gained for much of their produce, while peace within the realm, a stable government and the expansion of overseas trade were bringing increasing prosperity to a sizeable section of the population. This was reflected in the houses they built, and which can still be seen scattered up and down the country as a tangible memorial of the age.

At the top end of the scale were the great houses, such as Sir John Thynne's Longleat and the Earl of Pembroke's Wilton in Wiltshire, Christopher Hatton's Holdenby in Northamptonshire, Thomas Sackville's Knole and the Sidney family's Penshurst in Kent, Lord Burghley's Theobalds in Hertfordshire and Bess of Hardwick's Hardwick Hall in Derbyshire. These were houses built, or re-built, deliberately to impress and to show off their owners' wealth and status. Some, like Holdenby and Theobalds, both now long-vanished, were built with entertaining the Queen very definitely in mind. Elizabeth held Council meetings or received ambassadors at both houses, so they had to be big enough and grand enough for the purpose, with a Presence Chamber or High Great Chamber, a set of state apartments and a Long Gallery.

The gallery had become an essential feature of any important house and was used for entertaining, dancing, games and as an exercise area when the weather was bad. The gallery at Theobalds measured 123 ft and at Hardwick it is 170 ft long. All big houses retained a Great Hall, but this was being used less and less for its original purpose as communal living and dining-room for the household. Private dining parlours and withdrawing rooms were now provided for the owner and his family, while the Hall became more of a vestibule or ante-chamber, where guests were received and the inevitable hordes of upper servants and hangers-on gossiped and lounged and played cards.

One step below the palatial extravaganzas like Theobalds and Hardwick came manor houses such as Montacute in Somerset, Charlecote and Compton Wynyates in Warwickshire, Speke Hall near Liverpool and Little Moreton Hall in Cheshire. At the same time all over England a comfortable middle class of yeoman farmers and small-town merchants and clothiers were building themselves solid new dwellings containing as many as eight or ten rooms.

Although the half-timbered 'black-and-white' style of architecture has come to be regarded as typically Elizabethan, styles and materials varied according to local habit and availability. Where stone was easily come by, as in Cornwall, the North country, the Cotswolds and some parts of the Midlands, then obviously it was sensible to use it. The biscuit-coloured sandstone of Hardwick Hall, for instance, was cut from the quarry just below the house. In Dorset and Devonshire farmers lived snugly behind cob walls made of a mixture of mud, straw, chalk and rubble. In the south-east and East Anglia, brick and flint were used for building, while pargetting, or decorative exterior plasterwork, was a particular feature of Norfolk and Suffolk. Wood, however, remained the most important single structural component of the great majority of houses, and massive oak beams were incorporated in modest farmhouses and cottages.

The better type of newly built yeoman farmer's house consisted of a hall, where the family lived, ate and entertained their guests; a parlour, which often seems to have contained the best bed and was probably more for show than anything else; and a kitchen. Upstairs would be three or four bedrooms. The master and his wife occupied the headroom, or the room at the top of the stairs, while opening off on either side would be sleeping quarters for children and servants. This arrangement meant that everyone had to pass through the main bedroom on their way to bed – a useful aid to maintaining discipline. Attached to the house would be a variety of other buildings such as dairy, bakehouse and brewhouse.

Everywhere people were building with domestic comfort in mind. The nobility no longer needed to cumber themselves with moats and bastions and other such defensive outworks, and William Harrison noted the increasing use

Grace in glass and stone
Hardwick Hall in Derbyshire, one of a number of houses built or rebuilt by the formidable Countess of Shrewsbury, is the only one to have survived in its original form. Bess's initials ('E.S.' for Elizabeth Shrewsbury) cap the six towers. The plans of the architect, probably Robert Smythson, were subject to constant revision by Bess herself. She was determined that her new house should be 'lightsome', and during the building insisted on 'highing' the great windows still further.

of glass by ordinary people who had previously made do with panels of horn or a simple wooden lattice work to fill their window spaces. Glass was still quite a valuable commodity, however, and seems to have been regarded as part of the movable furnishings of a house; two yeomen, John Tyther of Shropshire and John Butler of Surrey, specifically mention their glass windows as well as their wainscoting as bequests in their wills.

The wealthy lined their walls with tapestry, usually depicting a biblical or classical scene, which served not only for decoration but also to help keep out the icy draughts which whistled through even the grandest mansion. This habit was widely copied, and every reasonably well-to-do household could boast some hangings of arras, while others would have a painted cloth on the walls of the parlour. To judge from the evidence of surviving wills and inventories, the average farmer would possess some 8 to 12 pairs of good homespun linen or hempen sheets, with pillows, bolsters and coverlets, perhaps half a dozen silver spoons and up to a dozen or so pieces of pewter or brass, together with the usual kitchen equipment of pots and pans, earthenware bowls, kettles and cutlery.

Carpets on the table and windows of glass

Furniture in Elizabethan terms included wall and bed hangings and also carpets, which were far too precious to put on the floor and were used instead as table coverings. Wooden furniture was still fairly sparse, even in wealthy homes, and a yeoman farmer was unlikely to own more than a cupboard for displaying his modest collection of plate, a table, some benches and stools, two or three chests in which to store linen, money and precious documents, and perhaps two or, at most, three bedsteads. These could be of the more primitive trestle type, but the prosperous yeoman or tenant might well have one or even two beds made by a carpenter. Very few people, though, were rich enough to have a bed to themselves, and the majority of farmhouse servants would still sleep on straw palliasses on the floor. The furniture in great houses was becoming more elaborate and elegant – 'a drawing table carved and gilt' and a walnut table inlaid with chessmen, dice and musical instruments can still be seen at Hardwick – but farmhouse furniture was usually of oak, made by a local joiner and built to last for generations, solid, heavy and foursquare.

There is little doubt that the comfortable classes, especially in the south of England, were growing more comfortable, with their new parlours (sometimes built on to an existing house), their glazed windows and smokeless interiors. More and more houses were being built with chimneys, or having chimneys added, to carry the smoke from the cooking fire. At the same time, many cottagers and labourers in less prosperous parts of the country still lived very much as their forefathers had done, in one or two-roomed mud-floored dwellings often shared with the beasts. This kind of house would be built of rough-hewn local stone, cob or wattle and daub and thatched with rye straw. Its occupants' wordly goods were likely to consist of no more than the clothes the householder and his family stood up in, some straw mattresses with hempen

Half-timbered hall
The 'black-and-white' half-timbered style of house is still thought of as being most characteristically Elizabethan. Little Moreton Hall in Cheshire, built by the Moreton family early in the reign, is probably the most picturesque surviving example. William Harrison, writing in the 1570s, remarked that 'the ancient manors and houses of our gentlemen are yet and for the most part of strong timber, in framing whereof our carpenters have been and are

worthily preferred'. Timber was used to decorate the exterior walls as well as for the main framework of the house, since wood was available in plenty from the forests which still covered much of the country. In other areas, stone, brick and flint were the most frequently used building materials.

sheets, a chest or coffer, a couple of stools and a trestle table, an iron cooking pot, a few crocks and wooden trenchers and drinking vessels. Such a cottage served as little more than a sleeping and cooking place and a shelter from the weather.

Even lower down the scale were the shacks of mud and straw, often erected overnight on a patch of waste ground by enterprising or desperate squatters, relying on their traditional but precarious right to be left undisturbed if smoke could be seen rising from a hole in the roof by morning.

The practice of converting large areas of arable land into sheep-runs had been a burning issue during the 1530s and 1540s, leading to riots and uprisings and angry, though exaggerated, complaints that 'sheep were eating men'. By Elizabethan times the price of wool had dropped sharply and as a result some pasture land was returning to tillage, but the gradual process of enclosing the common fields continued. Historians differ as to the exact causes and effects of these enclosures, but put at its simplest, the so-called 'agrarian revolution' of

Breaking the soil

Work on the land without mechanical aids was necessarily a hard and back-breaking business, as is demonstrated by this labourer who is attacking the soil with a mattock. Preparation of the soil for planting crops started early in the year for, as the farming writer Thomas Tusser advised:
'Who breaketh up, timely, his fallow or ley,
Sets forward his husbandry, many a way.'

the 16th century was the inevitable and sometimes painful consequence of the transition from a feudal to a capitalist economy.

Society in medieval England had been organised on the basis of the manorial village, each surrounded by two or three large unfenced arable fields, with some meadow land and common rights in the adjoining pasture and woodlands. The lord of the manor had his own 'demesne', cultivated by his dependent villagers, and the rest of the available land was divided in varying amounts among the villagers, who held it in return for service rendered to their lord. This was subsistence farming, each community, in theory at least, raising enough grain and meat and dairy produce to feed itself, its members bound to the soil they tilled and relying on their overlord for protection and justice.

By the year 1500 money rents were increasingly taking the place of personal service, while those whose holdings were insufficient to support them and their families worked on the lord's demesne for wages. The peasants were being released from their former and often burdensome obligations, but they were also losing their former security of tenure. The world was becoming a bigger, more sophisticated place, and land was becoming a marketable commodity. Inflation may have been an alien word to the 16th-century peasant farmer, but he was soon to feel its effects.

Enclosures to make farming pay

The lord of the manor, with his position to keep up and his greater dependence on manufactured and imported goods, had been the first to feel the impact of steeply rising prices, which were generally attributed to the sudden influx of gold and silver from the New World. His immediate reaction was to raise rents where he could, and to try to make more profitable use of his land – his only capital asset. This, in turn, frequently meant enclosure, for the open-field system was a wasteful one. A man farming, say, ten acres, would have 20 separate half-acre strips in the common field, and it was obviously more economic to consolidate these individual scattered holdings into a single block fenced off from its neighbours.

In places where enclosure meant no more than the parcelling out of the village land into small farms by mutual consent, the result was beneficial to all concerned. Equally, in places where an energetic landlord enclosed and reclaimed some of the surrounding waste of moor, heath or cleared woodland, this benefited the community as a whole by increasing productivity and providing employment. Unfortunately, however, enclosure could also mean wholesale landgrabbing by the rich at the expense of the poor cottagers, and an erosion of the cottagers' rights to gather fuel and feed their beasts in the common wood and pasture.

Those who did best out of rising prices and improved methods of husbandry were the yeomen farmers – known to contemporaries as the 'forty shilling freeholders', as they were judged to gather at least this sum in annual revenue from their lands. These yeomen were free men, born English, and their place in the social hierarchy came just below anyone entitled to call himself 'gentleman'. They could be summoned for jury service, and were eligible to vote at parliamentary elections. They also filled the unpaid, time-consuming and often thankless parish offices of constable, churchwarden, overseer of the poor, bridgewarden and so forth. As freeholders they were in an enviable position. They might still have to pay some nominal fixed rent to a landlord, but for all practical purposes they were the owners of their land, and as a class they were growing richer, often earning considerably more than 40 shillings in yearly revenue. Many of them were able to buy up the lands of unthrifty gentlemen and send their sons to grammar school, to the university and the Inns of Court.

Below the freeholders came various types of tenant. Commonest were the copyholders or customary tenants, who held their land by ancient custom and owned, if they were lucky, a copy of the manorial court roll confirming their title. Copyholders, though, could be dispossessed and were required to pay a steadily increasing fine to the landlord each time their property passed from father to son. Leaseholders, by contrast, would have a lease for a fixed term. Most leasehold farmers were doing so well that even when their rents rose from £4 to £50 or £100 a year, they were still able to save enough to buy a new lease when the old one ran out.

Least fortunate were the tenants-at-will, who had no security and were at the mercy of an enclosing or money-grubbing landlord. These were the smallholders, with two or three acres in the common field and common rights enabling them to graze a cow on the village pasture, and to gather fuel and feed a pig in the woodland; they supplemented their meagre living by hiring themselves out part-time to a neighbouring farmer. If they lost their holding,

Grinding the corn

Water-mills were a common feature of the pastoral scene, grinding the corn for almost every village which possessed a suitable stream. Here the wheel can be seen turning, while the great circular millstones lean against the walls of the mill. A sack containing more grain for the miller is slung across the back of a horse that is being led from the neatly fenced farmstead in the background.

they became landless labourers working on other men's fields for wages fixed locally by the Justice of the Peace. Skilled workers could earn up to sixpence a day, but the ordinary field labourer got about twopence or threepence. All too often an evicted cottager, unable to find work or fiercely reluctant to lose his independence, 'dropped out' of society, joining the growing numbers of masterless men aimlessly begging and stealing their way about the countryside.

The problem of the vagabond or sturdy beggar, resulting in large part from the break-up of the old manorial system, remained a serious social evil throughout the Elizabethan period and one which the government made strenuous efforts to remedy. Household servants and other workers such as shepherds and ploughmen, normally hired by the year, were obliged by law to finish their term of employment and could not leave or be dismissed before the end of the term without good reason. If an able-bodied man, or woman, was genuinely unable to find work, either in his or her own trade or in husbandry, then the parish authorities were required to find or create work for them. Those who refused to work were to be sent to the nearest House of Correction, while those discovered roaming the country without visible means of support were liable to a variety of harsh penalties which included being 'grievously whipped', or branded through the gristle of the right ear and put in the stocks, before being returned to their native parish by the shortest route. These punitive measures seem to have done little to reduce the numbers of determined rogues and vagabonds, who preferred to take their chance on the open road rather than accept the drudgery of the ordinary labourer's lot.

For all those who lived on or by the land, which meant some nine-tenths of the Queen's subjects, life, by modern standards, was hard, laborious and restricted; for those in the lower strata of society it was almost unimaginably so. The day's

Scenes of country life
This cushion cover embroidered in silks and silver thread displays a wide range of wild life, from caterpillar to peacock, butterfly to stag. The symmetrical design includes a realistic portrayal of many typical countryside scenes. A hound pursues the stag; the huntsman blowing his horn is balanced on the opposite side by a falconer with a hawk on his wrist. Wild flowers grow between the laden fruit trees.

work normally began with daylight which, in summer, would be around 3 a.m. Now, wrote Nicholas Breton, 'the cock calls the servants to their day's work . . . the milkmaids begin to look toward their dairy, and the good huswife begins to look about the house: the porrage pot is on for the servants' breakfast, and hungry stomachs will soon be ready for their victual'.

Dawn start to a day of toil on the land

Breakfast, which town dwellers and late risers often went without, was considered essential for those who had to be up and about their business by cock-crow, but it was not a leisurely meal, merely 'a snatch to wake fellows'. By 4 a.m. the farmhouse would be fully astir. 'Now are the horses at their chaff and provender,' says Breton, 'the servants at breakfast . . . and the shepherd with his dog going toward the fold.' By five, the maids would be milking and the labourers already hard at work in the fields. In the farmyard it was time to feed the poultry and give the hogs their swill, while indoors the women and girls, their housework done, would be busy at their spinning wheels. Weaving, though also a cottage industry, was generally regarded as a man's job, but the wives and daughters of cottagers and yeoman farmers found the spinning of wool and flax a useful means of augmenting the family income.

The farmer's wife was a key figure in the rural economy for, as Thomas Tusser in his *Five Hundred Points of Good Husbandry* put it, 'Husbandrie weepeth, where huswiferie sleepeth'. On the vast majority of farms and small-holdings, the dairy, vegetable plot and poultry yard were the housewife's responsibility. She had to know enough about animal husbandry to be a judge of a milch cow and a laying hen. She did her own milking, reared the calves and made her own butter and cheese, with the assistance of a dairymaid. The farmer's wife took her own produce to market and, traditionally, her profits were her own to dispose of. The good housewife, too, took a pride in her thrift and careful management. She saved all the feathers from her poultry for beds and bolsters, spun the flax for her own linen, made her own thread from nettles, and made and mended all the family's clothes.

Nothing was ever wasted in such a household, nothing bought that could possibly be made or grown at home. Buttermilk and household scraps went to the pig and chickens, home-grown wool and leather provided the farmer's breeches and jerkin, his wife's plain kirtle and petticoat. Rush-lights – peeled rushes dipped in tallow – were also homemade, and so was soap, by a laborious process involving mutton fat and an alkali obtained from wood ash. Wash-day was hard labour which involved steeping and then beating the heavy linen with wooden bats, before bleaching, smoothing and folding; this effort was only undertaken every three months or so.

The country housewife did her own baking and brewing and knew all about the techniques of preserving food – how to cure bacon and hams, how to salt the meat from the autumn slaughtering which must last through the winter, to store fruit and vegetables for the long months when no fresh produce would be available, to make jellies, conserves and pickles to vary a monotonous diet

Milking the cow
Sentimental Elizabethans were apt to regard the milkmaid with her pail over her arm as a romantic symbol of the joys of country life. But there was nothing carefree or romantic about the reality of a milkmaid's life, which meant getting up in icy winter dawns to go about her work with chapped and chilblained hands.

Making the butter
The hard and tedious job of churning the milk for butter was another of the many tasks which fell to the dairymaid's lot. All farms and most country households made their own butter, either for sale or their own use, and many superstitions were attached to churning. A variety of charms were muttered by the sweating milkmaid to make the butter come.

Honey from the hives
Sugar was a rarity in Elizabethan times, and honey was the principal form of sweetening used in most kitchens. Bee-hives made of plaited straw stood in every large garden, and maintaining the hives and processing the honey was one of the responsibilities of every conscientious housewife.

Threshers at work
Threshing – separating the grain from the chaff – was an autumn task, and the steady rhythmic 'thump thump' of the flail was a familiar sound around the farm after harvest. In a good year it brought the comforting promise of a good profit and full bellies. In a bad year, it meant anxious times for the farmer and his dependants.

and conceal the taste of anything which might be going 'off'. The housewife who neglected to plan her winter stores would suffer the ultimate shame of seeing her family go hungry.

Any housewife worthy of the name possessed a good general knowledge of sick-nursing and rudimentary doctoring, which in turn required an understanding of the medicinal properties of plants and herbs. In many families recipes for salves, cordials, poultices, possets and other sovereign remedies were handed down from mother to daughter, and some women with a special gift or interest in the subject would experiment on their own account. The really dedicated housewife also found time to make wines and syrups, pot-pourris and pastilles to be burned in a sickroom or to sweeten the air. As well as all these activities she had to find time for the ordinary chores of cooking, scouring and sweeping, nursing and caring for the children.

Housewives who served an entire community

The larger the household, the greater the housewife's responsibilities. She had to watch over the moral and physical welfare of the servants, keep them from idleness and teach them their duties. No matter how large her staff, she still supervised all the main departments – kitchen, pantry, buttery, stillroom, laundry and dairy – to ensure that waste and pilfering were kept to a minimum. She would doctor the family and household and often the surrounding neighbourhood as well, setting broken bones and dressing wounds and sores. She would always be prepared to offer hospitality to passing travellers and chance guests, and remember her Christian duty to care for the needs of her husband's poor tenants and dependants. She would be responsible for ordering supplies of anything which could not be made or grown on the estate, and in her husband's absence or incapacity she would manage the estate.

Few great ladies shirked their housewifely responsibilities. Bess of Hardwick certainly did not, and nor did Lady Margaret Hoby, a wealthy and deeply religious woman, who lived at Hackness, near Scarborough, and kept a diary of her daily doings. She superintended the dyeing and winding of yarn, the making of wax candles, sweetmeats and preserves, and would sit spinning or sewing with her maids while a devotional book was read aloud.

Lady Margaret also worked in her garden – 'went to take my bees and saw my honey ordered' runs one entry in her diary – and took an active part in running the estate: 'I was busy weighing of wool till almost night.' She rode about with her husband visiting their various farms, and discussed estate business with him. She often 'went abroad among the haymakers', and on other occasions could be found walking in the fields 'to see some wheat', talking to the ploughmen or to 'the new miller', supervising the sowing of five pecks of rye, 'busy about setting corn', receiving corn after harvest and measuring corn 'to see what provision we had'. She was tireless in visiting and tending the sick, helped poor women at their confinements, and makes frequent references in her diary to reading or talking to her 'old women' or her 'good wives'.

The civilising influence of educated, public-spirited ladies like Margaret Hoby was enormously important in the small communities where they lived, while the local manor house or 'great house' which, like a modern factory, provided employment for a whole district, was a vital economic and social centre.

Filling food, without ceremony, for the midday break

By 10 a.m. preparations for the midday meal would be well under way in manor and farmhouse kitchens up and down the country. 'The trenchers must be scraped,' says Nicholas Breton, 'and the napkins folded, the Salt covered and the knives scoured and the cloth laid, the stools set ready and all for the table. There must be haste in the kitchen for the boiled and the roast, provision in the cellar for wine, ale and beer. The pantler and the butler must be ready in their office . . . The ploughman now begins to grow towards home, and the dairy-maid after her work, falls to cleansing of her vessels. The cook is cutting sops for the broth and the butler is chipping of loaves for the table.'

In great houses like Longleat and Hardwick, dinner was served with a ceremony only slightly less elaborate than that observed at Court, but in the average farmhouse meals were straightforward affairs. In a well-run household everyone washed first and one of the children would be called on to say grace, before the farmer and his wife and those of their employees whose contracts entitled them to board and lodging got down to eating.

The food would be plentiful and filling, but plain. A dish of porrage would have been set cooling for the ploughfolk, and a great loaf and cheese put on the table. Beef and bacon, mutton, veal and poultry were all part of the prosperous

In the village street
Elizabethan notions of hygiene were casual and primitive. Housewives emptied their slops out of upstairs windows, while dunghills were left to accumulate in the street for scavenging pigs, dogs and rats, and became fertile breeding grounds for disease. The children playing and villagers going about their business in this cheerful street scene are unconcerned about the dangers of infection and too accustomed to the all-pervading smells even to notice them.

Travelling shop
The pedlar or packman trudging the country lanes in all weathers with his pack on his back was always a welcome visitor to the inhabitants of isolated villages and lonely farmsteads. This pedlar is offering daggers, spoons, pipes and combs, but many such travelling salesmen carried a wide variety of other small goods, including ribbons, laces, pins, looking-glasses, toys and trinkets.

yeoman's daily fare. Those living near a river or the sea-coast also ate a good deal of fish – mackerel and herring seem to have been the most popular – but the rest had to make do with dried or salted fish for Lent and on fish days. Fridays and Saturdays were statutory fish days when no meat was supposed to be eaten, and during the 1560s Wednesdays were added. This was not for religious reasons, but to encourage the fishing industry and maintain the strength of the fishing fleet – an essential training ground for seamen.

Cottagers and labourers lived on a largely vegetarian diet of so-called 'white meats' – that is, milk, buttermilk and whey, eggs, butter and cheese – with an occasional piece of bacon or a fowl. Bulk was provided by coarse rye or barley bread and porrage of peas, beans and oatmeal, turnips and cabbage – supplemented, of course, by a rabbit or a hare or whatever else could be scrounged or snared for the pot. In summer, too, the peasant could vary his rations with greenstuff, either growing wild or cultivated in his own plot, and with fruit and berries from the woods and hedgerows. Generally speaking it was not an unhealthy diet (though it must often have been a very dull one), but in winter poor people living on bread, salt bacon and dried peas were liable to suffer from scurvy caused by a lack of Vitamin C.

Except at busy times like haymaking and harvest when every available pair of hands was needed out of doors, the midday dinner, served about 11 o'clock, was the main event of the day and normally occupied the best part of two hours, including a pause for digestion when man and beast rested from their labours. 'The birds of the air are at juke (perched) in the bushes,' wrote Nicholas Breton. 'The lamb lies sucking, while the ewe chews the cud, and the rabbit will scarce peep out of her borough.' Even the humble labourer, who carried his dinner in a bag and ate it under a tree, was by law allowed a proper interval for relaxation. By the terms of the Elizabethan Statute of Artificers, which fixed working hours for artificers and labourers (5 a.m. to 7 or 8 p.m. from March to September, from dawn till dusk between September and March), employers were obliged to give their workers two hours off during the day for meals and 'drinkings', and from May to August labourers were entitled to an additional half-hour for a midday nap.

Justices who kept local government running

By 1 o'clock everyone was back at work. Indoors the housewife would be at her spinning wheel or busy in her kitchen or stillroom, and the dairymaid would be getting ready for the afternoon milking, while in the fields the men would be back at their endless toil. If the farmer's wife and the lady of the manor were busy and important people, so too were their husbands, and the average country gentleman who took his duties at all seriously had very little time on his hands. Many held office as Justices of the Peace, responsible to the Lords Lieutenant and, through them, to the Privy Council for the maintenance of the Queen's peace.

The justices were the mainstay of the Tudor system of local government, dealing with a hundred and one matters such as the control and licensing of

eas gesserunt, tribuantur.

Off to market

The farmer's wife was traditionally responsible for the dairy and poultry yard. She took her own produce – butter, cheese, eggs and fowls – to market and, by equally time-honoured custom, the profits were her own to spend as she liked. This countrywoman, in her best apron and kirtle, is carrying live poultry to market.

taverns and ale-houses, the maintaining of highways and bridges, and the building of gaols and poorhouses. A considerable part of their work was concerned with the administration of the Poor Laws, for as well as appointing three or four 'substantial householders' to act as overseers of the poor in every parish, any complaints against the overseers had to be referred to the justices. They were also empowered to arbitrate in disputes between master and servant, to fix local wage rates, order the whipping of beggars and vagabonds, suppress unlawful hunting and games, disperse riots and report those who failed to attend the parish church.

The JPs of the county, meeting at quarter sessions, heard a wide variety of cases. They committed the more serious offenders to the Assizes; but since all felonies except petty larceny – the theft of goods worth less than twelvepence – were subject to the death penalty, at least half the men and women condemned to death in England (estimated at about 800 annually) were tried and sentenced by the magistrates at quarter sessions. In addition to his public obligations, the country gentleman was expected to dispense hospitality to his neighbours and tenants. He had to look after his estates and business interests, while his leisure moments were likely to be occupied with the field sports – hunting, hawking, fishing and coursing – to which Englishmen of all classes were so much addicted.

The yeoman or tenant farmer also had certain public duties which were difficult to avoid, but if he was wise, his day was spent attending to his own affairs, rising at cock-crow to set his labourers to work and then going out himself about the fields. 'The best manure is the master's foot' was a common saying. Most Elizabethan farmers worked as hard as their hired hands, for most of them operated on narrow margins. A series of bad harvests, an outbreak of cattle disease or a sudden drop in prices could spell disaster even to prosperous yeomen whose lands brought them in an average income of between £300 and £500 a year, unless they had been able to put something aside to tide them over hard times. Lesser men, worth no more than £40 or £50 a year, lived permanently at or very little above subsistence level.

Sowing by hand, while oxen pull the plough

By modern standards farming methods were primitive – in many parts of the country oxen were still used to draw the plough – and every operation, from seed sowing to harvest, had to be done laboriously by hand. Root and winter crops were still unknown, and so were chemical fertilisers. Except by letting fields lie fallow, little was done to restore fertility, and the value of manure or compost was only just beginning to be understood. On many farms dung was collected, dried and burned as fuel, while straw was the principal winter feed for cattle. Nor was any systematic use made of the night soil, and the household refuse heap, or midden, was generally left to accumulate by the back door until it became too much even for the hardened Elizabethans and was burned. Marl and lime, however, were used. In Cornwall seaweed and sand were spread on the fields, and in Sussex, Kent and Suffolk pebbles from the shore were burned and used as fertiliser. In Hampshire and some other places river mud or 'moore earth' was dredged up for the same purpose, and towards the end of the century farmers in Middlesex were experimenting with dung from the London stables.

Probably no section of the community was more set in its ways and more suspicious of new-fangled ideas than the average small farmer, but interest in improving profits and yields certainly existed – especially among forward-looking agriculturists in the south-east who were learning to specialise in beef, corn and fruit for the insatiable London market. Books on farming practice, too, were proliferating and Thomas Tusser's homely *Five Hundred Points of Good Husbandry* went through about a dozen editions between 1557 and 1593.

The average farmer can have had little energy left for reading by the time he came in for his supper. This was usually only a snack – a handful of raisins soaked in hot milk or a roasted apple – eaten about 5 o'clock or later in summer

The working countryside
Some four out of five of the people of Elizabethan England lived on the land and got their living by it. The reconstruction on pages 136–7 shows a typical, busy rural scene. In the foreground are the sheep (1) on whose backs so much of England's prosperity still rested. The farm cart (2) is made of a simple board framework, and in the field below haymakers are hard at work with their big wooden rakes (3). On the left more workers pile the hay into another cart (4). Every scrap of grassland was mown, for the hay was precious as the only winter feed for cattle, and at haymaking time every able-bodied member of the local community was expected to turn out to help. By the river stand two farms. The one on the left (5) is the larger and richer, with its big barn, the farmhouse with a smoking chimney and another, smaller house with galleried living quarters. This farm also has its own well with a pulley for raising the water. The second farm (6) is smaller, thatched and timbered: local materials were always used for building. Both types of farm might be owned by yeoman freeholders, or else leased from the local lord of the manor. The fields in the foreground use the river and tree-line as natural boundaries, but on the hillside the older form of strip

when work continued out of doors as long as the light lasted. By dusk everyone would be ready for bed, and even in winter the farmer and his family did not keep late hours. There were some jobs which could be done indoors in the evenings, but Anthony Fitzherbert, in his *Boke of Husbandry*, advised the farmer to calculate the cost of fire and candlelight against the value of the work done. It might be more economical in the long run to send everyone to bed early and work by daylight. Thomas Tusser recommends bed after supper for both maidens and men, 'in Winter at nine and in Summer at ten', but first the animals must be settled and fed and everything secured for the night.

The countryman's year, from seed-time to harvest

As the countryman's day followed its inexorable, unchanging routine, so, too, did the countryman's year. Thomas Tusser's farming year begins with the Michaelmas quarter-day at the end of September, when the harvest has been gathered and the autumn gales were beginning to strip the trees, while hogs in the woodland browsed contentedly on the fallen acorns. This was the time for picking apples and other fruit for the winter store, for sowing white-wheat and rye and ploughing the barley-land 'dry as ye can'. Young rams and bulls must be gelded, and the boar brought into his sty. Bracken for the animals' bedding should be gathered in cowshed and stable, logs and/continued on page 138

cultivation (7) is still being practised, and cattle graze on the common pasture (8). The windmill (9) was used for grinding corn. Everyone lived within walking distance of his work, and the small group of cottages (10) half-hidden in the trees would accommodate those families who owned a minor stake in the common-strip fields and also worked part-time for the bigger farms close by. Unmarried workers, men and women, lived in the farmhouse, being hired by the year at a hiring or 'mop' fair.

The copyhold home
*The typical home of the
'copyholder', or cottager, was of
'one bay's breadth'. A bay
measured 16 ft, the space
between the crucks or bending
beams which stood at each end
of the bay to support the roof.
This kind of one-roomed or
two-roomed mud-floored
dwelling, built of local materials
and shared with the beasts, was
often little more than a sleeping
and cooking place and shelter
from the weather. This cottage,
however, has a chimney.*

A barn for the grain
*With rising food prices the
better-off copyholder could afford
to extend and improve his
house and out-buildings and
own a sizeable, snugly thatched
barn to store his grain and
fodder and farm implements.*

continued from page 135/kindling stacked for fuel, and all those other little outside jobs around the farm which have been overlooked during the busy summer months attended to – such as making buildings and fences tidy and weather-proof before winter's rains and storms.

In theory, each parish was responsible for the upkeep of roads and bridges, being required by law to elect a surveyor to serve for one year. The more prosperous members of the community were supposed to provide men and materials for roadworks, while the poorer sort had to give their labour for eight hours a day on four consecutive days when called upon. In practice, this was not a very successful system; William Harrison complained that the rich evaded their share, and the poor so loitered in their labour that scarcely two good days' work got done. Human nature being what it is, surveyors would make use of their term of office to improve those lanes and paths leading to their own farms or pastures, while neglecting the highway – occasionally throwing a barrowload of stones or a pile of brushwood over the more glaring deficiencies. As a result, the generally 'noisome' and dangerous condition of the roads remained a national scandal; even the main trunk routes out of London were little more than cart tracks.

Saving food for winter's lean days

November was slaughtering time, when pigs were killed and cattle which could not be fed through the winter were slaughtered for meat. Shortage of winter feed, in an age when turnips and other roots were grown only in the kitchen garden, was the 16th-century farmer's greatest headache and the chief brake on progress in animal husbandry. As much meat as possible was salted, pickled, soused, brawned or smoked in the farmhouse chimney for the lean days ahead; but even so, everyone could expect to have his belly comfortably filled by fresh-killed meat from All Hallows until the Christmas feast. The thresher was busy in the barn providing grain for bread and beer, and straw for the surviving livestock, but the husbandman must be constantly on his guard to prevent waste and pilfering. Out of doors the vegetable garden was dug and tender plants protected from frost, and once ploughing was over the horses were stabled for the winter.

Little could be done in the fields during December, except hedging and ditching if the weather permitted. This was the season when milk froze in the pail and icicles hung by the wall, but it was possible to keep warm by chopping or splitting logs. The stalled cattle had to be fed and tended, and the farmer could use this slack time to fit new handles to forks and rakes, and sharpen blunt tools on the whetstone. After the twelve days of Christmas, when everyone made merry and the more fortunate ate plentiful goose and roast beef came Plough Monday when, if the weather was kind, outside work began again. The wise farmer would also go out and look at his pasture, removing stones and other obstructions and filling up holes.

As the days began to lengthen, the tempo increased. Lambs were born on fat grounds, and the shepherd worked overtime. Early calves were given to the housewife to rear, and gardeners sorted seed saved from the previous year, as the first welcome signs of spring could be seen in swelling buds and occasional balmy days.

By mid-February the spring ploughing should be well under way, and by March the year's work was in full swing. Wheat, oats and barley were sown, along with peas and vetches, and small boys were employed to throw stones at the plundering birds. The housewife was busy in her garden, and Thomas Tusser lists an impressive number of plants and herbs for salad, stewpot and stillroom. Many are familiar – lettuce, endive, artichokes, cucumber, radish and mustard, spinach, leeks, mint, thyme, sage, rosemary and lavender. Others less familiar are bloodwort, to staunch bleeding, liverwort, eye-bright, horehounde, and lovage for gallstones. February, March and April were always hungry months – it was no accident that Lent was a fast – and it came as a relief all round when the starving cattle could at last be turned out to grass.

Throughout May and June the women and children were out weeding and picking stones from the fallow ground. It was hard, back-breaking work, but warm weather and the sight of the growing crops helped to keep everyone cheerful. At the beginning of May the lambs and ewes were separated and some ewes kept for milking; the yield of five ewes equalled that of one cow. May and June was also shearing time, always an occasion for merry-making.

The sheep were washed first, preferably in running water, and sheared two days later, after the fleeces had dried. In big sheep-farming areas, such as the

Guardian of the flocks

England's prosperity still depended heavily on the export of wool and woollen cloth, and the shepherd caring for the huge flocks which roamed the rich pasturelands of the Midlands and the south was an important member of the rural community. Sheep offered a low-cost, high-return crop to the farmer and landowner, but by Elizabethan times the international price of wool was dropping. The process of enclosing large areas of common or arable land for pasture was therefore slowing down.

Sussex Downs and the Cotswolds, teams of expert shearers, each working under a captain, moved from farm to farm, and the shearing ended with a special supper at which ale flowed freely. Arable farmers were busy with their second ploughing of the fallow ground. Then came haymaking, when every able-bodied man helped. Every patch of ground was mown; even if the grass was poor, it would all help the livestock to get through the winter.

Haymaking was followed by harvest, the climax of the farming year, and again every able-bodied man, woman and child would be out in the fields under the August sun. Wheat, oats and rye were reaped, the barley was mown and flax and hemp pulled. After the last sheaf was safely under cover came the harvest-home supper, a specially lavish meal provided by the farmer for all his workers, accompanied by more drinking, dancing and the singing of traditional songs. But there was no time, even now, for too much celebrating. The gleaners followed the reapers into the fields, and an industrious family could glean enough grain to keep them in bread for a year. Then, by immemorial custom, the cattle were turned on to the stubble, while in the barns the seed corn was being threshed and the whole cycle was ready to begin again.

A nation indebted to the frugal farmer

The Elizabethan countryman and his family lived hard and worked hard. For many of them, food in their bellies, a roof over their heads and a fire on the hearth marked the limit of their expectations, and by no means all of them achieved even these modest ambitions for all of the time. A bad harvest could

Oxen at the plough
Being stronger and cheaper to maintain than horses, oxen were widely preferred as draught animals for ploughing and harrowing. The ideal plough is described by the farming writer Thomas Tusser as being in eleven parts. It was still a cumbrous, medieval affair, though by Elizabethan times shod with iron.

Sowing the seed
Sowing was usually done 'broadcast', as the sower is doing in this illustration to an Elizabethan ballad, after the ground had been harrowed by the scratch plough in the background. The idea of 'setting' seed, or sowing it in drills, although recommended by the writers of agricultural manuals as being 'much more profitable and less chargeable', did not become general practice until the 18th century.

mean real hardship and a series of bad harvests, such as occurred during the 1590s, could mean starvation. For the farm labourer, living on a few pence a day in his tiny, damp cottage, life was little more than a harsh, unremitting struggle for existence. Yet the absence of any serious rural discontent during the Queen's reign indicates that by and large the cottagers were managing, if not much better, then certainly no worse than their forefathers. In some ways, of course, things *were* better. There was civil peace, a man could claim the protection of the law and, though some landlords were oppressive, the general trend was towards enlightenment.

For the new rural middle-class things were definitely improving, and the yeoman, sturdy, thrifty and frugal, was able to pursue with increasing success the ideal as described by Thomas Tusser:

Good farm and well stored, good housing and dry,
Good corn and good dairy, good market and nigh.

With the aid of 'good shepherd, good tillman, good Jack and good Jill', husband and huswife were filling their coffers, educating their children and contributing to the nation's prosperity. These were people who never travelled further than the nearest market town, who took no interest in extravagant new fashions and knew little or nothing of the expanding horizons of trade and adventure visible from London. Nevertheless, they made up the solid backbone of Elizabethan England without whom the glittering achievements of the age would not have been possible.

Harvest time

Harvest was the climax of the agricultural year, when every able-bodied man, woman and child turned out to help in the fields. Here, the master and his dog are keeping a watchful eye on the reapers. Like every other farming task, cutting the corn was done entirely by hand but a considerate employer would give his workers gloves, and everyone was spurred on by the thought of the lavish harvest-home supper to come.

Tudor gardens

PLANTS TO HEAL AND ADORN, LAID OUT IN FORMAL
PATTERNS THAT TAMED NATURE

Iris, in an embroidered panel

A lover's garden
*In a walled garden set with herbs,
the lover in the medieval* Roman
de la Rose *attains the rose,
symbol of his lady's love. The
wall is topped by a trellis for
climbing plants.*

The Elizabethans were enthusiastic and knowledgeable gardeners, from the housewife tending her vegetable plot to the great Lord Burghley supervising the laying out of his pleasure gardens at Theobalds in Hertfordshire. Love of flowers was a national characteristic, and Shakespeare's plays are full of references to gillyflowers, lady's smock, cuckoo bud, heartsease and love-in-idleness. Every cottage had a flower patch tucked in among the herbs and salads. Every manor house had its ornamental garden laid out with formal flower beds, shrubs – sometimes clipped into elaborate topiary shapes – trellis arches, shady walks and green alleys. A large house might have an artificial mount with a path winding to the top, a rose garden and a pond garden.

The knot garden
*Small beds edged with bricks or
low hedges of lavender, rosemary
or box were the basis of the typical knot garden (left). The beds
were set in a formal pattern with
paths of coloured gravel.*

Flowers in needlework
*From the mid-16th century,
many new plants reached England. This embroidered panel from
a series at Hardwick Hall shows
a tulip, introduced from Turkey
in about 1578, like the iris.*

Brought to book

John Gerarde's Herball *of 1597 was the first accurately illustrated work on botany to appear in England. In the second edition, published in 1633, the English names of plants were given for the first time. Most of the plants listed by Gerarde had medicinal uses; rock samphire, for instance, was widely recommended as an aid to digestion.*

Velvet rose   Yellow rose   Rock samphire   Thorny samphire

On a monastic pattern

The small enclosed garden (right), derived from the old monastery garden, was typical of the period. Paths and beds were geometrically arranged, and urns, balustrades and arbours were also common features. The well is handily placed for watering; elsewhere gardeners pumped water from large tubs.

A frame for Montacute

Owners of stately homes such as Montacute (below) in Somerset regarded their gardens as extensions of the house, designed to complement it with straight and curved lines, formal avenues of trees and carefully placed fountains and statuary. Tender plants were grown in tubs which could be carried indoors for the winter.

Music for diners and dancers

*Every great household employed professional musicians to entertain the family and their guests and provide music
for dancing. These four musicians from a painted frieze in the Great Chamber of Gilling Castle,
North Yorkshire, are playing viols and lutes, both favourite instruments
of the time, and have their music books beside them. Music was an essential part of Elizabethan life, and
anyone with the least pretensions to culture was expected
to be able to play an instrument, to read music and to take a part in the singing which was a regular after-dinner
amusement. The Queen herself was an accomplished performer on lute
and virginals, and music-making, both amateur and professional, was a favourite recreation at Court.*

CHAPTER SIX

Merry England

A NATION RELAXES AT FAIRS AND ON
FEAST DAYS, WHILE NOBLES HUNT, MUSICIANS FLOURISH AND
LONDONERS FLOCK TO THE NEW THEATRES

Much time is wasted now away,
At pigeon-holes, and nine-pin play,
Whilst hob-nail Dick, and simp'ring Frances,
Trip it away in country dances;
At stool-ball and at barley-break,
Wherewith they harmless pastime make . . .   Anon

---

*T*he Elizabethans worked hard but they also played hard, and although the idea of taking a fortnight's summer holiday would have astonished them, their year was well broken up by festivals and outings. For the rural community the most important of these were the regular fairs and markets at which business was combined with pleasure.

Every town of any consequence held a weekly market, usually on Saturday or Sunday, where the local farmers and their wives would come bringing their produce to sell, to buy such necessities or luxuries as could not be grown or made at home, to meet their neighbours, pick up the local news and drink a pot of ale at the tavern in the market place.

At Michaelmas the small farmer with his rent to pay came to sell his harvest grain for what he could get. Bigger men, who could afford to wait, would hold back until prices rose – a practice known as 'engrossing' which was frowned on by the authorities, especially in times of shortage. The government did its best to prevent hoarding and profiteering by means of Orders, Proclamations and market regulations circulated to the local justices. 'Forestalling' – the buying or contracting for a crop before it reached the market, and 'regrating' – buying in the market to re-sell elsewhere at a higher price, were both strictly controlled, and limits set to the profit that could be made. However, as the population grew, and more and more big farmers took to specialising in grain, in beef or dairy cattle, and in sheep, the justices had increasingly to use their discretionary powers to grant licences to middlemen, or 'badgers' as they were called, to buy and sell at a small profit in order to relieve shortages in other parts of the country.

Distribution and transport were a constant headache to buyer and seller alike. Road transport was slow and expensive at the best of times, while in winter it was impossible to move heavy goods by road. The most important grain markets, therefore, were always to be found on or close to a navigable river, at places like Abingdon and Reading and Ross-on-Wye, and in parts of the Midlands, Yorkshire and East Anglia.

Poultry, butter, eggs and cheese were sold at local markets, as well as some livestock – especially pigs, which could not be driven over long distances. Farmers who specialised in sheep and cattle normally attended one or other of the spring and autumn fairs to buy and sell stock. Fairs were held at numerous

Dancing on the green
Dancing was a pastime for everyone – from the Queen and her courtiers performing the sophisticated steps of a galliard or pavane to a cheerful group of boys and girls romping on the village green on a summer evening. Country or 'round' dances, like the one depicted here, were popular at every level of society. People also danced round the maypole, in spite of Puritan disapproval. They danced at weddings and feasts, and they danced in the hall or barn at Christmastime.

centres up and down the country. Every considerable town had its annual fair, and many had more than one. Some were larger and more famous than others, but all played a vital part in the economy of the region they served.

Most fairs had their own speciality. There were sheep fairs in Dorset, in East Anglia, at Skipton and Kettlewell in Yorkshire, in the Cotswolds and at Shrewsbury. There were horse and cattle fairs, cloth fairs, cheese fairs and the famous Nottingham Goose Fair, held in October and lasting for three weeks. Outside London, one of the biggest livestock markets was held in September at Barnet, where Scottish and Welsh drovers brought cattle which had been fattened on the way on the lush English pasturage. There were other cattle fairs at Gloucester, Hereford, Chester, Oswestry, Rugby, Northampton, Leicester, Norwich and Bury St Edmunds.

As well as these, there were the 'Mop' or hiring fairs, usually held at Michaelmas or Martinmas, when the rates of pay for the coming year were fixed by the magistrates and when farm workers looking for jobs offered themselves for hire, each with the emblem of his or her trade – the housemaid her mop, the shepherd his crook, the waggoner his whip, the dairymaid her

Gossip at the market
Every town of any size held a weekly market, when people from the surrounding villages came in on foot or on horseback to do their shopping, see their friends and exchange local news and gossip. Farmers' wives brought eggs, butter, cheese and poultry for sale. Their husbands bought and sold livestock, and at Michaelmas the tenant farmer came to sell his harvest grain. Market day was important in the economic life of the neighbourhood, but it was also a social occasion, eagerly looked forward to as a break in the harsh monotony of daily routine.

pail. The bargain between master and servant would be sealed with the payment of earnest money, known as the hiring penny, which would quickly be spent on a 'fairing' of ribbons, trinkets or sweets at one of the booths. The Mop fair was always an occasion of special jollity, for it might be the one time of the year when people of an entire neighbourhood came together with money in their pockets.

Probably the biggest and most famous English fair was Stourbridge Fair near Cambridge, where from August 24 to September 12 a field between the Newmarket road and the River Cam was transformed into a great wholesale market selling anything and everything, but best known for woollen cloth sold in a great square of booths known as the Duddery – after 'duds', an old colloquial term for clothes – which attracted dealers from all over the country. There was a famous Easter Fair at St Ives in Huntingdon, a Whitsun Fair at Lichfield, a September Herring Fair at Yarmouth, a Michaelmas Fair at Bedford, a great midsummer fair at Winchester, and the famous Bartholomew's Fair in London, held at Smithfield at the end of August.

Fairs where pleasure followed business

In medieval times, merchants from France, Spain, Italy, the North German Hanseatic towns and the Low Countries had all come to do business at the big fairs in the south and east of England, bringing silks and velvets, furs and amber, Flemish linen and Gascon wine to exchange for English wool and tin, lead from the Derbyshire mines and iron from the Sussex forges. By the Elizabethan period the fairs were losing their international flavour, but they remained important centres of home trade where, traditionally, local families and the stewards of great households stocked up for the year and had a real day out when the buying and selling was over.

Every fair brought swarms of showmen into the town, troupes of strolling players, travelling menageries, prize-fighters and cheapjacks selling, in the word of the pedlar's cry, 'all that maids lack from head to heel' – combs and garters, gloves, laces, silks, and ribbons and looking glasses. Here the maidservant could spend her year's wages on the pretty things she never saw at any other time. The young men bought presents for their sweethearts, while more sober folk took the opportunity to lay in supplies of necessities for farm, kitchen and store-cupboard.

This was the countryside's annual glimpse of the outside world – a chance for the young people to snap up the new ballad sheets, to dance to the latest tunes and gaze wide-eyed at the jugglers, acrobats and wild-beast shows; a chance for farmers to compare notes and prices; for their wives to enjoy a shopping spree; and for the rougher element to drink too much strong ale, known as huff-cap, angels' food or dragon's milk at the taverns and drinking-shops which sprang up overnight at fair time, and to get into fights and brawls, all too often ending up with broken heads and empty pockets.

Apart from the visit to the fair, amusements in the country were strictly home-made. Many holidays and festivals associated with the Roman Church had

Fiddler at the feast
The Elizabethans played as hard as they worked and were always ready to find an excuse to enjoy themselves. The fiddler, who might be a respectable local man practising an honest trade by day, or an itinerant vagabond making his way from village to village, was always in demand to play at a wedding or feast or just to accompany an impromptu dance in the farmhouse kitchen or on the village green.

Keyboard for a queen

The virginals, the commonest of Elizabethan keyboard instruments, resembled the harpsichord in having quills that plucked the strings – unlike the piano where the strings are struck by hammers. Queen Elizabeth herself was an accomplished player upon the virginals, and this richly decorated instrument belonged to her. The immense popularity of the virginals encouraged composers to write skilfully and copiously for it.

vanished, officially at least, with the Reformation, but many were still celebrated, along with others which had been old when Christianity was young.

The old year was ushered out and the New Year ushered in with the Christmas feast, which traditionally lasted from Christmas Eve to Epiphany, or Twelfth Day, and sometimes longer. The twelve days of Christmas were the nearest thing to a holiday season, when work was more or less suspended and everyone celebrated in an outburst of eating, drinking and hospitality. Manor and farmhouse would be decorated with boughs of holly, ivy, bay, laurel and holm-oak. This was not only a country custom. 'Against the feast of Christmas,' wrote the London chronicler John Stow, 'every man's house, as also the parish churches, were decked with holm, ivy, bays, and whatsoever the season of the year afforded to be green. The conduits and standards in the streets were likewise garnished.'

Feasting and revelry at Christmas

On Christmas Eve the Yule Log was brought in – a massive piece of tree-trunk large enough to burn on the open hearth for the whole of the holiday – and on Christmas Day everyone went to church before sitting down to the most sumptuous meal the family budget could rise to. In noble households this was an occasion for serving dishes like boar's head, peacock pie and elaborately sculpted and gilded castles of sugar and marchpane (marzipan), while the minstrels played in the gallery of the Great Hall. Humbler people feasted on beef and mutton, roast or boiled, geese, hens and capons, and even the poorest could be assured of a good dinner provided by charitable neighbours. Christmas was, above all, a time for keeping open house for family and friends, when the poorer sort went the rounds singing carols, and the mummers performed their antics in the hope of some seasonable reward.

To mask and to mum kind neighbours will come
With wassails of nut brown ale;
To drink and carouse to all in this house,
As merry as bucks in the pale;
Where cake, bread and cheese is brought for your fees
To make you the longer stay.

The universities, the Inns of Court and, according to John Stow, 'the house of every nobleman of honour or good worship' still observed the ancient custom of appointing a Lord of Misrule, or 'master of merry disports', to preside over the Christmas revels – a heathenish custom much disapproved of by the Puritan writer Philip Stubbes, who wrote angrily: 'First, all the wild heads of the parish . . . choose them a grand-captain (of mischief), whom they ennoble with the title of my Lord of Misrule, and him they crown with great solemnity and adopt for their king. This king anointed, chooseth forth twenty, forty, three-score, or a hundred lusty guts like to himself to wait upon his lordly majesty, and to guard his noble person . . . They bedeck themselves with scarves, ribbons and laces, hanged all over with gold rings, precious stones and other jewels: this done, they tie about either leg twenty or forty bells, with rich handkerchieves in their hands, and sometimes laid across over their shoulders and necks, borrowed for the most part of their pretty mopsies for bussing them in the dark. Then have they their hobby horses, dragons and other antiques, together with their bawdy pipers and thundering drummers, to strike up the devil's dance withal: then march these heathen company towards the church and churchyard, their pipers piping, their drummers thundering, their stumps dancing, their bells jingling, their handkerchieves swinging about their heads like madmen, their hobby horses and other monsters skirmishing amongst the throng . . . like devils incarnate, with such a confused noise, that no man can hear his own voice.' Stubbes was a prejudiced observer, but he has given us a marvellous word-picture of a band of Elizabethan 'lusty guts' in full cry.

The Christmas holidays were a time for indoor amusements – for gathering

Orchestra for a king
The popularity of music at Elizabeth's court was a tradition that went back to the time of her father, Henry VIII. In this illustration from Henry's own psalter, musicians are seen playing a pipe and tabor (drum), trumpet, harp and clavichord. Henry VIII had a large collection of musical instruments, and gathered a group of musicians from England and abroad to play them. He also composed music himself, particularly for dancing, and set verses to his own tunes.

For fun and for food
Fishing was a sport enjoyed by men and women. Many gentlemen had their own private fish-ponds or stretches of river. Fishing also had a more practical aspect. In days of slow and difficult transport, people living more than a few hours' journey from the coast never saw fresh fish unless they could catch their own.

Pewter plate for the feast
Pewter, an alloy of tin and lead which can be highly polished, was gradually superseding wooden vessels on Elizabethan tables, and most better-off households boasted a dozen or so pewter plates and cups which could be brought out for special occasions.

round the fire, drinking mulled ale, roasting chestnuts and listening to a storyteller. There was usually someone in the village with a special talent for telling spine-chilling tales of ghosts, spirits and fairies, and he or she would be in great demand at Christmastime. Dancing was always a favourite pastime, and after dinner the hall would be cleared for vigorous country dances like Sellinger's Round, Rogero, the Hay, Hunting of the Fox, Tom Tyler and John Come Kiss Me. The Elizabethans also enjoyed boisterous games of the kind now more commonly associated with children's parties, such as Hoodman Blind, or Blindman's Buff, and Hide-and-Seek. Other Elizabethan specialities were Shoeing the Mare and Dun is in the Mire – a game which involved trying to lift a heavy log of wood and then dropping it on the toes of the other players.

The less energetic played word and guessing games, shovel-board, or shove-groat (the Elizabethan equivalent of shove ha'penny), skittles, billiards and Troll-My-Dame, a form of bagatelle. Draughts and chess were both popular among the more sophisticated and so was backgammon, generally known as Tables. Gambling with dice and cards was also a popular indoor sport. Dice-games included Hazard, Novum and Tray-trip, probably won by throwing a three, and there were numerous different card-games. Primero, played by four players using 40 cards, was the most fashionable game, played a great deal at Court. In addition there was Trump, or Ruff, the precursor of whist; Gleek, played by three people; and many others now vanished, with names like Noddy, Post and Pair, Loadum and Maw.

A round of festivals, sacred and secular

When Christmas had come and gone, the next thing to look forward to was Shrove Tuesday. Shrovetide had always been a carnival time, an opportunity for a final fling before the rigours of Lent; and although the Protestant Church disapproved, Shrove Tuesday continued to be celebrated with pancake-tossing, cock-fighting, plays and football matches. The London apprentices regarded Shrove Tuesday as their particular holiday, a time to 'take the law into their own hands and do what they list', which usually appears to have meant rioting through the bawdy houses. Mothering Sunday, which fell during Lent, was also a holiday, when traditionally young people away from home, at school, in apprenticeships or domestic service, were given time off to visit their parents, take them gifts and eat simnel-cakes baked for the occasion.

Then came Easter, when every good Christian took communion and everyone who could contrive it had something new to wear. Then, as now, the custom of giving coloured or decorated eggs was widespread and in some parts of the country young men went 'pace-egging' – rolling eggs downhill, a custom said to be symbolic of the stone being rolled from Christ's tomb. The week after Easter was known as Hock-tide; in some places, especially Reading and Coventry, on Hock Monday the men seized and held the women of the town to ransom and on Hock Tuesday the women did the same to the men, the money raised going to the church funds.

May Day, the most important spring festival, had nothing to do with the

Church, for the ancient custom of going a-maying was unashamedly pagan in origin. John Stow says that 'on May-day in the morning, every man would walk into the sweet meadows and green woods, there to rejoice their spirits with the beauty and savour of sweet flowers, and with the harmony of birds, praising God in their kind'. This may well have been true for the more serious-minded, but there is little doubt that for most people it was the frolicking round the maypole which really mattered. The Londoners erected a great maypole in Cornhill by the parish church of St Andrew Undershaft, and every village and town in the country had its maypole and May-games.

Naturally the Puritans disapproved, and Philip Stubbes let fly another angry but informative broadside on the subject. 'Every parish, town and village assemble themselves together, both men, women and children, old and young . . . and either going all together or dividing themselves into companies, they go some to the woods and groves, some to the hills and mountains . . . where they spend all the night in pleasant pastimes, and in the morning they return, bringing with them birch, boughs and branches of trees to deck their assemblies withal. And no marvel, for there is a great lord present amongst them, as superintendent and lord over their pastimes and sports, namely, Satan, prince

At the chess board
Board games such as chess, draughts, backgammon (known as Tables) and a similar game called Tric-Trac were popular indoor pastimes. The long tables in the newly fashionable long galleries of the great houses were also used for games like the modern shove ha'penny.

If on your man you light
The first draught shall you play,
If not tis mine by right
At first to lead the way

of hell. But their chiefest jewel they bring from thence is their Maypole, which they bring home with great veneration, as thus: they have twenty or forty yoke of oxen, every ox having a sweet nosegay of flowers tied on the tip of his horns, and these oxen draw home this Maypole (this stinking idol rather), which is covered all over with flower and herbs, bound round about with strings and sometime painted with variable colours, with two or three hundred men, women and children following it with great devotion. And thus being reared up, with handkerchiefs and flags streaming on the top, they straw the ground about, bind green boughs about it, set up summer halls, bowers and arbours hard by it; and then fall they to banquet and feast, to leap and dance about it, as the heathen people did at the dedications of their idols, whereof this is a perfect pattern.'

The morris dancers, with Robin Hood and his Merry Men, Maid Marian, the Dragon, the Fool, Tom the Piper and the Hobby Horse, were an essential feature of the May Day revels – fragments of which still survive in the Padstow

At the card table
Elizabethans were great card-players – the court cards of the modern pack are still depicted in Tudor dress, the queen wearing the steep gabled head-dress fashionable in the early 16th century. The gentlemen here are playing primero, in which each player is dealt four cards, each card having three times its original value; this was a favourite game at Court,

and bore some resemblance to poker and piquet. Other popular card games included One and Thirty, Pope July, Gleek (similar to rummy), and the precursor of whist, known variously as Ruff, Triumph or Trump. Everyone gambled at both cards and dice, and this knowing-looking foursome appear to be playing for high stakes, judging by the piles of coins lying on the table.

Hobby Horse and the Helston Floral Dance. The party went on all day and all night, with drinking and dancing and other activities inevitably associated with scampering about the woods at night. 'I have heard,' remarked another moralist with gloomy relish, 'of ten maidens which went to fetch May, and nine of them came home with child.'

Whitsun was a favourite time for Church Ales, when the church wardens organised the brewing of a specially potent ale and sold it to all-comers in the churchyard or the church itself in order to raise funds for the parish. This was another opportunity for a party, when the young people danced on the green to the music of pipe and tabor, played chasing and catching games like Prisoner's Base, Barley Break or Last-in-Hell, and worked off their high spirits with leaping and wrestling matches, while their elders played bowls or sat gossiping under the trees. As well as the Church Ales, most villages had their own feast days, which were usually associated with the patron saint of the parish church.

On Midsummer Eve bonfires were lit and in London, at least until the middle of the century, the custom of the midsummer Marching Watches was kept up, when the militia or train bands paraded through the streets by torchlight, accompanied by pageants, processions of civic dignitaries and morris dancers, and the citizens decorated their doorways with greenery. Then came Harvest Home, followed by the traditional Michaelmas feast of goose, fattened on the stubble-fields, and finally All Hallows Eve with its remembrance and pro-pitiation of the souls of the dead, a time when ghosts and witches were abroad and 'soul-cakes' were baked.

In November the Londoners had their Lord Mayor's Show, and for the Elizabethans the year ended with an occasion peculiarly their own. This was the celebration, on November 17, of the anniversary of the Queen's accession to the throne, or Queen's Day as it became known. The custom of observing 'the sacred seventeenth' as a public holiday seems to have originated spon-taneously during the upsurge of patriotic fervour which followed the Pope's excommunication of the Queen in 1570. What is certain is that by the 1580s Queen's Day had become a major and official national festival, when the good Protestant people of England could legitimately rejoice for purely Protestant reasons. At Court the day was marked by the Accession Day Tilts, and all over the country there were bonfires, firework displays, bell-ringing, plays, pageants and special sermons.

Archery, tennis and the thrill of the chase

There was little in the way of organised sport in Elizabethan England, although the authorities encouraged athletic pastimes such as running, leaping, wrest-ling, throwing the sledge (hammer) and running at the quintain. This had originally been a military exercise for pages and squires which was performed on horseback, and involved trying to hit a swinging target with lance or stave; however, by Elizabethan times it was degenerating into a rough sport which was often seen at country weddings.

Het Haene gefecht Jn Engelandt.

At the cockfight

The staging of contests between specially bred game-cocks was first introduced into Britain by the Romans and, like bull-baiting and bear-baiting, was a favourite Elizabethan spectator-sport among all classes. It seems to have been particularly associated with the pre-Lent festivities of Shrove Tuesday. Cockfighting has given several familiar phrases to the language. 'To live like a fighting cock,' or live in luxury, is an allusion to the pampering and good feeding that the birds received to increase their mettle and stamina. The word 'cockpit' – the small arena where the fights were staged – is still used for an enclosed space like the cockpit of an aircraft.

The regular practice of archery, once a vital military exercise, was still, in theory at least, compulsory for all able-bodied Englishmen between the ages of 17 and 60, and the inhabitants of every town were supposed to maintain the butts, or practice ground, and use them 'on holy days and other times convenient'. But in spite of various Acts of Parliament passed during Henry VIII's reign and still on the Statute Book, the age of the long-bow was passing into history, and by Elizabethan times archery had become little more than just another leisure activity.

Young men in every age have enjoyed kicking a ball about, but Elizabethan football was frowned on by respectable parents and schoolmasters, since it was liable to degenerate rapidly into a free fight, with the players more interested in kicking one another on the shins than in scoring goals. Probably the best known Tudor ball-game is tennis; this, of course, was 'real' tennis, a game of French origin played on an enclosed court with rackets and a small leather ball stuffed with hair. Henry VIII had been an enthusiastic tennis player, and the game was an exclusively royal and aristocratic pastime. The lower orders played hand-ball – a game rather like fives – but bowls was popular with all classes.

The most universally popular outdoor activity, though, was hunting in its various forms – stag-hunting, falconry or hawking, and hare-coursing with greyhounds. Shakespeare's plays bristle with allusions to all these pursuits, and the technical terms used in them were familiar parts of everyday speech. It was a rough age, when physical pain and suffering were an inescapable part of everyone's experience, so perhaps it is not surprising that the Elizabethans had no feeling of repulsion about cruelty to animals. Certainly all classes were addicted to such bloody and barbarous entertainments as bull and bear-baiting, where the tethered animal was baited by mastiffs. Famous fighting bears like 'Harry Hunks' and 'the great Sackerson' were national idols, and Paris Garden in Southwark, the centre of the 'sport', drew immense and noisy crowds every Sunday, so that a 'bear-garden' remains the proverbial synonym for a place of disorder.

Philip Stubbes also inveighed against bear-baiting, which he considered 'a filthy, stinking and loathsome game'. 'What Christian heart,' he demanded, 'can take pleasure to see one poor beast to rend, tear and kill another, and all for his foolish pleasure?' But despite the increasing weight of Puritan disapproval against bear-baiting, dancing, football, May-games and Church Ales, the unregenerate English clung tenaciously to their old feasts, festivals and amusements, as well as eagerly welcoming new ones. Tobacco first came to England in 1565, introduced from the New World by Sir John Hawkins and made fashionable by Walter Raleigh. It was smoked in clay pipes by both men and women, and was sold in taverns and alehouses, by grocers, chandlers and apothecaries. According to Barnabe Riche, writing early in the 17th century, there were 7,000 shops in London alone selling the 'sovereign weed', and a lively controversy already existed between smokers and non-smokers.

Plays and players find powerful backers

Probably the most famous innovation in the field of entertainment in Elizabethan times was the commercial theatre. There was nothing new about watching and performing plays. On the contrary, there was a long tradition of drama in English culture, with its mummings and folk-plays. There were the medieval mystery and miracle plays, performed in many towns by the religious guilds under the auspices of the Church; those of York, Chester and Coventry were the most famous. Plays and 'interludes' had long been presented at Court and in noblemen's houses at Christmas and other special occasions, and for centuries little groups of strolling players had wandered through the country performing from the back of a cart, in inn yards and on temporary stages erected in the market place or churchyard.

After the Reformation and the consequent disappearance of so much religious ritual and colour from people's lives, interest in and desire for purely secular drama naturally increased, and at the beginning of the Elizabethan period the theatre acquired new and powerful patrons at the new Court. Robert Dudley, later Earl of Leicester, who was said to have 'loved a play and players', was an especially influential figure, and as early as 1559 had formed his own company of actors. Others followed his lead, and soon other companies were being formed under the patronage of the Lord Admiral, the Lord

Trained to kill

Falconry, the killing of wild birds by a hawk trained to return to its perch on the falconer's wrist, was an ancient and aristocratic sport very popular with the Elizabethan gentry. The hawks were mostly imported from Norway and bought and sold at St Botolph's Fair at Boston in Lincolnshire. The maintenance and training of hawks was expensive and complicated, and falconry had a language of its own. The word 'mews' was originally the place where hawks were confined while they 'mewed', or moulted.

Sighting the quarry
For the Elizabethans stag-hunting remained the king of field sports. Wild red deer still roamed the shrinking forests and the sparsely populated areas of Cumbria, Wales, Exmoor and Dartmoor. More numerous were the fallow deer preserved in gentlemen's parks up and down the country to be either driven and shot with a cross-bow, or else hunted by packs of hounds. Every gentleman hunted – there was a saying that 'he cannot be a gentleman which loveth not hawking and hunting' – and every true Elizabethan thrilled to the excitement of the chase.

Chamberlain, the Earl of Pembroke and Lord Strange. This system, under which the actors wore their lord's badge and could appeal to him for support against unsympathetic civic authorities, gave the profession a recognised status and also a necessary measure of protection, for an Act of Parliament of 1572 declared that 'common players in Interludes and Minstrels, not belonging to any Baron of this Realm or towards any other honorable Personage of greater degree, which shall wander abroad and have not Licence of two Justices of the Peace at the least . . . shall be taken adjudged and deemed Rogues, Vagabonds and Sturdy Beggars'. Actors were slowly becoming organised and respectable and, in 1583, received the ultimate seal of social approval with the formation of the company of Queen's Men.

In London during the 1560s plays continued to be performed in inn-yards – The Cross Keys in Gracechurch Street, the Bull in Bishopsgate Street and The Belle Sauvage on Ludgate Hill being favourite locales. The City fathers, however, remained uniformly hostile to the players who, they alleged, were attracting large crowds of undesirables, encouraging the poor to waste their money and corrupting youth by their brazen and shameless posturings. In the early 1570s the Court of Common Council made a determined attempt to suppress the 'sundry inconveniences' caused by the players. It was not successful. The habit of play-going was now too firmly entrenched and the players themselves too powerfully protected to be dislodged. They were, in fact, already an established part of the London scene and, in 1574, the Earl of Leicester's Men were granted a Royal Patent licensing them to perform 'Comedies, Tragedies Interludes and Stage Plays' in the City of London and elsewhere, subject only to the censorship of the Master of the Revels and with the proviso that performances must not be given 'in time of common prayer or in the time of great and common plague'.

Two years later, James Burbage, one of Lord Hunsdon's Men, decided that the time had come for the company to acquire its own premises, where it could exercise its craft without risk of harassment by the City authorities and without having to share its takings with rapacious innkeepers. Burbage therefore took the lease of a site in Shoreditch on the edge of Finsbury Fields, just outside the City boundary and there, in 1576, he erected the first purpose-built commercial playhouse, called simply The Theatre. The Theatre did well and within a year it had a neighbour, The Curtain – named after the curtain wall of the enclosure of the old Holywell Priory in which it stood.

Burbage, with his sons Cuthbert and Richard, the great tragic actor, were soon to have a rival in Philip Henslowe, who went into partnership with his son-in-law, the actor Edward Alleyn, and in 1585 built The Rose in Southwark.

On the tennis court
Tennis in Tudor times meant 'real' or royal tennis, a game imported from France and played in an enclosed space, as in the foreground of this Flemish painting. Henry VIII had been an enthusiastic and tireless tennis player, but it was not a game for ladies, and in Elizabeth's reign was no longer quite so fashionable. Once the Earl of Leicester and the Duke of Norfolk almost came to blows in the Queen's presence after a game of tennis.

GLOBE. SOUTHWARKE.

The 'Wooden O'

The Globe theatre is the best known of all the Elizabethan playhouses because of its close association with William Shakespeare, who owned an eighth share in it. Erected on Bankside by the Burbage brothers in the winter of 1598–9, it became the permanent home of the Lord Chamberlain's Men. It was the most popular theatre in London and the model on which many later theatres were based. Fire was the greatest threat to these wooden playhouses, and the Globe was burned down in June 1613 during a performance of Shakespeare's Henry VIII. It was rebuilt the following year and survived until 1644, when it was finally demolished to make room for housing.

Henslowe also had an interest in an unnamed playhouse in Newington Butts. Towards the end of the 1590s, after a long series of disputes with their ground landlord, old Burbage's sons dismantled The Theatre and transferred it bodily south of the river, where it was reborn as The Globe, the most famous of the Elizabethan playhouses. Also on the South Bank was The Swan, and in 1599 Philip Henslowe and Edward Alleyn built yet another theatre, The Fortune, in Cripplegate. As well as these public playhouses, there were the so-called 'private theatres', of which the best known was at Blackfriars, where the Children of Paul's – that is, the choristers of the cathedral – and the Children of the Chapel Royal performed before rather more select audiences than those which frequented The Rose or The Globe. The Elizabethan playhouses disappeared in the upheavals of the next century, but in 1989 builders excavating the foundations of a new office block on the South Bank uncovered the south-west wall of The Rose theatre, and strenuous efforts have since been made to preserve this romantic fragment of national heritage. Despite their popularity, the actors' life remained precarious. Apart from the normal hazards of the profession – a touring company would sometimes come to grief and go bankrupt – and the fact that, outside the circle of enthusiasts, they were still regarded as rogues and vagabonds, their chief enemy was the plague. The players also had to be careful not to tread on politically sensitive toes in the entertainments they presented; anything which could be construed as criticism of the state or its policies, or which might offend people's religious susceptibilities or tend to create civil disturbance was strictly forbidden.

Tragedy and triumph
The Tragedy of Romeo and Juliet, *based on an old story which first appeared in print in 15th-century Italy, was written about 1595, when William Shakespeare (far right) had finished serving his apprenticeship in the theatre. By the mid-1590s he had become securely established in his profession of actor and playwright. Backed by the wealthy Earl of Southampton, he became a shareholder in the Lord Chamberlain's Men, a company formed in the general reorganisation which took place in the London theatrical world in 1594. This step put William Shakespeare well on his way to the modest but comfortable fame and fortune he enjoyed during the remainder of his career.*

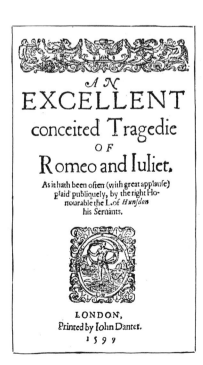

The labels in the drawing read: *tectum*, *porticus*, *sedilia*, *orchestra*, *ingressus*, *mimorum ædes*, *proscænium*, *planities siue arena*.

On the boards

Francis Langley, owner of a pleasure ground on the South Bank, built The Swan theatre in 1594–5. This drawing – the only contemporary representation of the interior of an Elizabethan playhouse – shows the stage jutting out into the open yard, where the 'groundlings' paid one penny admission fee. At the back of the stage are two doors for entrances and exits, leading to the dressing-rooms. Above this is the Lord's room for distinguished visitors, which could also be used for balcony scenes or musicians. Two columns on the stage itself support the canopy, and all round are covered galleries with accommodation for an orchestra, and seats and boxes for the better-off spectators.

Amateur theatricals continued to be a favourite form of amusement, and working alongside the professional theatre and feeding it with talent was a vigorous school of classical drama at both the Universities. The playwrights John Lyly and George Peele had both been nurtured at Oxford , while Thomas Nashe, Robert Greene and Christopher Marlowe were Cambridge men. Until his death at the age of 29 in a tavern brawl at Deptford in 1593, Christopher Marlowe, son of a shoemaker from Canterbury, dominated the theatrical scene. Marlowe was something of a hell-raiser and was at one time suspected of atheism by the authorities, but his plays – *Tamburlaine, The Jew of Malta, The Tragical History of Dr. Faustus* and *Edward II* – were all box office successes for Edward Alleyn and the Lord Admiral's Men, and broke new ground with the subtlety of their characterisation and rich use of language.

By no means all the new wave of Elizabethan dramatists had had the benefit of a university education. Thomas Kyd, author of *The Spanish Tragedy*, was a

Londoner, the son of a scrivener or copyist, and Ben Jonson, another Londoner, had begun his career by following his step-father's trade of bricklayer. The most famous of them all had not even had the advantage of a London background. William Shakespeare, born in 1564, son of a glover in the little Warwickshire town of Stratford-upon-Avon, came to seek his fortune in the big city some time between 1585 and 1592. The date most often suggested is 1587, when several companies of actors, including the Queen's Men and Leicester's Men (both of whom were under strength) visited Stratford on tour. His early years in London remain obscure, but he must certainly have been attached to one or other of the theatrical companies; the first recorded performance of one of his own works was *Henry VI*, billed as Harey the Sixth, put on by Lord Strange's Men at The Rose theatre in March 1592.

From hired man to greatest dramatist

Shakespeare would have been a hired man, not having the capital to buy himself a shareholding, and is variously said to have got his start by holding the horses of members of the audience, or acting as prompter's assistant. He was probably the Elizabethan equivalent of assistant stage manager – understudying and playing small parts as well as being employed as a copyist and re-write man, adding topical jokes and allusions to old material. He was making his way, though, and earning a reputation for civility, reliability and honesty.

In 1593 Shakespeare was lucky enough to find a patron in the 19-year-old Henry Wriothesley, Earl of Southampton. Southampton was a prime example of Elizabethan gilded youth – nobly born, romantically handsome, a little wild and more than a little spoilt. But he was also wealthy, open-handed, an enthusiastic playgoer, well educated and intelligent. An ambitious man of letters could hardly have asked for a better sponsor, and the first of Shakespeare's works to appear in print – the long poems *Venus and Adonis* and *The Rape of Lucrece* published in 1593 and 1594 – were both dedicated to Southampton. It was Southampton who gave his protégé the money – probably £100 – which enabled him to buy a shareholding in the Lord Chamberlain's Men; this was a new company formed in 1594, with Richard Burbage as leading actor and Will Kempe as the comedian.

Shakespeare was now securely established – *Romeo and Juliet, A Midsummer Night's Dream, Richard II* and *The Merchant of Venice* were all written between 1594 and 1597 – and by 1597 he had made enough money to buy himself a smart new house in his native Stratford. He went on acting as well as writing – there is a tradition that he played the Ghost in the first performance of *Hamlet* in the autumn of 1600 – and by the end of the reign he had few serious rivals for the position of England's leading dramatist.

Shakespeare was, above all, a practical man of the theatre, a hard-working craftsman who aimed to give the public what it wanted – from blood and guts to romance and broad comedy, plus plenty of good, rousing patriotic history to suit the mood of a nation which had just succeeded so triumphantly in defeating the Spanish Armada. Neither he nor his contemporaries can ever

Favourite clown
Richard Tarleton was, with Will Kempe, one of the two best-loved Elizabethan comedians. A short, stocky man with a broad nose and a squint, Tarleton was a natural clown. People began to laugh the moment he appeared on stage, and the Queen once 'bade them take the knave away for making her laugh so excessively'. Tarleton died in 1588 in a Shoreditch brothel, and was buried in Shoreditch church.

'Faerie Queen' poet
His long epic poem celebrating Elizabeth, The Faerie Queene, *made Edmund Spenser one of the most praised poets of his day. He received a royal pension of £50 a year after its publication, but was forced to spend a good deal of his time seeking patronage and preferment.*

Work for the printer
The art of printing with movable type had been introduced from Germany in the 15th century, and English printers were seldom short of work. The Elizabethans had an insatiable appetite for reading material of every kind.

have dreamed that he would come to be venerated as one of the greatest poetic writers the English-speaking world has ever produced. Generally speaking, the Elizabethans regarded the writing of poetry as a courtly art, and their most admired poet was young Philip Sidney who by the end of the 1570s, had begun to follow in the tradition of Sir Thomas Wyatt and the Earl of Surrey a generation earlier.

Philip Sidney was an aristocrat to his fingertips, nephew of the Earls of Leicester and Warwick, brother-in-law of the Earl of Pembroke, and accustomed to moving in the highest circles. An accomplished horseman and athlete, a generous patron of the arts, a scholar and a creative artist of the highest quality, he was the epitome of an Elizabethan gentleman and courtier. His sweet nature, his staunch Protestantism and his noble death at the Battle of Zutphen after giving his own drink of water to a dying soldier at his side turned him into a national hero.

The 'courtly' school of lyric poets included such men as Thomas Sackville, Fulke Greville, Walter Raleigh, the Earl of Oxford and Sir Edward Dyer who all helped to make Elizabethan England 'a nest of singing birds'. But apart from Shakespeare probably the best known Elizabethan poet today is Edmund Spenser, hailed in his own time as a second Chaucer. Spenser was not himself an aristocrat or a courtier, his background was middle-class, but he found a patron in Philip Sidney and became a member of the literary circle led by Sidney and his friends. Spenser is best remembered today for his epic poem *The Faerie Queene*, one of the longest poems in the language, which began to appear in 1590. Intended as a romantic, historical allegory celebrating the age and its Queen, it is full of thinly veiled allusions to contemporary events and characters. 'In that Fairy Queen,' wrote Spenser in his 'Prefatory Letter', 'I mean glory in my general inclination, but in my particular I conceive the most excellent and glorious person of our sovereign the Queen.'

A spate of books, despite cost and the censor

The Elizabethan age produced, in addition to the work of the major poets and playwrights, an enormous output of books of all kinds – technical treatises, textbooks, satire, works of travel, history and topography, translations from the classics, books on religious, political and philosophical subjects, novels, romances and a vast quantity of pamphlets, tracts and broadsheets on matters of topical interest. Authors, though, did not make their fortunes. John Stow, for instance, received '£3 and 40 copies for his pains' for his *Survey of London*, and Ben Jonson was given 20 shillings as an advance on a new play in December 1597 but apparently failed to deliver the manuscript. One can see why a patron was so important to a struggling author. The gentlemen amateurs, of course, expected to pay to have their works printed, but books and verses often circulated in manuscript for several years before they were published. Philip Sidney's *Arcadia* was written between 1580 and 1583 but not printed until 1590. Scriveners were employed to make copies which would be handed round among the author's friends, and a good deal of pirating went on.

The Stationers' Company, incorporated in 1557, controlled the printing and publishing trades which, like so many other things, were centred on London, and severe penalties were enforced against those who imported books from abroad or operated secret or unlicensed presses. Books, like plays, were subject to censorship, designed to prevent the dissemination of subversive material, especially of a religious nature, and 'no manner of person' was allowed to print 'any manner of book or paper of what sort, nature, or in what language soever' without a licence in writing from Her Majesty, by six members of the Privy Council, by the Archbishops of Canterbury and York, or the Chancellors of the two universities.

It was the responsibility of the publisher of any new work to get the manuscript approved and licensed by the Privy Council before entering it at Stationers' Hall. He might be a printer himself, but if not he would then contract for the printing to be done. Some printers employed literary men as editors or readers, but usually an author saw his own book through the press, reading the proofs and having the type corrected on the spot. The maximum number of copies for any one edition had been fixed by the Stationers at 1,250. If more were needed, the type had to be set up again. The object of this regulation was to ensure an even distribution of work among printers, but few serious or expensive books can have sold anything approaching this number.

In general, the standard of English printing and book production was considered inferior to that of the Continent. Large and important books were

Among the shepherds

Apart from The Faerie Queen, *the poet Edmund Spenser's best-known work is* The Shepherd's Calendar – *a series of 12 pastoral poems, one for each sign of the Zodiac – published in 1579 and dedicated to Sir Philip Sidney. This scene from April, under the sign of Taurus, shows a group of musicians playing on lyre, viol, lute and pipe in praise of the Queen. She stands, sceptre in hand, receiving homage while the shepherds go about their business in the background.*

bound in leather and illustrated sparingly with copper-plate engravings, a very costly process. At the cheaper, and more remunerative, end of the trade, books and pamphlets sold for sixpence or a shilling (the equivalent of modern paperbacks) were illustrated with woodcuts and either just sewn together or roughly bound in a limp vellum cover. Publishers and booksellers congregated in and around St Paul's Churchyard where they sold their wares on open stalls, attracting throngs of browsers and inpecunious students as well as buyers, while ballads and broadsheets were hawked by street-sellers and sold by cheapjacks at fairs and markets up and down the country.

Music, the art of servant and monarch

With the spread of literacy and respect for education fostered by the new grammar schools the book-loving public was undoubtedly increasing, but the music-loving public was larger still, and in the general flowering of the arts which characterised the second half of the Elizabethan period music took a pre-eminent place. The Elizabethans were enthusiastic amateur music-makers and music was an essential part of everyday life enjoyed by all classes – from those whose melodies came from the cries of vendors of hot mutton pies, new oysters and lily-white mussels, from the itinerant ballad-singers or the fiddler at a village wedding, to the elegant gentleman serenading his lady with the latest air by Dowland or Orlando Gibbons, or a group of courtiers listening to a consort of viols at some nobleman's house. Every great household employed its own musicians, and even in middle-class establishments a servant who could play an instrument or sing to entertain the company was highly prized. Anyone with the least pretension to culture was expected to be able to perform

Scholar and poet
Among all the handsome, gallant, witty and talented young men who made the Elizabethan Court such a brilliant social and intellectual centre, Sir Philip Sidney – poet, scholar, athlete and gentleman – held a special place. Best remembered today for his sequence of sonnets, Astrophel and Stella, *addressed to Lady Penelope Rich, Sidney also showed himself a generous patron to other writers.*

Honours for a hero
Born an aristocrat and courtier, Philip Sidney's noble death at the Battle of Zutphen at the age of only 32 made him a national hero. He was given a state funeral in St Paul's Cathedral – the first time this honour had ever been granted to an Englishman not of royal birth.

on an instrument and read music at sight. 'Supper being ended,' wrote one gentleman, 'and music books according to the custom being brought to the table, the mistress of the house presented me with a part, earnestly requesting me to sing. But when after many excuses, I protested unfeignedly that I could not, everyone began to wonder and some whispered to others demanding to know how I was brought up.'

The Queen herself was a skilful performer on the lute and virginals – a keyboard instrument something like a harpsichord – and the Scottish envoy Sir James Melville records in his memoirs that during his visit to Court in 1564 he was taken up to a quiet gallery by Lord Hunsdon to hear the Queen, alone in her chamber, playing 'excellently well' on the virginals. As soon as she saw that she had an audience, however, she got up, pretending to be angry and 'alleging that she used not to play before men, but when she was solitary, to shun melancholy'. Elizabeth employed a large number of professional musicians, mostly Italians, and through the Chapel Royal encouraged composers of Church music, while the Children of the Chapel were famous both as choristers and boy actors.

Of native Elizabethan musicians, Thomas Tallis and William Byrd, organist of the Chapel Royal, were primarily composers of Church music and between them provided the new Anglican Church with a wealth of anthems, chants and hymn tunes still familiar today. They also wrote chamber and instrumental music, especially Byrd, who was known as the 'Father of Musicke'. Orlando Gibbons also wrote for the Church, but is probably best remembered today for his madrigals – an Italian import, yet forever associated with the England of Elizabeth. There were many other music-makers, including John Dowland, whose compositions for voice and lute are unsurpassed; John Wilbye, another notable composer of madrigals; Thomas Weelkes, organist first at Winchester College and then Chichester Cathedral; Thomas Morley and Thomas Tomkins. At no other period has England produced such an array of musical talent.

Combinations of instruments as in a modern orchestra were still in the experimental stage and, in any case, 16th-century composers and musicians had fewer instruments at their disposal. The lute was the favourite instrument for solo performance and for accompanying a solo voice. The viol, similar to a violin, was made in four sizes and usually kept in sets, known as a chest of viols. A consort of viols constituted a chamber-music ensemble. For music out of doors, there was the hautboy, a wooden double reed instrument, the sackbut or trombone, the trumpet and drum.

Craftsmanship to adorn great houses

While rich in poets, playwrights and musicians, England had less to offer in the field of painting. Portrait painters were much in demand – everybody who was anybody had his or her likeness painted – but the fashionable artists, men such as Marcus Gheeraerts and Daniel Mytens, came mostly from abroad. Only in the art of 'painting in little' was the native school supreme, as exemplified in the work of the miniaturists Nicholas Hilliard and his pupil Isaac Oliver.

A musical best-seller
John Dowland published his First Booke of Songes or Ayres in 1597. It became a best-seller, running into four editions, and was the first of many issued by him and other popular composer-musicians. Dowland based many of his melodies on familiar folk-tunes, adding lute accompaniments within the range of amateur performers and often setting his music to poems which were works of art in their own right.

Instrument of the age
The lute was so popular an instrument that a variety of forms developed. The chittarone, which could be 6 ft tall, had an elongated neck to carry long bass strings attached to an additional peg-box. This model is carved from Italian pine, with ebony and ivory veneer.

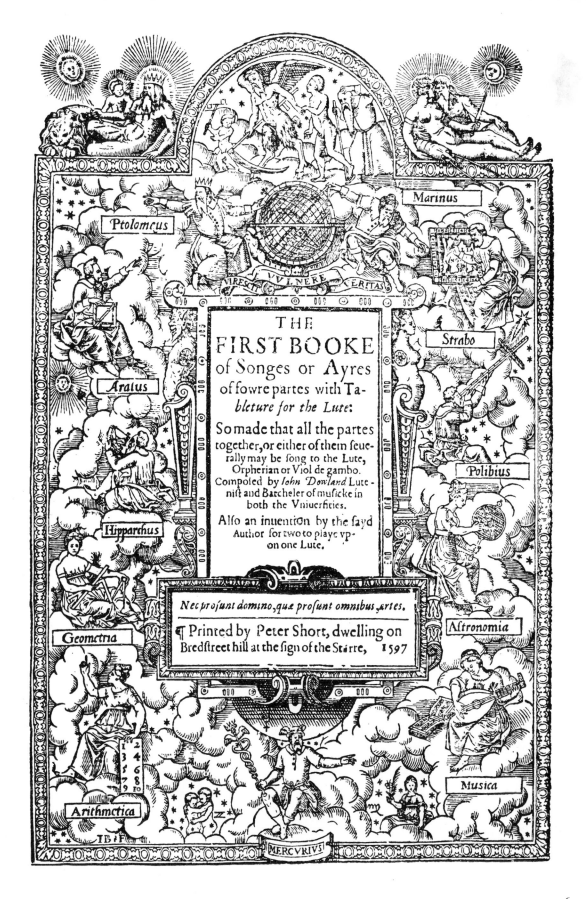

THE FIRST BOOKE

of Songes or Ayres of fowre partes with Tableture for the Lute:

So made that all the partes together, or either of them seuerally may be song to the Lute, Orpherian or Viol de gambo. Compoſed by *Iohn Dowland* Luteniſt and Batcheler of muſicke in both the Vniuerſities.

Alſo an inuention by the ſayd Author for two to playe vpon one Lute.

Nec proſunt domino, quæ proſunt omnibus artes.

¶ Printed by Peter Short, dwelling on Bredſtreet hill at the ſign of the Starre,　1597

Of the domestic arts, for which the great country houses made such a splendid background, English gold and silversmiths' work could more than hold its own with the rest of Europe, and examples of their craft still survive in the shape of the great standing cups and bowls and massive 'salts' which were so popular and so typical of the age. In the inventory of the contents of Hardwick House a gilt salt cellar weighing 62 oz. is listed, and another of gold and crystal weighing $5\frac{1}{2}$ oz. Porcelain, agate and crystal were often mounted in gold or silver, and the Earl of Leicester once gave the Queen a 'porringer of bloodstone, garnished with four feet and two handles of gold, made like snakes'.

The quality of English needlework was also deservedly famous. The huge tapestries which covered the walls of the great houses were woven in professional workrooms, but the bed-curtains, counterpanes, hangings, cushions and needlework 'carpets' which covered every available surface in houses like Hardwick were worked by hand by professional and amateur embroiderers. As well as these, the fashion for decorating caps, gloves, purses, baby clothes, shifts, smocks, men's shirts, the velvet bindings of books – everything, in fact, that was capable of being embroidered – offered ample scope for all those thousands of ladies and gentlewomen who 'wrought needlework'. Some ladies, such as Mary, Queen of Scots, a notable exponent of the art, employed a professional to draw patterns for them, but the artistically inclined would create their own designs, to a high standard of taste and skill.

The Elizabethans at play ranged from the brutal crowd baying for blood at a bear-baiting (or an execution) to the exquisite bejewelled youth singing of Arcadian shepherdesses, to the accompaniment of his lute; from a romping crowd of boys and girls dancing round a village maypole, to the knights in all their panoply of archaic chivalry jousting before the Queen at the Accession Day Tilts. These varied diversions illustrate vividly the many-textured quality of life in 16th-century England, with its astonishing contrasts between barbarism and refinement, innocence and sophistication. It was a world in which theatre audiences demanded their money's worth in blood-boltered corpses and yet produced poetry which sings as sweetly today as it did 400 years ago – a world which enjoyed childish games, yet staged Court masques of bafflingly intricate intellectual symbolism.

Court miniaturist

Nicholas Hilliard was the first English miniaturist and the originator of a new style of English painting. Among his miniatures are a dignified self-portrait only $1\frac{5}{8}$ in. in diameter (left) and a portrait of Henry Percy, 9th Earl of Northumberland (far left), lying pensively face on hand in a meadow. Percy's scientific interests earned him the nickname of the 'wizard earl'. Nicholas Hilliard became Court painter and goldsmith, designing Elizabeth's Great Seal. He painted several miniatures of the Queen, who told him that she most admired the Italian School which showed the face without shadows. Hilliard therefore painted his first likeness of her out of doors, in an open alley unshaded by trees and giving the effect of bright light on her clear pale face.

Youthful melancholy

This exquisite miniature, only 5½ in. tall, so redolent of the elegance, poetry and courtly romance characteristic of the closing years of the Elizabethan Age, is probably Nicholas Hilliard's masterpiece. The identity of the melancholy young man leaning against a tree among roses remains a mystery. It has been suggested, however, that the subject may have been the young Earl of Essex who, at 19, so captivated the ageing Queen that he became her constant companion and was regarded by an approving and sentimental public as the 'new adopted son' of royal grace.

Jewels and coins

ARTISTRY IN MINIATURE FOR PERSONAL ADORNMENT AND MONEY RESTORED TO ITS REAL VALUE

Jewel for a hat
Special jewels were designed to be pinned to the flat cap clinging precariously to the head of a young man-about-town, or on the front of a high-crowned beaver hat. This $2\frac{3}{4}$ in. high hat-jewel, made of coloured enamel set with gems, depicts St George slaying the dragon.

Elizabethan jewellery was strongly influenced by Renaissance designs and by the work of European craftsmen. The Queen's jewellers were mainly French, but the English were learning fast and the miniaturist Nicholas Hilliard designed several well-known pieces. Pearls were immensely popular – Elizabeth had some fine specimens, and wore them constantly. Apart from the influx of precious metals from the New World, gemstones from America and the Far East were more widely available than ever before. Enamel work, too, was popular. The art of cutting or faceting stones had not yet been fully developed, so they would often be 'foiled', or backed with coloured enamel.

Early Tudor coins were made of solid gold or silver, but Henry VIII started the practice of 'debasing' the coinage – that is, alloying it with base metal. Elizabeth, with the support of her financial adviser Sir Thomas Gresham, was able to reverse this process, which was bad for trade and confidence, and by 1561 had restored the coinage to its former purity. The pound in Elizabethan times was probably worth more than 150 times as much as it is today.

A goldsmith's wares
This fine hoard of jewellery, the stock of a London goldsmith's shop, was hidden in Cheapside early in the 17th century, perhaps at a time of plague or civil disturbance, and found in 1911. It reveals the wide variety of beautifully made luxury goods available to the middle-class citizens of Elizabethan London, in contrast with the jewels and other precious objects that belonged to aristocratic families of the time and survived in the possession of their descendants.

Christian convert

The conversion of St Paul is depicted on a hat-badge. This and other fine Renaissance jewels are among the Waddesdon Bequest, left to the British Museum by Baron Ferdinand de Rothschild.

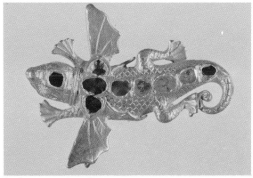

A charm against fire

A vast amount of treasure was believed lost in the Spanish ships wrecked after the defeat of the Armada. This golden salamander, a charm against fire, was retrieved from the wreck of the Gerona off Ireland.

Sovereign

Angel

Half-crown

Shilling

Pendants, with pearls

The elaborate and exquisite craftsmanship of Elizabethan times is evident in this group of pendants, designed to be hung on a gold chain, or silk ribbon or cord, worn round the neck and often pinned to the doublet or gown bodice. Most of the pendants have pearls hanging from them. The subjects of the designs include, from left to right, a sea-dragon, a Renaissance-style set-piece representing Charity, a warrior on horseback and a fruit motif in emeralds. The three-masted ship (right) made of enamelled gold, is Venetian work.

Coins of the realm

The fine sovereign of 23 carat gold was worth 30 shillings and represented about six months' wages for a skilled workman receiving food and drink from his employer. The angel (which showed the Archangel Michael on one side) was 22 carat gold and worth 10 shillings – the annual wage of an average maid-servant. The half-crown and shilling were silver coins.

'And I saw a beast coming up out of the sea . . .'

In October 1517, Martin Luther nailed to the church door at Wittenberg a protest against the sale of indulgences.
His act led to the social and intellectual revolution of the Reformation. Luther's translation of the Bible,
published in 1534, contains this representation of the seven-headed beast of the Book of Revelation which might
also have illustrated the feelings of orthodox churchmen about the monster unleashed in their midst.

CHAPTER SEVEN.

Belief and superstition

AS CHURCHGOERS ACCEPT
THE QUEEN'S RELIGION, PLOTS ABOUND,
PURITANS AGITATE AND
WITCHES AND WIZARDS STILL
CAST THEIR SPELLS

One matter toucheth me so nearly as
I may not overskip – religion, the ground on which
all other matters ought to take root,
and being corrupted, may mar the whole tree.

Queen Elizabeth I

The first nonconformist
The 14th-century 'father' of English religious nonconformity, John Wycliffe criticised abuses in the Church and attacked such fundamental Roman Catholic doctrines as confession and priestly absolution. His followers were known as Lollards, from a Dutch word meaning 'mumblers' or 'mutterers' of prayers, and preached against the worldliness of the Church.

For the Elizabethans every aspect of life – literally from the cradle to the grave – was influenced and coloured by their religion. The Anglican Church established in 1559 was essentially a compromise, received with gloomy disappointment by Catholics and radical Protestants alike. The Catholics regarded it with horror, and the Spanish ambassador told King Philip that England had fallen into the hands of 'a daughter of the Devil'. The more zealous Protestants, on the other hand, regretted that so much of what John Jewel, the new Bishop of Salisbury, called 'the scenic apparatus of divine worship' had been retained; the bishop criticised the Queen and her advisers for clinging to the old-fashioned idea that 'the Christian religion could not exist without something tawdry'.

It is less easy to be certain about what the English people thought of their new Church, but the majority of them were ready to give it a cautious welcome. After the upheavals of the past decade, many people were anxious for a religious settlement which would offer a middle way for moderate-minded men and women who wanted nothing more to do with Rome and were drawn by the logic, accessibility and commonsense appeal of the Protestant faith, but who still enjoyed a bit of decent ceremonial and music with their churchgoing.

The Queen and her more conservative-minded subjects would have almost certainly preferred a return to the form of Anglo-Catholicism introduced by Henry VIII. However, the opposition of an articulate and well-organised group of radical members in the House of Commons had been too strong for her, and the Book of Common Prayer, which came into use on Midsummer Day 1559 as the only legal form of public worship, was firmly based on the Protestant prayer book introduced in 1552, during the reign of Edward VI. The Latin Mass, restored by Queen Mary, was once more abolished in favour of a Protestant communion service; all 'images, shrines, tabernacles, roodlofts, and monuments of idolatry' were removed from the churches, the altars replaced by communion tables and the number of festivals and holy days reduced.

Under the new dispensation the clergy were once more allowed to marry. Queen Elizabeth never became entirely reconciled to the idea, and popular prejudice was against it, but here too the reformers had got their way. What with hardly knowing from one reign to the next whether they were legally married or not, and having to put up with disparaging remarks from old-fashioned parishioners, the pioneer generation of vicarage ladies must have led a precarious and harassing existence.

Martyrs to their faith
The persecution of Protestants during the reign of Queen Mary Tudor, when some 300 people, including 60 women, were burned at the stake, cast a shadow of gloom and disgust over the country. These five martyrs are being burned at Smithfield in London. Most of the victims of the Marian persecution were humble people who died in agony in their local market-place for what they believed to be God's truth. From their ashes rose the fear and hatred of Rome which were to persist through centuries of English life.

Their husbands, too, had been living through difficult times. After two violent changes of direction in less than ten years, the general state of the English church at the beginning of the Elizabethan Age was confused, and Bishop Jewel was appalled by the wilderness of superstition which had sprung up in the darkness of the Marian times.

Allowing for a certain amount of exaggeration by the incoming Protestants, there is no doubt that the bishops who took over from the Catholic hierarchy appointed by Queen Mary had a formidable task before them. It was fortunate that Matthew Parker, Elizabeth's first Archbishop of Canterbury, was a moderate man of tact and patience. Under his skilful guidance the Anglican Church gradually took hold, so that by the 1580s it was strong enough to withstand attack from both within and without.

Although it began with a fresh bench of bishops, the Church of England kept the existing priesthood which, with few exceptions, accepted the new order, outwardly at least, without demur. The parish priests were nearly all poor men who had become accustomed to being told what to do by the central government, and their standard of education was generally low. Nor, it seems, was illiteracy the worst of their shortcomings. According to the Protestant historian John Strype, corruption and absenteeism were rife, while many parsons, vicars and curates had got into the habit of haunting taverns and alehouses, giving themselves to drinking, rioting and gambling. Other frequent accu-

A Bible in English

The complete English Bible, translated by Miles Coverdale and printed in 1537, was followed two years later by a revised version known as the Great Bible, which every parish church was required by law to display for public reading. This illustration shows trumpeters honouring the Ark of the Lord, after David brought it to Jerusalem. The Great Bible went through six more editions by 1541, and its influence was immense and far-reaching.

sations – 'almost in every parish', says Strype – concerned fornication, keeping other women besides their wives, and having bastard children. The low morale of the clergy was reflected in an acute shortage of parish priests – so acute, in fact, that the authorities had to go on employing many of the older generation of priests whose conformity was doubtful, and fill the gaps with laymen pressed into service as readers.

A ready response to the Protestant revival

One fact which emerged clearly out of all this religious confusion was the apparently spontaneous collapse of Roman Catholicism in England – despite the fact that during Queen Mary's reign the great majority of people had gone to Mass without protest and generally behaved like good Catholics. The committed Protestants, whose vigour and efficient organisation did so much to gain them victory in 1559, still represented a small section of the total population.

In 1559 every Englishman and woman over the age of 35 had been baptised and brought up in the Church of Rome. It was still only a dozen years since Henry VIII's death, and his Church had retained so many of the elements of Catholic practice that the ordinary layman could have been excused for hardly noticing the difference. The Edwardian revolution had lasted a bare six years before the pendulum swung back again, so that most people were still far more accustomed to the Catholic form of service than to any other.

On the other hand committed Catholics, like committed Protestants, were in a small minority. Certainly a new and untried Queen could never have imposed a Protestant settlement on a nation of devout Catholics. In the event, the great majority of the laity, like the priesthood, did conform. They continued to attend their parish churches, partly in order to keep out of trouble, partly from sheer force of habit and, habit being what it is, presently became absorbed as communicating members of the new Church.

Of course there were positive as well as negative reasons for this. Many people much preferred to worship in their native tongue; a significant number of devout Catholics had been reluctant to give up their English Bibles during Mary's reign. Also, no reasonable man could deny that some measure of reform was long overdue. The moribund state of the Church of Rome in the first half of the 16th century was by no means confined to England, but by the time Rome had begun to put her house in order the English people had finally turned their backs on the Mother Church.

Possibly the strongest reason for this rejection was the fact that Roman Catholicism had become un-English. England's ties with Rome had never been as binding as those of some other European countries, and English Protestantism at grass-roots level had always been closely connected with the growth of nationalism and national pride. The medieval system under which Church and state had existed side by side as interdependent but separate bodies, each exacting their own measure of allegiance, had been destroyed by Henry VIII's Reformation. It was Henry who had first equated Roman

The first prayer book
The first English Book of Common Prayer, based on the Roman breviary and translated by Archbishop Cranmer, came into use in 1549, two years after the death of Henry VIII. It was superseded in 1552 by a more radical version which completed the process of transforming the sacrifice of the Latin Mass into an Anglican communion. In 1559 the Elizabethan Prayer Book came into use as the only legal form of public worship.

Martyrs' biographer
John Foxe, in his Acts and Monuments, *related the sufferings of the Marian and other Protestant martyrs in graphic detail. The 'Book of Martyrs', as it was popularly known, first appeared in 1563 and was soon to be found in every church and household.*

Reluctant Archbishop
Matthew Parker, Elizabeth's first Archbishop of Canterbury, was a scholarly, retiring man. But he had once been chaplain to Anne Boleyn who, just before her execution, commended her daughter to his care. 'If I had not been so much bound to the mother,' Parker told a friend, 'I would not so soon have granted to serve the daughter in this place.'

Catholicism with treason, claiming that allegiance to the Pope – that is, to a foreign power – could no longer be regarded as compatible with a subject's duty of allegiance to the Crown.

The dilemma facing patriotic Elizabethan Catholics was neatly summed up in the Oath of Supremacy, which declared the Queen's highness to be 'the only supreme governor of this realm . . . as well in all spiritual or ecclesiastical . . . causes as temporal', and which went on to renounce the jurisdiction of any 'foreign prince, person, prelate, state or potentate'. This oath, rejecting the spiritual authority of Rome, was one which no true Catholic could conscientiously swear, but the stigma of implied disloyalty attached to refusing it proved too much for most Englishmen. Besides this, the memory of the martyrs of Mary's reign, together with her disastrous Spanish marriage, had polluted Catholicism in the popular mind with the taint of foreign interference and oppression.

Exiles and recusants keep the 'Old Faith' alive

The 'Old Faith' of Roman Catholicism did not disappear. It went underground, as other old faiths had done before it. Those who clung to the old ways, from conviction or from stubborn conservatism, were divided roughly into three groups. At one end of the scale were those who could not live under the authority of a Protestant state and sought refuge in Spain or Italy. Other committed Catholics, like William Allen and Edmund Campion who left their university posts at Oxford, gathered in northern France and Belgium – especially at Louvain, which had a long-standing connection with the family of Sir Thomas More. These refugees, condemned to a lifetime of exile, were men of ability and initiative who exerted an influence out of proportion to their numbers and represented a considerable loss to their native land.

Among the Catholics who stayed at home, two sub-divisions soon began to appear. These were the hard-core, or 'recusants', who refused to conform, and a much larger group known as 'Church papists' by the Protestant establishment and 'schismatics' by their more resolute fellow Catholics. These people attended services at the parish church often enough to avoid prosecution, while continuing to practise their own religion in secret as and when they could.

In the early days of the reign this was not too difficult, particularly in the north and west, and in other areas where the leading family was Catholic. Many clergymen were still prepared to say Mass and administer the sacrament in private, while at the same time officiating in the Protestant Church. Sympathetic householders often gave shelter to Catholic priests who had been deprived of their livings in 1559, passing them off as tutors or poor relations.

The Queen and the Council were well aware that Catholicism was by no means dead, but to the regret of her more zealous advisers, Elizabeth always refused to sanction anything in the nature of a witch-hunt. Her government maintained that provided the Queen's subjects obeyed the law – that is, attended the state church – and otherwise behaved themselves, they would

Colchester captives

The Home Counties and East Anglia were strongholds of Protestantism, and this illustration from Foxe's Acts and Monuments *shows a party of victims of the Marian persecution – 'godly and faithful Christians, apprehended about Colchester, pinioned in one band' – being brought under guard to London. There are several women in the group, two of them named as Margaret Field and Agnes Whitlock, and their costume places them as ordinary working people.*

not suffer molestation 'by way of examination or inquisition of their secret opinions in their consciences'.

The Queen's well-known distaste for 'making windows into men's souls' did not, however, mean that she was prepared to allow her subjects freedom of worship. In the 16th-century context this would have been an invitation to chaos. In a society which – for all its surface sophistication – remained basically primitive, violent and lawless, organised religion supplied a vital unifying and disciplinary force. The corporate act of Common Prayer emphasised and symbolised those concerns shared by every member of the community. The Church alone provided the framework of moral teaching on which society rested; and the Church alone was in a position to apply supernatural sanctions to enforce its teaching.

It was therefore essential for the state to insist on a common religious observance upholding the established order. Since conformity was most important among the educated and all those in positions of authority and influence, the Oath of Supremacy was exacted from every office holder under the Crown, from members of Parliament, mayors, magistrates, schoolmasters

and anyone taking holy orders or university degrees. Any clergyman who used any other form of service than the Book of Common Prayer, or spoke against it, could lose a year's income and go to prison for six months for a first offence, lose all his benefices and go to prison for a year for a second offence, and suffer life imprisonment for a third. Any layman who spoke slightingly of the Prayer Book, or took part in any other form of service, could be fined 100 and 400 marks respectively for a first and second offence (a mark was a unit of currency worth thirteen shillings and fourpence), lose all his goods and go to prison for life for a third offence. Anyone absent without good reason from the local parish church on Sundays and holy days could be fined twelvepence for each offence, or suffer 'censure of the church'. This could involve lesser or greater excommunication which, in its turn, involved the loss of certain civil rights. For example, an excommunicated person's evidence was considered worthless in a court of law.

A papal bull sparks Protestant fury

The Queen undoubtedly hoped that, given time and patience, the problem of the Catholic minority would solve itself, as the old generation of priests died off and a new generation of schoolchildren educated on sound Protestant principles grew up. But, unhappily for many people, all hopes of a peaceful solution were destroyed by outside events, which were to turn the religious question into an increasingly bitter and bloody battle.

The first of these events was the dramatic appearance in England of Mary, Queen of Scots. Although Mary Stuart was to remain a political prisoner for the rest of her life, the mere fact of her presence in the country gave the English

A gentle cleric martyred
Thomas Cranmer, a don at Jesus College, Cambridge, brought himself to royal notice in 1529 by suggesting that the 'Great Matter' of Henry VIII's divorce from his first wife should be referred to the universities of Europe. Four years later the king chose him to be the first post-Reformation Archbishop of Canterbury. Cranmer duly pronounced Henry's first marriage to be null and void, and in September 1533 he stood god-father to the infant Elizabeth. A gentle, kindly man, he possessed genuine humanity and humility in an age not noted for such qualities in its public figures.
Tried for treason and heresy under Mary, and faced with excommunication, degradation and martyrdom, Cranmer's courage failed him and he made several recantations of his faith. But this did not save him from being burned at the stake. In his last moments outside St Mary's Church in Oxford (left), an ageing, white-bearded man in a ragged gown, he found the strength to thrust his right hand which had signed the recantations into the fire, and held it there until he collapsed in the smoke and flames.

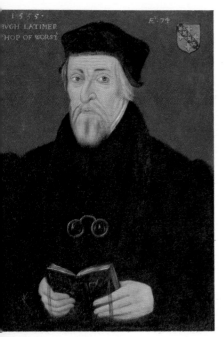

Oxford martyr

*Hugh Latimer, Bishop of
Worcester, was an outspoken
preacher against social in-
justice, and in 1553 he supported the claims of Lady Jane
Grey against Mary Tudor.
Condemned to death for heresy
in 1555, he and Nicholas
Ridley suffered together.
Latimer's last words to Ridley
as they stood bound to the
stake outside the walls of
Oxford have rung down the
ages: 'Be of good cheer, Master
Ridley, for we shall this day
light such a candle, by God's
grace, in England as shall never
be put out.'*

Catholics and their foreign sympathisers a figurehead and a focal point for intrigue. It was no coincidence that Mary's arrival should have been closely followed by the Northern Rising – the first and only serious civil disturbance of the reign. Although not primarily an affair of Catholics versus Protestants, the rebellion rapidly became an affair of the old against the new, and its success could only have benefited the Catholic cause.

In 1570 the Pope, encouraged by garbled reports of the rising in the north which reached him from the English exiles, issued his Bull *Regnans in Excelsis*. This formally denounced the Queen of England as a bastard, a heretic and a usurper, and absolved her Catholic subjects from their allegiance to her. The bull infuriated all good Protestants, and made life very much more difficult for all loyal and peaceable Catholics.

In 1572 came the revelations of the so-called Ridolfi Plot, the first of a series of conspiracies aimed at deposing Elizabeth and replacing her by her Catholic cousin Mary, Queen of Scots. In August of the same year the Protestant world was outraged by the atrocity of the St Bartholomew's Day Massacre, when the Catholics of Paris rose against their Huguenot countrymen, slaughtering thousands of men, women and children.

By the mid-1570s, therefore, Protestant opinion was hardening. At the same time the English government was alarmed and irritated by the arrival in England of the first of the missionary priests trained at the seminary at Douai. This was the brainchild of William Allen, a Lancashire man who did more perhaps than any other single individual towards keeping Roman Catholicism alive in England. Allen's faith was not of the kind which admitted compromise, and he had abandoned a promising academic career at Oxford to join the exiled community in Belgium. But William Allen was not content to wait passively, hoping for better times to return. He realised as clearly as Queen Elizabeth that once the last representatives of the pre-Reformation English priesthood were gone, 'no seed would be left hereafter for the restoration of religion, and that heresy would thus obtain a perpetual and peaceful possession of the realm'. In 1568, therefore, he decided to set up a centre for exiled scholars like himself, where the flame of resistance could be kept alight and from which it might one day be possible to send emissaries to rally the faithful.

Through Allen's inspiration and hard work the English College at Douai grew and flourished. As its fame spread a steady stream of students and visitors began to flow through its ever-open doors. Six years after its foundation, the first contingent of priests was ready to leave for 'the English harvest'. More soon followed, and by the end of the 1570s at least 100 missionaries had been sent across the Channel. These devoted, dedicated and highly trained young men were a very different breed from the old, ignorant so-called 'mass-monger', who all too often had done little more than gabble his unintelligible Latin prayers over an uncomprehending and indifferent congregation. Although these new missionaries came too late and were too few in numbers to reverse the Protestant tide, they did succeed in breathing new life into the dying embers of English Catholicism.

The missionary priests naturally gravitated to Catholic neighbourhoods, where they found shelter among sympathisers in 'safe houses', but they faced constant danger and almost certain death if they were caught. Robert Parsons, a Jesuit priest, has left a vivid description of the atmosphere in one of these households while a priest was being entertained. 'Sometimes when we are sitting at table quite cheerfully, conversing familiarly about matters of faith or piety, it happens that someone knocks on the front door a little more insistently than usual, so that he can be put down as an official. Immediately, like deer that have heard the huntsman and prick up their ears, all stand to attention, stop eating and commend themselves to God in the briefest of prayers. No word or sound of any sort is heard until the servants come to report what the matter is. If it turns out that there is no danger, we laugh at our fright.'

Priests in hiding as 'treason' laws bite

Many Catholic families had already taken the precaution of providing secret places where a wanted man could be concealed in an emergency. As time went on, the construction of 'priests' holes' became a highly skilled and specialised craft; Nicholas Owen, son of an Oxford carpenter, was its most famous practitioner. But in the early days the hiding places were often amateurish affairs, known to too many people, so that the priests would prefer to take refuge out of doors in woods and thickets, lying in ditches or even holes in the ground.

As the success of the English mission spread and other training centres for missionary priests were set up, more and more Catholics were becoming 'reconciled' to their Church, refusing to attend Protestant services and smuggling their children abroad to be educated. At a time when the menace of international Catholicism was looming ever larger in Protestant eyes, and the recurring plots against her life and throne were causing acute alarm in the country at large, the Queen was forced to adopt a harsher attitude towards her Catholic subjects. During the early 1580s, the penalties for hearing Mass were increased, and the fine for non-attendance at church was raised from twelve-pence a week to a crippling £20 a month. The priests working to persuade the Queen's subjects to leave the Church of England and accept the authority of Rome were in future to be considered guilty of high treason, and any person who harboured or assisted them would be guilty of felony.

Although the recusancy laws were still not always strictly enforced and not all the captured priests suffered the full punishment for treason, there is no doubt that many members of the Catholic minority did suffer grievously for their faith. It is estimated that altogether about 200 priests and laymen were executed, and another 50 or so died in prison.

It was a grim business, but given the climate of the times it might have been very much worse. If the Queen had allowed herself to be carried away by the prevailing mood of anti-Catholic hysteria in the House of Commons, religious persecution on the continental model could well have been seen in England. As it was, her stubborn refusal to be panicked into regarding all Catholics as potential traitors went a long way towards calming the situation. At no time

Bishop in torment
Nicholas Ridley, Bishop of London, was like Latimer a supporter of the cause of Lady Jane Grey. Condemned with Latimer, Ridley's death was an especially horrible one. Many of those burned at the stake were quickly suffocated by the smoke, and sometimes well-wishers placed bags of gun-powder among the faggots to ensure that the end came quickly. But in Ridley's case the wood was damp and the fire slow to burn, and he died in long-drawn-out agony.

were the English Catholics ever in danger from Protestant mob violence – not even when a Spanish invasion fleet was sailing up the Channel within sight of the coast.

Puritan zealots excite the Queen's wrath

Elizabeth had a good deal of sympathy for those Catholics who did not allow their faith to interfere with their loyalty, and she protected some known Catholics attached to the Court – the musician William Byrd was one of them. She had no sympathy, however, for the radical Protestants who, by the 1570s and 1580s, had begun to attack the Anglican settlement from within. These radicals, or 'Puritans' as they were dubbed in an apparent reference to the 'purity' of their religion, were still hoping to achieve their aim of remodelling the Church of England on Calvinist or Presbyterian lines and purging it of the last remaining vestiges of what they saw as 'Romish idolatry'.

The Puritans wanted to do away with the wearing of surplices and vestments, the use of the ring in marriage, making the sign of the cross at baptism, the churching of women and kneeling at communion. They wanted to abolish the bishops and to replace them with a system of church government by ministers and lay elders. The extremer elements even visualised the destruction of the cathedral churches where, a Puritan writer alleged, 'the time and place of God's service, preaching and prayer is most filthily abused in piping

Missionaries of the Pope
Edmund Campion and Robert Parsons are the best-known of several hundred Catholic missionary priests who infiltrated Elizabethan England. In this Protestant print, Parsons is shown holding out his papal licence. Both men joined the Jesuits after brilliant academic careers at Oxford, and both arrived in England together in the summer of 1580. Campion was captured hiding in a priest's hole at Lyford Grange near Oxford in 1581 and was hanged, as shown on the left. Parsons escaped to France.

with organs, in singing, ringing and trolling of the Psalms . . . with squeaking of chanting choristers'. If these 'sinks of iniquity' were swept away, it was argued, their revenues could be used to maintain a learned ministry.

Although there were probably never more than a few hundred Puritan activists, they formed a powerful, well-organised group, totally committed to the righteousness of their cause. Their rigidly anti-Catholic position won them widespread sympathy from the public, who saw them as diligent watch-dogs barking against the Papist wolf, and they had strong support in the House of Commons. They could also count on influential backing in high places. Francis Walsingham, Francis Knollys, the Earl of Leicester and even Lord Burghley himself were known to sympathise with at least some of their objectives.

Only the Queen remained implacably hostile to the Puritans. Elizabeth detested doctrinaire zealots of whatever complexion, but she detested the joyless authoritarianism of the Calvinists most of all. She saw clearly that the logical outcome of the system of discipline being advocated by the Puritan faction would be the end of royal supremacy as established by Henry VIII, and envisaged the monarchy as being subjected to a parcel of Bible-punching upstarts licensed to pry into the affairs of their betters.

The Queen had never forgiven that rugged Calvinist John Knox for his *Blast . . . Against the Monstrous Regiment of Women* – a pamphlet written in the 1550s attacking women rulers in general, but the regimes of Mary of Guise in Scotland and Mary Tudor in particular. Nor had she forgotten Calvin's own teaching that subjects had a positive duty to overthrow and spit upon an ungodly prince. Throughout her reign Elizabeth fought tenaciously to keep the stealthy encroachment of Puritanism at bay.

'Good and godly exercises' mark Sunday in church

The two extremes of Catholicism and Puritanism aroused intense passions in certain quarters, but the vast majority of ordinary, respectable, God-fearing Elizabethans were little affected by the religious controversies raging over their heads. The vast majority continued to obey the summons of the church bells on Sunday, to take communion two or three times a year and to subscribe quite contentedly to the doctrine of the Church of England as set out in the Thirty-Nine Articles.

Morning service in the parish church began at 7 o'clock. After a certain number of psalms had been read, says the Rev. William Harrison, a parish priest and author of the *Description of England*, there were two lessons, the first taken from the Old Testament, the second from the New. Then came the Litany, and 'this being done', Harrison continued, 'we proceed unto the communion, if any communicants be to receive the Eucharist; if not, we read the Decalogue (that is, the Ten Commandments), Epistle and Gospel, with the Nicene Creed, and then proceed unto an homily or sermon, which hath a psalm before and after it, and finally unto the baptism of such infants as . . . are brought unto the churches'. Afternoon prayers began at 2 o'clock, when there would be more psalms and lessons, perhaps another sermon and the young

Bedside communion
Religion affected the life of every Elizabethan from birth to death. To give the sacrament to the sick and dying, priests used a travelling communion set. This set, dating from 1534, contains a silver-gilt chalice and paten for wine and wafer, and a bottle for wine or holy oil.

Hiding for a priest
The Catholic missionaries, who began to appear in England during the 1570s led hunted lives, and many Catholic households provided hiding places for them. These priests' holes, as they were known, were concealed in chimney-stacks, under floorboards or within the thickness of the walls. This one is hidden below the floor of a gallery at Sawston Hall, near Cambridge.

people of the parish would be catechised 'by the space of an hour'. 'Thus,' observed Harrison complacently, 'do we spend the Sabbath day in good and godly exercises, all done in our vulgar tongue, that each one present may hear and understand the same.'

Unfortunately, there was still a serious shortage of educated men coming into the ministry, due largely to the fact that many of the smaller country livings were worth no more than from £10 to £30 a year before the payment of first fruits and tenths – taxes due to the government. According to Harrison, 'of a benefice of twenty pounds by the year, the incumbent thinketh himself well acquitted if, all ordinary payments being discharged, he may reserve thirteen pounds, six shillings and eightpence towards his own sustentation and maintenance of his family'. In the circumstances it was scarcely surprising that 'the greatest part of the more excellent wits choose rather to employ their studies unto physic and the laws, utterly giving over the study of the Scriptures for fear lest they should in time not get their bread by the same'.

Thanks to the efforts of the Elizabethan bishops – a hard-pressed and often maligned body of men – standards and conditions were gradually improving, but the average country parson remained a poor man, farming the glebe land assigned to him as part of his benefice and, like most small farmers, relying heavily on his wife's assistance in the dairy and poultry yard. Nevertheless, although he might often be less well off than some of his parishioners and was unlikely to possess a university degree, he was still an important member of the local community, a natural arbiter of disputes among neighbours, and a representative, however humble, of the authority of the Established Church.

A Church that set rules for everyday behaviour

The consciousness of this authority formed a very real part of everyone's daily life, and was by no means confined to Sundays. It made itself felt from the moment of birth – all parents being expected to present their babies for baptism at the parish church during the first month of their lives. (Catholic mothers-to-be would frequently leave their homes and go into hiding in another part of the country in order to evade this obligation.) As the child grew, parents or employers had to see that he or she went to church and learnt the catechism in preparation for confirmation at the age of 14. No person ignorant of the catechism or the Ten Commandments was allowed to communicate. All schoolmasters had to be licensed by the bishop of the diocese, as did doctors and midwives. All couples had to have their banns of marriage published in the parish church and go to the parish church for the ceremony. Equally, everybody made their last journey to the parish church to be laid to rest in the churchyard among their friends and neighbours.

In a well-run parish, day-to-day supervision was exercised by the churchwardens, who were empowered to close the alehouses during the hours of Common Prayer, and to seek out and report those who did not come to church or otherwise failed to perform their religious duties. The wardens, as the people's representatives, were also responsible for keeping an eye on the vicar,

Foe to women's rule
Queen Elizabeth never forgave John Knox for his vitriolic attack on women rulers in his Blast . . . Against the Monstrous Regiment of Women. *Knox had imbibed the doctrines of Calvinism while exiled in Germany and Geneva during the reign of Mary Tudor. When he returned to Scotland in 1559 he was largely responsible for establishing the Church of Scotland on Presbyterian lines.*

making sure that he wore his surplice, made the sign of the cross at baptism and so on, and reporting him to the bishop if he did not.

The Church enforced discipline through its own courts. As well as dealing with such matters as marriage and divorce and the probate of wills, these courts were concerned with a wide variety of misdemeanours, including adultery, fornication, defamation, Sabbath-breaking, witchcraft and blasphemy. The man who quarrelled with his wife or worked on a holy day and the woman who gossiped maliciously about her neighbours or had an illegitimate child were both liable to be presented at the Archdeacon's court to be sentenced to a fine or, more often, some humiliating penance, such as having to stand up in church before the congregation in a white sheet. More extreme cases could be punished by excommunication which, in its severest form, involved being made virtual outlaws from society.

To modern ears this sounds like intolerable interference with personal liberty, but the Elizabethans were accustomed to the concept of an authoritarian state. However, judging by the number of cases of people presented for sleeping, spitting, swearing, jostling, scoffing and, on one occasion, letting off a gun in church, they did not allow themselves to be unduly overawed by the

Ducking a scold

The ducking stool was widely used as a punishment for 'common scolds' or nagging, quarrelsome women. Dipping in the local pond or river was thought to be the quickest and most effective method of quelling even the noisiest virago. Suspected witches were also ducked or 'swum'. If the unfortunate creatures drowned, they were considered to have been guilty. If they were lucky enough to float, they were judged innocent.

A 'witch' dispatched

*The Scriptures stated un-
equivocally that 'thou shalt not
suffer a witch to live', and
many a poor old woman whose
eccentric habits or disfigured
appearance made her an object
of fear and repulsion to her
neighbours was condemned
on the slenderest evidence.
Sometimes, too, a respectable
working woman would be
accused of 'over-looking' an
hysterical girl and harassed
into a 'confession'.*

Open-air pulpits

*Country clergymen often com-
plained that their parishioners
'love a pot of ale better than a
pulpit, and a corn-rick better
than a church-door', but most
educated Elizabethans had an
insatiable appetite for sermons.
The open-air pulpit at Paul's
Cross in the cathedral churchyard was a focal point of the
Queen's London, where fashionable preachers could be certain
of a large and attentive audience. A gallery in the north
wall of the cathedral choir faced
the pulpit cross; here Queen
Elizabeth listened to a sermon
by the Bishop of Salisbury after
the defeat of the Armada
in 1588.*

system. Sermons were an important vehicle for government propaganda in an age when the pulpit was the only regular medium of mass communication, but congregations did not always sit in docile silence to be indoctrinated. On the contrary, they seldom hesitated to heckle an unpopular or long-winded preacher. When the curate of Stogursey in Somerset went on too long, he was told loudly that it was time he came down so that the maids could get to the milking, and when a rector in Essex discoursed on the subject of Adam and Eve making themselves coats of fig leaves, one wit promptly demanded to know where they had got the thread from. Released from church, the men would stream noisily into the nearest tavern, and many were the mournful complaints from moralists and clergy about the invincible ignorance, indiffer- ence and irreverence of the lower orders.

While the arrangements for getting people to church and generally watch- ing over their manners and morals appeared to be comprehensive, in practice a sizeable minority continued to be largely untouched by the civilising influence of Christianity. This was especially true of people who lived in the remoter areas of forests, marsh and heathland, and of those who had opted out of society in favour of the vagabond life. Nor did everyone who went to church swallow the church's teaching whole. Some defiant, and admittedly often pot- valiant, individuals would openly declare their scepticism before a shocked or admiring audience in the alehouse. At the other end of the intellectual scale were the original and inquiring minds who found it hard to accept scriptural infallibility or biblical chronology. These included men like Francis Bacon, Christopher Marlowe and Walter Raleigh – who once, in conversation with the vicar of Winterbourne, went so far as to question the existence of the soul, thus laying himself open to a charge of atheism.

Worship encouraged by a Bible in English

The average Elizabethan Anglican seems to have regarded his churchgoing as part of his moral and social duty as a good citizen, as an integral part of everyday life, without ever thinking very seriously about it. On the other hand, the Catholics, hearing their proscribed Mass in fear and secrecy in barns, attics or caves, did not have the monopoly of religious conviction, and there was undoubtedly much genuine and deeply felt devotion among Protestants.

The publication in 1539 of the first generally available English Bible, based on the translations by Tyndale and Coverdale, had an electrifying effect on an increasingly sophisticated and literate public. To the average concerned and educated laymen it meant that he was for the first time in a position to study and interpret the Word of God for himself, and this in turn had led to the exhilarating realisation that it was possible for ordinary men and women to make their own approaches to the Almighty without being entirely dependent on the priest to act as intermediary. For many thousands of people the discovery of the Scriptures, and with it a whole new world of delights in which the spirit could find its own refreshment, brought a sense of emotional and intellectual release which transformed their outlook on life. By the middle

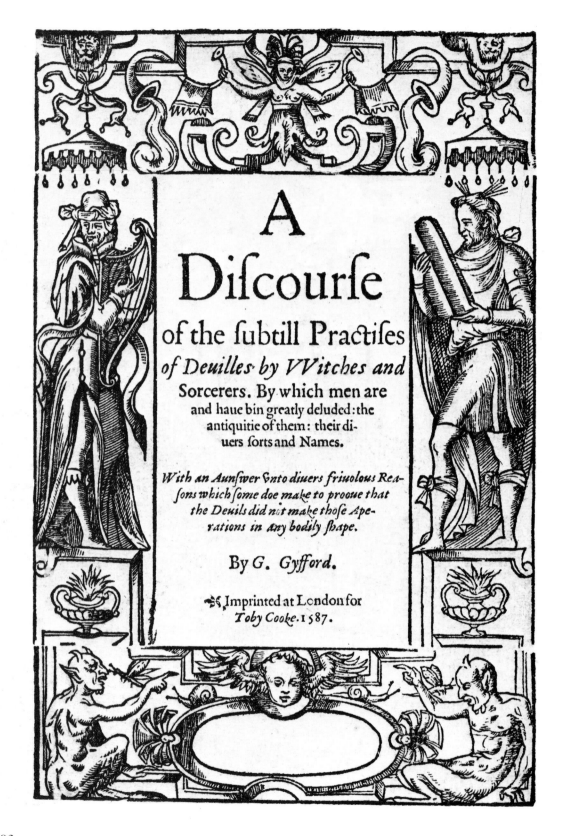

A

Difcourſe

of the ſubtill Practiſes
of Deuilles by VVitches and
Sorcerers. By which men are
and haue bin greatly deluded: the
antiquitie of them: their diuers ſorts and Names.

With an Aunſwer vnto diuers friuolous Rea-
ſons which ſome doe make to prooue that
the Deuils did not make thoſe Ape-
rations in any bodily ſhape.

By G. Gyfford.

Imprinted at London for
Toby Cooke. 1587.

years of Elizabeth's reign a whole generation had been reared on the English Bible. Every family with any pretensions to culture possessed a copy and, thanks to compulsory churchgoing, every child grew up familiar with the sonorous beauty of its language.

Protestantism had always laid great stress on the importance of private prayer, while playing down the more outward and sacramental aspects of religious observance. Family prayers were an established institution in all well-conducted households, but in those with leanings towards Puritanism a considerable amount of time was also spent in meditation, study and discussion of the Gospels.

Charms to heal the sick and tell the future

Across the not-very-clearly defined frontier dividing religion from superstition, 16th-century Anglicans, Puritans and Catholics alike could unite in their common belief in the supernatural, and in the existence of magic, sorcery and witchcraft. Witchcraft was not necessarily always evil. Every village, small town and city neighbourhood had its 'cunning man' or 'wise woman' who could count on a steady stream of clients. These 'charmers' offered a wide range of services – from medical and veterinary care to the recovery of lost or stolen property, the tracing of missing persons and fortune-telling and divination of the future. They were mostly widely employed for healing the sick, especially for lifting curses or driving out evil spirits. Some specialised in particular ailments, such as the cure of ringworm, tetter-worm and canker-worm (people with weak backs went to Mother Phillips on Bankside), while others claimed to be able to tackle anything.

The methods practised by witches and wizards usually involved the touching and saying of prayers or magic formulae over the patient. Many of these formulae were extremely ancient, handed down by word of mouth through countless generations until their original meaning had been lost. Some were debased versions of Christian prayers, and some were the old Latin Catholic prayers which had by now acquired a supernatural aura. Other charmers made use of the Hebrew names for the divinity, reflecting an ancient belief in the magical power of holy names, and others again were extremely simple. For example, for a burn or scald:

Two angels came from the West.
The one brought fire, the other frost.
Out fire! In frost!
In the name of the Father, Son and Holy Ghost.

For toothache, the sufferer had to write three times on a piece of paper:

Jesus Christ for mercy sake
Take away this toothache.

Then, having repeated the words aloud, he burned the paper. Charms were often written down and worn as amulets. Many magical practitioners were,

'Suspicions' under fire
Witchcraft became the subject of much earnest intellectual debate in the later years of Elizabeth's reign, especially among Puritans. George Gifford, a parson at Maldon in Essex, published his Discourse of the Subtle Practises of Devils by Witches and Sorcerers *in 1587. Belief in witchcraft was obligatory, for, it was claimed, 'the word of God doth plainly show that there be witches'. However, Gifford, a comparatively enlightened individual, thought that 'the raising up of suspicions and rumours' was all too often the cause of innocent persons being accused and innocent blood being shed.*

Dancing round the Devil
The belief that witches danced in a circle round their master, the Devil, at witches' Sabbaths was prevalent among the more credulous Elizabethans. So, too, was the belief that the cat or toad or suchlike creature, which might be some old crone's only companion, was a 'familiar', housing an evil spirit. But there is nothing to suggest an organised witch-cult in the England of Elizabeth.

A witches' Sabbath
This early 17th-century Flemish impression of a witches' Sabbath (opposite page) illustrates the unhealthy obsession with witchcraft and the black arts which permeated society in mainland Europe. In England, however, witchcraft trials remained sufficiently unusual to excite special interest, and outbreaks of witch-hunting were sporadic affairs. They usually occurred in places where the local Justice of the Peace had a fixation upon the subject. Essex, a centre of Puritanism, seems to have been particularly afflicted in this respect.

of course, merely charlatans, while others may well have possessed a healing touch, plus a useful knowledge of herbal medicine. All clearly had an understanding of basic human psychology, and such is the power of suggestion that they were often able to achieve cures. In any case, there is no reason to suppose that they did any more harm than conventional doctors.

Magical healing was regarded with some suspicion by the Church, hence the normal inclusion of a version of a Christian prayer so that the wise man or woman could claim to be merely assisting a client with the power of prayer. But one form of magic healing which remained entirely respectable was cure by royal touch. This was the ritual, inaugurated by Edward the Confessor, of touching for the King's Evil. Properly speaking, the Evil was scrofula, or struma, a tubercular inflammation of the lymph glands of the neck probably caused by infected milk, but it was also taken to include a variety of complaints affecting the head, neck and eyes, especially sores, swellings and blisters. Elizabeth touched regularly for King's Evil — it was an important factor in maintaining the royal mystique – and her 'cures' were cited as evidence that the Pope's excommunication had had no effect on the sacred and supernatural aspect of her office.

When it came to recovering stolen property, the cunning man had a high success rate. It usually only needed to be known that his services had been called on for the missing article to reappear as if by magic. Fortune-tellers and astrologers had to move with circumspection to avoid charges of sorcery, but there were several well known and fashionable 'wizards' with lucrative practices, for example, Simon Forman and William Lilly, while the Queen herself consulted and patronised the famous Dr Dee.

Witches blamed when accidents befell

Belief in witches was widespread and had Scriptural authority, but there is little evidence of any systematic witchcult in 16th-century England. The vast majority of witchcraft cases coming before the courts involved an old, ill-favoured woman of the poorest class, dependent on her neighbours' charity for survival, who was refused when she came begging. If any misfortune subsequently overtook the uncharitable neighbour, his family or livestock, suspicion of witchcraft would fall on the unfortunate crone – the result of a mixture of resentment, superstition and guilty conscience. At the same time, these outcast old women – or, more rarely, old men – would sometimes deliberately cultivate a reputation for possessing the evil eye as a means of defence against a hostile world and of extorting blackmail from neighbours afraid of offending them.

Accusations against alleged 'witches' were occasionally brought by hysterical girls and harmless individuals persecuted; and if a person 'pined away' for no obvious reason, it was generally put down to their having been 'overlooked' or ill-wished. Similarly, if an apparently healthy person suddenly dropped dead, there was no medical expert to diagnose a cerebral haemorrhage or a coronary and the general verdict would be that the deceased had been be-

witched. But there was no sadistic obsession with the subject.

The Elizabethans were heirs to a rich and varied folklore, and many were the tales of ghosts and hobgoblins, of demons with glaring eyes and claws like a bear, of witches, changelings and firedrakes (comets) told round the fire on winter evenings, sending nervous folk to bed starting at their own shadows. Most country people believed implicitly in the existence of such bugaboos, and it took a hardy soul to pass through the churchyard after dark.

Ghosts were known to walk at midnight. They would not speak unless challenged, and then only to those for whom they had a message, while the crowing of the first cock sent them gibbering and squeaking away. Crossroads, where criminals and suicides were commonly buried, were notoriously haunted spots. In marshy places the will o'the wisps would lure an unwary traveller to his doom. In Norfolk the wayfarer was in danger of meeting Black Shuck on his wanderings, and numerous roads were frequented by headless horsemen or packs of phantom hounds.

Puck, otherwise known as Robin Goodfellow or Lob-lie-by-the-fire, was a mischievous domestic sprite for whom the wise dairymaid would always remember to leave out a bowl of cream, and those up and about early enough on summer mornings might have the good fortune to see the fairies dancing. Fairies, if kindly treated, were usually beneficent spirits, but they were not entirely to be trusted; the puny, wizened baby wailing fretfully in its cradle might well be a changeling replacing the bonny human infant stolen by some fairy mother. A knife hung over the cradle was believed to keep a sleeping child from harm – fairies were known to be afraid of iron – and salt was a protection against witches and evil spirits.

Owls and comets as the heralds of doom

Signs, omens and portents were taken seriously, especially by farmers, fishermen and seafarers, and everyone's daily life was riddled with superstition. It was bad luck to hear an owl hoot or a raven croak, or to see a hare run across one's path. Anybody who stumbled on the threshold of a door would be sure to find trouble within, and it was unwise to begin an enterprise or a journey on a Friday. To talk of marriages in a sickroom foreshadowed death, and a person whose name was mentioned frequently on a deathbed would not long survive.

Any natural cataclysm or phenomenon was taken to presage disaster, and great alarm followed the appearance of a comet in 1577. The Queen boldly flung open a window in Richmond Palace to gaze at it, exclaiming impressively, if a little obscurely: *'Jacta est alea'* ('the dice is thrown'), while her courtiers huddled fearfully in the rear, prophesying doom.

The Elizabethans lived in a romantic, mysterious world where marvels and prodigies of all kinds were to be expected. John Stow explained the accident of a church spire struck by lightning as the work of a devil who had actually been seen entering the belfry window; Stow himself claimed to have often examined the marks left by his claws. There was also the circumstantial tale of the

From a pagan past
The 'wild man' was a popular figure in Elizabethan pageantry. In one of the entertainments provided for the Queen by the Earl of Leicester at Kenilworth in 1575, a 'savage man' nearly caused an accident by throwing away his club – a young oak sapling – and causing her horse to rear. The wild man, or Green Man or Jack-in-the-Green, had long associations with rural folklore, and could trace his pedigree back to pagan spirits dwelling in trees and forests.

The Smithfield Ghost

Crossroads, where criminals and suicides were commonly buried in unhallowed ground, were notoriously haunted places, but the Smithfield Ghost, dressed most respectably in a lawyer's gown, was said to pass through London's Smithfield Market every Saturday night, snatching joints of meat from the butchers' stalls. The haunting of Smithfield may have arisen from its association with the religious martyrs who were burned there.

Raising a ghost

Few ordinary Elizabethans would willingly venture into a graveyard after dark, but to the scientist and astrologer Dr John Dee ghosts were objects of scientific curiosity. In this illustration from Dr Dee's writings, he and his friend Edward Kelly are seen invoking the spirit of a dead person. Dee also used Kelly as a medium in crystal-gazing sessions, seances and other experiments with the paranormal. Dee enjoyed the patronage of the Queen, but Kelly came to a violent end in Prague.

'strange and terrible wonder' which took place in the parish church at Bungay, when the devil, in the shape of a black dog, fell upon the congregation during a thunderstorm, wringing the necks of two of the worshippers and clawing another man's back so that his skin shrivelled 'like leather scorched in a hot fire'. Scarcely a village did not possess its own ghost or bogey, scarcely a common was without its fairy ring, and travellers' tales of dragons, unicorns, two-headed serpents and men whose heads grew below their shoulders found an eager and credulous public.

In this same world, some men were beginning to push back the frontiers of knowledge which would lead to the age of reason and of science, while others still believed that tumours could be removed by stroking with a dead man's hand, that a salamander's skin would protect one from sunburn and that a large house spider swallowed alive in treacle was a certain cure for ague.

Weapons of war

MEDIEVAL COMBAT GIVES WAY TO THE FIREARM, BUT
ARMOUR STILL GLEAMS IN THE TILTYARD

Apart from a few professional captains, there was nothing approaching a regular army in Elizabethan times. Men of substance were required to provide equipment and horses according to their incomes, and when soldiers were needed they had to be levied from musters of the militia – which comprised, in theory at least, every able-bodied man between the ages of 18 and 60. It was an unsatisfactory and antiquated system, usually producing reluctant, semi-trained armies, and wide open to corruption.

The most important development in weaponry and warfare generally was the development of the firearm to replace the archer with his longbow and the heavily armoured cavalry. The earliest hand-guns, however, were cumbersome and unreliable. The match, or fuse, and the charge of gunpowder had to be kept dry, and the guns were slow to load and fire. But by the beginning of the 1580s the last English longbow had been hung on the wall.

Firearm finery
This ornate matchlock musket is inlaid with bone and ivory and bears the arms of the Haberdashers' Company. Beside it is a flask for gunpowder.

Knights 'at full tilt'
Mounted knights in medieval panoply demonstrate the art of jousting or tilting. The object of this war-game was to shatter the opponent's lance and throw him from his horse.

Armour for an earl

This suit of armour made for the Earl of Cumberland by German craftsmen was for ceremonial use. The officer in the field wore a buff or leather coat, and a steel helmet and breast-plate.

A musketeer's load

The early musket needed a flask of gunpowder, a bag of bullets, several yards of slow match, wadding of paper or tow, and flint or steel for lighting the match – all slung at the waist.

At long range and close quarters

Rockets guided by sticks like a modern firework and fired by gunpowder were a siege weapon developed by French and Italian military experts. In this French illustration of 1598 the rocket is fired from a grooved ramp, elevated by a cross-beam. Gunpowder was also used in grenades (below), hurled among enemy troops and exploding into lethal flying fragments of iron.

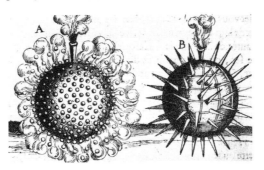

Lighting the fuse

Cannon which fired iron, bronze or stone projectiles were chiefly used for battering a fortified target, but often a great deal of time, money and effort were expended to little effect.

The first 'bayonet'

The pike – an 18 ft long wooden shaft tipped with a pointed head of iron or steel – was the infantryman's standard weapon. He also carried a sword and dagger for hand-to-hand combat.

Across the ice to find the riches of the Indies
*English and Dutch explorers braved the dangers of Arctic waters in their search for a northern passage to
the Far East, which would break the Spanish and Portuguese monopolies of the southern sea routes to America and the Far East.
Much time was wasted and many lives lost on the quest for the legendary North-West Passage, while
the Dutchman Willem Barents made three unsuccessful expeditions from Holland between 1594 and 1597 in search of a
North-East Passage by way of Siberia. Here his ship is seen trapped in the ice, as his crew collect driftwood.*

CHAPTER EIGHT

The new found lands

LURED BY ADVENTURE AND EASY BOOTY,
ENGLAND'S CAPTAINS WIN
MASTERY OF THE SEAS, DISCOVERING
NEW MARKETS AND
FOUNDING THE FIRST COLONIES

To seek new worlds, for gold, for praise, for glory . . .   Sir Walter Raleigh

*F*or very many Elizabethans the world was a small place, bounded by their own village, by the fields they tilled and the market town where the annual fair was held. For the Oxfordshire farm labourer, for the Cheshire dairymaid, for the shepherd tending his flock on the Lincolnshire Wolds, London was as fabled a place as far Cathay, and about as inaccessible.

People living in the southern coastal regions, and those who had received a little schooling, were vaguely aware of lands beyond the sea inhabited by Frenchmen, papists, Turks and wild Indians, but there is no evidence that they were greatly interested. On the contrary, secure in their well-known conviction, recorded by a visiting ambassador, 'that there are no other men than themselves and no other world but England', the islanders were apt to dismiss all things foreign with contempt and suspicion.

For the landed gentleman or professional man who had been to grammar school and university, and had even travelled abroad on business or to acquire social polish, the known world also centred on his own island and on western Europe, which was bounded on the north by the Baltic and the Hanseatic League of North German ports and on the south by the Mediterranean. Poland, a country of constantly changing frontiers, was generally regarded as being the easternmost boundary of Christendom, since its king had fought against the Turks. Nearer home were the Netherlands, traditional allies and trading partners; France, still regarded as the ancestral enemy by conservative Englishmen and deeply distrusted, and Spain, the arch-enemy. Most educated men knew something of Italy and Italian culture – everyone who had been to school was, perforce, well acquainted with the civilisation of classical Rome – while the better educated knew something of classical Greece.

Outside these narrow limits, geography became hazy. Beyond Poland were the Russians or Muscovites, the dominions of the Grand Sophy of Persia and, further east still, the Spice Islands. Somewhere to the west lay the Indies and the Spanish Main. South of the Mediterranean were the Moors and the pirates of the Barbary Coast. The rest was *terra incognita* – a nebulous region of seas and islands, snow and ice, savages, monsters and miracles – and most sensible people, preoccupied with the day-to-day affairs of the estate, parish and farm, the little town and its concerns, were content to let it go at that. The early Tudor monarchs, preoccupied first with the business of securing their dynasty and then with matrimonial, religious and other problems at home, had shown no particular curiosity about geographical matters either. As a result, England had lagged well behind the other European powers in the great race to discover, domesticate and exploit the new worlds beyond the seas.

By the time Queen Elizabeth came to the throne, it was well over a century

Prester John's land
The Portuguese, encouraged by their enterprising prince Henry the Navigator, first began to find their way into the Indian Ocean during the second half of the 15th century. By 1558, when this map was drawn, the coast of Africa was fairly accurately known, and dotted with place names, though the interior remained a mystery. Sitting enthroned in Ethiopia is Prester John, the legendary figure who was believed to rule over a mighty Christian empire at the heart of pagan Africa. Prince Henry's seamen constantly sought news of Prester John in their explorations of the coast. Portugal had papal authority for regarding the Indian Ocean as its private property, and did its utmost to discourage heretical and piratical trespassers such as the English.

Encounter in the Arctic

Polar bears were a frequent hazard for Willem Barents and his crew in their search for a North-East Passage. The search had begun with an expedition led by Sir Hugh Willoughby in 1553. Willoughby's ship became trapped in the ice off Lapland. In 1594 Barents renewed the search, and the Barents Sea, between the North Cape and Novaya Zemlya, is named after him.

since the Portuguese had begun to colonise the Atlantic islands and to nose their way cautiously down the west coast of Africa; more than half a century since their navigators had rounded the Cape of Good Hope, sailed to India and back, and taken possession of Goa and the Molucca or Spice Islands. It was more than half a century, too, since Christopher Columbus, the Genoese visionary and soldier of fortune, had sailed westwards expecting to find the coast of Asia for the King and Queen of Spain, making instead his momentous landfall in the Bahamas.

During that half century the Portuguese had founded their African and far eastern empires and colonised the coast of Brazil; while the Spanish *conquistadors* had opened up and ransacked the Caribbean, the whole of Central America, Mexico and Peru. The Spaniards had also reached across the Pacific to the Philippines, and were beginning to probe northwards into Florida and the unexplored lands beyond.

Through Arctic seas to trade with Russia

By the 1550s and 1560s, therefore, Portugal had established a monopoly of the immensely rich trade in spices, ivory, silks, calicoes and precious stones from the Far East; while an apparently inexhaustible stream of gold and silver from America was flowing into the King of Spain's treasury. By the time the English began to wake up to the realisation of lost markets and missed opportunities, there seemed nowhere left to go but north. Back in the early years of the century the Venetian John Cabot and his son Sebastian had sailed out of Bristol to begin the search for the legendary North-West Passage which

would, it was hoped, provide a short cut to China through Arctic waters. Although the Cabots reached Newfoundland and explored the coast of Nova Scotia, their voyages were a commercial failure. They found no gold or spices, no China or Japan, and hence received no further financial backing.

In 1553 another attempt was made, this time in a north-easterly direction, and on May 10 an expedition led by Sir Hugh Willoughby, with Richard Chancellor of Bristol as his second-in-command, sailed down the Thames on the ebb tide. The ships were given a triumphant send-off, recorded in a contemporary account by Clement Adams, a teacher in the royal household. As they passed Greenwich Palace 'the Courtiers came running out, and the common people flocked together, standing very thick upon the shore: the Privy Council, they looked out at the windows of the Court, and the rest ran up to the tops of the towers'.

The expedition itself, though it did achieve some useful results, proved less than triumphant. Willoughby and Chancellor were separated in a storm off the Norwegian coast and when his chief failed to appear at the rendezvous at Vardo on the north-eastern tip of Norway Chancellor went on alone. In the words of Clement Adams, 'Master Chancellor held on his course towards that unknown part of the world, and sailed so far, that he came at last to the place where he found no night at all, but a continual light and brightness of the sun shining clearly upon the huge and mighty sea'. Chancellor found his way into the White Sea, 'a certain great Bay which was of one hundred miles or thereabout over', and reached the Russian village of Archangel in time to pass the winter there. Willoughby's ship, however, was caught in the ice off

Envoys from Ivan's Russia
Although Sir Hugh Willoughby's expedition failed to find a North-East Passage to the Orient, his second-in command, Richard Chancellor, reached the Russian port of Archangel and travelled overland to Moscow, where he obtained trading rights from Ivan the Terrible. After 250 years of virtual isolation from the West under Tatar rule, Russia was keen to forge links with other countries. This painting of 1576 shows Russian envoys, followed by merchants carrying furs for trade, visiting the court of Holy Roman Emperor Maximilian II at Rosenburg, in present-day Poland.

ÆTATIS SVÆ LVIII
Anno Dñi 1591

Lapland, and the bitter cold (and, very probably, scurvy) killed everyone on board before the spring.

Chancellor, meanwhile, having learned that 'this country was called Russia, or Muscovy', set out overland from Archangel on the 'very long and most troublesome' journey to Moscow, where he was received in the Kremlin by the Tsar, Ivan the Terrible. Undismayed by the strangeness of his surroundings and the barbaric splendour of the Tsar's Court, Richard Chancellor 'did his duty to the Emperor after the manner of England', and this meeting between the Bristol sea-captain and the Tsar of All the Russias resulted in the opening of the first trading links between the two countries. The Muscovy Company was formed to develop the Russian market, and soon English cloth, tin and paper, as well as wine, raisins and other goods imported from southern Europe, were being exchanged with the Russians for rope and cordage (always in demand for the navy), whale oil, tallow, caviare, sealskins and flax.

Much of the Muscovy Company's early success was due to the efforts of its principal agent, Anthony Jenkinson. An energetic and enterprising individual who was already experienced in the Levant trade, Jenkinson first went to Moscow in 1557 and quickly won the Tsar's confidence. The following year he travelled down the Volga to Astrakhan, a distance of 600 leagues (about 1,800 miles), crossed the Caspian Sea into Turkestan and joined a camel caravan bound for Bokhara. Jenkinson's plan was to try to follow the ancient silk route through Central Asia. He succeeded in reaching Bokhara, after an adventurous journey during which he was feasted on horseflesh and mare's milk by the local Tartar chieftains, his caravan was attacked by armed robbers and he was forced to travel for four days without water through 'a wilderness of sand'. But he came to the conclusion that the country was too poor, the people too wild and barbarous for 'any good trade there to be had worthy the following'.

Hunger, disease and danger the seaman's lot

Four years later the intrepid Jenkinson was off again, this time to the southern shores of the Caspian and Persia to explore the possibility of opening up a way into India. He was politely received by the Shah's officials, and the Muscovy Company carried on some profitable business with Persia until 1579, when a victorious Turkish army barred any further access to English merchants. Jenkinson's experience taught him that overland trade with the Far East by way of Russia was not a practical proposition. Accordingly, the Company sponsored two other attempts to find a north-eastern sea passage to China, but on both occasions the pack ice, the terrible cold and storms of the Siberian coast defeated them.

Meanwhile other merchant venturers were turning south. In August 1553, three months after Willoughby and Chancellor had left for Arctic waters, 'two goodly ships', the *Lion* and the *Primrose*, sailed from Plymouth bound for the Gold Coast. Here the dangers were hostile Portuguese and, especially, fever. On that first West African voyage only 40 out of 140 crew members survived –

Reformer of the navy
John Hawkins, a native of Plymouth, came of solid merchant stock and began his career in trading ventures to West Africa and the Caribbean. But his true fame lies in his services to the Elizabethan Navy Board. During his period as Treasurer he set himself to root out the corruption and pilfering which he found at every level, and made many enemies in the process. He brought the Queen's ships to such a fine state of readiness that the Lord Admiral could tell Lord Burghley in 1588: 'I have been aboard of every ship that goeth out with me and in every place where any may creep, and I do thank God . . . that there is never a one of them that knows what a leak means.'

one of them being Martin Frobisher, an orphan lad from Yorkshire sent to sea by his uncle.

Conditions on board the small, overcrowded and often unseaworthy vessels seem horrific by modern standards, with the crews packed like sardines into their insanitary, verminous quarters for months at a time. Although fresh water and provisions were always taken on whenever possible, the seamen's ordinary diet consisted of salt pork, beef and fish, biscuit, wine and beer.

In theory, every man and boy (and many crew members were quite young boys) was supposed to receive a pound of biscuit and a gallon of beer per day and a pound of beef or pork with dried yellow peas on Sunday, Monday, Tuesday and Thursday. On the other days of the week every mess of four men was allowed a side of salt fish, usually ling or cod. In practice, food on board ship, especially on a long voyage, was often in short supply (sometimes seriously so) and often bad. Drinking water, stored in wooden casks, quickly became foul, and victuallers were well known for their habit of charging top prices for putrid meat, stale beer and maggoty biscuit.

In the circumstances, disease was rampant. Malaria and yellow fever, food poisoning, dysentery, typhus and scurvy all took an appalling toll of Elizabethan seamen. Scurvy in particular, that 'plague of the sea and spoil of mariners', as John Hawkins called it, was estimated to have killed 10,000 sailors in 20 years. It was not unusual for at least half a ship's crew to die during a voyage. Supernumeraries were carried to make up for the expected mortality, thus increasing the overcrowding and likelihood of infection. A large ship carried a crew of several hundred, but some vessels were lost because there were just not enough men left alive to work them.

All the same, in spite of a more than fifty-fifty chance of dying miserably, far from home – not to mention the risks of perishing in the tropical storms or frozen wastes of uncharted oceans in leaky little ships in which most people today would hesitate to cross the English Channel – there was apparently never any shortage of volunteers from the seaports of the south and west. The lure of adventure, plus the dream of making a fortune, continued to outweigh the terrors, dangers and hardships of a mariner's life.

Slaves from Africa sold for sugar and pearls

John Hawkins of Plymouth, a smooth-spoken, ambitious young sea-captain, had been giving serious consideration to ways of breaking into the West Indian trade. This was jealously guarded by the Spanish government which, although it granted concessions to certain foreigners, insisted that all goods must be shipped in Spanish vessels and must pass through the port of Seville. But John Hawkins had some useful contacts in the Canary Islands, where he was able to pick up valuable information about the needs of the Spanish colonists. The most urgent of these, it seemed, was labour for the mines and sugar plantations.

Since the native population of Central America ungratefully died on their new masters when put to heavy work, labour for the plantations had to be

Drake, sea-dog extraordinary
By the mid-1580s Sir Francis Drake was by far the most internationally famous Englishman of his day, and to his own countrymen he had become a national hero. A first-hand description of Drake sent to King Philip of Spain by the Spanish factor for Hispaniola early in 1586 called him 'a man of medium stature, blond, rather heavy than slender, merry, careful. He commands and governs imperiously . . . Sharp, restless, well-spoken, inclined to liberality and to ambition, vainglorious, boastful, not very cruel.' Drake's arrogance and vaingloriousness made him enemies at home, but his prowess and achievements in his chosen sphere have never been matched.

Drake's Drum
At the beating of this drum, now preserved in the Great Hall of Buckland Abbey, Drake's crew mustered for battle against the Spanish Armada on the deck of the Revenge *in July 1588. After the defeat of the Armada, the drum became a source of popular legends. According to one, it will beat of its own accord if England ever faces a Spanish threat again.*

SIC PARVIS MAGNA

imported, and cargoes of Negro slaves were already being shipped across the Atlantic. Owing to the complicated system of restrictions and licences imposed by Madrid, slaves were expensive and scarce, and Hawkins, having learned that 'store of Negroes might easily be had upon the coast of Guinea', felt that here might be an opportunity for an enterprising businessman. He managed to get financial backing from a syndicate of London merchants, and in October 1562 sailed from Plymouth with three ships and 100 men.

After calling at Tenerife to consult his Spanish friends, Hawkins went on to Sierra Leone where he seized, partly by his own sword and partly from Portuguese middle-men, a haul of about 400 blacks. He then set course for the Caribbean by the southerly trade-wind route.

This first incursion into forbidden territory went off smoothly. Hawkins found a ready market for his wares among the Spanish planters on the island of Hispaniola (occupied today by Haiti and the Dominican Republic) and brought home a cargo of hides, ginger, sugar and pearls which paid a handsome dividend for his London backers. No one saw anything in the least immoral about slave-trading and Hawkins, encouraged by his success, planned another expedition for the autumn of 1564.

This time he took his cargo of black slaves not to the Islands but across to the Spanish Main itself – the northern coast of South America from the Orinoco delta to the Panamanian Isthmus, now Venezuela and Colombia. He found that although strict orders had been issued from Spain prohibiting the colonists from trading with him, the officials on the spot were only too ready to connive. After a token show of resistance, for the benefit of their home government, they allowed business to proceed as briskly as before. On the return journey Hawkins called at the French settlement on the coast of Florida, sailed on a reconnaissance up the eastern coast of North America as far as the Newfoundland fisheries, where he took on a consignment of salt cod, and finally arrived home at the Cornish port of Padstow in September 1565. His prosperous voyage showed a very satisfactory 60 per cent profit.

Battle that began a struggle for mastery

John Hawkins' third West Indian expedition left Plymouth in October 1567. He had two of the Queen's ships with him, the *Jesus of Lubeck*, a large but dilapidated vessel bought second-hand from the Hanseatic League more than 20 years earlier, and the *Minion*, plus four other ships and a force of 400 men, among them a young kinsman of his by the name of Francis Drake. This voyage was ill-fated from the start. On the fourth day out the fleet ran into a storm off Cape Finisterre which the *Jesus of Lubeck*, leaking like a sieve, only just survived. The situation on the Guinea coast, where a state of undeclared war now existed with the Portuguese, was also unsettled and Negroes were less easy to come by. However, after entering into an alliance with one of the warring native chiefs, Hawkins was able to collect enough prisoners from the defeated tribe to make his journey worthwhile.

Once on the Spanish Main, the pattern of previous years was repeated. The

The coconut cup

In the tropics Drake and his crew followed the example of the local inhabitants in using coconuts as a source of food. They brought some of the fruit home with them, and Drake had one coconut mounted in silver filigree to make this drinking goblet. It is engraved with the Drake arms and the royal emblems, and is kept today in the wardroom of HMS Drake at Devonport, together with Drake's sword.

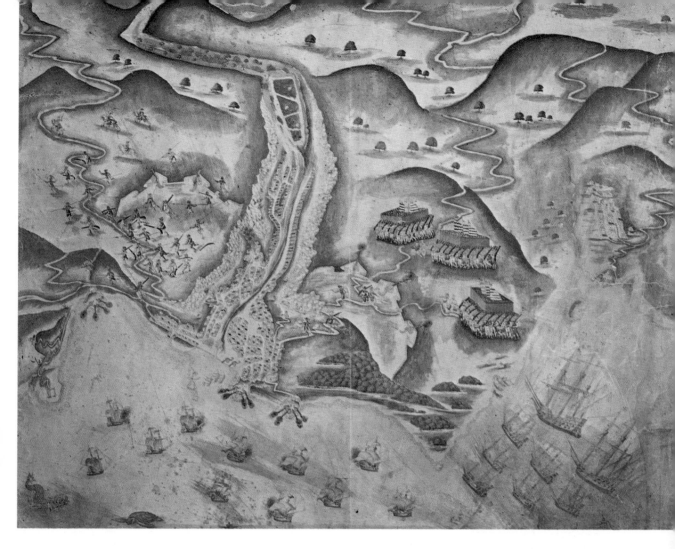

The sack of Santiago

In November 1585, an English fleet under the command of Francis Drake bore down on the settlement founded by the Portuguese at Santiago in the Cape Verde Islands. This vivid contemporary painting shows the inhabitants fleeing before Drake's advancing formations. The town was burned to the ground, but Drake failed to find any treasure and he also failed in his plan to intercept a Spanish bullion fleet on its way home from the West Indies.

colonists were as anxious as ever to do business, but there were signs of increasing nervousness among King Philip's officials. By the end of July 1568 Hawkins had disposed of his slaves and was ready to sail for home, but west of Cuba the ships were caught by a severe storm. It was too much for the *Jesus of Lubeck*. Her seams parted, water flooded into her hold and her rotten upper works were carried away. Clearly she was in no state to face the Atlantic, so Hawkins was forced to seek shelter in the Mexican port of San Juan de Ulua. Here, by ill luck, the Spanish *flota*, or treasure fleet, was about to arrive from Spain on its annual visit to collect the year's output of silver from the Mexican mines.

The English could have prevented the *flota* from entering until they were ready to leave, but to have done so would have been an act of provocation tantamount to a declaration of war – especially as the Spanish fleet was carrying Don Martin Enriquez, the new Viceroy of Mexico who ranked next to King Philip in importance. Hawkins, therefore, reluctantly made room, after first extracting Don Martin's pledged word that he would be allowed to refit and revictual unmolested. But to Don Martin, Hawkins and his men were heretics and pirates with whom no gentleman was required to keep faith, and as soon as the *flota* was safely berthed the Spaniards prepared to attack.

Francis Drake, commanding the 50 ton bark *Judith*, got safely away, but the *Jesus of Lubeck* and three other English ships had to be abandoned. The remainder of the 200 or so survivors of the Battle of San Juan de Ulua escaped on board the *Minion* with their lives but very little else. With hardly any food or water their plight was desperate, and 100 men were put ashore, at their own request, to give themselves up. They subsequently fell into the hands of the Inquisition, and Robert Barrett of Saltash, master of the *Jesus*, was taken to Spain to be burned at the stake in Seville market-place. Of the others, only two ever returned to their native land to tell the story of their sufferings.

Those who stayed with the *Minion* had a nightmare journey home. 'Our men being oppressed with famine died continually,' wrote John Hawkins sadly, 'and they that were left grew into such weakness that we were scantly able to manage our ship.' When the *Minion* finally staggered into Mount's Bay in Cornwall at the end of January 1569, the Spanish ambassador in London heard that there were only 15 survivors still on board. No English seafaring man ever forgot or forgave the Spanish treachery at San Juan de Ulua, and the incident marked a turning point in Anglo-Spanish relations. It marked the end

Under sail – on a sea-chest
Galleons in full sail decorate the underside of the lid of the cypress chest that formed part of the furnishings of Drake's cabin in the Golden Hind. *The vessel in the centre is the* Golden Hind *itself, in which in 1580 Drake completed his voyage round the world, the first by an English ship. Drake's vessel was originally called the*

of all hope of peaceful trading expansion in the New World, and the beginning of the long struggle for control of the sea.

The next 20 years belonged to the sea-dogs and privateers, but especially to Francis Drake. Born in Tavistock about 1541, Drake was brought up on the Medway, near Chatham Dockyard, where his father was a naval chaplain, and served his apprenticeship on an old coaster trading between the Thames and the French channel ports before graduating to take service with his influential Hawkins relatives. He was a sturdy young man, rather below average height, with bright twinkling blue eyes, reddish hair and a broad West Country brogue. He was to become the darling of Elizabethan England and the most famous private citizen in the Western World. European princes clamoured for his portrait; the Spaniards, who called him (among other things) *El Draque*, the Dragon, believed he was a wizard who carried a magic mirror in his cabin which enabled him to see over the horizon.

A revenge on Spain by sea-dog Francis Drake

After the disaster at San Juan de Ulua, Drake had dedicated himself to the pursuit of his private war with the King of Spain. Although he never achieved his self-stated ambition of coming face to face with Don Martin Enriquez and showing him 'how to keep the word of a gentleman', he was, over the years, to exact a very satisfying revenge.

In his famous expedition of 1572–3, Drake remained at large on the Spanish Main for more than a year. With two small ships, the *Pasco* (70 tons) and the *Swan* (25 tons), and a combined crew of 73, he spread alarm and despondency throughout the Caribbean and came home to Plymouth with booty valued at £40,000. During this voyage he had brought his men to the very mouth of 'the treasure house of the world' at Nombre de Dios, had penetrated deep into the Isthmus of Panama, sighted the Pacific Ocean, and only narrowly failed in his attempt to ambush a mule train carrying silver from Peru.

Drake's astonishing exploit was achieved partly by careful planning; he had made at least one and possibly two reconnaissance trips between 1570 and 1571. He had also made friends with the Cimaroons, an embattled community of runaway slaves and aboriginal Indians living in the wilderness of the isthmus, who loathed the Spaniards and acted as guides and spies for the English. Another factor in Drake's success was first-rate seamanship, and the fact that the small English ships were able to use long oars known as sweeps to row away from pursuit in the frequent calms of the area. They were also able to sail in shallow water where the larger Spanish galleons could not follow them. But probably the real explanation lies in Drake's own genius, his magnetic personality, his gift for leadership, his daring and brilliant opportunism.

In 1577, with an impressive list of backers headed by the Queen herself, Drake was ready to try his luck again. He sailed from Plymouth in the 100 ton *Pelican*, a tough, armed merchantman, and four other ships, of which the *Elizabeth* (80 tons) was the largest. About 160 men sailed with the little fleet. Apart from the seamen, there was a chaplain, an apothecary, a shoemaker, a

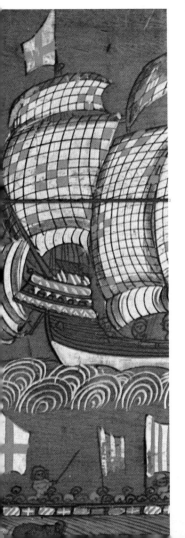

Pelican, but he renamed it off South America in honour of his patron at court, Christopher Hatton, whose coat of arms featured a hind. Drake always travelled in style. A four-piece orchestra accompanied him on his voyage round the world, and he dined to the music of trumpets and viols, from silver plates edged with gold and decorated with his coat of arms.

The Armada Jewel
This jewel, according to tradition, was given by the Queen to her old friend and Vice-Chamberlain Sir Thomas Heneage, after the defeat of the Spanish Armada. It shows on one side the Queen in profile, and on the other the Ark of the Protestant church tossed on troubled waters, with the inscription Saevas tranquilla per undas *('calm through the savage waves'). Nicholas Hilliard designed the jewel, which is $2\frac{3}{4}$ in. high, made of enamelled gold set with diamonds and rubies.*

tailor, a band of musicians, some soldiers and ten gentlemen adventurers. The fleet also carried four pinnaces (eight-oared ships' boats which were taken out in sections to be reassembled at need), provisions for 18 months, a smith's forge, tools for digging and cutting down trees and a useful store of weapons.

The fleet's destination was unstated, but this time Drake was not making for the Caribbean. Instead he set course for the southern tip of South America. Off the Cape Verde Islands a Portuguese vessel bound for Brazil was captured and added to the strength, together with its Portuguese pilot. This pilot, Nunez da Silva, was greatly impressed by the way of life on board ship maintained by Francis Drake – always known as 'the General' – who dined off silver plate to the music of trumpets and viols. Da Silva also noticed how interested Drake was in charts, astrolabes and compasses, and that he spent a good deal of time sketching. This was to record the appearance of a strange coastline, the look of an important landfall as approached from the sea; captains with no talent for drawing usually took an artist along with them. Prayers were held regularly on board the *Pelican*, the General reading the lessons, leading the psalm-singing and sometimes preaching the sermon too.

A traitor court-martialled in Patagonia

Drake's own men would have followed him anywhere, but during that Atlantic crossing there were signs of dissension on the other ships, apparently fomented by the gentlemen adventurers. The chief trouble-maker was Thomas Doughty, and at Port St Julian, an inhospitable spot on the inhospitable coast of Patagonia, Drake held a court martial at which Doughty was accused of incitement to mutiny and of practising 'conjuring' – that is, of using witchcraft to conjure up bad weather – and condemned to death. A good deal of un-certainty still surrounds this episode, but probably the real trouble lay in the jealousy which existed between the 'gentlemen' – landsmen seeking adven-ture and profit – and the professional seamen, aggravated by the natural strains and stresses affecting an expedition sailing in strange waters.

Drake was a ruthless man and clearly believed that to attempt to follow the traditional custom of command exercised by a council of equals on a venture of this kind would quickly lead to disaster. There was room for only one commander-in-chief, and like it or not the gentlemen must learn to 'haul and draw' with the mariners. To drive this point home Doughty, justly or unjustly, had to be sacrificed. There was apparently no ill-feeling. On the day of the execution Doughty and Drake took communion together. Afterwards they dined together and drank a farewell toast, but when the victim's head had been struck off Drake ordered it to be held aloft while he pronounced the customary formula: 'Lo, there is the end of traitors!'

The expedition's troubles were not yet over. The 30 ton *Marigold* sank with all hands in a storm near the western end of the Straits of Magellan, and the *Elizabeth* gave up and turned for home. Drake, alone in the *Pelican*, now rechristened the *Golden Hind*, was driven helplessly south before the gale, incidentally making the important discovery that the Straits were not, as had

Opponent of the Armada

The Lord Admiral, Lord Charles Howard of Effingham, later Earl of Nottingham, was a member of the powerful Howard clan and related to the Queen on her mother's side. Although not a professional sailor, he possessed qualities of tact, generosity, fairness and firmness which made him an ideal commander of that rugged bunch of individualists who sailed from Plymouth Sound to meet the Spaniards in 1588. He genuinely loved the navy – 'our ships do show themselves like gallants here', he wrote from Plymouth. When the battle was over he did his utmost to provide help and shelter for the seamen dying of typhus on the streets of Margate, for 'it would grieve any man's heart to see them that have served so valiantly to die so miserably'.

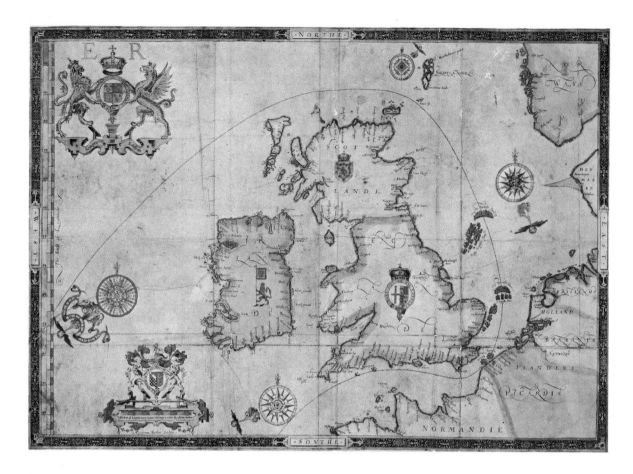

been supposed, a channel separating South America and the continent of Terra Australis Incognita. The *Golden Hind* was battered by more than a month of terrible weather, worse than any man on board had ever known, 'neither hath there been such a tempest so violent and of such continuance since Noah's flood'. At last the storm blew itself out, the wind veered and Drake was able to make headway to the north. After an encounter with hostile Indians on the coast of Chile, Drake paid a call at Valparaiso, capturing a Spanish ship laden with 25,000 pesos of 'very fine and pure gold'.

After so many months at sea the *Golden Hind* was in urgent need of a refit. In December 1578 Drake put in at Salada Bay, where the ship was scraped and tallowed, the ballast (into which most of the sewage drained) was cleaned out and renewed, and the last of the pinnaces brought out from England was put together by the carpenters. All vessels on long voyages carried skilled carpenters, shipwrights and sailmakers, who accomplished miracles in the hidden bays and deserted beaches of the New World.

Once more ready for anything, Drake resumed his leisurely cruise along the undefended coasts of Chile and Peru, picking up prizes of jewels and gold and silver bullion as he went, and causing consternation among Spaniards faced with the horrifying realisation that English corsairs were at large in the Great

The course of the Armada
Defeated in a battle off Grave-lines in August 1588, the battered Spanish Armada ran northwards before the wind, chased by the English, to about the latitude of the Firth of Forth. The Spanish ships vanished into the northern mists, and for weeks Europe hummed with rumours concerning their whereabouts. Then the survivors began to limp home. Of the 130 ships which had set sail from Lisbon, only some 70 returned.

South Sea. Off Panama, the English corsairs caught up with the *Cacafuego*, another treasure ship in which they found 'jewels, precious stones, thirteen chests full of pieces of eight, fourscore pound weight of gold, and six-and-twenty ton of silver.'

The *Golden Hind*, weighted down with treasure, continued her journey north, past the area of Spanish occupation and up the so far unexplored west coast of the North American continent. Drake may have been hoping to find the mythical 'Strait of Anian', believed to be the western outlet of the elusive North-West Passage, and he seems to have sailed as far as Vancouver Island, possibly even further, before turning south again. On the Californian coast, a little to the north of modern San Francisco, he went ashore to take a look at the land he had christened New Albion, leaving behind an English sixpence and a metal plaque announcing that this was a dominion of Queen Elizabeth.

It was time to think of going home, and in July 1579 the *Golden Hind* sailed westward across the Pacific – the first English ship to do so. Her journey took her to the Spice Islands where she added a cargo of cloves to the riches in her hold, and Francis Drake struck up a useful friendship with the Sultan of Ternate, an island of New Guinea, who proposed an alliance with England against the Portuguese. Then, somewhere south of the Celebes, among the uncharted shoals and islands of the South Seas, the voyage nearly came to an abrupt end as the *Golden Hind* ran on to a submerged reef. It was the sort of mishap which every seaman dreaded. The guns and some of the precious cloves were jettisoned and the crew fell most earnestly to their prayers, but once again Drake's luck held. The wind, which had been holding them fast, eased and the staunch little ship slid free and floated intact.

Drake refitted again, revictualled on the south coast of Java and set course for the Cape of Good Hope. There were no further alarms, and in September 1580 the *Golden Hind* entered Plymouth Sound after an absence of nearly three years. She had accomplished an epic feat of sailing round the world – the first by an English vessel, and the first by any nation since the Magellan voyage nearly 60 years before. Drake had brought home 59 of his original crew of 80 (a remarkable achievement in itself), booty valued at £600,000 and a boost of incalculable value for English national pride and international prestige. The *Golden Hind* was sailed round to the Thames and moored at Deptford, where for many years she remained as one of the sights of London; there in April 1581, Queen Elizabeth, accompanied by the French ambassador, came on board to knight Sir Francis Drake.

Quest for the North-West Passage

Although Drake had failed to find any trace of an outlet during his exploratory trip up the coast of New Albion, the search for a North-West Passage had by no means been given up. Many geographers still held to Sebastian Cabot's view that the North American continent tapered to a point at the northern end of Labrador, and that an open channel existed, leading in a south-westerly direction to the fabled riches of Cathay and Zipangu (China and Japan).

Victory medal
This gold medal struck to commemorate the victory over the Armada represents Britain as an island fortress, with at its heart a single bay-tree, struck by lightning but unharmed. The inscription reads Non ipsa pericula tangunt *('Not even dangers affect it'). The medal, which is $2\frac{1}{4}$ in. high, was presented to the officers who commanded the ships of the British fleet.*

217

The first coloniser

Sir Humphrey Gilbert, a leading exponent of the advantages of planting settlements in North America, sailed from Plymouth for Newfoundland in the summer of 1583. At St John's, already a flourishing fishery and trading post, he formally took possession of the territory on behalf of the Queen and 'the advancement of the Christian religion'. Newfoundland can, therefore, claim to be the oldest Crown colony. Gilbert was lost on the way home on board the tiny Squirrel *which he stubbornly refused to leave, possibly to disprove rumours that he was afraid of the sea, and his half-brother Walter Raleigh took up his unfinished task.*

The advantages of such a route seemed obvious to informed Elizabethan opinion. Not only would it be very much shorter than the voyage through the Straits of Magellan or round the Cape of Good Hope, but it also offered 'no manner of danger of any foreign princes or pirate' – in other words, the English would have it to themselves. In June 1576, therefore, Martin Frobisher left in the 25 ton bark *Gabriel* for a voyage of exploration in northern waters. He passed the southern extremity of Greenland and sailed up the gloomy coast of Labrador, with its 'monstrous high islands and mountains of ice fleeting and driving with the winds and tides'. Missing the entrance to Hudson's Bay, he sighted Baffin Island and found a long inlet, which he named Frobisher Strait – now known more accurately as Frobisher Bay.

Here the *Gabriel*'s crew encountered Eskimos fishing from leather kayaks who came aboard bringing salmon and seal flesh which they ate raw, to the disgust of the English, and trading furs for bells, looking-glasses and other toys. Friendly relations were, however, abruptly severed when five seamen, going trustfully ashore, were captured with the ship's boat and never seen again. Martin Frobisher, a man of astonishing physical strength, lifted one Eskimo, kayak and all, into the *Gabriel*, whereupon the captive, 'for very choler and disdain . . . bit his tongue in twain within his mouth'. In spite of this, he survived to reach England, but then died of a cold taken at sea. Without the ship's boat, Frobisher was unable to do much more in the way of inshore investigation and returned home announcing confidently that the geographers were right and that he had found their Passage.

Fortunes lost in a 'gold rush' fiasco

Frobisher, a hard-bitten, hard-up professional sea-captain with a rather shady past, seems to have been more concerned to tell his patrons what they wanted to hear than with serious exploration. He brought back with him as a souvenir a lump of black ore picked up off Baffin Island, and this was regarded with much the same awe as a sample of moon rock today. A rumour soon circulated that the mysterious ore contained gold. The result was a hectic rush to promote further voyages, as a result of which a good many people, including the Queen herself, lost their investments, while the whereabouts of the North-West Passage remained as problematical as ever. After this gold fiasco, enthusiasm for Arctic ventures waned noticeably in financial circles. However, John Davis, a fine seaman and scientific navigator, made three journeys to the north-west during the 1580s, reaching a record 73 degrees of latitude and doing more for the geography of the region than any of his predecessors.

Popular interest in oceanic exploration continued to be concentrated on the search for gold – and on the satisfaction to be derived from pulling the noses of the proud Spaniards. In the City, the expansion of trade and the opening up of new markets was still the prime factor; while in the Queen's Council chamber they were considering how best to use the exploits of Francis Drake and his fellow sea-dogs to bring pressure to bear on the King of Spain, as the threat of war in Europe seemed imminent. But before the end of the 1570s a group of

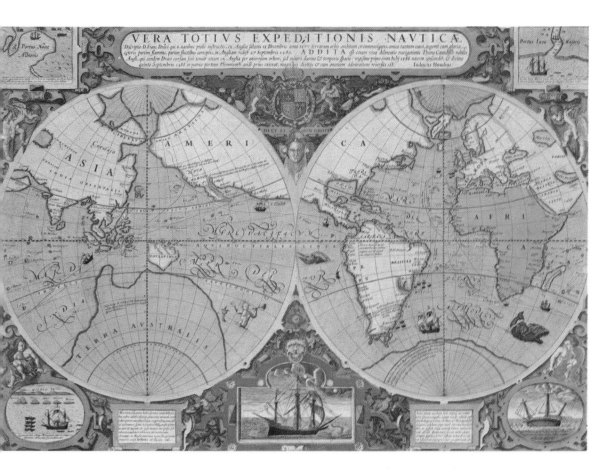

Around the world

This map of the two hemispheres by a 16th-century Flemish cartographer, published in 1589, is the earliest map of Francis Drake's voyage round the world. It traces his route across the Atlantic, through the Straits of Magellan and up the western seaboard of North America to Nova Albion. The Golden Hind's journey then took her across the Pacific, through the East Indies and into the Indian Ocean. She rounded the Cape of Good Hope and sailed into Plymouth Sound on September 26, 1580, when her captain's first anxious question was: 'Does the Queen still live?'

enterprising and far-sighted Westcountrymen, headed by Richard Grenville, Humphrey Gilbert and Walter Raleigh, had begun to turn their thoughts to colonisation and the possibilities of 'planting' permanent English settlements on the eastern seaboard of North America.

One of the most enthusiastic advocates of 'Western Planting' was the geographer and chronicler Richard Hakluyt. He pointed out that colonisation would help to solve the twin problems of Elizabethan society – over-population and unemployment – by providing an outlet for those 'many thousands of idle persons . . . which, having no way to be set on work, be either mutinous and seek alteration in the state or at least (be) very burdensome to the common wealth, and often fall to pilfering and thieving and other lewdness, whereby all the prisons of the land are daily pestered and stuffed full of them'. Secretary of State Francis Walsingham was also in favour of the idea, and in June 1578 Humphrey Gilbert was granted Letters Patent by the Queen authorising him to discover and occupy lands not already in the possession of other Christian princes.

In the first instance, interest was focused on Newfoundland, where there had been a flourishing cod fishery since the beginning of the century and which was the only part of the American continent at all well known to the

English. Anthony Parkhurst, a Kentish gentleman who worked with the Bristol merchants and had made a number of journeys with the fishing fleets, had written an optimistic report pointing out that as well as the fishery, which would increase in value and usefulness if a permanent settlement could be established, the colonists could work the plentiful deposits of iron and copper ore in the area. There would be unlimited fuel available for smelting from the local pine forests, which could also supply masts for small ships, and there was no lack of water-power for driving sawmills. Food should present no difficulty either. The climate was temperate and the soil fertile, so that grain and fruits could be grown and cattle raised. In addition to all these advantages, Newfoundland was easily accessible, the voyage taking no more than three or four weeks in favourable conditions.

The Queen smiled on the venture, though she invested no money in it, and by the summer of 1583 Humphrey Gilbert had gathered enough support to equip a fleet of five ships – the *Delight*, the *Bark Raleigh*, provided by Walter Raleigh who was Gilbert's half-brother, the *Golden Hind* (not Drake's), the *Swallow* and the tiny *Squirrel*.

A fleet sails to found the first colony

The expedition sailed from Plymouth in June. 'We were in number in all about 260 men,' wrote Edward Hayes, captain of the *Golden Hind*, 'among whom we had of every faculty good choice, as shipwrights, masons, carpenters, smiths and such-like requisites to such an action; also mineral men and refiners. Besides, for solace of our people and allurement of the savages, we were provided of music in good variety, not omitting the least toys, as morris dancers, hobby horses, and May-like conceits to delight the savage people, whom we intended to win by all fair means possible.'

Things began to go wrong two days out from Plymouth when the *Bark Raleigh*, at 200 tons the largest ship of the fleet, suddenly turned for home, giving 'contagious sickness' on board as her excuse. The rest struggled on in fog, rain and contrary north-west winds which drove them so far south that it was seven weeks before they sighted land again. Edward Hayes noted several wonders on that 'uncomfortable coast' including 'mountains of ice driven upon the seas', amazing quantities of fish and whales, and on an island named Penguin 'a fowl there breeding in abundance almost incredible, which cannot fly, their wings not able to carry their body, being very large (not much less than a goose) and exceedingly fat'.

The fleet finally gathered in the harbour of St John's where, on August 5, Humphrey Gilbert formally took possession 'to the behalf of the crown of England and the advancement of the Christian religion'. Newfoundland thus became the first outpost of empire, and the oldest Crown colony.

After a stay of three weeks in Newfoundland, during which the expedition was royally entertained by the English merchants already in residence, and feasted on 'fresh salmons, trouts, lobsters and other fresh fish brought daily unto us', Gilbert moved on, being anxious to explore further south before

Buccaneer from the north
Martin Frobisher was a pugnacious Yorkshireman with enormous physical strength, who lifted one Eskimo, kayak and all, on board the Gabriel *during his 1576 expedition. He served as vice-admiral in Drake's 1585 voyage to the West Indies, but the two men later quarrelled. Frobisher commanded the* Triumph *in the Armada campaign and was knighted for his part in the fighting. He figured in buccaneering ventures throughout the 1580s and 1590s, but died of wounds in 1594.*

A clash with the Eskimos
Off Baffin Island, Eskimos fishing from kayaks (opposite page) at first brought furs to the crew of Martin Frobisher's ship, the Gabriel, *in exchange for trinkets. But Frobisher's men soon found the Eskimos treacherous, and were revolted by their eating habits. Despite many failures and disappointments, the search for a North-West Passage to the Pacific and the fabled riches of Cathay (China) and Zipangu (Japan) continued throughout the Elizabethan age.*

deciding where to 'plant' the colonists. Not everyone went with him. There had been the usual quota of casualties from dysentery and other ills, while some had lost their enthusiasm for life in the New World. The sick and the faint-hearted were therefore sent home in the *Swallow*, which was already in disgrace for having robbed an innocent fishing boat, and on August 20 the *Delight*, the *Golden Hind* and the *Squirrel* sailed for the mainland. Disaster struck nine days later somewhere off the coast of Nova Scotia, when the 120 ton *Delight*, whose crew had been 'keeping so ill watch that they knew not the danger', ran aground on a shoal in rain and thick mist and broke up, with the loss of all but a handful of the 100 men aboard her.

This 'heavy and grievous event' was the end of the venture. Gilbert had lost most of his provisions and all his colonists on the *Delight*, together with his German assayer of metals and some precious specimens of ore said to contain silver. There was nothing for it but to return to England. Gilbert was sailing in the *Squirrel*, which was dangerously overloaded with guns and other impedimenta, 'too cumbersome for so small a boat that was to pass through the ocean sea at that season of the year'. But when his well-wishers tried to persuade him to transfer to the *Golden Hind* he refused, saying: 'I will not forsake my little company going homeward, with whom I have passed so many storms and perils.'

Edward Hayes could only shake his head over this 'wilful resolution', believing that Gilbert's stubbornness was due to a rash determination to disprove unkind rumours that he was afraid of the sea. On Monday, September 9 the *Squirrel* was 'near cast away' in heavy seas north of the Azores, but when the *Golden Hind* approached within hailing distance Gilbert could be seen sitting aft with a book in his hand. 'We are as near to heaven by sea as by land,' he told her, in a manner 'well beseeming a soldier resolute in Jesus Christ,' as Edward Hayes could testify. That night the look-out on the *Golden Hind* saw the *Squirrel*'s light disappear and in the morning there was no sign of her. The little ship had been 'devoured and swallowed up of the sea'.

Failure of an experiment in Virginia

In 1584 Walter Raleigh took up his half-brother's unfinished task, sending out a small reconnaissance party to explore further south. The expedition made its landfall among the islands lying off what is now the coast of North Carolina and went ashore on Roanoke Island, where they found woods full of tall, sweet-smelling timber trees and alive with deer, conies, hares and fowls. The soil was 'the most plentiful, sweet, fruitful and wholesome of all the world', according to Arthur Barlowe, one of the captains, and the natives were friendly, bringing the strangers gifts of melons, walnuts, gourds, cucumbers and corn, or maize, 'which groweth three times in five months'. The Indians readily traded skins for hatchets, knives and axes, but one brave was most pleased with a bright tin dish which he hung round his neck, making signs that it would defend him from his enemies' arrows. Arriving at an Indian village on the north of the island, the English were welcomed by the chieftain's wife, who

Waiting for the tide
Elizabethan seaports, especially those along the southern coasts, were scenes of bustling activity. The quayside buildings in the reconstruction on pages 224–5 are based on surviving buildings in the Barbican area of Plymouth. Bales and barrels of cargo are being loaded and unloaded (1) from the store and warehouses of the wealthy merchants. In the foreground a group of children (2) greet their father, who is approaching in a small boat (3). One of the children carries his midday meal in a covered basket, while gulls hover expectantly overhead. The harbour is crowded with shipping. On the left is a big English galleon (4), probably the flagship of her owner, an eminent Elizabethan of the status of Walter Raleigh or the Earl of Cumberland. His emblem is proudly emblazoned on the stern castle (5), and the great man himself is being rowed out to embark (6). On the right is an armed trading vessel (7), her gun ports visible (8) and her crew working aloft on the rigging (9). In the background are another galleon (10)

dried their wet stockings in front of a great fire, washed their feet in warm water and made 'great haste to dress some meat for us to eat'. They seemed, in fact, to have stumbled on an earthly paradise, inhabited by people 'most gentle, loving and faithful, void of all guile and treason, and such as lived after the manner of the golden age'.

Encouraged by these reports, Walter Raleigh christened the new territory Virginia in honour of the Virgin Queen, the full sunshine of whose favour he was currently enjoying, and in April 1585 a fleet of seven ships under the command of Richard Grenville left for Roanoke Island. A hundred or so colonists were planted there, under the charge of Ralph Lane, one of the Queen's equerries, and Grenville sailed for home in August, promising to return the following spring with supplies and reinforcements.

The experiment was not a success. The settlers relied too heavily on the Indians for food, and as a result their honeymoon period with the tribes quickly came to an end. They also discovered that the islands, so idyllic in fine weather, were unpleasantly exposed to squalls and hurricanes, as well as being surrounded by shoals and shallows which made exploration of the mainland and its resources difficult and dangerous. (The colony of Virginia eventually took root further north, on the shores of Chesapeake Bay.)

Grenville's relief expedition was delayed, and when /continued on page 226

and one of the sturdy, tub-like Dutch trading vessels (11) which constantly plied in and out of the English ports. The surface of the water is alive with small craft passing between the bigger ships as they wait for wind and tide.

continued from page 223/Francis Drake called at Roanoke on his way back from the Indies in June 1586, he found the colonists disillusioned and disenchanted. The opportunity of escape offered by Drake's visit was too tempting to be resisted, and they clamoured to be taken home. When Grenville finally arrived about a month later the settlement was deserted.

In spite of this disappointment, Raleigh was ready to try again. In July 1587 another batch of colonists, this time including some women, was landed on Roanoke, and on August 18 the first English child was born on American soil – a girl christened, inevitably, Virginia. But Walter Raleigh's second attempt at 'the planting of his country of Virginia' was to end in tragedy. Lacking a strong leader, the colonists quarrelled among themselves and insisted on sending their Governor, John White, back to England to organise a regular supply system. White reached Southampton in November and, with the support of Raleigh and Grenville, started equipping another expedition to sail in the spring. But the next year was 1588, the year of the Spanish Armada, and there were no ships to spare for side issues like Virginia. It was 1590 before John White was at last able to set out for America again; when he arrived he found no survivors on Roanoke Island, which became known as the Lost Colony.

This was the end of Elizabethan colonial efforts. By the mid-1590s Grenville was dead and Raleigh's attention had been diverted to Guiana and fruitless voyages up the Orinoco River in search of El Dorado, 'the golden one' – a city believed to exist somewhere on the Amazon where gold was to be had for the picking up. When a permanent settlement was founded on the shores of Chesapeake Bay, it bore the name of another sovereign – Jamestown. But although they had failed, the Elizabethans had led the way. Valuable knowledge and experience had been gained by the pioneers, without which the achievements of the next century would have been impossible. Thomas Hariot, who went with the 1585 expedition as a scientific observer, drew up a *Brief and True Report of the New Found Land of Virginia* which is a classic of its kind, while John White's maps and sketches of the New World provide a unique record of North America in its age of innocence.

Piracy that brought riches – or ruin

Despite a slow start, by the last decade of the Elizabethan period England had emerged as a first-rate maritime power. After the Armada, the Venetian ambassador in Paris remarked that the English had now proved they were the skilled mariners rumour reported them to be, and in 1590 a Dutch merchant living in the Azores gave it as his opinion that the English had become lords and masters of the sea and need care for no one.

Throughout the 1580s and 1590s privateering and the raiding of Spanish ports, begun by Drake in reprisal for San Juan de Ulua, continued unabated. Most of the profits – which in a good year could amount to several hundred thousand pounds – passed into the hands of syndicates of hard-headed merchants in London, Bristol and Plymouth dealing in prize cargoes of relatively prosaic commodities like ginger, sugar, cochineal and hides. But the un-

Proud adventurer
Sir Walter Raleigh was famous for the elegance and extravagance of his dress. This miniature by Nicholas Hilliard shows him wearing a great wheel-ruff edged with lace and a bejewelled cap. From the beginning of his career Raleigh was disliked for his pride and overbearing manner, and nicknamed 'that Great Lucifer' by his enemies.

Landfall in the New World
In 1584 a small reconnaissance party was sent by Sir Walter Raleigh to explore the coast of North America with a view to planting a colony there. The expedition landed on Roanoke Island, off the coast of what is now North Carolina, and returned with such enthusiastic accounts of woods alive with game, and fruitful and wholesome soil which bore three crops of maize in five months, that they seemed to have stumbled on an earthly paradise. They failed to notice that the island, idyllic in fine weather, was subject to violent storms in the hurricane season, and was surrounded by shoals and shallows which made further exploration hazardous.

Their greene corne.

Corne newly sprong.

Their sitting at meate.

The place of solemne prayer.

horse wherin the Tombe of their Herounds standeth.

SECOTON.

A Ceremony in their prayers w
strange iestures and songs dansing.

A welcome turned sour
*The Indian woman welcoming
early settlers in Florida was
painted by John White, the
artist who accompanied Sir
Walter Raleigh on his 1585
expedition. An early reconnaissance party found the native
people 'most gentle, loving and
faithful, void of guile and
treason', and the aborigines
welcomed the strangers as gods.
But this state of affairs did not
survive closer acquaintance.*

Life before the colonists
*This water-colour of the Indian
village of Secoton, North
Carolina, showing the villagers'
huts, their fields of maize, their
'place of solemn prayer', their
religious ceremonies and 'their
sitting at meals', provides a
unique record of North America
in its age of innocence. It was
painted by John White, whose
paintings and maps remained
the authority for this part of
the coast until long after his
own day.*

quenchable hope of one day seizing some great merchant ship stuffed with gold
and spices, such as would make a man rich beyond his dreams, operated
powerfully on all sorts and conditions of the Queen's subjects. Outstanding
among them were men like Walter Raleigh and the Earl of Cumberland, who
financed and led their own expeditions, but nearly all the leading figures at
Court put money into privateering ventures. The Queen herself was often a
shareholder, more than once going into partnership with the Earl of Cumberland in his regular prize-hunting forays.

In 1592 one such venture, financed jointly by the Queen, Cumberland,
Walter Raleigh and a group of London businessmen intercepted a huge
Portuguese carrack homeward-bound from the East Indies. The *Madre de Dios*
– at 1,600 tons one of the largest ships afloat – was laden with gemstones and
spices, perfumes and rare drugs, with silks and calicoes, priceless Oriental
carpets and porcelain, elephants' teeth, coconuts and ivory, and was probably
the richest prize ever taken. There was an orgy of looting and wild scenes at
Plymouth, as the London dealers jostled one another on the quayside to buy up
treasures dirt-cheap from ignorant seamen. Robert Cecil, old Lord Burghley's
son and a rising man in the government, who was sent hurrying down to
restore order, swore that everyone he met within 7 miles of Exeter stank of
musk and ambergris.

Windfalls like the *Madre de Dios* were rare. By no means every privateering
expedition showed a profit, and some of the gentlemen amateurs ruined
themselves. The Earl of Cumberland himself died heavily in debt. Nor did all the
English sea-dogs triumph over the Spaniards. Drake's friend John Oxenham
attempted to seize the Isthmus of Panama and cut off the Peruvian silver
carried overland from Panama, but was himself captured and hanged, while
many another Elizabethan seaman, falling into Spanish hands, ended his days
on the gallows, at the stake or as a galley slave chained to an oar.

Cannons and trumpets sound at Drake's death

As time went on, the Spaniards learned how to defend themselves and their
treasure more efficiently. When Francis Drake led his last expedition to the
Indies in 1596 he found that times had changed. The good old days when
Spain's colonial outposts had been a happy hunting ground for roving bands
of marauders were gone for ever. The expedition failed in its twin objectives of
taking a galleon laden with gold and silver ducats stranded at Porto Rico, and
cutting the treasure trail across the isthmus. The old pirate's luck had turned
at last. Drake died of a virulent form of dysentery somewhere off Puerto Bello.
They buried him at sea, 'slung atween the round shot in Nombre Dios Bay', as
Henry Newbolt's poem recalls, saluted by all the cannon in the fleet, 'the
trumpets in doleful manner echoing out this lamentation for so great a loss'.

Exploration went on, of course. Ten years earlier Thomas Cavendish had left
Plymouth to emulate Drake's great feat of circumnavigation. He followed
Drake's course through the Straits of Magellan and, like Drake, raided the
coasts of Chile and Peru, although less profitably. He did, however, succeed in

A briefe and true report of the new found land of Virginia:

of the commodities there found and to be raysed, as well marchantable, as others for victuall, building and other necessarie vses for those that are and shalbe the planters there; and of the nature and manners of the naturall inhabitants : Discouered by the *English Colony there seated by* Sir Richard Greinuile *Knight in the* yeere 1585. which remained vnder the gouernment of Rafe Lane Esquier, one of her Maiesties Equieres, during the space of twelue monethes : at the speciall charge and direction of the Honourable SIR WALTER RALEIGH Knight, Lord Warden of the stanneries ; who therein hath beene fauoured and authorised by her Maiestie and her letters patents:

Directed to the Aduenturers, Fauourers,

andWelwillers of the action, for the inhabiting and planting there:

By *Thomas Hariot*; seruant to the abouenamed *Sir Walter*, a member of the Colony, and there imployed in discouering.

Imprinted at London 1588.

A 'brief and true' report
Thomas Hariot, an observer with an interest in mathematics, astronomy, anthropology and navigation, possessed a truly scientific mind. He accompanied the Virginia expedition of 1585, and his Brief and True Report is a sober and accurate account of the flora and fauna of the new-found land of Virginia, based on careful observation. It describes the nature of the soil, the manners and customs of the native people and their methods of agriculture, as well as their ideas and beliefs, for Hariot learned enough of their language to be able to communicate with them.

Bird of good omen
The long, slender wings, hooked beak and forked tail of the frigate bird of the South Atlantic are accurately caught in John White's drawing. The frigate bird does not alight on water, so the sight of it was welcomed by mariners as a sign that land was near. To most people in Britain, however, such birds were as believable – or unbelievable – as tales of sea-serpents, unicorns, or men whose heads grew beneath their shoulders.

capturing the *Santa Ana*, a galleon eastward bound from Manila laden with silks and other rich goods from China. He returned by way of Java, across the Indian Ocean and round the Cape of Good Hope. Cavendish was the first Englishman to call at St Helena, and arrived home just in time to hear of the defeat of the Armada.

For every 'prosperous voyage', however, there were two or three which ended in disaster. A well-equipped expedition led by John Fenton and aiming for China achieved nothing. The fleet hung about off the coast of West Africa while the captains quarrelled about the course and the crews died of fever, and eventually returned home empty-handed. Another West Country venture was baulked in the Straits of Magellan by contrary winds and storms. Two of the ships foundered with all hands and a third was wrecked off Cherbourg on the homeward voyage, so that only four out of the original crews of more than 300 men survived.

Eastward bound, in search of trade

In 1591 Thomas Cavendish set out again for the Far East with three large and two small ships, and this voyage, like Fenton's, ended in tragedy. The ships were rotten, there was no spare canvas or cordage, provisions were short, the weather bad and there was dissension among the officers. The result was a nightmare of sickness, starvation and suffering. A crew member on board the *Desire*, captained by John Davis, records that 'our men were not able to move; their sinews were stiff, and their flesh dead, and many of them (which is most lamentable to be reported) were so eaten with lice, as that in their flesh did lie clusters of lice as big as peason, yea and some as big as beans'. In the Straits of Magellan the starving men killed penguins for food, but the meat putrefied, breeding a plague of maggots – 'a most loathsome and ugly worm an inch long' – which threatened to devour the ship. 'The more we laboured to kill them, the more they increased; so that at the last we could not sleep for them, but they would eat our flesh and bite like mosquitos.'

Soon after this, a horrible form of scurvy broke out. 'Our men began to fall sick of such a monstrous disease as the like was never heard of; for in their ankles it began to swell; from thence in two days it would be in their breasts, so that they could not draw their breath . . . For all this divers grew raging mad, and some died in most loathsome and furious pain. It were incredible to write our misery as it was; there was no man in perfect health but the captain and one boy.' Out of a crew of 91 only 16 survived this terrible ordeal, and of the 16 only five were in a state to work the ship and get her back to Ireland.

The chief motivating force behind all this suffering and endeavour was the search for trade, becoming more and more necessary as the war with Spain closed so many of England's traditional European markets. Trade with the Baltic, which yielded timber, tar, turpentine, hemp and flax, and nitre for gunpowder, in exchange for kerseys (woollens) and other cloths, was very important and continued under the control of the Eastland Company, as did the Muscovy Company's operations in Russia. But the lure of the East was

The fish that flies
John White's drawing of a flying fish is typical of his carefully observed studies of the creatures of the New World. The Elizabethan explorers saw many strange sights, and brought home travellers' tales that were often greeted with scepticism at home. White's studies enabled the interested few to separate fact from fantasy.

Plant with a future
*Of all the plants introduced
from the New World, the
humble potato was to have the
greatest effect. Its first mention
in print occurs in 1596; the
plant is here seen in an
illustration from John Gerarde's
Herball of the following year.
In the early days the true
Virginian potato was often
confused with the sweet potato,
or yam, a native of Mexico.
Potatoes, like tomatoes or 'love-
apples', were originally thought
to possess aphrodisiac qualities.
Walter Raleigh is traditionally
credited with introducing the
potato into Ireland, with far-
reaching consequences.*

still strong, and in the early 1580s steps were taken to revive England's trade with the Levant. An experienced and influential merchant, William Harborne, was sent to Constantinople as ambassador to the Sultan's Court, a new Company – the Turkey or Levant Company – was set up, and in spite of some trouble with pirates in the Mediterranean, a flourishing commerce developed. The Turkey merchants exported English cloth, tin, pewter and rabbit skins and imported silk and cotton goods, carpets, currants, olive oil, soap, indigo and spices.

In India, a step towards an empire

Looking further afield, two adventurous English traders, John Newbury and Ralph Fitch, pioneered the overland route to India, sailing from Falmouth to the Middle East in the *Tiger*. Newbury and Fitch travelled across the Syrian desert by camel-train and on down the Euphrates to Babylon. Soon afterwards they came upon a strange sight, pointed out by the locals as the entrance to Hell – 'a mouth that doth continually throw forth against the air boiling pitch with a filthy smoke'. It was oil, of course. They reached Ormuz on the Persian Gulf, where they fell foul of the Portuguese, and from thence to India. In Goa they were thrown into prison again, but escaped and penetrated to the Court of the Great Mogul at Agra and Fatipur.

After this Newbury turned for home, but vanished somewhere along the route. Fitch went on, down the Ganges, by sea to Pegu (Burma), to Siam and the Malay coast. He survived and got home after an epic journey lasting eight years, to find he had been presumed dead and his goods divided.

Virginia's staple crop
*Tobacco was introduced from
America by John Hawkins at
least as early as 1565 and was
originally prized as a medicinal
plant for purging the body of
'superfluous phlegm and other
gross humours'. The habit of
smoking tobacco in a long-
stemmed clay pipe was made
fashionable at Court by Walter
Raleigh, and rapidly became
popular with all classes. By the
end of the Queen's reign, the
English were to be observed
constantly puffing tobacco at
public gatherings. It became the
staple crop of the new colony
of Virginia and enabled the
American settlements to
survive economically.*

Fashionable fruit
The 'pyne frute' or pineapple, a native of Central and Southern America brought home by the explorers, became a popular table delicacy in Europe. It was also often carved in stone as an architectural motif. The pineapple remains a tropical fruit, but many other flowers and fruits introduced from the New World, such as the nasturtium, the Michaelmas daisy, the lobelia, the tomato and the potato, have settled comfortably into English gardens.

Meanwhile, the 'direct' sea route to the East via the Cape of Good Hope was being explored by the English – and the Dutch. After several false starts and the usual quota of calamities, James Lancaster (who was learning to defeat scurvy by dosing his men with lime juice) finally got through, laded pepper at Sumatra, established an English 'factory' or trading post in Java and returned safely with all his four ships. In January 1601 the East India Company received its royal charter, and the first steps towards empire had been taken.

Not that the idea of empire had yet occurred to anyone, except possibly a few visionaries like John Dee and Richard Hakluyt. It would be easy to exaggerate the effect of oceanic exploration on the ordinary men and women of Elizabethan England, the great majority of whom lived out their lives without ever seeing the sea, let alone a foreign country. News of great exploits such as Francis Drake's voyage round the world, the defeat of the Armada or the Earl of Essex's triumphant raid on Cadiz spread by word of mouth and were celebrated in ballads and broadsheets; but less spectacular achievements, even if more important from the commercial and geographical point of view, were of interest only in seafaring and trading circles. The Queen encouraged any promising-looking trading enterprise, but cherished no dreams of empire and had invested neither ships nor capital in any of Raleigh's colonial ventures.

Like the Eskimos and Red Indian braves occasionally brought home as trophies, the new foods – the potato, the tomato and Indian corn – were long regarded as mere curiosities. It would be for the next generation, who found things less to their liking at home, to take seriously to the idea of making a new life in a New World.

'Revenge' commander
Richard Grenville is best remembered for his epic fight off Flores in the Azores in August 1591. Grenville, commanding the 500 ton Revenge, *was cut off by a Spanish fleet and insisted on taking on the enemy single-handed. When most of the crew had been killed and he himself fatally wounded, Grenville ordered the master gunner to blow up the* Revenge. *But the surviving crew members insisted on surrender, and Grenville, a harsh-tempered, violent man, was carried on board the Spanish flagship. There he died, grumbling about those traitors who had crossed his will.*

233

Hearts of oak

SHIPWRIGHTS GIVE THE NAVY A FAST-MOVING FLEET TO SCATTER THE ARMADA

The Elizabethan navy which fought the Spanish Armada in 1588 was quite a small fleet. It numbered only 34 ships, of which no more than 21 were of the first line, and even these varied considerably in tonnage and fighting power. The ships were not kept continually at sea. It was very expensive to keep a sizeable warship in commission, and except in time of danger or when they were being used for a special expedition the royal ships were laid up in harbour and their crews paid off. But when the Queen's navy did take to the sea it was among the best afloat. In times of emergency it was supplemented by privately owned armed merchantmen, and other smaller craft including fishing vessels and coasters. Against the Armada, these totalled about 140.

Before Elizabethan days, a warship was regarded as being little more than a floating platform for artillery and soldiers, who would grapple and board the enemy. The mobile fighting ship armed with heavy guns capable of firing broadside was still a comparatively new development, but it was one in which English sailors and shipwrights had taken the lead. The traditional tall, top-heavy galleons had their high forecastles and sterncastles lowered, and new vessels were built to a sleeker, modern design.

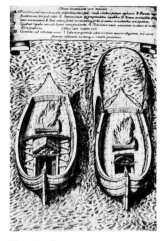

Floating furnaces
Fire was the greatest hazard facing any 16th-century ship, with its mass of highly inflammable timber, cordage and sails. Fire-ships – small unmanned vessels filled with pitch and dry timber and sometimes with gunpowder – would be set alight and cast adrift where the wind could carry them into the enemy at anchor.

On the drawing board
Elizabethan shipwrights are shown at work in an illustration to a manual on shipbuilding by Matthew Baker who, with Peter Pett, was one of the Queen's shipwrights at the royal dock-yard at Chatham. Under the supervision of John Hawkins they were largely responsible for building and rebuilding the navy to the new designs.

A new fighting ship

A design by Matthew Baker shows the new type of English warship. It has less freeboard, or distance from deck to waterline, than its predecessors, and less clumsy masts and rigging. His studies of the fish led Baker to give his ship a longer keel in proportion to the beam than earlier vessels, giving greater manoeuvrability.

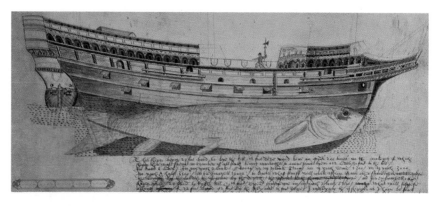

Fire from the sea

The English dealt the Armada a crippling blow when they sent fireships into the Spanish fleet as it lay anchored off Calais (below). The Spanish commanders fled in confusion, and their troubles were aggravated by lack of food, water, ammunition and a deep-water anchorage. The towering forecastles make the Spanish ships look huge, but in fact there was little difference in tonnage between the Spanish and English ships. The biggest ship in either fleet was the 1,100 ton Triumph, commanded by the English seadog Martin Frobisher.

Spanish supply ship

El Gran Grifon, 'The Griffin', was the flagship of the 25 supply ships which accompanied the Spanish Armada. She was wrecked off Norway.

England's flagship

The Ark Royal was the flagship of the English Admiral, Lord Howard of Effingham, in the battle against the Armada. Reputedly unmatched for sailing qualities, she was a good example of the new design of warship, built low at the head but high at the stern.

Help from the skies for a wandering mariner
*In an age of expansion and exploration, mathematicians and astronomers all over Europe turned
their attention to improving means of navigation, and numerous learned manuals made their appearance throughout
the 16th century. Sightings were particularly difficult to take from the decks of pitching vessels,
and the mariner in this illustration from Jacques de Vault's* Cosmographia *of 1583 has taken his navigational
instrument ashore on a tropical island to determine his position by the stars.*

CHAPTER NINE

Scientists and charlatans

AS COAL, IRON AND WOOL START AN INDUSTRIAL
REVOLUTION, ALCHEMISTS STILL SEEK MAGIC GOLD AND DOCTORS
LOOK TO THE STARS AND THE 'HUMOURS'

Come, Mephistophiles, let us dispute again,
And argue of divine Astrology.
Tell me, are there many heavens above the moon?
Are all celestial bodies but one globe,
As is the substance of this centric earth?   Christopher Marlowe, *Dr Faustus*

*I*n an age which has come to take marvels such as colour television, supersonic flight and organ transplants for granted, it is easy to underestimate the scientific achievements of the time of Elizabeth. In fact, the second half of the 16th century saw the beginning of a great revolution in man's attitude to the nature of his environment, and the dawn of a new rational approach to physical science by a pioneering band of astronomers, mathematicians and geographers.

The most influential of these pioneers was a Polish physician and astronomer, Nicolaus Copernicus who, in 1543, first put forward the view that the earth rotated on its axis and, with the other planets, orbited around the sun. This notion ran directly counter to the previously accepted picture of an immutable universe drawn by the ancients, who saw the earth as a fixed centre around which the sun and other heavenly bodies revolved in separate, concentric spheres.

Copernicus himself, a cautious man, did not claim the results of his observations and calculations to be more than an informed guess, and they were not finally confirmed until Johannes Kepler and Galileo published their treatises early in the 17th century, but his ideas were taken up eagerly by other astronomers and gained a number of supporters in Tudor England. Robert Recorde, John Field, John Dee, Thomas Digges, William Gilbert and Thomas Hariot were all 'Copernicans' and kept in close touch with their European colleagues; John Dee, in particular, had an international reputation among scholars and scientists.

Outside scientific circles, most people preferred to go on believing in the traditional plan of the cosmos laid down by the Egyptian astronomer Ptolemy in the 2nd century AD, which had become deeply embedded in the language of poetry, philosophy and daily life. Of far greater interest to most people was the closely related 'science' of astrology – the Elizabethans frequently used the terms 'astronomy' and 'astrology' interchangeably. In the 16th-century context this was quite logical. Astronomy was the study of the stars and their movements, while astrology was the no-less-important study of the effects of those movements. It was widely believed that the planets and the signs of the Zodiac exercised a profound influence over human affairs and that men's fates and natures were governed by their stars, so that many prominent Elizabethans were in the habit of consulting their favourite astrologer before taking

The 'wizard' from Wales
The Welshman John Dee (1527–1608) was an eminent scholar of wide-ranging interests. He was highly respected as a mathematician, geographer and astronomer, but he was also cloudily obsessed with astrology and other, more occult arts. The Queen was interested in Dee's work, and fixed the day of her coronation by his astrological advice. During her reign she visited Dee more than once at his house at Mortlake, and gave him her personal assurance that he might do what he would in philosophy and alchemy and none should 'check, control or molest' him.

Johannes Dee.
Anglus
Londinensis
Æt. suæ
67

ISRAELIS VICTRIX SACRA

Est PETRUS a Superis mihi datum nomen in Astris
Incola mox fuium dum TUBA cantar adest
Subditus [et] Daemon [et] virtute gemiscit
Euge! animi mactus, Victor ab hoste redis

any important decision in the course of their lives.

It was customary in upper-class families to have horoscopes cast for their children. Astrologers based their calculations on 'nativities' – that is, on maps of the sky as it appeared at the moment of a client's birth. By comparing the inborn tendencies revealed by the nativity with what was known of the future movements of the heavens, they were able to make 'elections' – that is, to choose the best times for cutting hair or nails, having a bath, taking physic, having blood let or undergoing surgery. Medicine and astrology were still closely allied, for just as it was believed that the moon caused madness, so it was thought that the various parts of the human body were ruled by particular signs of the Zodiac.

The astrologer also advised his clients as to the most propitious moment for starting on a journey, getting married, closing a business deal or applying for a new job. The Queen herself had consulted Dr Dee over the date of her coronation. Most astrologers were prepared to answer all kinds of personal questions concerning sex, the interpretation of dreams, when a rich relative was likely to die, how a business venture was likely to prosper, and so on.

The fortune-telling aspect of astrology was frowned on by the Church, and the Puritan writer Philip Stubbes vigorously denounced all 'astrologers, astronomers and prognosticators'. Their art, he said, was based on nothing but 'mere conjectures, supposals, likelihoods, guesses . . . conjunction of signs, stars, and planets, with their aspects and occurrents, and the like, and not upon any certain ground, knowledge, or truth, either of God or of natural

Goddess of love and joy
A lightly clad Venus (left) holds a horn and scroll inscribed with symbols. The illustration is from an astrological work by John Dee, Tuba Veneris, *'The Horn of Venus'. All Elizabethans believed to some extent in the principles of astrology, which held that men's destinies were shaped and governed by the heavenly bodies. The planet Venus naturally came to be associated with the Roman goddess of beauty and sensual love, and in astrology signified joyfulness, laughter, dancers, players, musicians and messengers of love.*

A soul for sale
Christopher Marlowe wrote his Tragical Historie of Dr. Faustus *in about 1592, not long before his death. Based on the character of Johann Faust or Faustus, a German magician and astrologer supposed to have possessed supernatural powers, the play mirrored the popular interest in such matters, and enjoyed an immediate success. Faust is said to have sold his soul to the Devil in exchange for another 24 years of life in which he would have all pleasure and all knowledge at his command. Many versions of the story have appeared over the centuries.*

A teller of fortunes
The zodiacal signs at the side of this illustration indicate the fortune-teller's stock-in-trade. Almost every Elizabethan would at some crisis in his or her life consult an astrologer, fortune-teller or other 'wise man'. Many prominent men – the Earl of Leicester among them – employed a private astrologer and seldom took an important decision without his advice.

reason'. As time went on, a new mood of scepticism and commonsense was beginning to reject the more obvious absurdities of astrology, so that by the end of the Elizabethan age it was falling into disrepute and into the hands of charlatans and swindlers. All the same, there is no doubt that the popular passion for astrology had served to stimulate the serious study of astronomy.

Another branch of science which depended on an improved understanding of astronomy was oceanic navigation. Here the Spanish and Portuguese were the pioneers, and the English mariners profited by their experience. However, since the English did much of their sailing in northern waters they soon encountered special problems. Apart from the variation of the compass and oceanic currents which could take a ship several hundred miles off course, there was the added difficulty of fog and cloud which sometimes made observation of the stars impossible for days at a time. This stimulated work on developing the compass, in which the English took the lead.

In 1574 William Bourne of Gravesend, a gunner by profession, published a standard manual on navigation in which he gave instructions on how to find the latitude 'where the sun doth not set under the horizon'. He provided tables of the sun's declination north or south of the celestial equator by which to calculate latitude, and urged ships' masters to record the variation of the compass 'at every place they come to'. In 1585 Robert Norman, a seaman and compassmaker, announced his important discovery of the dip of the magnetic needle – the result of 20 years' experience at sea.

Instruments to aid navigation at sea

By this time the best mathematical brains in the country were applying themselves to the problems of navigation, and much useful work was being done on navigational instruments. Thomas Hood of Cambridge had designed a new cross-staff described as 'perhaps the first nautical instrument devised to measure the sun's altitude by indirect observation'. William Barlow, the son of a bishop, invented an improved compass, and Thomas Hariot designed an improved device for taking altitudes at sea, called a back-staff because the observer turned his back to the sun, so avoiding glare. He also compiled the first table of amplitudes – the angular distance of the sun from the horizon – which made it possible to correct the compass daily at sea, at sunrise or sunset.

Elizabethan scientists were practical men who did not remain secluded in their studies or laboratories. On the contrary, they frequently accompanied the explorers to test their navigational and mathematical theories in the field. Nor did they attempt to confine themselves to a single discipline. 'I have taken all knowledge to be my province,' wrote Francis Bacon, the great Elizabethan intellectual – a claim which seemed in no way unreasonable to his contemporaries. Thomas Digges, the astronomer who was among the first to come to terms with the concept of an infinite universe, did not think it beneath his dignity to apply his mathematical genius to the more mundane matters of military fortification and ballistics. William Gilbert, whose work in the field of electro-magnetism set English science on the road to the discoveries of Isaac

A sighting at sea

A compass, indicating the position of north, and a primitive form of sextant, measuring the angle of the sun's rays, enable a mariner aboard a wave-tossed vessel to calculate his approximate longitude. Precise time-keeping was necessary to fix longitude with any precision, and accurate calculation only became possible in the 18th century with the development of a chronometer suitable for use at sea.

Rings around the globe

The armillary sphere – this one is dated 1568 – was a skeleton celestial globe, consisting of metal rings revolving on a central axis within a wooden horizon. The rings represent the equator, the tropics, the arctic and antarctic circles and the two colures, or great circles, which intersect at the poles and divide the equinoctial and ecliptic into four equal parts.

Newton and Michael Faraday, was also a well-known medical practitioner and President of the Royal College of Physicians.

Gilbert's mind was essentially modern; the Welshman John Dee, probably the best remembered Elizabethan scientist, was more representative of his age. Dee's obsession with astrology and the cabbalistic arts has damaged his reputation as a serious scholar, but he was in fact a man of enormous learning; another mathematical genius and an experimental and theoretical scientist second to none in his time.

A vain search for the 'philosopher's stone'

The Queen took a serious interest in Dee's work and visited him more than once at his house by the Thames at Mortlake. On one of these occasions she came with the Court and Privy Council, intending to inspect his famous library of more than 4,000 books, but hearing that his wife had just died, she contented herself with taking a look at his 'magic mirror' – perhaps a telescope – which he brought out to her. 'Her Majesty,' says Dee, 'being taken down from her horse by the Earl of Leicester at the church wall at Mortlake, did see some of the properties of that glass, to her Majesty's great delight.' On another occasion, when Elizabeth was passing through Mortlake in her coach on her way from Richmond to London, she turned down by the church to stop at Dee's garden gate, beckoning him to come and kiss her hand and asking him 'to resort to her court'.

THE MARINERS MIRROVR
Wherin may playnly be seen the courses, heights, distances, depths, soundings, flouds and ebs, risings of lands, rocks, sands and shoalds, with the marks for thentrings of the Harbouroughs, Havens and Ports of the greatest part of Europe: their seuerall traficks and commodities. Together with the Rules and instrumēts of NAVIGATION.
First made & set foorth in diuers exact Sea Charts, by that famous Nauigator Lvke Wagenar of Enchuisen. And now fitted with necessarie additions for the use of Englishmen by ANTHONY ASHLEY.
Herein also may be understood the chiefe exploits lately atchiued by the right Honoable the L. Admirall of England &c, with her Maiestie Nauie: and some former seruices don by Sr that worthy Knight, Sr FRANCIS DRAKE.

244

Dee was an earnest and influential promoter of oceanic exploration and expansion. He was consulted by all the voyagers, especially in connection with the North-West and North-East Passages, and it was he who first used the phrase 'the British Empire', in connection with ocean voyages and colonies in the New World. But forward-looking though he was in some respects, he also wasted time and energy down the unprofitable blind-alleys of alchemy, searching for the elixir of life and the so-called 'philosopher's stone' which, it was optimistically believed, could turn base metals into gold.

Alchemy was founded on the false theory of the essential unity of matter. The alchemists assumed that all substances were composed of one primitive matter, capable of taking on different forms by the imposition of different qualities, such as heat, cold, dryness and moisture. It therefore seemed to follow that if these qualities could be abstracted by chemical processes, the primitive matter could be laid bare, and by further treatment transformed into whatever substance was required. Alchemy was officially illegal in England, and Dr Dee, who had been appointed royal adviser on mystic secrets, pursued his arcane researches under royal protection.

In 1565 a Dutchman, Cornelius de Lannoy, was allowed to set up a laboratory in Somerset House, on the strength of his promise to produce 50,000 marks worth of pure gold annually at a moderate charge; but two years later he had been committed to the Tower for deceiving the Queen's majesty. All the same, the hope of finding some method of transmuting base metal into gold naturally died hard, and as late as the 1590s Lord Burghley was trying to find out if there was any truth in the claims of a certain Edward Kelly to have discovered a 'magic powder' which could perform the desired transformation.

On a more practical level, the science of metallurgy was well developed, especially in Germany. The uses and properties of the principal metals and their alloys were known and understood by all the advanced nations, and by

Charting the oceans

The early Elizabethan voyagers sailed on literally uncharted oceans. The only charts then available were little more than mere maps of the European coastlines. The first marine atlas was published in Antwerp in 1584, and appeared in this English translation (left) four years later. Down the side of its ornate title page appear navigational instruments in use at the time: quadrant, mariner's astrolabe, cross-staff, lead-line, dividers and compass.

Tools for the navigator

The increase in ocean voyaging brought an urgent need for improved navigational aids. Instrument-makers showed ingenuity and skill in producing devices such as the navigational dividers and the compass. English sailors, particularly, needed an improved compass, because they did much of their sailing in northern waters where weather conditions could make astronomical observations impossible for days at a time. Its basis was an iron needle, magnetised by a lodestone to point to the north and pivoting on a central pin around a card marked with the principal directions.

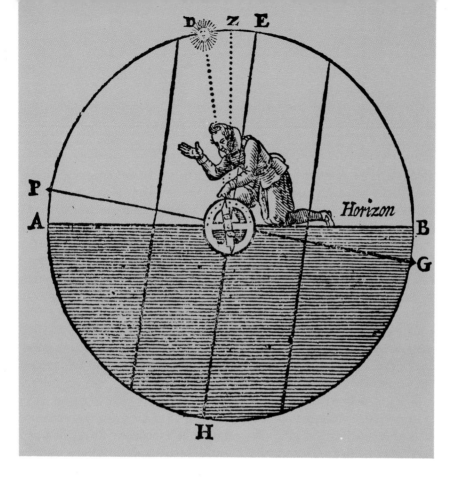

the late 1560s brass was being manufactured for the first time in England, with the assistance of German capital and expertise.

The branch of science which affected the ordinary man and woman most directly was medicine, but in this field few noticeable advances were made during the Elizabethan period. The English medical profession was already well organised. The College of Physicians had been established in 1518 and the Company of Barber Surgeons in 1540, but although Henry VIII founded professorships of medicine at Oxford and Cambridge, most ambitious young doctors preferred to go abroad to study if they could.

Four 'humours' that ruled the body's health

A great deal of valuable new medical research was going on in the European universities during the 16th century, especially at Padua and Basle, but in England the College of Physicians still clung obstinately to the medieval theory of 'humours'. This held that four humours, or fluids, went to make up the composition of the human body – blood, phlegm, yellow bile or choler, and black bile or melancholy – and that a predominance of any one of these determined the temperament of the individual as sanguine, phlegmatic, choleric or melancholic. In a healthy person the humours were more or less evenly balanced. Disease was caused by an excess of blood, phlegm or black or yellow bile, for which the only remedy was to try to restore the balance by diet, bleeding or purging. Upper-class Elizabethans were much addicted to swallowing purgatives in order to keep themselves 'in health' – a habit strongly

Measuring the heavens
Many of the instruments which early astronomers used to measure sun and star altitudes were works of art in themselves. The astrolabe (below) consisted of brass rings, divided into degrees and representing the sky and the relative position of certain fixed stars, with a movable sight rule pivoting upon the centre. The user rotated the sight rule until it pointed at the star, then read off the altitude on the outer ring. Mariners used simplified astrolabes to determine latitude and time, and illustrated handbooks (left) showed navigators how to use them in various circumstances – including 'How you shall find the height when you are right under the sun'. Francis Drake took a special interest in all navigational instruments, and whenever he captured a prize ship he always looked first at the charts, astrolabes and compasses carried on board.

discouraged by the Queen, because it meant that useful councillors and courtiers were liable to be out of action for days as a result.

Surgeons ranked below physicians in the professional hierarchy, and the College of Physicians did its best to prevent them from practising physic, although in the provinces and country places surgeons often seem to have set up as general practitioners. There was no surgery as the term is understood today. A person who developed appendicitis was likely to die of it. Surgeons studying anatomy were permitted to dissect the corpses of convicts, but their day-to-day work consisted chiefly of letting blood by cupping or leeches, lancing abscesses, treating wounds and fractures, performing amputations (usually cauterising the stump with pitch) and pulling teeth, the only form of dentistry available, and all without the benefit of anaesthetics.

The humblest members of the medical profession were the apothecaries, who belonged to the grocers' guilds and sold sweets, perfumes, cosmetics and fancy goods as well as drugs. A compound known as Venice treacle was a favourite medicament, but towards the end of the period new drugs like senna, aloes and nux vomica were coming into use as a result of increasing trade with the east.

The usual fee for a doctor's visit seems to have been an angel – a gold coin worth ten shillings. This was beyond the means of poorer people, who therefore relied either on home doctoring and their granny's herbal recipes, on the services of the local white witch or on the numerous quacks who practised

Lessons of the lodestone
The typical Elizabethan scientist was the mathematician, and the age produced several who did pioneer work in the closely related fields of astronomy and navigation. In this engraving by Johannes Stradanus, an astronomer-mathematician named Flavius seeks a way of calculating longitude by using the magnetic properties of the lodestone which floats on a board in a bowl of water in the foreground. A pet dog lies at the foot of his master's chair, and other instruments of the cosmographer – globe, hour-glass, sextant – fill the study.

under a limited licence granted by the Barber Surgeons. As the name suggests, barbers also practised as surgeons, and let blood as well as shaving people; the striped red and white barber's pole is a relic of this. (The trade of barber was not separated from the practice of surgery until 1745.) Other unqualified practitioners travelled round the country to the annual fairs under no licence at all, peddling their pills and potions to a credulous public.

Poor people, of course, suffered from all the ills associated with lack of hygiene, bad housing and inadequate diet. Farm labourers and their wives became twisted with rheumatism as a result of being out of doors in all weathers and living in damp, cold cottages. By the end of the winter, especially after a bad harvest, the poor would often have a mild form of scurvy caused by diet deficiencies. Typhus, variously known as gaol fever or ship fever, was endemic in the slums – no one had yet recognised that it was carried by lice – and was only remarked upon when a judge or magistrate caught it from the prisoners he was trying.

Sickness from poor food and hard living

Most illnesses were no respecters of rank. Rich as well as poor lived in draughty, uncomfortable conditions and suffered from colds, coughs and rheumatism. High-born ladies, surrounded by the best available attention, died of puerperal sepsis, or childbed fever, just as often as the labourer's wife giving birth with the assistance of the village midwife, or with no assistance at

Disappointed genius
Philosopher, natural scientist, essayist, lawyer and indefatigable seeker after knowledge, Francis Bacon (far left) possessed one of the most brilliant and wide-ranging minds of the Elizabethan age. Able, ambitious and well-connected, the young Bacon seemed set for an equally brilliant public career. But although the Queen appeared to enjoy his conversation and occasionally took his advice, she thought him unreliable and consistently refused him preferment. For all his intellectual attainments, Bacon suffered a lifetime of disappointment and frustration. This page from one of Bacon's notebooks (left) describes improvements he planned to make to his garden at Gorhambury, Hertfordshire. They include a lake with various islands, one 'where the fayre hornbeam stands with a stand in it and seats underneath', one 'with rock', one 'with a grotto' and another 'mounted with flowers in ascents'.

A surgeon's silver
However primitive the instruments used in medicine and surgery even in royal palaces, they were ornamented with the extravagance typical of the period. This silver instrument box belonged to John Vicary, chief surgeon to Henry VIII. It bears the royal arms in enamel. Vicary was Master of the Barbers' Company in 1540, when it united with the Fellowship of Surgeons to form the Company of Barber Surgeons.

The quest for gold
In the heart of a furnace, this hopeful alchemist seeks the magic reaction which will turn base metals into gold or silver. The practice of alchemy, officially illegal in England, continued in secret. It was a complex blend of astrology, chemistry and magic, founded on the false theory that all substances were composed of one matter.

all. Young girls suffered from green-sickness, a form of anaemia, and rich and poor alike died of tuberculosis, a complaint which carried off at least three members of the royal house of Tudor, while many undiagnosed cases of 'wasting sickness' were probably cancers of stomach or bowel.

Rich and poor alike suffered from dysentery, caused by tainted food and known as the flux, sometimes the bloody flux, for which the remedy was the application of a drench, or enema. Rich and poor also came down with ague, a form of malaria endemic in the numerous undrained, marshy areas of Elizabethan England, such as the Fen Country, the Thames estuary and in London itself, around Lambeth and Westminster. The most prevalent variety in England was 'benign tertian' in which the ague, or feverish, shivering fits occurred every third day. In quartan ague, the parasites took 72 hours to mature, causing a fit every fourth day. English malaria, of course, was nowhere near as serious as the malignant form found in the tropics, where as early as 1572 the merchant Henry Hawks had noticed a connection between the mosquito and the disease.

Upper-class Elizabethans were martyrs to gout – which was probably more often arthritis, another condition unknown to Tudor medicine – and to stone in the kidneys. They were extremely health-conscious, and their letters are full of detailed descriptions of their aches and pains, and the remedies they were trying. Some took the waters at Bath, or at Buxton in Derbyshire, a fashionable Elizabethan spa. No doubt the poor suffered just as severely, but they suffered

Equipment for the surgeon
The sight of this travelling sur-
geon's chest, with its gruesome
array of pincers, knives and
scissors, can have done little to
reassure the trembling patient.
The illustration appears in a
manual for surgeons by William
Clowes, published in 1588.
Surgery, still largely a matter
of amputations, blood-letting,
setting broken bones and pulling
teeth, did begin to make some
advances under the stimulus of
the Spanish war, which made
work on the treatment of gun-
shot wounds a question of
urgent practical necessity.
Clowes himself worked as a
surgeon with the army and
navy in action.

in silence, having neither the skill to record their symptoms nor the opportunity to do anything much to alleviate them.

One disease which apparently claimed a higher mortality from the upper-classes was the so-called sweating sickness, thought to have been introduced into England by the mercenary soldiers who accompanied Henry VII from France in 1485. The 'sweat' sounds like a particularly virulent form of influenza, often fatal within hours, and remained a scourge throughout the first half of the Tudor century, before it suddenly vanished or mutated.

Another scourge which hung heavily over Elizabethan England was the plague or Black Death. There were two forms of this particular horror – pneumonic, which caused acute inflammation of the lungs and was the deadlier of the two, and bubonic, which affected the lymphatic glands, producing the characteristic buboes, or black swellings, in groin and armpit. The two forms were often present together, and the great epidemic which swept across Europe in the 14th century, decimating whole populations, was probably chiefly pneumonic.

The lonely deaths of victims of the plague

Of all the ills which Elizabethan flesh was heir to, none was more dreaded than the plague, partly no doubt because of the sense of helplessness it brought – during a bad outbreak there was literally nothing anyone could do about it – and partly because of the terror of being left to die alone. 'If a man be sick of a fever,' remarked the preacher William Bridge, 'it is some comfort that he can take a bed-staff and knock, and his servant comes up and helps him with a cordial. But if a man be sick of the plague, then he sits and lies all alone.'

Another frightening aspect of the plague was its mysteriousness. No one knew 'whence it cometh, whereof it ariseth and wherefore it is sent', although various explanations were offered – the most popular being that it was God's instrument for the punishment of sin. Another suggestion was corruption of the air – and as recently as 1891 it was being said that plague was a soil poison generated by the products of decay. A third explanation was astrological. It was noted during the 1603 epidemic, that there was a conjunction of Saturn and Jupiter in Sagittarius, preceded by an eclipse of the sun.

The Elizabethans knew about infection and contagion, and dogs, cats and pigs were all blamed for spreading the plague, but no one thought of the rats and their fleas which swarmed through the close-packed wood and plaster houses, feeding on the piles of rotting garbage in front of every door or on the entrails and blood (both animal and human) casually dumped in the streets by the butchers and barber surgeons.

Plague, of course, attacked every class, but the well-to-do were normally able to avoid the worst of it by leaving town during the summer months when it was most prevalent. There were always several hundred plague deaths in the slums in warm weather and epidemics every ten years or so during the Elizabethan period; particularly severe ones occurred in 1563–4, during the early 1590s, and again in 1603, when more than 30,000 died in London.

Drugs for the sufferer

An engraving of 1600 illustrates the state of contemporary medicine – and points a moral. The patient in bed has syphilis, and the picture on the wall of his bedroom depicts the loose living that led to his predicament. In the adjoining room, the doctor's assistants are making up a drug called hyacum, a decoction made from Peruvian tree bark which was first used as a cure for venereal disease at the beginning of the 16th century.

Although unable to prevent its outbreaks, the civic authorities did their best to contain the ravages of the disease when it arrived by issuing a stream of 'plague orders'. Infected houses were to carry a placard bearing the words 'Lord have mercy upon us' enclosed in a red circle. Their inhabitants were supposed to remain isolated for 20 days or more, their wants being supplied by the wealthier members of the parish. Theatres and other places of entertainment were closed and, since there was a strong notion that plague and filth went together, great efforts were made to clean up the streets and force people to burn or bury their rubbish.

Sensible citizens co-operated and took their own precautions. The actor Edward Alleyn advised his wife, left behind in London while he was away on tour during the epidemic of 1593, to 'keep your house fair and clean, which I know you will, and every evening throw water before your door, and have in your window good store of rue and herb of grace'. But a strange form of morbid hysteria often attacked the population at plague-time, and nothing would stop crowds of sight-seers, even women with young children, from gathering at mass burials and standing over the open plague-pits. Nor, of course, was it possible to enforce the isolation of contacts. People had to get about to earn their living, and all the surveyors and constables appointed by the parish could not prevent them.

Sufferers were advised to stay quiet and warm in bed, with little to eat. Some doctors lanced the buboes, for it was believed that unless the poison was released it would go inwards and kill the patient. A warm poultice made of

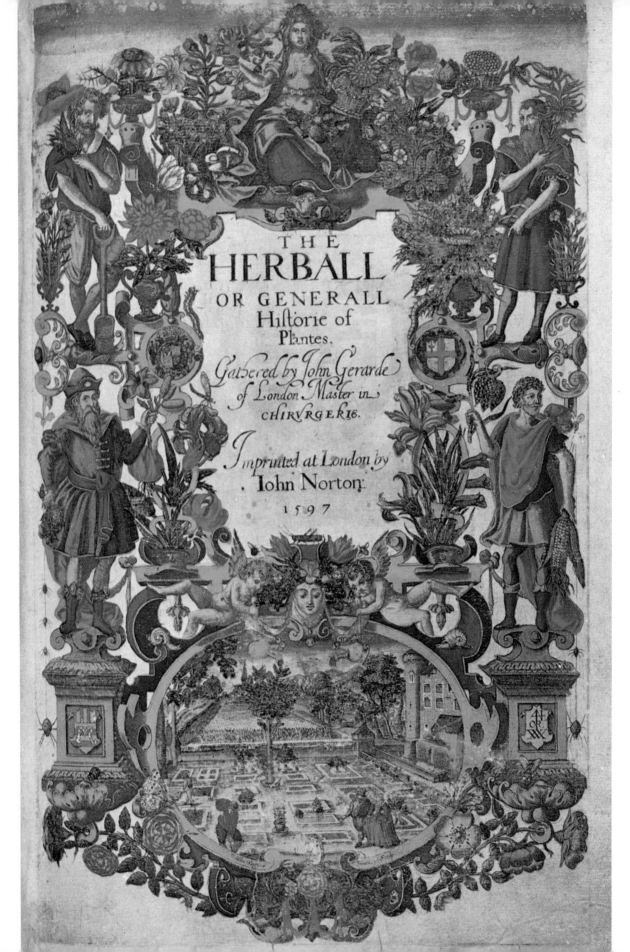

THE
HERBALL
OR GENERALL
Historie of
Plantes.

Gathered by John Gerarde
of London Master in
CHIRVRGERIE.

Imprinted at London by
Iohn Norton.
1597

onions, butter and garlic could be used to draw out the venom, or a live pullet could be held against the plague sores until the unfortunate bird died. Onions, cloves, lemons, vinegar, wormwood – in fact almost any pungent or aromatic substance – were thought to ward off infection, and all sorts of remedies and preservatives were recommended, including tobacco, arsenic, quicksilver and dried toads. Everyone had their favourite nostrum for plague – from a lily root boiled in white wine to a noxious-sounding draught concocted of salad oil, sack and gunpowder – but all were agreed that the sovereign specific for drawing out poison and provoking a sweat was powdered unicorn's horn. Needless to say many unscrupulous quacks grew rich on the sale of this rare commodity, said to be worth 'half a City'.

On the whole, perhaps one is driven to the conclusion that those Elizabethans who contrived to keep out of the doctors' hands were the lucky ones. The Queen certainly appears to have thought so, for the royal physicians lamented the fact that Her Majesty frequently disregarded their advice and refused to submit to their recommended programmes of purging and bleeding. All the same, some progress was being made. The war with Spain and the increase in the destructive power of firearms had made work on the treatment of gun-shot wounds a matter of urgent practical necessity, and surgeons were beginning to discover that bleeding could be staunched by other methods than cauterisation with boiling tar. Timothy Bright's *Treatise of Melancholy*, which appeared in 1586, was an early and thoughtful study of some aspects of mental illness, and the great Dr Harvey was also an Elizabethan, although his discovery of the circulation of the blood was not published until 1616.

When dragons seemed as real as dogs and cats

The natural sciences of botany and zoology both received considerable stimulus from the discoveries of Elizabethan explorers. As early as the 1560s efforts were being made to apply scientific methods to the description and classification of plants, and take the herbal arts out of the realm of folklore. William Turner, with his *New Herball*, was a pioneer in this field. In 1577 John Frampton published his *Joyful News out of the New World*, the first English account of the vegetable products of America, and in 1597 came John Gerarde's famous and lavishly illustrated compilation – *The Herball or General Historie of Plants* – which was long regarded as the classic work on the subject.

Most Elizabethan surveys of the animal kingdom, however, were not far removed from medieval bestiaries with dragons, griffins, cockatrices and basilisks rubbing shoulders with more familiar dogs, cats and lions – it was, after all, an age when anything still seemed possible. The greatest scientific naturalist of the age was the German–Swiss Conrad Gesner, whose work was first popularised and translated in 1607 by Edward Topsell in *The Historie of Fourefooted Beastes*, but Thomas Hariot included a carefully factual list of the fauna to be encountered in Virginia in his *Brief and True Report* on the 1585 expedition. Nevertheless, mythological creatures such as mermaids continued to appear in serious catalogues until the mid-17th century.

The earliest plant guide
John Gerarde's Herball *(opposite page), which appeared in 1597, was one of the first encyclopaedias of garden plants in English. The plants listed were chiefly used for medicinal purposes. Herbal medicines were far more widely used than the noxious mixtures of the apothecaries, and every housewife possessed some knowledge of the properties of the various herbs.*

Beasts real and imaginary
The unfamiliar animals of newly discovered lands seemed no more and no less improbable to people in England than the mythical beasts that figured in the medieval bestiaries. Pictures of a tiger and a unicorn are among more than 100 panels embroidered on velvet wall-hangings by Mary, Queen of Scots and the Countess of Shrewsbury in about 1570, while Mary was a prisoner at Tutbury Castle in the custody of the Earl of Shrewsbury.

The general attitude towards domestic animals was strictly utilitarian and cruelty was often sickening, but the English passion for horses and dogs was already well known, and English mastiffs or bandogs were famous. Many ladies kept lap-dogs – usually some kind of spaniel – as pets, and monkeys were also popular. When Katherine Grey, the Queen's cousin, was imprisoned in the Tower after her unwise secret marriage to the Earl of Hertford, she was allowed to keep her pet dogs and monkeys, in spite of the damage they caused to government property. The cat remained a working animal, and a good mouser was always greatly prized. However, cats were also regarded with superstitious dread by foolish people and, along with toads, often believed to be witches' 'familiars'.

Coal for export, and a flourishing iron industry

Although much useful scientific groundwork was done during the second half of the 16th century, especially in the area of higher mathematics, the Elizabethans were above all practical people who liked their science to have a practical application to such matters as gunnery or navigation. They were inclined to distrust thinkers and intellectuals as atheists, and even mathematicians were liable to find themselves regarded as wizards or 'conjurers' – all the mysterious symbols which appeared in their work looking suspiciously diabolic to the ordinary layman.

Most characteristic of the period were the strides being made in the industrial and technological fields. It has been suggested that the origins of the Industrial Revolution can be traced to developments in the Elizabethan era, and certainly the coal-mining industry, the foundation of England's later industrial supremacy, expanded dramatically during the Queen's reign. This was largely due to the late Tudor 'energy crisis', caused by the steady erosion of the woodlands, the growth of the population and the increasing demands of industry, and enterprising landowners in the Midlands, Yorkshire, Derbyshire and South Wales were busy sinking pits on their estates.

Poet's patron as pet lover
Cats and dogs were often kept as household pets, and the Earl of Southampton had his cat included in the portrait which he commissioned as a memorial of his captivity in the Tower of London. According to tradition the cat found her way across London and climbed down a chimney to join her master in the Tower, where he was imprisoned for his role in the Essex rebellion. Earlier in his career the Earl, Henry Wriothesley, had been William Shakespeare's patron, and it was his gift of £100 which enabled the young man from Stratford to buy himself a shareholding in a theatrical company.

New World, new creatures
When Sir Walter Raleigh tried in 1585 to establish a permanent settlement on Roanoke Island, off North Carolina, he took with him the artist John White to paint the men, plants, birds, fish and other creatures of the New World. These elegant drawings of a crab and a flamingo are typical specimens of the vivid record that White brought back from three journeys to North America, to give people in England a glimpse of the lands to which settlers were being encouraged to travel. White became Governor of Roanoke, but the colony was eventually lost.

Tapping wealth underground
Metal-working and mining made great strides during the Elizabethan age. Here miners can be seen at work underground, while above a prospector is divining with his forked rod. The English, however, still depended heavily on continental expertise: the Germans, and Austrians from the Tyrol, were the acknowledged leaders in the science of metallurgy. England was rich in mineral resources, and two new companies, the Mines Royal and the Mineral Battery Works, were set up for the purpose of exploiting the copper-bearing areas of the Lake District and other parts of north-west England.

The great bar to progress was difficulty of transport. Since the only practicable method of carrying coal in bulk was by water, its use and supply continued to be effectively limited to the region of the coalfields or to coastal and riverside communities. At Wollaton in Nottinghamshire, for example, Sir Francis Willoughby was able to transport his coal by barge on the River Trent, and did very well out of it, but the chief centre of the industry remained concentrated in the Tyneside area. The Newcastle Society of Hostmen, comprising the leading burgesses of the town, quickly established a monopoly of the trade, sending up the price of 'sea-coal' from four to nine shillings a chauldron (36 bushels).

By modern standards, these Elizabethan collieries were small, primitive affairs, each consisting of one pit and its workings, but some of the production figures are impressive. In the year ending 1594 nearly 36,000 tons of coal were exported from Newcastle in fleets of colliers which also provided a useful nursery for seamen. London took some 15,000 tons a year – the rest going mostly to the Netherlands and other European countries.

In the Kent and Sussex Weald, where iron had been smelted for generations, coal would have been particularly valuable, but all Elizabethan attempts to use it in the smelting process proved unsuccessful. The secret of producing coke for use in furnaces was not discovered until the 18th century, and the iron-founders had therefore to rely on the diminishing supplies of charcoal for fuel.

Decoration for a fireplace

The increasing use of coal for heating brought a steady demand for cast-iron firebacks which, like so many Elizabethan domestic artefacts, were often extremely decorative. The Sussex Weald was the great centre for iron-founders who, since medieval times, had used charcoal from the forest as fuel in their furnaces, and water-powered bellows to fan the flames. The introduction of blast furnaces, with their tall, enclosed hearths, enabled higher temperatures to be achieved, producing molten metal which was run off into bars or moulds.

At work in the forge

The blacksmith, or ironsmith, was a skilled and important member of the rural community who did far more than shoe horses. He would make plough-shares and make or repair all the simpler iron tools and utensils used in manor or farm-house. In his forge, surrounded by the tools of his trade, he hammers a lump of molten metal into shape on his anvil, while a metal rod heats in the fire. A north wind (septentrio) fans the flames, and fumes escape to the south (auster).

The industry, however, flourished, and it is estimated that there were about 100 iron-mills and forges at work in the Weald in Tudor times. The old method of making iron, known as the bloomery, where a lump of hot metal was hammered out directly into shape while still malleable, was being rapidly superseded by the blast furnace, introduced from the Continent, which ran molten metal into a mould, producing cast iron. Iron cannon were first cast at Buxted in Sussex in 1543, and there was a growing demand for cast-iron fire-backs for coal fires. There were iron-founders, too, in the Forest of Dean and Cannock Chase, and iron-works around Walsall which concentrated on the manufacture of bits, stirrups, spurs and buckles for harness. Parts of Stafford-shire and Worcestershire formed the centre of the nail-producing industry, and by the end of the reign Sheffield steel and cutlery were gaining an inter-national reputation for excellence. Already the pattern of English industrial development was forming.

Mineral riches fuel new industries

Although progress in iron and steel-making was somewhat hampered by its inability to make use of coal, other manufacturing industries did benefit from coal – especially glass-making, soap-boiling, brick-making, sugar refining and salt evaporation. One new enterprise on Tyneside, using coal for the process of extracting salt from sea-water, employed 300 workers.

England was rich in mineral resources, and interest in mining was by no means confined to coal. 'Tin and lead,' wrote William Harrison, 'are very plentiful with us, the one in Cornwall, Devonshire, and elsewhere in the north,

Historian and map-maker
John Speed, a tailor by trade, was one of many popular historians who were hard at work throughout the Elizabethan period to appease the insatiable public appetite for historical writings. Speed made maps and wrote a History of Great Britain . . . from Julius Caesar . . . to King James, *first published in 1611. Another tailor, John Stow, produced a great work on the history and topography of his beloved City of London, while William Camden, master at Westminster School and friend of Lord Burghley, produced the nearest work that exists to a contemporary political history of the reign.*

the other in Derbyshire, Weardale and sundry places of this island; whereby my countrymen do reap no small commodity, but especially our pewterers, who in times past employed the use of pewter only upon dishes, pots, and a few other trifles for service here at home, whereas now they are grown unto such exquisite cunning that they can in manner imitate by infusion any form or fashion of cup, dish, salt bowl, or goblet, which is made by goldsmiths' craft, though they be never so curious, exquisite and artificially forged.' Pewter was usually sold by the 'garnish', or set of 12 platters or dishes; according to Harrison: 'In some places beyond the sea, a garnish of good flat English pewter of an ordinary making is esteemed almost so precious as the like number of vessels that are made of fine silver.'

Tin and lead, of course, had been mined since pre-Roman times (England was still the largest tin-exporting country), but in the 1560s the need for brass for the new cannon led to the opening-up and serious exploitation of the copper-bearing areas of the Lake District and north-west. Two new companies, the Mines Royal and the Mineral and Battery Works, were set up, and several well-known people, including Lord Burghley, the Earls of Pembroke and Leicester and the Duke of Norfolk, took shares in them. A search for calamine, or ore of zinc, to mix with the copper revealed useful deposits in the West Country, and rolling mills for the manufacture of sheet metal and drawing mills for wire were built – a wire works in the grounds of Tintern Abbey employed 100 men. English brass was at first considered inferior to the continental product, but by the end of the century English cannon had won such a high reputation abroad that competition for them was keen. They were exported, with and without licence, until Walter Raleigh complained that, while at one time 'one ship of her Majesty's was able to beat ten Spaniards', the enemy now possessed so much English ordnance that 'we are hardly matched one to one'.

Foreign help for metal work and weaving

In the development of both mining and metal-working England depended heavily on German help, and German miners were brought over to work in the new copper mines of the north-west. In other industries, too, the Elizabethans turned to more highly industrialised European nations for assistance, and as time went by and France and the Netherlands were devastated by religious civil wars, peaceful England benefited from her neighbours' misfortunes. At the beginning of the Queen's reign, Antwerp had been the financial capital and greatest port of Europe, but by the end of the 1560s the city was in arms against its Spanish overlords and much of its trade and business supremacy had passed to London.

Protestant refugees from France and Flanders streamed across the Channel, bringing their skills in silk and linen-weaving, glass-making, engraving and printing with them. In some places this caused a good deal of resentment among the English workers, but the government encouraged the immigrants who brought extra prosperity into the south and east. By the early 1570s there was a sizeable community of weavers in Norwich and another at Colchester. There were silk-weavers at Canterbury, thread-makers at Maidstone and sailcloth-makers at Ipswich, while the newcomers also brought glass-making to the Sussex Weald and the Forest of Dean.

It would be quite misleading to picture any of these activities in terms of modern factories or industrial estates. The Elizabethan industrial worker was a craftsman or craftswoman, and Elizabethan industry was still a small, patchy affair of individual workshops, usually family concerns, carried on at home and nearly always combined with the cultivation of a plot of ground, the keeping of a cow, a pig and a few hens. This was especially true of the wool trade, the mainstay of England's economy, in which the various processes of carding, spinning, weaving, fulling (cleansing and thickening) and dyeing were done by out-workers in their own homes.

In the North, the industry remained largely in the hands of small independent producers and traders, working for a profit rather than a wage. The farmers brought their raw fleeces to the local fair or market and sold them to the spinners, who would bring the yarn back to sell to the weavers. The weavers, in turn, sold their product to the clothiers, who, after fulling and

Portrait of a county
Leader among Elizabethan map-makers was the Yorkshireman Christopher Saxton, whose maps are works of beauty in themselves. This map of Cheshire includes a detailed inset of the city of Chester, with a list of its principal places of interest, and illustrations of county history and activities ranging from the 15th-century Battle of Blore Heath to the production of salt for which Cheshire was already noted.

sometimes dyeing, would market the finished cloth to merchants either in London or abroad. In the more progressive south, where the industry was organised on an altogether bigger scale and required more capital, the entrepreneurs – the wool-brokers and clothiers – controlled the whole of the manufacturing process, 'putting-out' the raw material to their workers and paying piece-rates.

There had been some technical advances in the textile industry, too, such as the introduction of the stocking knitting frame, but in general it followed its medieval pattern. Spinners and weavers worked in their own cottage kitchens and weaving sheds, doing as much or as little work as they needed to support their families, and growing some at least of their own food on their own patch of ground.

Wages remained pitifully small, around fourpence or sixpence a day, while food prices rose steadily, and the small independent craftsmen possessed little or no bargaining power. In times of economic recession, the clothiers, themselves often operating on narrow enough margins, simply laid off the outworkers, leaving them to the doubtful mercies of parish relief.

In spite of the undoubted advances, both scientific and technological, which were being made, ordinary people's lives were as yet little affected by them. It would be another 200 years before the Industrial Revolution had gathered enough momentum to begin to break up the age-old pattern of grinding manual labour geared to the changing seasons, or the patient handcraftsmanship of weaver, potter and metal-worker, carpenter, printer and glass-blower. Another 300 or so years would pass before antisepsis, anaesthesia and antibiotics began to take some of the terror out of illness, or modern technology to relieve the daily drudgery hitherto taken for granted.

But in spite of its harshness and uncertainty, life was sweet to the Elizabethans. Perhaps its very uncertainty and fleeting quality helped to heighten their awareness of its pleasures, while at the same time breeding a natural fatalism. 'Adieu, farewell earth's bliss!' wrote the poet Thomas Nashe in the plague year of 1593

This world uncertain is:
Fond are life's lustful joys,
Death proves them all but toys.
None from his darts can fly;
I am sick, I must die –
Lord have mercy on us!

Rich men, trust not in wealth,
Gold cannot buy you health,
Physic himself must fade.
All things to end are made,
The plague full swift goes by,
I am sick, I must die –
Lord have mercy on us!

Mapping the Queen's realm
The Elizabethan age saw a great upsurge of national pride, and with it a corresponding increase of interest in England's history and topography among the new educated middle-class. Christopher Saxton's complete atlas of England and Wales, which appeared in 1579, was the first national atlas to be produced by any country. The frontispiece shows the Queen, crowned and robed in majesty, surrounded by an elaborate Renaissance decoration of columns, cameos and cherubs, surmounted by the royal arms. The verse below is said to have been written by Alexander Nowell, Dean of St Paul's, and celebrates the peace of Elizabeth's rule, while other nations are at war.

Clemens et Regni moderatrix iusta Britāni
Hac forma insigni conspicienda nitet.

Tristia dum gentes circum omnes bella fatigant,
Cæciq́ errores toto grassantur in orbe.
An·Dñi   pace beas longa, vera et pietate Britannos: 1579
Iusticia moderans miti sapienter habenas.
Chara domi, celebrisq́ foris, longiæuaq́ regni
Hic teneas, regno tandem fruitura perenni.

In brick and stone

CRAFTSMEN LABOUR TO BUILD AND ADORN THE HOMES
OF NOBLES AND YEOMAN FARMERS

'Fieldhead' four-poster

This oak-panelled bedroom at Oakwell Hall, West Yorkshire – the 'Fieldhead' of Charlotte Brontë's novel Shirley *– displays that important Elizabethan status symbol, the four-poster bed. The chest at the foot of the bed would have been used to store documents and deeds.*

The building boom which began after the Reformation, when the vast monastic estates passed into lay hands, continued throughout Elizabeth's reign, reflecting the growing self-confidence of a nation which knew it was going up in the world. The houses themselves – from splendid mansions such as Longleat and Hardwick Hall to the sturdy functional dwellings of the yeoman farmers which still decorate our landscape – show clearly the rising standards of comfort which people were coming to expect.

Men were no longer building simply to defend themselves from attack or to provide shelter for their families, but to show off new wealth and status. Old men remarked on 'the multitude of chimneys lately erected'. Windows which had once been filled with lattice work or panels of horn were being glazed. Rooms were being panelled and wainscoted, and walls lined with tapestry.

Villages, too, were enlarged and improved: a virtually complete Elizabethan village street survives at Chiddingstone in Kent. Building was not confined to the countryside, and towns such as Shrewsbury, Exeter, Oxford and Bristol were substantially rebuilt. The Queen alone seems to have been unaffected by the building craze, for no new royal palaces were built during the reign. Elizabeth preferred to let her subjects provide the grand new mansions, and made use of them when it suited her convenience in the course of her 'progresses' round the country.

Romans on a brick

This Tudor brick found in Thames Street, London, is decorated with the figures of Roman soldiers leading two captives. It is an example of the craftsmanship of a period which was ready to add ornamentation to the most mundane of objects.

Heraldry in glass

Coats of arms accurately portrayed in stained glass decorate the windows of the library of Montacute House, in Somerset. The library was formerly the house's great chamber.

Artistry on the walls

The High Great Chamber at Hardwick Hall still contains the tapestry hangings designed for it in the 1590s. It also contains several pieces of original furniture and a fine frieze in painted plasterwork by a local craftsman, Abraham Smith.

A frame of timber

Many Elizabethans' prosperity was founded on sheep-farming, especially in East Anglia and the Cotswolds. This fine timber-framed house in Lavenham in Suffolk belonged to a 16th-century wool merchant. The speciality of Lavenham was its blue cloth, stamped with a fleur-de-lys trademark introduced by the Flemish weavers who taught Englishmen their craft.

A castle in stone

Kenilworth Castle, near Warwick, was granted to Robert Dudley, Earl of Leicester, by Elizabeth in 1563. He rebuilt it and in 1575 entertained the Queen to the 'Princely Pleasures of Kenilworth', which lasted for nearly three weeks.

A palace in brick

The Old Palace at Hatfield, Hertfordshire, is all that remains of the Tudor building which originally belonged to the Bishops of Ely. It was here that Elizabeth held her first Council meeting in November 1558 and appointed William Cecil, later Lord Burghley, to be her Secretary of State.

The Chariott drawne by foure Horses vpon which Charret
stood the Coffin couered wth purple Veluett and vpon
that the reprefentation, The Canapy borne by fix Knights.

The Queen's funeral sees a nation united in mourning

Queen Elizabeth's funeral took place on April 28, 1603, five weeks after her death, and more than 1,000 people –
from the humblest servants of the royal scullery and woodyard to the greatest nobles in the land –
went to make up the procession to Westminster Abbey. This contemporary painting shows the hearse, drawn by
four horses arrayed in black velvet, surrounded by cloaked and hooded mourners carrying
the banners of the royal arms. On the coffin lies a life-size wax effigy of the Queen dressed in her parliament robes,
with a crown on her head and a sceptre in her hand.

footemen.

Gentlemen Pentioners

Gentlemen Pentioners

CHAPTER TEN

The end of an era

A FAVOURITE'S TREASON CLOUDS ELIZABETH'S LAST YEARS:
HER MEMORIALS ARE A PROUD, PATRIOTIC NATION AND A RICH LEGACY IN
BUILDINGS, PORTRAITS AND LITERATURE

265

There will never Queen sit in my seat, with more zeal to my country,
care for my subjects, and that sooner with willingness will venture her life for
your good and safety than myself. For it is not my desire to live
nor reign longer than my life and reign shall be for your good. And though you
have had, and may have many princes more mighty and wise sitting in
this state; yet you never had, or shall have any that
will be more careful and loving.   Elizabeth I's 'Golden Speech' to Parliament in 1601

*T*he last two decades of the Elizabethan period saw the great flowering of the age. These were the years of Philip Sidney, of Marlowe and Shakespeare, of Ben Jonson and Edmund Spenser, of Walter Raleigh, Francis Drake and the brilliant young Earl of Essex; years when England's international prestige soared to a peak it would not reach again for centuries; years of expansion and increasing national prosperity.

Yet those were also, paradoxically, years of crisis and of acute political and economic anxiety. Later generations have tended to look back on the Elizabethan age as one of history's more striking success stories – but this was not always how it appeared to the Elizabethans themselves.

Throughout the 1580s Protestant England lived in constant and active dread of Catholic subversion from within and Catholic encirclement from without. This dread sometimes came perilously close to panic, but while fears of Popish plots and of the invading armies of anti-Christ may have been exaggerated, they were very understandable. If Queen Elizabeth had died or had been assassinated during the lifetime of Mary, Queen of Scots, her Catholic cousin and heiress, there can be little doubt that the country would have been plunged into a religious civil war as devastating as that which ravaged 16th-century France. Equally, if the Spanish army in the Netherlands had succeeded in crossing the North Sea in the summer of 1588, it would undoubtedly have made short work of England's enthusiastic but untrained and ill-equipped citizen army.

After the execution of the Queen of Scots and the resounding defeat of the Spanish Armada, much of the popular alarm subsided, but the war continued and was a heavy drain on the Crown's resources. Despite the triple and quadruple subsidies voted by Parliament towards the end of the reign, the system by which the leading members of the tax-paying classes were left to assess themselves for tax purposes naturally did little to tap the country's growing wealth. As a result, the rich of Elizabethan England grew steadily richer while the monarchy grew poorer; the Queen, faced with ever-increasing calls on her purse, was forced to sell Crown lands in order to make ends meet.

During the 1590s the political scene was dominated by the troubles in Ireland. To the average Elizabethan Englishman, Ireland was a soggy, savage

Time and Death in waiting
This memorial portrait of Queen Elizabeth flanked by the ominous figures of Time and Death was painted after she herself was dead. It shows her as a tired old woman in pensive mood – something she would never have allowed in her lifetime. Perhaps the unknown artist was remembering stories put about by the friends of the Earl of Essex, telling how the Queen would sit alone in the dark and weep for the Earl after his execution. Elizabeth certainly suffered from occasional moods of depression during her last years, but her melancholy was more likely to have been caused by physical weariness and the knowledge that the days of her greatness were inevitably coming to an end.

wilderness where no sensible person would willingly set foot. The matter-of-fact English saw nothing romantic or admirable about this remnant of ancient Celtic civilisation which, by an odd quirk of history and geography, had survived into the 16th century. On the contrary, they were shocked by the backwardness and barbarity of the 'wild Irish', and irritated by the inefficiency and laziness of a people whose favourite pastimes appeared to be cattle raiding and tribal warfare.

Revolt in Ireland 'beyond the Pale'

Successive Tudor sovereigns had made well-meaning attempts to introduce their Irish subjects to the benefits of the English way of life. However, the task of grafting a totally alien system of law, language and land tenure on to a primitive and uncomprehending pastoral society by peaceful means was beyond the capacities of the Tudor administrative machine. In the opinion of those on the spot, the only way by which Ireland would ever be brought into what the Earl of Surrey, Lord Deputy under Henry VIII, called 'good order and due subjection' was by outright conquest, but this was always regarded as a last resort.

Serene in victory
The 'Armada Portrait' shows the Queen with her hand on the globe and the crown at her side, while behind her are two windows – one showing the advance of the dreaded Spanish fleet, the other its humiliating defeat. As with so many of the Queen's portraits, this was not intended as a conventional likeness, but as a symbolic image of the monarch whose crown has vanquished the powers of darkness and whose hand now covers the whole world.

During the Elizabethan period, the government pursued a policy of colonising Ireland with English settlers, in the hope that they would introduce modern methods of cultivation and generally help to anglicise and subjugate the natives. Sir Richard Grenville and Walter Raleigh both invested heavily in the Irish 'plantations', and so, to a lesser extent, did the poet Edmund Spenser. But the scheme was not a success. The newcomers led an uncomfortable and precarious existence, constantly harassed by the wild Irish much as the early American colonists were harassed by wild Indians, and few of them stood the course. By the 1590s Ireland seemed further away than ever from the ideal of peaceful integration. English influence was effectively confined to the area round Dublin, known as the Pale. In the north, rebellion was simmering under the leadership of the Ulster chieftain, Hugh O'Neill, Earl of Tyrone, who dreamed of driving out the English and setting himself up as High King of an independent Celtic Ireland.

In the summer of 1598 Tyrone inflicted a crushing defeat on an English army at the Battle of the Yellow Ford. The Irish problem was transformed overnight into an Irish crisis, as the spark of revolt ran like wildfire through the whole country. Everywhere the tribes were out, emerging from their impenetrable bogs and mountains to indulge in an orgy of killing, looting and burning, and the English settlers had to run for their lives to the doubtful sanctuary of the towns. Even the Pale could no longer be regarded as safe, and Queen Elizabeth was faced with yet another grim and urgent challenge to the security of her realm – for Ireland was England's vulnerable back door, offering a strategic bridgehead to an invader, and Tyrone was known to be in regular communication with Spain.

A challenge from the young Earl of Essex

The Queen was now in her mid-sixties, but as alert, formidable and autocratic as ever. André de Maisse, a French diplomat, who saw her several times during the winter of 1597, thought that apart from her face, which looked old, and her teeth, which were bad, it would not be possible to see a woman of so fine and vigorous disposition. 'It is a strange thing,' he observed, 'to see how lively she is in body and mind, and nimble in everything she does.'

All the same, Elizabeth was now an old woman by the standards of her day and, at the end of her life, was to know the loneliness of one who had outlived her generation. Nearly all the men associated with the years of her greatness were gone by this time – the Earl of Leicester, whose name had been so closely linked with hers, Christopher Hatton who, alone of all her favourites, had remained single for her sake, dour Francis Walsingham and her cousin Henry Carey, Lord Hunsdon. When, in August 1598, old Lord Burghley died, it was a break with the past more complete than any other, and the Queen felt it bitterly. She and Burghley had worked together in close partnership for very nearly 40 years – a partnership unique in English history – and it was noticed that for months after his death she could not speak of her old friend without tears coming to her eyes.

Spanish adversary
The Queen's old adversary, King Philip of Spain, died five years before her in 1598. They had become brother and sister-in-law in the far-off days when Philip, as a young man of 27 with yellow hair and beard, landed at Southampton to be married to the sad Queen Mary Tudor in Winchester Cathedral. It is said that the Prince of Spain was impressed by the red-headed Princess Elizabeth, and for a few weeks during the summer of 1555 made it his business to try to win her friendship.

Knave

The Pope Consulting with
his Cardinalls & Contributing
a Million of Gold towards the
Charge of the Armada —

VI

The Lᵈ Admirall Howard
Knighting Thomas Howard,
the Lord Sheffeild, Rogᵗ Townsen,
Iohn Hawkins, and Martir
Forbisher for their good service

VI

Arthur Lᵈ Grey, Sᵗ Francis
Knolles, Sᵗ Iohn Norris,
Sᵗ Richard Bingham, Sᵗ Rog
Williams & others in a Councell
of War consulting how ẙ land
Service should be Ordered

King

The Army of 1000 horse, and
22000 Foot, which ẙ Earle of
Leicester comanded when hee
Pitched his Tents att Tilbury

III

Queene Eliz: wᵗʰ Nobles and
Gentry and a great number
of people giving God humble
thanks in Sᵗ Pauls Church
and having set upp theEnsignes
taken from the Spaniards

IIII

Queene Eliz: Riding in Triumph through London in a
Chariot drawn by two Hor-
ses and all ẙ Companies
attending her wᵗʰ their Baners

Like many ageing people, the Queen found it difficult to understand the new generation growing up around her, and one member of it had begun to cause her acute anxiety. The handsome, high-spirited young Earl of Essex has often been described as the darling of her old age, though it would be more accurate to think of him as one of its greatest headaches. Essex had breeding, courage, ability and immense personal charm, but he was also spoilt, ambitious and essentially unstable. Not content with the honourable career of 'domestical greatness', as Francis Bacon called it, which would have been his for the asking, he yearned for military glory; in 1596 he distinguished himself in the brilliantly successful raid on the Spanish port of Cadiz, returning home to a hero's welcome. His youth, his striking good looks, his open-handed generosity and his martial valour all combined to make him a favourite with the London crowds, but at Court two distinct and increasingly hostile factions were emerging. On one side stood Essex and most of the younger element, who looked to him as their natural leader; on the other the party that favoured peace with Spain, headed by Lord Burghley's son Robert Cecil, who had inherited his father's former office of Secretary of State.

The Queen did her best to keep a balance. She was undoubtedly fond of Essex and enjoyed his company – she never lost her eye for an attractive man – but it was soon noticed that while the Earl seemed able to get anything for himself, including plenty of expensive presents, the Queen would give nothing to his friends. She had no intention of allowing him to build up too large a following, no matter how he coaxed.

Playing-card heroes

Several heroes of Elizabeth's time are depicted on these playing cards from the so-called Armada pack, engraved in 1680 as a protest against James II's leanings towards the Catholic Church. They include Lord Howard of Effingham, Sir John Hawkins, Sir Martin Frobisher, Sir John Norris and Sir Roger Williams. The Pope is shown as the Knave, contributing gold to finance the Spanish Armada. The Earl of Leicester, depicted as the King of Hearts, is seen pitching his camp at Tilbury in 1588, while the last two cards show the Queen giving thanks at St Paul's for the defeat of the Armada, and her triumphal procession through London.

A Deputy rides out

Sir Henry Sidney, seen riding out from Dublin Castle, was the most successful Elizabethan Lord Deputy in Ireland. During his term of office in the 1560s and 1570s he recommended the planting of English colonies, and the building of roads and bridges in Ulster – the wildest and most backward of the provinces. Sidney saw the breaking of the power of the tribal chiefs as being the way to 'civilise' Ireland. Sir Henry was the father of Philip Sidney, the poet.

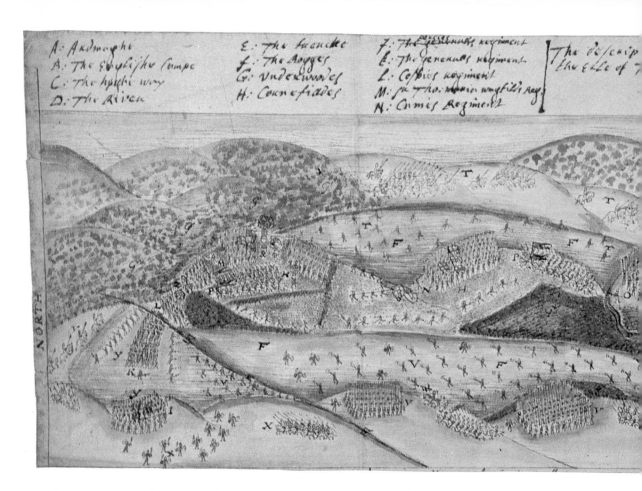

A: Ardmaghe
B: The Englishe Campe
C: The highe way
D: The River
E: The Trenche
F: The Bogges
G: Underwoodes
H: Corne fieldes
I: The [...]uks Regiment
K: The Generalls Regiment
L: Coshies Regiment
M: [...]Tho [...] wingfild's Reg
N: Cosmes Regiment

The descrip[...]
the Isle of [...]

Essex did not like being refused. In his arrogance and impatience he made the fatal mistake of underestimating Elizabeth, coming to see her as a tiresome old woman who, if she could not be cajoled, would have to be bullied. Not surprisingly this resulted in several furious rows between them, Essex sulking and storming, the Queen swearing angrily that she would break him of his will and pull down his great heart, and on one occasion publicly boxing his ears.

Arrest after a military debacle

In spite of the annoyance caused by his tantrums and his insolence and in spite of growing doubts as to his loyalty, the Earl of Essex was still a great man with an international reputation who was acknowledged as England's leading military commander. So, when it came to appointing a new Lord Deputy to suppress the rebellion in Ireland, the Queen had little choice but to send for Essex. Nevertheless, it turned out to be a serious error of judgement. After six wasted months of floundering through the Irish bogs, the Earl abandoned his command in despair and came rushing back to England, against all orders.

The Court was at Nonsuch, and Essex, covered in mud from his journey, burst unannounced into the Queen's bedroom, finding her, according to a contemporary account, 'newly up, with the hair about her face' and only half-dressed. Taken by surprise, she received him kindly – she had, at that moment, no means of knowing whether this might be the beginning of an armed *coup* – and the Earl left her presence thanking God that 'after so many troublous

Defeat at the Yellow Ford
This painting by the soldier John Thomas, who fought in Queen Elizabeth's Irish wars, shows the Battle of the Yellow Ford, on the Blackwater River near Armagh. Here, in the summer of 1598, the English army in Ireland was overwhelmed by the forces of Hugh O'Neill, Earl of Tyrone. The disaster of the Yellow Ford was the signal for a general rising of the tribes, and this transformed the Irish problem into an Irish crisis – especially as the rebel leaders were known to be in close touch with Spain. To deal

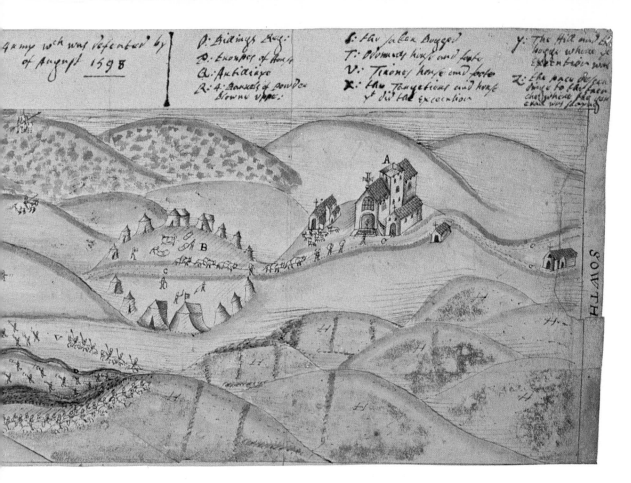

with the crisis, Elizabeth
appointed the Earl of Essex as
commander. He spent six
months in Ireland in 1599, but
his only real success was the
capture of Cahir Castle in
Munster. The Queen did not
regard what she termed 'the
taking of an Irish hold from a
rabble of rogues' as much of an
achievement. She watched in
frustrated fury from London as
Essex dissipated the strength of
a large, expensively equipped
army in pointless diversions in
the south, instead of tackling the
power base of the rebel Tyrone
in Ulster.

storms abroad, he had found a sweet calm at home'. But the calm was decep-
tive. When he saw the Queen again, she spoke to him sternly and ordered him
to explain himself to her Council. Two days later he was put under house
arrest in the custody of the Lord Keeper, Sir Thomas Egerton.

Elizabeth was furious with Essex and remained deaf to his impassioned pleas
for forgiveness, but she was in an awkward predicament. Essex had a tremen-
dous popular following, especially among the Londoners, and just now the
town was full of his henchmen, many of them deserters from Ireland. The
Queen had wanted to bring him to trial in the Star Chamber – not, she said, to
destroy him but just to make him know his duty. However, she was warned
that this might lead to violent demonstrations in his favour. Reluctantly she
abandoned the idea, and at once rumours began to spread that the Earl was
being condemned unheard. At last, in June 1600, he was summoned before a
special tribunal of Privy Councillors, who suspended him from his various
offices and decreed that his imprisonment should continue until the Queen
chose to be merciful.

In fact, by this time Essex was living in his own house again and by the end of
August he was free to go where he liked – except to Court, the only place that
mattered. By the end of the year he was approaching the last act of his tragedy.
He was a sick man by now, and probably more than a little mad. Heavily in
debt and despairing of ever being restored to favour, he became reckless. He is
said to have described the Queen as an old woman whose mind was as crooked

273

Widow of the famous
Frances Walsingham, daughter of Sir Francis Walsingham, Queen Elizabeth's puritanical Secretary of State, was the wife and widow of two notable personalities of Elizabeth's court. Her first marriage to Sir Philip Sidney ended tragically when he died of wounds received at the Battle of Zutphen. Her second, to the Earl of Essex, was abruptly cut short by the headsman's axe. In fact, Lady Essex can never have enjoyed much of her second husband's company, for the Queen had an aversion to wives and did not welcome her at court.

From triumph to disgrace
This portrait of Robert Devereux, Earl of Essex, was painted after his triumphant return from the raid on Cadiz in 1596. Essex was then at the height of his fame and popularity, his every public appearance drawing an eager, jostling crowd of admirers. But his career had only a few more years to run. The disastrous Irish campaign of 1599 ruined his military reputation, the Queen refused to forgive him, and the brilliant star of the late Elizabethan Court went down in debt, disgrace and futile rebellion.

as her carcass, and the doors of Essex House were thrown open to anyone who cared to enter. Here a rabble of impoverished lords and gentlemen who had lost out in the harshly competitive Elizabethan rat-race mingled with soldiers and captains discharged from the wars, and with the bully boys, petty criminals and professional trouble-makers who haunted the streets and taverns of the city. All were ready for mischief and united by their penury, their sense of grievance and their greed.

Wild plans were being made to seize the Court, force the Queen to reinstate the Earl of Essex in his several offices and dismiss his arch-enemy Robert Cecil. The Queen and Robert Cecil watched and waited. Then, on Saturday, February 7, 1601, some of the Earl's friends crossed the river to the Globe Theatre to persuade the Lord Chamberlain's company to put on a special performance of William Shakespeare's *Richard II*. When the actors objected that this was an old piece which would not fill the house, they were offered forty shillings to compensate them for any loss of takings.

To demand to be entertained by a play in which a reigning monarch is deposed and murdered was regarded as a deliberate piece of provocation, and that night Essex was ordered to appear before the Council. He refused to come. Next morning a deputation headed by the Lord Keeper and the Lord Chief Justice went to Essex House to try to restore order, only to be insulted and threatened by the jeering, jostling mob which filled the courtyard. It was many years since London had seen such a riotous assembly. The Queen's representatives were rudely seized and locked up in a back room, while Essex and about 200 of his followers attempted to raise the City, running armed through the Sunday streets crying that a plot was laid for his life and that England was sold to the Spaniard. The citizens, however, stayed indoors and by ten o'clock that evening it was all over. Essex was brought to trial, convicted of high treason and executed before the end of the month, acknowledging that he was thus 'justly spewed out of the realm'. With him went the last flicker of the old, turbulent baronial England, in which an over-mighty subject could challenge the central authority of the state.

As for the Queen, she would, said the Lord Admiral, Charles Howard of Effingham, 'have gone out in person to see what any rebel of them all durst do against her, had not her councillors with much ado, stayed her'. All the same, she had been very much upset by the treachery of her one-time favourite. Sir John Harington, her godson, reported that 'the many evil plots and designs hath overcome all her Highness's sweet temper. She walks much in her privy chamber and stamps with her feet at ill news and thrusts her rusty sword at times into the arras in great rage.' Even when the danger was over, the Queen still kept a sword by her table. She had worn 'but one change of raiment for many days, and swears much at those that cause her griefs, to the no small discomfiture of all about her'.

Hunts and feasts on the last royal progress

Abroad there was nothing but admiration for Elizabeth's handling of the Essex affair. 'She only is a king! She only knows how to rule!' exclaimed the King of France, and certainly there was little sign that her powers were failing. Her summer progress in 1601, the year of Essex's execution, took her to Reading and then on into Hampshire, where she stayed for nearly a fortnight at Basing as the guest of the Marquis of Winchester. There she entertained a grand ambassador's party from France which had been accommodated close by at The Vyne, the stately home of Lord Sandys. Extra plate, hangings and furniture were borrowed from the Tower and Hampton Court. There was hunting and feasting, and the Queen was able to boast 'that she had done more than any of her ancestors had ever done, or any other prince in Christendom was able to do – namely, in her Hampshire progress this year, entertained a royal ambassador royally in her subjects' houses'.

The Hampshire progress was to be the Queen's last long journey but 1602, the last full year of her life, was cheered by good news from Ireland, where the new commander-in-chief, Lord Mountjoy, had finally succeeded in bringing the situation under control. In April the Queen danced a galliard with the Duc de Nevers, another distinguished visitor from France, and on May Day she and the Court went a-maying in the woods round Greenwich. Although there was no royal progress that summer, she stayed at several of the great houses near London, finishing up at Oatlands, where Robert Cecil noted that she had not been in better health for years and was still riding 10 miles in a day and hunting.

In September the Earl of Worcester wrote to the Earl of Shrewsbury: 'We are frolic here at Court; much dancing in the Privy Chamber of country dances before the Queen's majesty who is exceedingly pleased therewith.' Later in the

At the inn door

Wayside inns in 16th-century England were the envy of foreign tourists, who praised their high standards of cleanliness, comfort and service. The hostelry shown in the reconstruction on pages 278–9, close to the gateway of the local manor house (1) is typical of the inns to be found in all towns on the main highways, providing oases of light and warmth for weary travellers on a stormy night. Torches of blazing pitch in metal brackets illuminate the scene (2). Mine host stands, lantern in hand (3), on the threshold beneath the flag that serves as an inn sign (4). An ostler (5) is coming out to help with the horses (6), which are being taken out of the traces of the coach in order to free the coach from the mud. Coaches were a fairly recent innovation, brought in from Germany and the Low Countries, but were still an uncomfortable means of transport. They had no springing, and their only real advantage over the farm cart lay in the protection they offered from the weather. This coach (7), of standard pattern, could accommodate three or four passengers and was drawn by four horses. The coachman sat up in front on a hard wooden bench seat (8) with a footrest. Most people, however, still travelled on horseback. Women sometimes

month another courtier remarked in a letter to the Countess of Shrewsbury: 'The best news I can yet write your ladyship is of the Queen's health and disposition of body, which I assure you is excellent good. And I have not seen her every way better disposed these many years.'

On November 17, the 44th anniversary of the Queen's accession was celebrated with the usual festivities, and the Court fool, who appeared on a pony no bigger than a bull mastiff, 'had good audience of her Majesty and made her very merry'. But not even Elizabeth was immortal. She had now entered her 70th year and Sir John Harington, who had come to town for the Christmas season, was shocked by the change he saw in her. 'Our dear Queen, my royal godmother and this state's natural mother, doth now bear show of human infirmity,' he wrote to his wife down in Somerset.

Harington found the Queen in 'a pitiable state' and tried to cheer her by reading her some of his witty verses. 'Whereat,' he said, 'she smiled once and was pleased to say, "When thou dost feel creeping time at thy gate, these fooleries will please thee less. I am past my relish for these matters." ' She was eating hardly anything and, for the first time, there were signs that her memory was beginning to fail. 'But who,' wrote Harington sadly, 'shall say that "Your Highness hath forgotten"?'

She rallied, however, and in January 1603 was once more said to be very well. On January 21 the Court moved to Richmond. /continued on page 280

rode their own horses but more often travelled pillion, sitting behind husband, father or servant like the couple in this inn yard (9). The yard itself is cobbled and there is a stone rim or edging round the inn, but the road surface is the usual mud (10). Few Elizabethans travelled for pleasure. The roads, even the main trunk routes, remained in a shocking state, and in winter were impassable for wheeled traffic. A journey from London to York would take at least six days.

Victor in Ireland
Charles Blount, Lord Mountjoy, was the Lord Deputy who finally suppressed the Irish rebellion led by the Earl of Tyrone. A quiet, bookish, unspectacular character, with an unexpected talent for command, he went reluctantly to Ireland and wore an extra pair of woollen stockings, three waistcoats and a warm russet scarf to protect himself from the rigours of the climate.

Royal sun after storm
The 'Rainbow Portrait' (opposite page), painted in about 1600, represents the Queen as the sun, a rainbow in her hand promising peace and fair weather after storm. Her hair is shown hanging loose, symbolising virginity, as does her low-cut bodice which is embroidered with spring flowers, another allusion to eternal youth. The coiled serpent worked on her sleeve is the ancient symbol of wisdom, and the eyes and ears which cover her cloak signify the all-seeing, all-hearing vigilance of the politic ruler.

continued from page 277/The weather had turned very cold, but the Queen insisted on wearing 'summer-like garments'. On February 6 she received the new Venetian ambassador, dressed in white and silver, her hair 'of a light colour never made by nature', and apparently in good spirits. Then, towards the end of the month, she lost her cousin and closest woman friend, the Countess of Nottingham. Her mood of depression returned, and this time she did not throw it off.

Early in March the Queen's young kinsman Robert Carey came down to Richmond and found her in one of her withdrawing chambers, sitting huddled on a pile of cushions. 'She took me by the hand,' he wrote, 'and wrung it hard and said, "No, Robin, I am not well"; and then discoursed with me of her indisposition, and that her heart had been sad and heavy for ten or twelve days, and in her discourse she fetched forty or fifty great sighs. I was grieved at the first to see her in this plight, for in all my lifetime before I never knew her fetch a sigh, but when the Queen of Scots was beheaded.'

Carey did his best 'to persuade her from this melancholy humour', but found it was too deeply rooted in her heart and hardly to be removed. This was on a Saturday. Next day the Queen was unable to go to church, and heard the service lying on cushions in her privy chamber. 'From that day forwards,' says Robert Carey, 'she grew worse and worse. She remained upon her cushions four days and nights at the least. All about her could not persuade her either to take any sustenance or go to bed.'

Death at Richmond Palace, 'mildly like a lamb'

The immediate cause of the Queen's last illness seems to have been a quinsy or severely ulcerated throat which made swallowing difficult and painful, but soon pneumonia set in. Still no one could persuade her to go to bed until, at last, her old friend Charles Howard, the Lord Admiral, was sent for. Partly by coaxing, partly by force, he got her off her cushions and into bed, but 'there was no hope of her recovery because she refused all remedies'.

Elizabeth had always said that she did not desire to live longer than would be for her subjects' good, and now it seemed as if she felt her task was done. Recently the coronation ring, outward and visible token of her symbolic marriage to the people of England which for nearly 45 years had never left her finger, had grown into the flesh and had to be cut away. It was an omen. The Queen grew worse and worse, said Robert Carey significantly, 'because she would be so'.

On Wednesday, March 23 she became speechless, and that evening the Archbishop of Canterbury prayed at her bedside 'till the old man's knees were weary' and he rose to leave her, but the Queen would not let him go, indicating by signs that she wished him to pray still. At last she sank into a coma and 'everyone departed, all but her women that attended her'. She died very peacefully – 'mildly like a lamb, easily like a ripe apple from the tree' – in the early hours of March 24, 1603. For very many of her contemporaries, England would never be the same again.

Queen Elizabeth was carried to her tomb in Westminster Abbey on April 28, at which time, John Stow recorded in his Annals, 'the City of Westminster was surcharged with multitudes of all sorts of people, in the streets, houses, windows, leads and gutters, who came to see the obsequy. And when they beheld her statue or effigy, lying on the coffin, set forth in royal robes, having a crown upon the head thereof, and a ball and sceptre in either hand, there was such a general sighing, groaning and weeping, as the like hath not been seen or known in the memory of man.' It was the end of an era, and as the new century, with all its strains and stresses, began to unfold, people looked back more and more nostalgically to the days of 'Good Queen Bess' until the Queen and her reign became surrounded in a golden haze of perfection.

In fact it was never quite so idyllic as that, but the achievements of the Queen and of the age which bears her name were phenomenal enough. When Elizabeth came to the throne England was an impoverished, factious, second-rate power, despised and discounted by its European neighbours. When she died, she left a strong, prosperous and self-confident nation, feared and respected by the whole civilised world.

A reign that gave England peace and prosperity

To her people, the Queen's greatest single triumph was undoubtedly the fact that, while successfully challenging the might of Spain, she had also succeeded in keeping the struggle against anti-Christ out of English territory. 'God, even our God, gave us Queen Elizabeth,' exclaimed the Bishop of Salisbury; 'and with her gave us peace, and so long a peace as England hath seldom seen.' Throughout the bloody wars which tore 16th-century Europe apart, no foot of English countryside was laid waste. No English farmstead was burned down, no English town was looted or put to the sword, no Englishman, woman or child slaughtered by an invading army. In all England during Elizabeth's rule, as the contemporary historian William Camden put it, 'never any mortal man heard the trumpet sound the charge to battle'.

The cost had been high, but for a country fighting for its life against a powerful and determined enemy, taxation generally remained astonishingly low. The brunt of the financial burden was borne by the Queen, and although in the long term this fatally weakened the monarchy, it enabled the nation as a whole to prosper and grow rich.

In a suddenly expanding world, the time of Elizabeth was an age of adventure and of opportunity seldom paralleled. The Elizabethan aventurers – tough, individualistic, self-seeking and all cheerfully convinced that God was an Englishman – went out to seize those opportunities. They were a comparatively small band, but in the opinion of Richard Hakluyt, writing the Epistle Dedicatory of his *Principal Navigations, Traffics and Discoveries of the English Nation*, the Queen's subjects had excelled all the nations and peoples of the earth 'in searching the most opposite corners and quarters of the world'. Hakluyt demanded 'Which of the kings of this land before her Majesty had their banners ever seen in the Caspian Sea? Which of them hath ever dealt

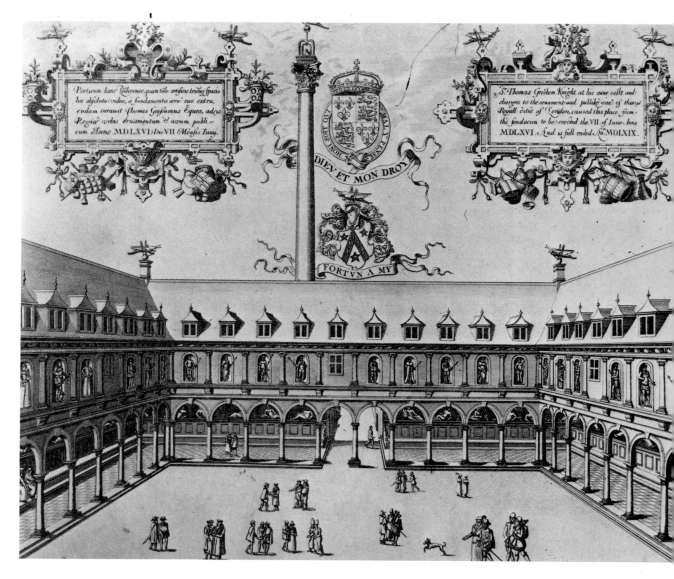

with the Emperor of Persia, as her Majesty hath done, and obtained for her merchants large and loving privileges? who ever saw before this regiment, an English Ligier [embassy representative] in the stately porch of the Grand Signior at Constantinople? who ever found English Consuls and Agents at Tripolis in Syria, at Aleppo, at Babylon, at Basra, and which is more, who ever heard of an Englishman at Goa before now? what English ships did heretofore ever anchor in the mighty river of Plate? pass and repass the unpassable (in former opinion) strait of Magellan, range along the coast of Chile, Peru, and all the backside of Nova Hispania, further than any Christian ever passed, traverse the mighty breadth of the South Sea, land upon the Luzones [the Philippines] in despite of the enemy, enter into alliance, amity and traffic with the princes of the Moluccas, and the Isle of Java, double the famous Cape of Bona Speranza, arrive at the Isle of St Helena, and last of all return home most richly laden with the commodities of China, as the subjects of this now flourishing monarchy have done?'

At home, the merchant class was flourishing as never before. Thomas

Merchants' shop-window
The growing prosperity of the City of London was reflected in the new Royal Exchange, built by the financier Sir Thomas Gresham for the use of his fellow merchants. It was given its royal title by the Queen in the course of a state visit to the City in January 1571. Sir Thomas let the shops in the arcade surrounding the main quadrangle of the Exchange rent-free for a year, on condition that the traders filled them with their best wares and illuminated them with wax lights for the occasion.

Wilson, writing of the state of England in the year 1600, declared that in his time he had known 24 aldermen in the city of Norwich 'which were esteemed to be worth £20,000 a piece, some much more, and the better sort of citizens the half'. But, Wilson went on, 'if we should speak of London and some other maritime places we should find it much exceeding this rate. It is well known that at this time there are in London some merchants worth £100,000, and he is not accounted rich that cannot reach to £50,000 or near it.'

Wilson's figures may be somewhat exaggerated, but great entrepreneurs like Andrew Judd, Thomas Gresham, Lionel Ducket, William Chester and Sir Thomas Smythe were able to live in princely fashion and buy themselves country estates; sooner or later every successful Elizabethan businessman invested in land. Lower down the scale, prosperous and ambitious yeomen – farmers, clothiers, graziers and tradesmen – were busy building themselves new houses, dressing their wives and daughters in silk and velvet, sending their sons to university, and setting themselves up as gentlemen.

Spires and shrivelled heads
Most of the familiar Elizabethan features of the London skyline survive in this mid-17th-century panoramic map. Churches thrust up a forest of spires and steeples, while the southern gateway of the Bridge is still decorated with a ghoulish pin-cushion formed from the shrivelled heads of executed criminals. Houses and shops had been a feature of the

The Tower

Bridge since soon after it was built at the end of the 12th century. Small vessels crowd the river above the Bridge, while larger, ocean-going craft throng in front of the Tower. In the foreground, St Saviour's Church, Southwark – later to become Southwark Cathedral – rises above an area of the South Bank that is becoming increasingly built up.

'As for gentlemen, they be made good cheap in England,' remarked another observer of the social scene. 'For whosoever . . . can live idly and without manual labour and will bear the port, charge and countenance of a gentleman, he shall be called master . . . and shall be taken for a gentleman.' Those wishing to do things thoroughly could pay a king of heralds to provide them with a coat of arms, not infrequently 'newly made and invented, the title whereof shall pretend to have been found by the said herald in perusing and viewing of old registers'.

This craze for gentility was scoffed at by moralists. 'Everyone vaunts himself,' complained Philip Stubbes, 'crying with open mouth, "I am gentleman, I am worshipful, I am honourable, I am noble" and I cannot tell what. "My father was this, my father was that." "I am come of this house, I am come of that . . .".' But the social climbers paid no attention. In a status-conscious age to become armigerous – that is, to win the right to bear a coat of arms – was a definite step up the social ladder, an achievement that mattered to the Eliza-

The Queen's successor

The son of Mary, Queen of Scots was a man of 36 when he finally succeeded Queen Elizabeth on the English throne. James I's personal habits were unattractive, and his pro-Spanish policy, his High Church views and his assertion of the doctrine of the Divine Right of Kings combined to alienate almost every section of the community. At the same time, James I was intelligent and strong-minded enough to maintain his authority without serious challenge during the 22 years of his reign. It is to his inspiration that the English-speaking world owes the Authorised Version of the Bible.

bethans. It mattered to William Shakespeare who, as soon as he had made a success in London, took steps to obtain a coat of arms for his father, impaling it with those of the Ardens, his mother's family.

The whole reign saw a steady rise of the gentry and professional middle-class – at the expense, it is sometimes said, of the aristocracy. But although the old feudal lords lost much of their political power under the Tudors, the aristocracy in general continued to prosper. Of course, some old families decayed and some, like the Nevilles and Dacres of the North, had been unwise enough to challenge the new order in the Rising of 1569. The Duke of Norfolk, England's premier nobleman and only duke, who counted himself as good a prince as any at home in his bowling alley at Norwich, also became foolishly and fatally involved in the intrigues surrounding Mary, Queen of Scots. The Earl of Essex and his crony the Earl of Southampton dabbled in treason, and the Earl of Oxford ruined himself by extravagance.

These, though, were the exceptions. The other great landed families – the Talbots and Stranges, Russells, Cavendishes, Pagets and Paulets to name but a few – stayed loyal to the Crown and wielded immense local influence. They, too, were growing richer on rising rents and the exploitation of the mineral resources on their estates, and Thomas Wilson estimated that the total revenue of the nobility in 1600 amounted to £220,000 per annum.

A new respect for the voiceless poor

As for the labourers and poor husbandmen, and tradesmen such as tailors, shoemakers, carpenters and bricklayers, their lives went on as they had always done, though of course they also benefited from the long Elizabethan period of peace and stable government. This, by far the most numerous section of the community, had 'no voice nor authority in our commonwealth, and no account is made of them but only to be ruled'. And yet, says Sir Thomas Smith in his treatise on the constitution written during the 1560s, 'they be not altogether neglected. For in cities and corporate towns for default of yeomen, inquests and juries are impanelled of such manner of people. And in villages they be commonly made churchwardens, ale-conners [inspectors], and many times constables, which office toucheth more the commonwealth, and at first was not employed upon such low and base persons.'

In good years the poor husbandmen lived well, feasting each other at weddings, churchings and christenings 'where it is incredible to tell what meat is consumed and spent, each one bringing such a dish or so many with him as his wife and he do consult upon'. In bad years they went hungry, making do with bread 'made either of beans, peas, or oats, or of all together and some acorns among, of which scourge the poorest do soonest taste, since they are least able to provide themselves of better'.

In really bad years, such as the great 'dearth' of the early 1590s, when a succession of drenching summers resulted in a series of ruined harvests, the poorest could starve to death, in spite of all efforts at relief. But they were still far better off than many of their European counterparts, for no contending

Reward from a king
This gold locket, enamelled and set with diamonds, contains a miniature of James I attributed to Nicholas Hilliard and dated about 1610. The locket, when closed with the hinged cover incorporating the monogram IR ('Jacobus Rex'), is about 3 in. tall. The King presented the Lyte Jewel to Thomas Lyte of Lyte's Carey in Somerset in recognition of services rendered in drawing up a royal family tree.

armies fought over their fields, no unpaid, mutinous soldiers rampaged through their villages and, while the Queen's government was often power-less to protect them from the worst effects of famine or economic recession, it never actively oppressed them. They might have no voice nor authority in the commonwealth, but they were still freeborn Englishmen who through their labour played, and knew they played, a vital part in the life of the country.

The population of Elizabethan England rose from approximately $4\frac{1}{2}$ million in 1558 to approximately 5 million by 1603, but it was still a small place, very much a family affair. The vast majority of people lived out their lives in the parishes where they were born, and the inhabitants of whole districts were bound together from the cradle to the grave by a complex web of custom and kinship, marriage ties and business partnerships, family loyalties and feuds.

The same men worked on the same land together from boyhood to old age. The women gossiped and sewed and span together, and helped at one another's childbeds. The children grew up together, the squire's son and the yeoman farmer's son sitting side by side on the benches of the local grammar school. Neighbour's boy married neighbour's girl and the village danced at their wedding. The parish went to church together Sunday by Sunday, and in the end neighbour lay beside neighbour in the graveyard outside. It is easy to be dazzled by the exploits of the glorious few, but equally necessary to remember that the solid, wholesome fabric of the nation from which they sprang was made up by the narrow, laborious lives of the many thousands of little people, whose written memorials consist of a few musty court records, the occasional letter or account book, but whose living memorial is the English landscape,

The final journey
The ladies of the Court – count-esses and viscountesses, earls' daughters and baronesses, with the Maids of Honour and the Privy Chamber – followed Elizabeth's funeral cortège on its way to Westminster Abbey, while the people of London crowded into the streets, filled every window and stood on the roof-tops to see the Queen go by on her last journey. There was,

Countesses Assistants. xiiij.   Countesses and Viscountesses.

the English tradition and culture they helped to create.

The legacy left by the Elizabethans, great and simple, still lies all about us. The houses they built and lived in can be seen up and down the country, from palaces like Longleat in Wiltshire and Hardwick, elegant and graceful on its Derbyshire escarpment, to the more typical manor and farm and town houses, half-timbered or local stone, rosy weathered brick or the elaborate plasterwork of East Anglia. Many of these houses are lived in to this day, and many an Elizabethan framework still lies hidden behind a Georgian or Victorian façade.

Works that survive, faces that remain familiar

says the tailor and chronicler John Stow, 'such a general sighing, groaning and weeping as the like hath not been seen or known in the memory of man'. Before the funeral procession, part of which is seen in this painting by William Camden, the Queen's coffin was brought by river to Whitehall Steps from Richmond Palace, where she died early in the morning of March 24, 1603.

Many of the beautiful and functional things that the Elizabethans made and wore can still be seen today, and the faces of the great and famous still gaze from their portraits: the Queen, elegant, high-nosed, with those strange moth's eyes which look as if they never slept; the Cecils, father and son, calm and watchful, with those formidably intelligent foreheads; Leicester in his prime, handsome and arrogant; Essex with the beard he grew after Cadiz; Raleigh, 'that great Lucifer' as his enemies called him, brilliant and restless; the Earl of Cumberland dressed for the tilt; Philip Sidney, scholar, poet, courtier and soldier, the model for Elizabethan youth; Richard Grenville, hot-eyed, with more than a hint of paranoia about him, and so many more. They can be seen on their tombs: Bess of Hardwick, business tycoon, dynast and dreamer of dreams, lying in state in All Saints Church, Derby; old Lord Burghley with his staff of office by the altar of St Martin's at Stamford; Black John Norris and his brother, two soldierly figures from a family which gave four sons to the

rles Doughters and Baronesses.   *Maides of Honor and of the priuy chamber.*

Queen and empress

In this portrait (opposite page) the Queen is represented as 'empress of the world', her feet firmly planted on a map of England. The portrait is thought to have been painted to mark the entertainment of the Queen by Sir Henry Lee at Ditchley, his Oxfordshire home, in 1592. Sir Henry was for many years the principal organiser of the Accession Day Tilts.

Tomb for a Speaker

Sir John Puckering was twice Speaker of the House of Commons and became Lord Keeper of the Great Seal in 1591. He died five years later and lies in stately effigy beside his wife on his tomb in Westminster Abbey. Below kneel the figures of their eight children; two carry skulls to indicate that they died before their father.

Queen's service, kneeling together in Westminster Abbey; and many more.

Still surviving are the love letters and business letters, the diaries and memoranda of these long-dead Englishmen and women. Their songs and plays and poetry form part of the well-loved and familiar furniture of English minds, for it was the Elizabethans – significantly the first generation to be brought up on the English Bible and Cranmer's prayerbook – who first fully explored and exploited all the rich beauty and variety of the language.

At the end of Queen Elizabeth's reign England stood at the beginning of a 250 year journey which would turn the nation from a small, fertile, well-wooded island living principally from agriculture and sheep-farming into a trading super-power and industrial giant, the ruler of the seas and centre of the world's greatest empire. This achievement stems in large part from the tradition set by the Elizabethan sea-dogs, indefatigably nosing their way through fields of ice and tropical hurricanes into the remotest corners of the earth in the little ships which sailed from Plymouth and Falmouth, from Bristol and Southampton and London River. To them, too, is owed the fact that the North American continent became English-speaking, perhaps their greatest legacy of all.

Gloriana: a memory that 'shall for ever live'

The English of Elizabethan England were a vigorous, thrusting, free-spoken people. Foreigners thought them courageous but notoriously fickle and light-minded. 'They are not vindictive,' wrote Emmanuel van Meteren, a Dutchman living in London, 'but very inconstant, rash, vainglorious, light and deceiving.' A German visitor to the capital complained of the rudeness of the Cockney street boys and apprentices, and found the Londoners a proud, overbearing lot. 'They care little for foreigners,' he commented, 'but scoff and laugh at them.'

They were a proud race, especially the Londoners, but they were also in their rough way a tolerant people in an age that was generally intolerant, and they were slow to rouse to anger.

Presiding over them, as she said, like a mother, the Queen remains the genius of the age. To us, as we look back across the centuries, the cult of Gloriana, the glorification and idealisation of an ageing, over-dressed woman into a curious amalgam of Protestant saint and classical goddess may seem excessive, even perhaps a little ridiculous, but to the Elizabethans, nurtured as they were on the Bible and the classics, it was entirely logical. In any case, by the 1580s and 1590s, Elizabeth had become an almost mystical symbol. She *was* Protestant England, and not only gave the nation a natural focal point for legitimate pride and patriotism but, in an age of transition when all sorts of upsetting ideas were beginning to work their way to the surface, she also represented continuity and inspired her people with an instinctive confidence that as long as she reigned the Protestant God would look after his own.

Four hundred years after her death she still gives Englishmen a legitimate cause for pride. 'No oblivion shall ever bury the glory of her name,' wrote her contemporary, the historian William Camden. 'For her happy and renowned memory still liveth and shall for ever live in the minds of men.'

The Elizabethan heritage

STATELY MANOR HOUSES AND HUMBLE FARMHOUSES
STILL BEAR WITNESS TO THE SKILLS OF ELIZABETHAN ARCHITECTS IN BRICK AND STONE, WHILE
MUSEUMS AND ART GALLERIES DISPLAY THE PAINTINGS, THE JEWELS, THE CLOTHES
AND OTHER CREATIONS OF A LIVELY AND INVENTIVE AGE. THIS A-Z GAZETTEER EXPLORES
THE RICH HERITAGE OF THE ELIZABETHAN AGE UP AND DOWN THE COUNTRY.

Adlington Hall *Cheshire*

An inscription carved into an oak beam in the Quadrangle at Adlington records that: 'Thomas Leyghe Esquyer . . . made this buyldinge in the yeare of O Lorde Gode 1581 and in the raigne of our Soveyraigne Lady Queen Elizabeth . . .'

Adlington has been the home of the Legh family for more than 650 years, and in that time the house has undergone many changes and additions. What remains of the exterior of Thomas Legh's 'buyldinge' is the Elizabethan east front, in typical Cheshire 'black and white'.

Thomas Legh's son, Sir Urian Legh (1566–1601), fought with the Earl of Essex in Spain and was knighted by him at the capture of Cadiz.

Adlington has a fine Elizabethan oak staircase, its newels surmounted by carved fir cones. In the Great Hall is an elaborate canopy with heraldic panels painted in 1581.

Adlington is 4 miles north of Macclesfield, off the A523.

Arreton Manor *Isle of Wight*

Arreton was granted to the Convent of Quarr after the Norman Conquest, but was taken over by the Crown at the Dissolution. The present house was built between 1595 and 1612.

The panelling in the Hall is late Elizabethan and the table is dated 1580. Also displayed in the Hall is a rare Elizabethan baby's bonnet. In the Long Room is the will of Barnaby Leigh, who farmed Arreton in Queen Elizabeth's time. The ghost of Leigh's little daughter, said to have been murdered by her brother, is supposed to haunt the house and gardens.

Arreton Manor remained Crown property until about 1628, when Charles I disposed of it to settle part of his debts to the City of London.

The manor is 3 miles south-east of Newport, off the A3056.

Arundel Castle *W. Sussex*

Portraits of a host of notable personalities of Tudor times are among the treasures of Arundel Castle, begun in the 11th century in a commanding position overlooking the valley of the River Arun and the seat since 1580 of the Howard family, dukes of Norfolk.

Arundel Castle became the home of the Howards when the 4th Duke of Norfolk married Lady Mary Fitzalan, daughter of the 12th Earl of Arundel. Their son, Philip, the 13th Earl, a zealous Roman Catholic, was in 1589 accused of conspiring with foreign Catholics and having a Mass said for the success of the Spanish Armada. He was convicted and imprisoned in the Tower of London, where he died six

years later. In 1970 he was canonised as Saint Philip Howard.

Both Lady Mary Fitzalan and the 4th Duke of Norfolk were painted by Hans Eworth. In the Dining Room of Arundel Castle are an illuminated prayer book and a gold rosary carried by Mary, Queen of Scots at her execution.

Ashley *Staffs.*

CHURCH OF ST JOHN THE BAPTIST The massive monument is that of Sir Gilbert Gerard, who died in 1592. A staunch Protestant, he had been imprisoned by Queen Mary for his support of Princess Elizabeth. When Elizabeth came to the throne she knighted him and appointed him Keeper of the Rolls and Attorney-General.

The life-size figures of Sir Gilbert and his wife, Anne Radcliffe, lie side by side: he is dressed in a full suit of armour, and his wife wears a richly ornamented dress. His son Thomas, Lord Gerard, kneels at his head, and at the back his four daughters are carved in relief.

The Gerard monument is the chief treasure of a church known to have been founded by 1205, but largely rebuilt in the Victorian age.

Ashridge *Herts.*

As a child, the future Queen Elizabeth spent much of her time at a converted 13th-century monastery at Ashridge. Here she was arrested in 1554, suspected of complicity in

Sir Thomas Wyatt's rebellion against her sister, Queen Mary.

The original monastery, founded in 1283, was seized by Henry VIII at the Dissolution. Henry left the house to Elizabeth in his will, but it was not handed over to her until 1550. In 1556 Elizabeth leased the property to a local farmer, Richard Combe; the original deed of lease, signed by Elizabeth, hangs in the library.

In the 19th century Ashridge was almost entirely rebuilt by James Wyatt, and little remains of the house Elizabeth knew. It is today a management college.

Ashridge is off the A4146, 5 miles north-west of Hemel Hempstead.

Avebury Manor *Wilts.*

A few miles from the great prehistoric stone circle of Avebury stands a gabled manor house, built during the 16th century, partly by Sir William Sharington, owner of the Bristol Mint, and partly by William Dunch, an auditor of the London Mint, who bought the house from Sharington. The south front was added by Sir James Mervyn, High Sheriff of Wiltshire, in 1600.

The Little Parlour, with its fine panelling, is dated 1560. The Great Parlour has a fascinating narrow-ribbed plaster ceiling. The fireplace in the bedroom was mentioned by the 17th-century antiquarian John Aubrey.

Portraits of the ancestors of the Marquess of Ailesbury, a former owner of Avebury Manor, still hang on the walls. One of these was Sir Edward Seymour, whose sister Jane married Henry VIII, and who, as Duke of Somerset, was Protector of the Realm in Edward VI's reign. Another was Seymour's son Edward, Earl of Hertford, who was imprisoned in the Tower by Elizabeth for marrying Lady Jane Grey's sister Katherine without permission.

The manor is off Avebury High Street, near the church.

Bacton *Heref. & Worcs.*

CHURCH OF ST FAITH The pride of this church is the unusual monument to Blanche Parry, who was one of Queen Elizabeth's ladies-in-waiting. Blanche is shown kneeling before the Queen, and the inscription reads: 'Allwaye wythe maeden queene a maede did ende my liffe.'

Basing *Hants.*

BASING HOUSE Brick walls, a gate-house and dovecote survive of a vast Tudor mansion built in the mid-16th century by Sir William Paulet, the 1st Marquess of Winchester. Elizabeth visited the house twice, in 1560 and 1601. In 1645 Cromwell's troops captured the house after a three-year siege and razed it.

The 3rd Marquess, William Paulet (1535–98) is remembered for a Latin acrostic he wrote. It consists of six lines of verse in which the initial letters of each line form the word *regina*, the last letters form *nostra*, and the initial letters of the words in the last line form *Angliae*, giving *Regina Nostra Angliae*, 'Our English Queen'.

There is a collection of Tudor and Elizabethan sculpture and pottery in the Old Bothy, built over the original powder magazine of the house.

The ruins of Basing House are 1½ miles east of Basingstoke, off the A30.

Beaupre *S. Glam.*

This Elizabethan mansion, now restored, has a fine inner porch, dating from 1600. Although mainly classical in design, it has a four-centred Tudor arch.

The home of the Basset family since the 13th century, Beaupre was extensively rebuilt during the 16th century by William Basset (d. 1586) and his son Richard, who added the porch. The family was ruined in the Civil War, and Beaupre was abandoned towards the end of the 17th century.

Beaupre is a mile south-west of St Hilary, off the A48 Cardiff–Bridgend road.

Berkeley Castle *Glos.*

Very few private houses are mentioned by name in Shakespeare's plays. Berkeley Castle, however, achieves that distinction in *Richard II* when Bolingbroke asks Northumberland:

'How far is it, my lord, to Berkeley now?'

Northumberland replies:

'Believe me, noble lord,
I am a stranger here in Gloucestershire.'

For the Elizabethan enthusiast, the 800-year-old castle has two points of particular interest.

In the 14th-century part of the building is Drake's Room, which contains his supposed cypress chest, part of the furnishings of his cabin aboard the *Golden Hind*.

In the gardens of Berkeley Castle is an Elizabethan terraced garden, with a bowling alley.

Berkeley Castle is 16 miles south-west of Gloucester, off the A38.

Berwick-upon-Tweed *Northld*

Between 1558 and 1560 the medieval walls of this fortified border town were massively reinforced with great bastions as a defence against the Scots.

The fortifications, designed by an Italian engineer, are among the finest of the 16th century in Europe.

Birmingham *W. Midlands*

BLAKESLEY HALL Amid the suburban sprawl of Birmingham stands this typical Worcestershire yeoman's house of the Elizabethan period.

The ground plan is L-shaped and, the construction is of timber frame and plaster. The interior has original partitions and a moulded stone fireplace. The hall, kitchen and Long Gallery are furnished with period pieces, and the bedroom has Elizabethan wall-paintings.

Blakesley Hall is at Yardley, $3\frac{3}{4}$ miles east of the centre of Birmingham.

Blickling Hall *Norfolk*

In the mid-15th century, Sir John Fastolf (*c.* 1378–1459), the soldier on whose name Shakespeare is said to have based that of Falstaff, sold the manor of Blickling to Sir Geoffrey Boleyn, a rich London merchant who was Lord Mayor in 1457. Sir Geoffrey was the great-grandfather of Anne Boleyn, and therefore Queen Elizabeth's maternal great-great-grandfather.

The present house was built by Sir Henry Hobart (d. 1625) who was Lord Chief Justice under James I. Building started in 1616 under the architect Robert Lyminge, who had built Hatfield House for the Cecil family. It has a warm red-brick façade, turrets and curved gables.

The interior has been altered over the centuries, but the grand staircase remains.

Blickling is $1\frac{1}{2}$ miles north-west of Aylsham on the B1354, 15 miles north of Norwich.

Borthwick Castle *Lothian*

Built in 1430 by the first Lord Borthwick, the Castle was held in the mid-16th century by the 6th Lord Borthwick, a supporter of Mary, Queen of Scots.

It was to Borthwick that Mary fled in June 1567, after her marriage to the Earl of Bothwell, the suspected murderer of her second husband, Darnley. On June 11, Lord Home's forces surrounded the castle. Bothwell escaped and later Mary followed him.

Borthwick is now a conference centre, but the Great Hall, with its huge fireplace and minstrel's gallery, has been preserved, and visitors can sleep in Mary, Queen of Scots' Bedchamber, in a bed made for Bonnie Prince Charlie.

Borthwick is off the A7, 11 miles south-east of Edinburgh.

Borwick Hall *Lancs.*

In 1567 Robert Bindloss, a rich wool merchant of Kendal, bought part of the manor of Borwick. In 1590 he set about transforming the 14th-century manor into a mansion.

The west wing, with its mullioned and transomed windows and lofty porch, is dated 1595. The baronial hall is of the same date. In the grounds are some long barns thought to have been built by Christopher Bindloss about 1600.

Borwick is 2 miles north-east of Carnforth, close to access point 35 on the M6.

Bosbury *Heref. & Worcs.*

CHURCH OF THE HOLY TRINITY The church contains two remarkable Elizabethan monuments.

The monument to John Harford is dated 1573 and is by the master craftsman John Guldo of Hereford. It shows a sarcophagus supported by two lions, with a recumbent effigy under a coffered arch, embellished with Tudor roses. The monument to Richard Harford and his wife, dated 1578, is also probably by John Guldo.

The church also has a 13th-century detached tower and the 16th-century chapel of the Morton family.

CROWN INN The Oak Room of this old inn has panelling dated 1571.

Boughton Monchelsea Place *Kent*

An Elizabeth mansion once owned by a supporter of the Wyatt rebellion against Queen Mary stands 300 ft above sea level and commands an impressive view of the heart of Kent, with Romney Marsh and the sea to the south-east.

In 1551 Robert Rudston, son of a Lord Mayor of London, bought the medieval hall-house at Boughton from his friend Sir Thomas Wyatt for £1,730. In 1554 Wyatt, outraged by Queen Mary's proposed marriage to Philip of Spain, raised an army of 'Men of Kent' and persuaded Rudston to join the rebellion. The uprising, in which Princess Elizabeth was accused of having a hand, was crushed and Wyatt was executed.

Rudston was sent to the Tower and his property was confiscated. In 1555, however, he obtained a pardon and repurchased Boughton from the Crown for £1,000. By 1575 he was building the mansion that, with later additions and alterations, exists today. It contains part of the original staircase, and many other features of the period.

Boughton Monchelsea is 5 miles south of Maidstone off the A229.

Bramhall *Greater Manchester*

BRAMALL HALL This largely 16th-century timber-framed mansion, with its spectacular 'magpie' black and white exterior, was for 500 years the seat of the Davenport family.

The house contains a collection of Elizabethan portraits, notably those of John and Margaret Warren of Poynton, dated respectively 1580 and 1595. The Warrens were the parents of Dame Dorothy Davenport.

In the Plaster Room is the

Davenport Heraldic Tapestry, woven between 1575 and 1580, which sets out the marriage alliances of the family. The central shield depicts a Tudor queen, almost certainly intended to be Elizabeth.

The Withdrawing Room is a grand interior, dated 1592. The intricate plaster overmantel bears the arms of the Queen.

Bramall Hall is at Bramhall south of Stockport, just west of the A5102.

Brockhall *Northants.*

The south front and the east side of this mansion are well-preserved examples of Elizabethan architecture. The north front is 18th-century Gothic.

The house has been for many centuries the home of the Thornton family. It is not open to the public.

Brockhall is off the A5, 5 miles east of Daventry.

Broughton Castle *Oxon.*

A moated manor house at Broughton was transformed into a Tudor mansion between 1550 and 1600 by Richard Fiennes and his son, also Richard. The elaborate plaster ceiling in the White Room bears at one end the initials R E F – Richard and Elizabeth Fiennes – and at the other the date 1599.

The Elizabethan additions include broad windows, making the interior of the castle exceptionally light and airy, and two ornate fireplaces. One of these, in French style, is believed to be similar to chimney-pieces made for Henry VIII for Nonsuch Palace.

The castle has been the home of the Lords Saye and Sele for more than 500 years.

Broughton Castle is 2 miles south-west of Banbury, on the B4035.

Buckland Abbey *Devon*

After sailing round the world in the *Golden Hind*, Sir Francis Drake sought a home in England that would suit his new-found fame and fortune. He coveted the converted Cistercian monastery of Buckland Abbey, which was owned by his rival, Sir Richard Grenville. Today Buckland Abbey is a museum and memorial to both men.

The abbey was built by Cistercian monks in 1278. After the Dissolution it was bought from the crown by Sir Richard Grenville whose grandson, the famous Sir Richard, completed its conversion. In 1581 Drake fulfilled his ambition to buy Buckland Abbey, after making an offer through a third party of some £3,400, which was accepted.

During the Civil War Grenville's grandson, another Sir Richard, succeeded in ousting the Drakes from Buckland, but in 1646, when the Royalists were defeated, the Drakes regained possession and it remained their family home until 1937.

The house is now a memorial to the vigorous, adventurous spirit of both Drake and Grenville. A notable relic is Drake's Drum, displayed in the Drake Gallery. Sir Henry Newbolt's poem *Drake's Drum* expresses the folklore that surrounds this drum, which is supposed to beat whenever England is in danger.

The Gallery also contains an oak chair made of timbers from the *Golden Hind*; Drake's will, signed by him as he lay dying off Puerto Bello in 1596; and the Letters Patent, bearing Elizabeth's Royal Seal, granting Drake command of the 1587 Cadiz expedition – the 'singeing of the King of Spain's beard'.

The plaster frieze put up by Grenville depicts a knight, his armour hung up, resting from activity, beneath a tree.

In the Gallery is a scale model of the *Golden Hind*. A collection of Drake's papers includes his detailed accounts for the ships that fought against the Armada. There are portraits of Queen Elizabeth, and of Drake as a young man.

The Drawing Room has portraits of Elizabeth; of Sir John Hawkins, Drake's kinsman and fellow-voyager; and of Drake himself, by Gheeraerts.

Among the many other maritime relics at Buckland are the banners which Drake commissioned to dress his ship overall when the Queen knighted him at Deptford in 1580; a mural, showing the positions of the English and Spanish fleets in July 1588; and Drake's coat-of-arms over the fireplaces of both the Great Hall and the Tower Room.

Buckland Abbey is near Yelverton, 11 miles north of Plymouth and west of the A386.

Bunbury *Cheshire*

CHURCH OF ST BONIFACE This mainly 14th-century church contains the elaborately decorated tomb of Sir George Beeston. When an elderly man, Beeston commanded the *Dreadnought*, one of the ships in the fleet that fought the Armada.

Burghley House *Cambs.*

England's largest surviving Elizabethan mansion, Burghley was built by Queen Elizabeth's Lord Treasurer William Cecil, the 1st Lord Burghley (1520–98). Burghley himself was responsible for the style of the house, which was built in three stages over 37 years, between 1552 and 1589.

The house has remained in the possession of the Cecil family to the present day. Over the centuries, succeeding Cecils have transformed much of the interior and put together one of the finest art collections in England.

The chapel is still in use, and the stairs that lead to it are dated 1560. The covers on the bed and chairs in the Queen's Bedroom are Elizabethan.

The Great Hall, perhaps the

outstanding feature of the house, was completed in 1560. It is 68 ft long, 30 ft wide and over 60 ft high. The splendid double hammerbeam roof, incorporating Gothic and Renaissance motifs, is one of the most noteworthy in England. The house contains portraits of Burghley and Elizabeth by Marcus Gheeraerts (c. 1510–90).

Burghley is a mile south-east of Stamford, Lincs. off the B1081.

Burnley *Lancs.*
TOWNELEY HALL An Elizabethan Long Gallery, 85 ft long, has panelled walls, a ceiling worked with the initials of members of the Towneley family, and some fine examples of period furniture.

The house dates from the 14th century, but has been greatly altered over the centuries, both inside and outside.

Towneley is 1 mile south-east of Burnley, on the A671.

Burton Agnes Hall *Humberside*
This delightful mansion was begun in 1598, and has been little altered since its completion in 1610. Outside, the building is in regular Tudor style, except for the bow windows, which were uncommon elsewhere at this period.

Inside there is a feast of Elizabethan decoration. The carving, plasterwork and panelling in the Great Hall are ornate, and so is the chimney-piece in the drawing-room. The staircase is richly carved, and there are several outstanding pieces of Elizabethan furniture.

Burton Agnes Hall was built by Sir Henry Griffith, who married Elizabeth Throckmorton of Coughton Court.

Burton Agnes is 6 miles south-west of Bridlington, off the A166.

Cadzow Castle *Strathclyde*
One of Scotland's romantic ruins,

brooding above the River Avon, Cadzow was the stronghold of the powerful Hamilton family. In 1568 Mary, Queen of Scots took refuge there after her escape from Loch Leven Castle.

Cadzow was the base of Mary's operations against the Earl of Moray's faction, but when the Hamiltons were defeated at the Battle of Langside on May 13 Mary fled south. For three days she lived in the open, eating oatmeal and sour milk, before spending a night at Dundrennan Abbey and then crossing the Solway to take refuge in England.

Cadzow is 2 miles south of Hamilton, west of the A72.

Carlisle *Cumbria*
CASTLE Mary, Queen of Scots arrived at Carlisle Castle in 1568 as an honoured guest; she remained there as a prisoner. After the rout of her forces at the Battle of Langside on May 13, Mary had fled to England, calculating that her cousin, Queen Elizabeth, would be more likely to restore her throne than the King of France, who was distracted by religious wars. It proved to be a fatal error of judgment.

The castle, built by William II about 1092, was largely demolished in the 19th century, and the apartments where Mary had been kept were lost. However, the 14th-century main gate, the central keep and Queen Mary's Tower have survived.

Castle Ashby *Northants.*
In the 1530s the castle at Ashby was reported by a contemporary chronicler to be 'now clear down'. A few years later the estate was bought by Sir William Compton, who had made a fortune in London. In 1574 Sir William's son, the first Lord Compton, began to build a grand new house.

Lord Compton's arms are displayed over the doorway in the south-west tower; the Compton family, Marquesses of Northampton, still live in the mansion.

The Great Hall is a notable Elizabethan interior, with its rib-vaulted undercroft, richly carved panelling, and galleries. The fireplace is particularly elaborate.

The building is approached by a $3\frac{1}{2}$ mile avenue through grounds laid out by Capability Brown.

Only the gardens are open to the public.

The castle is in the village of Castle Ashby, a mile north of the A428 Northampton–Bedford road.

Chard *Somerset*
A prosperous town in Elizabeth's time, thanks to the wool trade, Chard has a group of good Elizabethan buildings, collectively known as the Court House.

Other reminders of the era are the interior of the Choughs Hotel in the High Street and the Grammar School, founded in 1671, part of which is in a building dated 1583.

Charlecote Park *Warks.*
'He had . . . fallen into ill company . . . and some, that made a frequent practice of deer-stealing, engaged him in robbing a park that belonged to Sir Thomas Lucy of Charlecote, near Stratford.'

The 'he' is William Shakespeare, and the story of this traditional episode in his childhood appears in a biographical introduction to the 1709 edition of the plays, edited by Nicholas Rowe, who was made Poet Laureate in 1715.

It is likely enough that Shakespeare engaged in some deer-stealing episode, since his early work contains frequent references to hunting the deer. However, the tradition that the young Shakespeare was on one occasion caught, arraigned before Sir Thomas Lucy and either fined or flogged is almost certainly apochryphal; for his references to the Lucy family in *Henry VI* are perfectly friendly.

The Lucys had lived at Charlecote since the 13th century. When Shakespeare's contemporary, Sir Thomas, inherited the estate in 1551 he began to build the mansion that, with substantial 19th-century restoration, still stands today.

The spacious park, with its oak palings, ancient trees, and herd of fallow deer, survives much as Shakespeare would have known it. He would also recognise the gate-house which has survived unaltered, its patterned brick mellowed to a rosy pink.

Of the house itself, only the east front retains its original form and some of its original features. The arms of Elizabeth above the main doorway commemorate her visit in August 1572; the Queen was on her way to Compton Wynyates, having stayed with the Earl of Leicester at Kenilworth.

The interior of Charlecote is largely a 19th-century reconstruction. Throughout the stress is on Elizabethan and Shakespearean associations.

In the Great Hall stand a bust of the Queen, copied from the effigy on her tomb in Westminster Abbey, and a marble bust of Shakespeare. There are portraits of Elizabeth, Henry VIII, Queen Mary and Sir Thomas Lucy.

The third Sir Thomas, a literary scholar and friend of the poet John Donne, was living at Charlecote when Shakespeare, by then a country gentleman in his own right, retired to his house at New Place, Stratford.

Charlecote lies 5 miles east of Stratford-upon-Avon, off the B4086.

Chester *Cheshire*

The city's many architectural treasures include several Elizabethan buildings.

BISHOP LLOYD'S HOUSE This building in Watergate Street is the best example of carved timberwork in Chester. George Lloyd DD was Bishop of Sodor and Man in 1599, and later Bishop of Chester. The interior has original panelling and plasterwork, and a secret doorway and stair.

STANLEY PALACE The black-and-white half-timbered house in Watergate Street was built in 1591 by Sir Peter Warburton, who was Elizabeth's attorney for Cheshire and assisted at the trial of Essex in 1600–1 and Raleigh in 1603. It later became the town house of the Stanleys of Alderley.

TUDOR HOUSE This house in Lower Bridge Street dates from the late 16th century and has many unrestored features.

ABBEY SQUARE A row of 16th-century cottages stands on the east side of the square, which is part of the precincts of Chester Cathedral.

PIED BULL HOTEL Beyond the Town Hall square stands a hotel said to be the oldest licensed premises in the city. The façade is late 18th century, but inside there is good panelling and a fine Elizabethan staircase.

Chiddingstone *Kent*

The row of small 16th-century and 17th-century houses that faces the church of this unspoilt hamlet is virtually unchanged since Elizabethan times. In contrast to the great houses of noblemen and magnates, Chiddingstone provides a glimpse of how the humbler people of the age lived.

CHIDDINGSTONE CASTLE This Gothic Revival castle contains, among its varied collections of art and antiquities, paintings and relics of the House of Stuart, including portraits of Mary, Queen of Scots and her father, James V of Scotland.

Compton Castle *Devon*

In 1577 Sir Humphrey Gilbert of Compton Castle presented Queen Elizabeth with a treatise entitled *How Her Majesty may annoy the King of Spain*. Earlier he had written a draft plan for 'Queen Elizabeth's Academy', to train 'Her Majesty's Wards and others' for service in the army and navy. Yet another of Gilbert's writings, *A Discourse of a Discoverie for a new Passage to Cataia*, published in 1566, had inspired Sir Martin Frobisher to explore the North-West Passage.

Gilbert began life as a soldier. With his brothers John and Adrian and his step-brother Sir Walter Raleigh, he was one of the West Country group bent on voyages into and across the Atlantic. Sir Humphrey served in the defence of Le Havre in 1562–3, and then in Ireland where he was knighted by Sir Henry Sidney. In June 1583 he led an expedition of five ships to found a British colony in America.

Compton Castle remained the property of the Gilbert family until 1800. In 1930 Commander Walter Raleigh Gilbert repurchased it and restored it, and Gilberts continue to live there though the castle now belongs to the National Trust. The building dates mainly from the 14th to 16th centuries and is an unspoilt example of a medieval fortified house. The only known portrait of Sir Humphrey Gilbert hangs there.

Compton is 3 miles west of Torquay, off the A380.

Conwy *Gwynedd*

PLAS MAWR The title is Welsh for 'The Great Mansion' – and it was a great mansion that Robert Wynne set out to build in 1577.

Wynne was a typical Elizabethan adventurer. Scion of an ancient and distinguished Welsh family that claimed descent from Owain Gwynned, Prince of North Wales, Robert fought against the Turks in Hungary with the Emperor Charles V.

The great house he built when he returned from the wars was completed in 1580. Originally surrounded by extensive gardens it has been engulfed by the town of Conwy; yet it remains a monument to the man and his age.

The Banqueting Hall contains a fine fireplace, dated 1580, and some of the glass in the mullioned windows is original, as are the refectory table and oak wall-seats.

The Queen's Parlour derives its name from Elizabeth's initials over the fireplace. The plaster ornamentation in this room incorporates scores of crests and heraldic devices, and the black oak screen is richly carved.

Between the Reception Room, whose wall-seats and tables are original, and the Lantern Room is a secret chamber which once sheltered fugitive priests. The Lantern Room is said to be haunted by the ghost of Dr Dick, a 16th-century physician.

Cotehele House *Cornwall*

This mansion in woods above the Tamar was all but complete by the time Elizabeth came to the throne. It survives virtually unaltered – a fine example of an early Tudor squire's house.

Sir Richard Edgcumbe, who fought for Henry Tudor at the Battle of Bosworth in 1485, built the massive entrance gateway and gate tower, and also the chapel. His son, Sir Piers Edgcumbe, the owner from 1489 to 1539, was responsible for the Hall, with its timbered roof and large open fireplace.

The house remained untouched until 1627, when Thomas Coteele added the north-west tower. Coteele, a wealthy merchant, had come to England during Elizabeth's reign as a refugee from the Low Countries, then in the grip of the Spanish army. He lent vast sums to James I, and married his daughter to another Sir Richard Edgcumbe. Tradition has it that the merchant's treasure chests still lie secreted about the house.

Later in the 17th century the family chose to live at their other house, Mount Edgcumbe, overlooking Plymouth Sound, and from then on Cotehele was lived in only occasionally. It remained in the Edgcumbe family until 1947, when it was acquired by the National Trust.

Cotehele House is 14 miles north of Plymouth, about 3 miles south of the A390.

Coughton Court *Warks.*

A family that gave the Elizabethan age three of its most colourful personalities – a leading diplomat, a conspirator against the Queen, and the secret lover of Sir Walter Raleigh who later became his wife – had its ancestral home at Coughton Court. The family was that of Throckmorton, and the house as it now stands was built by Sir George Throckmorton, of an old Warwickshire landowning family, at the beginning of the 16th century.

His fourth son, Sir Nicholas Throckmorton (1515–71) was one of the most celebrated diplomats of Queen Elizabeth's reign. He became deeply involved in the problems presented by the activities of Mary, Queen of Scots, and was ambassador to France.

Sir Nicholas's daughter, Elizabeth Throckmorton, became lady-in-waiting to Queen Elizabeth. In 1592, however, she found herself a prisoner in the Tower of London, after her secret marriage to the Queen's favourite, Sir Walter Raleigh, and the birth of a child. In September of the same year Raleigh and his wife were released from prison.

A Throckmorton cousin, Francis Throckmorton (1554–85) was involved in the 'Throckmorton Conspiracy' to betray England's seaports and defences to Spain. Under torture, he confessed to treason and was executed at Tyburn. Conspiracy played a role in the history of Coughton Court again in 1605, when a group of conspirators involved in the Gunpowder Plot waited there for news of Guy Fawkes's enterprise.

The Tribune Room at Coughton has a portrait of Sir Nicholas and a moving relic of Mary, Queen of Scots. This is the chemise said to have been worn by the Queen at her execution at Fotheringhay Castle in 1587.

Coughton is 9 miles north-west of Stratford-upon-Avon off the A435.

Danny *W. Sussex*

The ghost of a grey lady is said to walk up the oak spiral staircase in the north wing of this Elizabethan mansion.

It was built between 1582 and 1595 by George Goring, whose son, also named George, began his successful career as a courtier under Elizabeth and was created Earl of Norwich by Charles I in 1645. The E-shaped design is typically Elizabethan, and although there have been later additions and alterations, the east front, with its rosy brick and lozenge patterns in darker brick, remains untouched.

Goring's mansion replaced a small Tudor farmhouse and was built on a site occupied by men since the early Iron Age. The remains of an Iron Age track can be seen in the gardens of the house.

The interior is rich in Elizabethan features, including the original staircase and panelling. In the entrance hall are carved heads in oak of ladies and gentlemen in Elizabethan costume. There are two fireplaces dated 1571, and a fine plaster ceiling.

In the fireplace of the Great Hall is a small collection of Elizabethan leather shoes, found when the old lodge was demolished in the late 19th century.

Danny is about a quarter of a mile off New Way Lane, a mile south-east of Hurstpierpoint.

Dartmouth *Devon*
Along the picturesque cobbled wharves of Bayard's Cove in Dartmouth, Sir Walter Raleigh and his half-brothers moored their ships. The town's renown for seamanship was such that it contributed no fewer than nine ships to the fleet that fought the Spanish Armada in 1588.

John Davis (1550–1605), a brilliant navigator, was born and lived at Stoke Gabriel on the River Dart.

DARTMOUTH MUSEUM In the Butterwalk, a row of colonnaded merchants' houses dated 1635–40, is a museum containing a model of Drake's ship, the *Golden Hind*.

Derby *Derbys.*
CATHEDRAL The early 18th-century cathedral, designed by James Gibbs, contains the monument of Elizabeth, Countess of Shrewsbury, better known as Bess of Hardwick, one of the great personalities of Elizabeth's reign.

Bess was certainly the ablest businesswoman of her day, a builder of palaces, the wife of four rich and well-known men and a dynastic schemer. Her monument is in a grandiose style befitting her wealth and power – as she assured by supervising its construction in her own lifetime.

Dover Castle *Kent*
One of the treasures of this Norman castle, called by the 13th-century chronicler Mathew Paris 'the key of England', is a brass gun nicknamed 'Queen Elizabeth's Pocket Pistol'. Being restored in 1992, it is, in fact, a 24 ft long cannon, cast in 1544 and presented to Henry VIII by the Emperor Charles V.

The gun has a calibre of $4\frac{3}{4}$ in. and is reputed to be capable of firing a 10 lb shot 7 miles. The barrel is elaborately decorated in the high Renaissance style, with acanthus leaves and allegorical panels. One of the breech-shields bears the Royal Arms of England.

Dundrennan Abbey *Dumfs. & Gall.*
On May 16, 1586, Mary, Queen of Scots spent the night at Dundrennan, an abbey founded by the Cistercians in 1142. It was to be the last night she ever slept on the soil of Scotland. The next day she crossed the Solway to England to seek the aid of Queen Elizabeth. She found not a sanctuary but confinement.

The abbey is now a ruin, but some of its stone was used to build a number of the houses in the little village of Dundrennan.

Dundrennan is 6 miles south-east of Kirkcudbright on the A711.

Edinburgh *Lothian*
The Edinburgh of the late 16th century is associated with two highly contrasted personalities: Mary, Queen of Scots, who was a Catholic, and John Knox, a preacher who was a scourge of Catholicism.

CRAIGMILLAR CASTLE Here Mary, Queen of Scots lived in 1566 after the murder of her secretary Rizzio in Holyrood Palace. It was at Craigmillar that the plot to kill Mary's husband, Lord Darnley, was hatched.

EDINBURGH CASTLE Here in 1566 Mary gave birth to her son James, later James VI of Scotland and James I of England.

JOHN KNOX'S HOUSE Dating from 1490, this is probably the oldest dwelling in the city. It was badly damaged by fire in 1544 when the English sacked Edinburgh, but was rebuilt and restored in 1561 and rented to John Knox, the Protestant reformer. On the second floor is a small room Knox used as a study, and next to it is the bedroom in which he died.

PALACE OF HOLYROODHOUSE King James IV of Scotland made Edinburgh his capital in 1498, and Holyroodhouse, originally the guest-house of an Augustinian abbey, was used as a palace. Mary, Queen of Scots lived there in the 1560s. Her apartments were on the second floor of the James V Tower. It was here, on the evening of March 9, 1566, that a gang of Scottish lords, headed by Darnley and Patrick, Lord Ruthven, burst in while Mary was entertaining a few friends to supper. They dragged Mary's Italian secretary, David Rizzio, into an adjoining room, where he was brutally stabbed to death within earshot of the queen, who was then nearly six months pregnant. She later insisted that Rizzio's murderers had hoped that the shock would cause her to miscarry and die.

The rooms, though altered in the 17th century, contain the original oak ceilings and wall-paintings. In Queen Mary's bedroom are two embroidered panels worked by her during her long imprisonment in England.

Exeter *Devon*

A canal cut during Elizabeth's reign enabled sea-going ships to sail up to Exeter, and so established the city's importance as a port.

Exeter was founded by the Romans, as Isca Dumnoniorum, in AD 50–55 and remained an important commercial centre through the centuries; in 1537 it was granted a charter by Henry VIII as 'the county and city of Exeter'. CATHEDRAL Exeter Cathedral was rebuilt in the 14th century in the Decorated style, and has the longest stretch of Gothic vaulting in England.

The monument to Lady Dodderidge, who died in 1614, shows a lady in Elizabethan costume, reclining on her side, her right hand grasping a skull. She wears a ruff, and the lace-work on her bodice is of carved alabaster. Lady Dodderidge's husband, Sir John Dodderidge (1555–1628) was MP for Barnstaple in 1588 and Solicitor-General to James I in 1604.

In the Cathedral Close is Mol's Coffee House, now an art shop. The arms of Elizabeth I are painted on a panel over the remarkable bay window on the first floor. This window stretches the entire width of the building, seeming to represent the stern of a 16th-century galleon.

Gawsworth Hall *Cheshire*

Mary Fitton, a well-known beauty at Elizabeth's court, had her home at Gawsworth Hall. She was a member of the Fitton family which held the ancient manor of Gawsworth between 1316 and 1662. Sir Edward Fitton (1527–79) was Vice-Treasurer of Ireland. He was succeeded by his son, also named Sir Edward (1548–1606), whose daughter, Mary, born in 1578, was appointed Maid of Honour to the Queen in 1596. She was celebrated at court for her grey-blue eyes and auburn hair, and her vivacity and skill at dancing. Her career ended in scandal when she was found to be pregnant by the young Earl of Pembroke.

The black-and-white house, which dates from the late 15th century, and its park have changed little from Queen Elizabeth's time. There is a fine mantelpiece, dated *c.* 1580, in the library, and the dining-room, with its long refectory table, is virtually untouched. In the drawing-room there is a portrait of Lady Fitton, wife of Sir Edward, with her children, Edward and Mary.

Gawsworth is 3 miles south-west of Macclesfield, off the A536.

Gilling Castle *N. Yorks.*

The Great Chamber at Gilling was built in 1585 by Sir William Fairfax on the medieval walls of the original manor house. It survived the 18th-century remodelling of the house and is today one of the most remarkable Elizabethan interiors in the country.

The Chamber is richly panelled in oak, inlaid with ebony and holly. Above the fireplace are the arms of Elizabeth I. A painted frieze runs right round the room; one section of it depicts an Elizabethan musical party, with ladies and gentlemen playing viols and lutes.

The castle houses Ampleforth College, and is open during school terms only. Telephone 04393 224.

Gilling is 12 miles south-east of Thirsk on the B1363.

Great Yarmouth *Norfolk*

ELIZABETHAN HOUSE MUSEUM On South Quay is a museum in part of a house built in 1596 by a Yarmouth merchant, Benjamin Cooper. Although the house now has a Georgian front, several Elizabethan rooms remain intact.

The oak-panelled dining-room has a carved chimney-piece, and on the first floor the drawing-room has a moulded plaster ceiling and an elaborate overmantel.

Hardwick Hall *Derbys.*

Built between 1591 and 1597 by the formidable 'Bess of Hardwick,' Countess of Shrewsbury, Hardwick Hall is probably the most beautiful Elizabethan house in England. On Bess's death in 1608 it passed to the Earls (later Dukes) of Devonshire, who preferred nearby Chatsworth as their seat.

Austere, symmetrical, almost unadorned except for the initials 'E.S.', for Elizabeth Shrewsbury, in proud relief on each of the six towers. Hardwick stands virtually as Bess and her architect, probably Robert Smythson, conceived it: 'Hardwick Hall, more glass than wall,' as an old saying describes it.

Many of the contents listed in Bess's 1601 inventory remain in the house to this day, and the great rooms evoke the opulence and confidence of the Elizabethan age. The High Great Chamber on the second floor has a plasterwork frieze by Abraham Smith, and Brussels tapestries of 1587.

The Long Gallery, an exceptional 166 ft in length, contains portraits of Bess, of two of her four husbands, and of Elizabeth I in a dress elaborately embroidered with animals and flowers.

The Withdrawing Room contains much of the finest furniture listed in the 1601 inventory, and in the Paved Room are two cushion covers embroidered by Mary, Queen of Scots while she was the Earl of Shrewsbury's prisoner. This room contains many of the finest embroideries in Hardwick Hall.

Hardwick is 6½ miles north-west of Mansfield, off the A617.

Hatfield House *Herts.*

No other place in England has such powerful associations with Queen Elizabeth's childhood and youth as Hatfield. It was there, in 1558, that the news of her accession as Queen was brought to her as she sat under an oak tree in the park.

The original house that Elizabeth knew, Hatfield Old Palace, was built in 1497 by Henry VII's minister Cardinal Morton. At the Dissolution of the Monasteries, Henry VIII took over the house and installed his children there.

After her mother, Anne Boleyn, was executed in 1536 Elizabeth was for a time neglected and even went short of clothes. Later, however, conditions improved. She was educated with her half-brother Edward, who reigned from 1547 to 1553, and showed talent as a classical scholar. In 1548, when she was 15, she was the target of Sir Thomas Seymour's attentions. Her steward and governess were arrested, and Elizabeth herself was rigorously interrogated by Sir Robert Tyrwhit. Seymour was executed later, for conspiring against Protector Somerset.

In Mary's reign, 1553–8, Elizabeth was once again almost a prisoner at Hatfield, though not without her entertainments, plays, bear-baiting and singing. On her accession Elizabeth held her first Council in the Great Hall of Hatfield.

All that remains of the Old Palace is the Great Hall, restored by the 4th Marquess of Salisbury in this century. Elizabeth's successor, James I, exchanged Hatfield for Theobalds, a house belonging to Robert Cecil (1563–1612), son of Elizabeth's great minister, Lord Burghley, and later 1st Earl of Salisbury. Cecil demolished three sides of the Old Palace and used the bricks to build the magnificent Jacobean house that stands today.

Hatfield is a treasure-house for the Elizabethan enthusiast. In the Marble Hall hang two of the most celebrated portraits of the Queen. The 'Ermine Portrait' by Nicholas Hilliard (1547–1619) shows Elizabeth with a live ermine, a symbol of purity and virginity, on her arm. The 'Rainbow Portrait', attributed to Isaac Oliver (d. 1617) shows her holding a rainbow, symbolic of peace, with the Latin motto *Non Sine Sole Iris*, 'no rainbow without the sun'. The sun, of course, was Elizabeth herself.

In the Long Gallery Queen Elizabeth's hat, gloves and stockings are displayed, together with a parchment roll, heavily illuminated and bearing hundreds of heraldic devices, which sets out Elizabeth's pedigree, tracing her ancestry back to Adam.

On the Grand Staircase is a picture of a white horse, traditionally held to be the one Elizabeth rode in the review of her troops at Tilbury before the Armada. In the showcases in the Library are letters from Elizabeth and Mary, Queen of Scots. In the Armoury is a collection of armour worn by men of the Spanish Armada, perhaps presented to Lord Burghley, and in the archway leading into the North Entrance Hall hangs Elizabeth's own saddlecloth.

Throughout the house there are portraits of noted Elizabethans, including Mary, Queen of Scots, probably by Hilliard; Lord Burghley; and Robert Cecil.

In the park, the site of Elizabeth's oak tree is marked by a monument.

Hatfield House is off the A1000 in Old Hatfield.

Hawthornden Castle *Lothian*

In the grounds of this mansion, rebuilt in 1638, stand the remains of a great sycamore tree under which two famous poets met in 1618. William Drummond (1585–1649), author of *Flowers of Zion*, published in 1613, was the owner of the house. Ben Jonson (1572–1637) was one of the most celebrated poets and playwrights of the Elizabethan and Stuart eras.

Jonson's play *Every Man In His Humour*, with Shakespeare in the cast, was produced by the Lord Chamberlain's company in 1598, and his *Sejanus* by Shakespeare's company at the Globe Theatre in 1603. He was the friend of Bacon and Shakespeare and enjoyed the patronage of the Sidney family.

Drummond wrote a detailed account of his conversations with Jonson. It records that when Jonson approached the sycamore tree Drummond greeted him: 'Welcome, welcome, Royal Ben.' To this Jonson quickly returned the rhyming reply: 'Thank ye, thank ye Hawthornden.'

Hawthornden is off the A6094 7 miles south of Edinburgh.

Hever Castle *Kent*

This late 13th-century moated castle incorporating a Tudor manor house, was inherited in 1505 by Sir Thomas Boleyn (or Bullen), the father of Queen Anne Boleyn and grandfather of Elizabeth I. One of the most able and ambitious courtiers of Henry VIII's reign, Sir Thomas made a brilliant marriage to Lady Elizabeth Howard, daughter of the 2nd Duke of Norfolk, and then set about arranging matches for his three children, Mary, Anne and George.

Boleyn's ambitions resulted first in triumph, then in tragedy. Mary became Henry VIII's mistress, but was soon discarded. Anne became his Queen, and was beheaded. George was involved in the fall of his sister, Queen Anne, and was also beheaded.

In the day when the Boleyns' star was in the ascendant, Hever Castle was supposed to be the house where Henry wooed Anne. On the stone newel of the circular stair in the Long Gallery, crudely incised, is the love cypher he used when writing to her. Below it is carved an executioner's axe. At the end of the gallery is the 'Lover's Window' where, according to folklore, Henry and Anne would sit together.

By the end of the 19th century Hever Castle had become a farm. The Great Hall was a kitchen, with hams hanging from the beams. The castle was rescued by the American millionaire William Waldorf Astor, who was created Viscount Astor of Hever in 1917. Lord Astor and his architect, Frank Pearson, meticulously restored the castle and built the Tudor village to the north of it as a way of enlarging the accommodation without touching the original fabric.

Hever is now a treasure-house of pictures and objects associated with Henry, Anne and Elizabeth. A portrait by Gheeraerts of Elizabeth hangs in the Entrance Hall, as does the Holbein portrait of Henry VIII. In the Inner Hall is a copy of the silver clock which was Henry's wedding present to Anne. The suit of baby's clothes was made by Elizabeth for the expected child of her half-sister Mary Tudor, wife of Philip II of Spain. There is also a portrait of Anne Boleyn.

In the Dining Hall is a door-lock with Henry's coat of arms. One of the suits of armour in this room belonged to Shakespeare's patron, the Earl of Southampton.

The fireplace and panelling in the Morning Room are Elizabethan, dated 1603, and the iron fireback bears the Queen's arms. A head-dress displayed is said to have been Anne Boleyn's. In the Long Gallery is a massively carved bed-head and

posts, and there is a collection of toilet articles reputed to have belonged to Queen Elizabeth.

Hever is 2 miles east of Edenbridge off the B2027.

Kenilworth Castle *Warks.*

On July 9, 1575 Queen Elizabeth arrived at Kenilworth to stay, for the third and last time, with her favourite Robert Dudley, Earl of Leicester, who had restored and added to the ancient castle largely for her benefit. The visit was the occasion for the most lavish royal entertainment in the castle's history.

At the Brays Gate the Queen was greeted with verses. Then, as she progressed towards the castle along a causeway across the artificial lake that surrounded the fortress, the Lady of the Lake and two nymphs appeared on the island. There were fanfares and music as the Queen passed into the inner court, and for the next 18 days the entertainments continued – fireworks, dancing, hunting, excursions on the mere in barges, tilting, feasting and bear-baiting – at a cost to the Earl of Leicester of £1,000 a day. Sir Walter Scott's novel *Kenilworth*, published in 1821, is a fanciful reconstruction of Elizabeth's visit to the castle.

Founded in about 1122 by Geoffrey de Clinton, Kenilworth had been one of the most important strongholds of medieval England. John of Gaunt, who held it from 1361 to 1399, converted it into a palace, and much of the ruined banqueting hall he built survives. In 1553 the castle was granted to John Dudley, Duke of Northumberland, who was beheaded by Mary in the same year. Elizabeth renewed the grant in favour of his son, Robert Dudley, who held the castle until his death in 1588.

The Gallery Tower is so named because Leicester converted the 12th-century defensive tower into an observation gallery from which tilting and jousting could be watched.

Leicester's Building, to the east of the outer court, was built to accommodate distinguished guests. In 1575 the chronicler Laneham described the 'rare beauty of building that his Honour hath advanced; all of hard quarry stone; every room so spacious, so well belighted and so high roofed within . . .'

Leicester's Stables, to the west of the outer court, are virtually untouched, except for the north end which has been rebuilt. The stables are 160 ft long. Leicester's Gate-house, converted into a house after the Civil War, bears the Earl's initials over the west porch, and on the ground floor there is a magnificent Elizabethan alabaster chimney-piece which is thought originally to have been in Leicester's Building. The gardens to the north of the Keep are a modern reconstruction of Leicester's original ornamental pleasure-garden.

Kenilworth Castle is on the western edge of Kenilworth, off the B4103.

Kirby Hall *Northants.*

Although now only a shell, Kirby is remarkable for its beauty and a certain French influence in its motifs.

Begun in 1570 by Sir Humphrey Stafford, Kirby was bought in 1575 by Elizabeth's favourite Sir Christopher Hatton, who continued to build. Hatton was made Lord Chancellor by Elizabeth on April 20, 1587. The relationship between the Queen and this dazzling young man, famed for his brilliance as a dancer and jouster, was close and affectionate. A handsome man, Hatton was intelligent, and a good servant of the state.

In the first half of the 17th century further work was carried out at Kirby. The building fell into decay during the 19th century.

Kirby is off the A43, 3 miles north-east of Corby.

Knole *Kent*

This vast, rambling mansion which, from a distance, appears more like a medieval city than a house, was built between 1456 and 1486 by Thomas Bourchier, Archbishop of Canterbury. It remained the property of the see of Canterbury until Archbishop Cranmer (1489–1556) was persuaded to hand it over to Henry VIII.

In 1566 Queen Elizabeth gave Knole to her Lord Treasurer, Thomas Sackville, the 1st Earl of Dorset (1536–1608). It was Sackville who, in re-modelling the exterior, largely created the house as it stands today. Shrewd, capable, rich and dour, Sackville epitomised his age. His father was Anne Boleyn's first cousin, and he exploited his kinship with Elizabeth in a long and highly successful political career. His passion for stateliness and grandeur is reflected in many of Knole's great rooms.

The fine Great Hall, built originally by Bourchier, remains as Sackville re-created it. The fire-dogs in the grate bear the arms of Henry VIII and the badge of Anne Boleyn. The Great Staircase was installed between 1605 and 1608, and its *trompe-l'oeil* paintings added.

The Galleries, a set of state apartments designed to impress the visitor with the wealth and power of the Sackville family, contain portraits of Lord Burghley and Sir Philip Sidney, in the Brown Gallery, and Henry VIII in the Cartoon

Gallery. Anne Boleyn's portrait hangs in Lady Betty Germain's Rooms and that of Sackville himself in the Great Hall.

The series of identically framed portraits in the Brown Gallery is a pictorial record of English history in the faces of its great men from the Plantagenets to the Stuarts.

Knole is off the southern end of Sevenoaks High Street.

Little Moreton Hall *Cheshire*

One of the most celebrated black-and-white half-timbered houses in the country, Little Moreton Hall was begun by Ralph Moreton in about 1480. In 1559 William Moreton added the two great bay windows in the north-east angle of the courtyard, and his son John built the Chapel and the whole of the south range of the house, including the gate-house and Long Gallery. The Moretons were prosperous landowners with an estate of 1,360 acres.

The heart of the house is the lofty Great Hall which is lit by William Moreton's massive bay windows. The round table on an octagonal base in the Withdrawing Room is probably the 'great Rounde table in the parlour' mentioned in the inventory of John Moreton's property in 1601, and valued at 10 shillings. The inventory also mentions 'one cupborde of boxes'; this is thought to be the large cupboard in the Great Hall, whose numerous small drawers were possibly used to store spices. The plaster chimney-piece in the Withdrawing Room bears the arms of Queen Elizabeth and the ceiling is very fine, its moulded timbers dating from 1559.

The Parlour contains fascinating wall-paintings, for which there was a vogue between 1570 and 1610. The paintings simulate panelling and incorporate biblical texts with

illustrations. There are biblical texts, too, in the Chapel, which dates from 1559–70. The Long Gallery has plasterwork based on designs from the 1556 edition of *The Castle of Knowledge* by the mathematician Robert Recorde.

Outside there is a reconstruction of an Elizabethan knot garden, based on a design in *The English Gardener* by Leonard Meager, published in 1688.

Little Moreton Hall is 4 miles south-west of Congleton.

Llanvihangel Court *Gwent*

Originally a medieval house, Llanvihangel was extensively rebuilt in 1559 in the Tudor style. In the so-called 'Queen's Bedroom' is an Elizabethan plasterwork ceiling, bearing an intricate pattern of intertwined hearts, Tudor roses, and fleur-de-lis.

A stained-glass window by Dudley Forsyth on the main staircase shows Elizabeth accompanied by Sir Walter Raleigh.

Llanvihangel Court, which in 1992 was not open to the public, is 4 miles north-east of Abergavenny off the A465.

Loch Leven Castle *Tayside*

Mary, Queen of Scots was imprisoned in Loch Leven Castle because escape from it was thought to be impossible. The five-storey tower house could be entered only by way of a ladder to the second floor; furthermore, it was built on an islet in the loch.

Mary was taken to the castle in May 1567 after capitulating to her rebel lords at Carberry Hill in an attempt to save the life of her husband, Bothwell. On May 20 the 'Casket Letters' were discovered; these were a series of letters and poems, kept in a silver casket, that allegedly implicated Mary in the murder of her previous husband Darnley. After her defeat, Mary was forced to abdicate in favour of her son.

Mary spent more than 11 months in Loch Leven Castle, during which time Elizabeth sent her a ring and a letter in token of favour for her cousin's cause. Then, on May 2, 1568 Mary proved that the fortress was not escape-proof after all. An 18-year-old admirer, Willie Douglas, let her out of a postern gate where there was a boat waiting to carry her to the shore. George Douglas, Lord Seton, and a strong bodyguard were there to meet her and escort her to the safety of Niddry Castle.

Loch Leven Castle is now a ruin, rugged and somewhat forbidding. It can be reached by ferry from Kinross.

London, Central

'At length they all to merry London came,
To merry London, my most kindly nurse,
That gave to me this life's first native source.'

So wrote the Elizabethan poet Edmund Spenser in his *Prothalamion*, published in 1596. Shakespeare wrote in *Henry V*:

'But now behold,
In the quick forge and working-house of thought,
How London doth pour out her citizens.'

Spenser was born in East Smithfield in 1552, and Shakespeare made his fame and fortune in the London theatre. In Elizabeth's time London was the largest capital city in Europe, with a population estimated at 90,000. But virtually nothing of the city Shakespeare and Spenser knew has survived. It was almost entirely destroyed in the Great Fire of 1666, or in subsequent redevelopment. Elizabeth's palace of Whitehall has

gone, and so has the string of mansions, the palaces of the nobility, that ran along the Strand.

Yet in spite of the Great Fire, 400 years of redevelopment, and the wartime Blitz, fascinating fragments of Elizabethan London can still be found; and London's museums and art galleries contain many treasures of the era.

BRITISH MUSEUM (BLOOMSBURY, WC1) The gold medallion struck to commemorate the defeat of the Spanish Armada in 1588 is one of the most treasured relics of the Elizabethan era in the museum. Others include the 'Warwick Gitterne', an instrument like a guitar, and a glass jug which may have belonged to the Queen.

The silver gilt 'Bacon Cup' was made for Elizabeth's Lord Keeper, Sir Nicholas Bacon (1509–79). The collections also contain Sir Walter Raleigh's silver seals and rings of Mary, Queen of Scots.

Among the manuscripts and documents are Shakespeare's signed will, the warrant for the execution of Mary, Queen of Scots, and Elizabeth's personal copy of Nicolay's *Navigations et Peregrinations*, bound for her by John Le Planche in 1568.

Not all the British Museum's treasures are always on display.

CANONBURY TOWER (CANONBURY, N1) is a rare survival from the 16th century. Begun in about 1520 by William Bolton, Prior of St Bartholomew's, it became towards the end of the century the home of Sir John Spencer, one of Elizabeth's richest subjects. Elizabeth interceded with Sir John on behalf of his daughter when she eloped with Lord Compton. Sir Francis Bacon later rented the house and is said to have planted the mulberry tree in the garden. The house contains Elizabethan panelling, and a plaster ceiling dated 1599.

GOLDSMITH'S HALL (FOSTER LANE, EC3) One of the prized possessions of Goldsmith's Hall is the golden cup from which Queen Elizabeth is said to have drunk at her coronation.

GRAY'S INN (FLEET ST, WC1) The gardens were originally laid out by Sir Francis Bacon in 1606. The Hall, where Shakespeare's *The Comedy of Errors* was first performed in 1594, was badly damaged during the Blitz, but the Hall Screen survived.

LINCOLN'S INN (WC2) The Gate-house, built in 1518, bears the arms of Henry VIII. The Old Buildings and the Hall date from between 1490 and 1520, and though restored are much as Elizabeth would have known them.

MIDDLE TEMPLE HALL (EC4) The magnificent Elizabethan dining-hall, built between 1562 and 1573, was badly damaged by wartime bombs but has been completely restored. The double hammerbeam roof is one of the finest surviving, and the oak screen is dated 1574. Among the many coats of arms that decorate the hall are those of Sir Walter Raleigh, in a window on the north side. At the west end is the dais on which Shakespeare's *Twelfth Night* had its first performance in 1601. The 29 ft 3 in. table on the dais is made of oak from Windsor given by Elizabeth. A smaller table has a wooden protective cover made of timber from Drake's ship, the *Golden Hind*.

MUSEUM OF LONDON (LONDON WALL, EC2) An extensive social history collection includes several important relics of Elizabethan times. The collection of jewellery known as the Cheapside Hoard is probably part of a city goldsmith's stock-in-trade, buried early in the 17th century. A plate bearing an illustration of the Tower of London and an inscription in praise of Elizabeth is the earliest piece of dated Delft ware, made in London by potters from the Low Countries.

NATIONAL PORTRAIT GALLERY (ST MARTIN'S LANE, WC2) Portraits of most of the major personalities of Elizabeth's life and reign start with the Holbein portrait of her father, Henry VIII, and include paintings of her sister Mary I, her brother Edward VI, Walsingham, Burghley, Salisbury and Leicester. There is a full-length portrait of Elizabeth herself, and one of Shakespeare.

ROYAL EXCHANGE (EC3) All that remains of the original Exchange, founded by Sir Thomas Gresham in 1568 and named 'Royal' for Elizabeth in 1571, is the pavement of the great central courtyard. There are statues of Elizabeth and Gresham.

ST BARTHOLOMEW'S The priory and hospital of St Bartholomew, founded in 1123, were dissolved by Henry VIII in 1539. The nave of the priory church was destroyed, but its Norman choir became the parish church of St Bartholomew the Great, which still stands.

The remainder of the priory buildings were put to secular use. In Elizabeth's time there were factories, an inn, a forge and stables within the precincts, and criminals were executed in front of the west gate, then the open space of Smithfield.

The loss of the hospital caused hardship among the poor, and Henry VIII refounded it, making it one of the oldest hospitals in Britain.

SOUTHWARK Elizabethan travellers going southwards left London by old London Bridge – then the city's only bridge across the Thames – and then passed through 'Long Southwark', a market street with many inns and taverns, including The Tabard (now The Talbot) dating back to Chaucer's time.

Just south of the bridge stood St Saviour's Church. The Norman .church was rebuilt in Early English style in the 13th century. The elaborate altar screen was installed 200 years later; this and the choir are all that remain of the church of Elizabeth's day, for the nave was rebuilt in 1890–7. The church was made the Cathedral of Southwark Diocese in 1905.

The George Inn in Borough High Street was built in 1677. With its galleried inner courtyard and dormer roofs it recalls the traditional taverns of Shakespeare's London.

STAPLE INN (HOLBORN, WC1) The row of shops facing High Holborn, with their projecting black-and-white fronts, appear on the street side of this small Inn of Court. They are among the few fragments of Elizabethan London that have survived.

TOWER OF LONDON The battlements of William the Conqueror's great stronghold, begun in 1078, cast their shadows over the reigns of the Tudor monarchs, darkening the life of Elizabeth herself and ending that of several people closely associated with her.

Elizabeth's mother, Anne Boleyn, was beheaded on May 19, 1536 in front of the chapel of St Peter ad Vincula, where she is buried.

In the crypt of the Chapel Royal in the White Tower are graffiti carved by rebels of Sir Thomas Wyatt's uprising against Queen Mary in January 1554. On Palm Sunday, March 18, 1554 Elizabeth was taken by boat from Whitehall to the Tower, accused of complicity in Wyatt's revolt. Like her mother before her she entered through Traitor's Gate. She was locked up in the Bell Tower; the section of the ramparts between the Bell Tower and the Beauchamp Tower, where she took her exercise, is known as 'Queen Elizabeth's Walk'. Elizabeth was exonerated of complicity in the rebellion and released on May 19. Wyatt, however, had been executed on April 11.

On February 25, 1601 Robert Devereux, Earl of Essex, once Elizabeth's favourite, was beheaded on Tower Green. His co-conspirator, the Earl of Southampton, Shakespeare's patron, was also imprisoned in the Tower.

Sir Walter Raleigh spent 12 years in the Tower after Elizabeth's death. Released in 1616 he enjoyed only two years of freedom, being imprisoned in the Bloody Tower again in 1618 and beheaded on October 29 in the same year. His portrait now hangs in the Bloody Tower.

Among the treasures of the Tower are many objects associated with Elizabeth and her family. The Crown Jewels date mainly from the Restoration, the original royal regalia having been melted down during the Commonwealth, but amongst the collection of plate is Queen Elizabeth's Salt, which dates from 1572–3.

The Armouries contain a collection of armour begun by Henry VIII. As well as Henry's own armour, made at Greenwich in 1540, the displays include armour that belonged to the Earl of Leicester, dated 1585, and the Earl of Worcester, dated 1570–80.

VICTORIA AND ALBERT MUSEUM (EXHIBITION ROAD, SW7) A virginal – a keyboard instrument similar to a spinet – that belonged to Queen Elizabeth is one of the principal items in the museum's Elizabethan collection. It also contains perhaps the most celebrated of all pieces of Elizabethan furniture, the Great Bed of Ware, mentioned in Shakespeare's *Twelfth Night*. There are fine examples of Elizabethan embroidery, and probably the best collection of miniatures in the country, including works by

Holbein, Oliver and Hilliard.

The museum also contains a complete Elizabethan interior, taken from Sizergh Castle, and the Armada Jewel portrait of the Queen.

WESTMINSTER ABBEY (SW1) Elizabeth lies in the elaborate chapel built by her grandfather Henry VII and begun in 1503. With her lies her sister Queen Mary and not far away, in the South Aisle, is Mary, Queen of Scots, reinterred there by her son James I in 1612.

Elizabeth's monument, with its lifelike effigy, was designed by Maximilian Colt and completed, in white marble, in 1607. In 1740 a memorial to Shakespeare, designed by the architect William Kent (1685–1748), was erected by public subscription; it includes a bust of Elizabeth.

The origins of the Abbey's Poets' Corner lie in the Elizabethan era, with the burial of Edmund Spenser in 1599. Michael Drayton and Ben Jonson were later buried there.

Westminster School, in the precincts of the Abbey, regards Elizabeth as its second founder. She re-established the school in 1560.

WHITEHALL (SW1) Beneath the Ministry of Defence building opposite Downing Street lies one of the few remaining fragments of the Palace of Whitehall, where Elizabeth had her main court. It is the Wine Cellar of Cardinal Wolsey's original palace, taken over by Henry VIII in 1529.

London, Greater

In Elizabeth's time the area now covered by Greater London was open countryside. In the succeeding centuries the capital grew, swallowing up rural villages like Chelsea, Tottenham and Harrow and burying the woods and meadows Elizabeth knew with streets of terraced houses. Yet even in this vast urban sprawl there are reminders and survivals of the Elizabethan age.

CHINGFORD In Ranger's Road, on the edge of Epping Forest, stands possibly the most surprising survival of all – Queen Elizabeth's Hunting Lodge. Built in the 15th century, it is a two-storey structure of an unusually elaborate design. The upper floor was open to the elements and was used as a combination of observation post and shooting platform. Hounds drove the deer in front of the lodge and the guests shot at them from the platform. Below the platform were living quarters. The lodge has an immense arch-braced roof, and an Elizabethan staircase with a rare square hollow newel. Closed during 1992.

ELTHAM PALACE There is a tradition that Edward III (1327-77) founded the Order of the Garter at Eltham. Henry VIII spent some of his childhood at Eltham, as did his daughter Elizabeth. Henry and Anne Boleyn visited her there in 1534, when she was a baby.

After becoming Queen, Elizabeth used Eltham as a hunting lodge. One of her favourites, Sir Christopher Hatton, was Keeper of Eltham, and arranged musical entertainments as well as hunting. Elizabeth's last visit to Eltham was in 1602, the year before her death.

Eltham was sacked and virtually demolished during the Civil War and very little of the original building remains. However, the Great Hall has been restored to the grandeur Elizabeth knew. The palace, off Eltham High Street, is at present occupied by the Institute of Army Education.

GREENWICH Elizabeth was born at Greenwich on September 7, 1533 and baptised three days later at the church of the Grey Friars. The palace at Greenwich had been a royal residence since the later 15th century – Henry VIII himself was born there – but was rebuilt by Charles II, then by William and Mary. It is now the Royal Naval College.

Behind the College lies another palace, the Queen's House, built by Inigo Jones for James I's queen, Anne of Denmark, and started in 1618. It now houses the National Maritime Museum, and among the collections are several items of Elizabethan significance.

Nicholas Hilliard's portrait of George Clifford, 3rd Earl of Cumberland (1558–1605) is the largest known picture by Elizabeth's court painter, who specialised in miniatures. A great landowner, impaired by gambling, Cumberland tried to restore his fortunes through privateering adventures. He financed ten expeditions against the Spanish in the West Indies and commanded the *Elizabeth Bonaventure* against the Armada in 1588. Hilliard's portrait shows him dressed as Queen's Champion at the Tilt.

The Armada Medal is a silver medal struck to commemorate the defeat of the Spanish Armada. It bears the legend *Flavit Jehovah et dissipati sunt 1588*, 'God blew and they were scattered', the word 'Jehovah' being written in Hebrew characters.

The Drake Silver Medallion is inscribed with a map by the great cartographer Michael Mercator (c. 1567–1614) showing Drake's famous circumnavigation in the *Golden Hind*. The map is one of the earliest to show the names of California and Virginia.

There is a fine portrait of Drake, dated 1591, by an unknown artist, an astrolabe that belonged to him and his lode-stone, or compass.

HACKNEY St John's or Sutton House, 2–4 Homerton High Street, was built in the first half of the 16th century and was the home of Thomas Sutton (b. 1531), who became Master of the Ordnance to Queen Elizabeth. At the Armada he commanded his own ship, the *Sutton*, and captured a Spanish galleon with £20,000 worth of cargo. His house is built on the traditional H-shaped plan, in red brick, with darker patterning. Many of the rooms contain fine linenfold panelling.

HAMPTON COURT Cardinal Wolsey's great palace, which he presented to Henry VIII in 1528 in a vain attempt to placate his jealous and suspicious master, was Henry's pride and joy. Queen Elizabeth visited the palace many times – although she preferred nearby Richmond.

The Anne Boleyn Gateway is so named because it was embellished during the brief marriage of Elizabeth's mother. There are some notable Tudor interiors, including the kitchens with their great ovens and spits. The Great Hall, 106 ft long, 40 ft wide, and 60 ft high, has a fine hammerbeam roof.

HAREFIELD The parish church has one of the most interesting interiors in England, rich in monuments from many eras. The most magnificent is the painted tomb of Alice, Countess of Derby, who died in 1636. The countess's second husband was Sir Thomas Egerton, Elizabeth's Chancellor, and their mansion, now demolished, was next to the church. There, in 1602, they entertained Elizabeth with a performance of *Othello*. The avenue of elms that once led up to the house is called the Queen's Walk.

The countess's monument shows Alice lying under a domed and curtained canopy, supported on Corinthian pillars and dressed as a great lady of the Elizabethan era, her golden hair spread on pillows.

Her three daughters, each one of whom married an earl, kneel beside her.

Harefield is 4 miles north of Uxbridge.

OSTERLEY PARK Though entirely rebuilt in 1761 by Robert Adam, Osterley Park has strong Elizabethan associations, and the Stable Block, behind the house, has been preserved very much as it was in the 16th century.

The first great house at Osterley was built by Sir Thomas Gresham (c. 1519–79), the richest merchant in Elizabethan England, and founder of the Royal Exchange in the City of London. Queen Elizabeth visited Osterley in May 1575.

ROMFORD The Cooke monument in St Edward's Church is characteristic Elizabethan work.

Sir Anthony Cooke lived at Gidea Hall, of which only the park remains. There, as Steward of the Liberty of Havering-atte-Bower, he entertained Queen Elizabeth.

In his monument Sir Anthony kneels, in Tudor armour, opposite his wife. Behind his wife are his four daughters, each of whom made a distinguished marriage. Mildred married Lord Burghley; Ann was the mother of Sir Francis Bacon; Katherine married Sir Henry Killigrew, one of the Queen's most trusted ambassadors; and Elizabeth married Lord Russell.

TOTTENHAM The pride of this North London suburb is Bruce Castle, formerly known as Tottenham Castle, a Tudor house now encased behind a Georgian façade, where Elizabeth stayed in 1578.

The name Bruce Castle recalls the early history of the building. In the 11th century the manor of Tottenham was held by the Earl of Northumberland, who married William the Conqueror's niece. Their daughter married a Scottish

prince, and in 1254 the property passed to Robert de Bruis (1210–95), the grandfather of Robert Bruce, who unsuccessfully contested the throne of Scotland in 1290. Edward I sequestered the manor in 1306, and in 1514 Sir William Compton acquired it and built a new house. It was his grandson who entertained Elizabeth and probably built the curious brick tower that stands in the garden.

Longleat *Wilts.*

Elizabethan architecture at its finest is represented by Longleat, completed in 1580. The finely proportioned exterior, symmetrical in plan with three tiers of huge windows, has never been altered since it was completed in 1580 for Sir John Thynne.

Thynne bought the old Augustinian priory in 1540, after the Dissolution. In the same year he began to build a great new house. In 1567, however, fire gutted much of the new building. When work began again in 1568 Robert Smythson, architect of Hardwick Hall and Wollaton Hall, was called in to direct operations.

By the time Sir John died in 1580 the new house was almost completed – at a total cost of £8,016 13s. 8¼d. Already Sir John, who had been Comptroller to Princess Elizabeth, had successfully entertained the Queen at Longleat in 1574.

Inside, the house has been considerably altered, mainly by Sir Jeffry Wyatville, between 1807 and 1811, but Sir John Thynne's Great Hall remains largely unchanged. The fireplace and Minstrels' Gallery were added about 1600. This room contains an oak table, 33 ft long, used for the game of shuffle-board and dated 1600.

Sir John founded Longleat's famous library which contains,

among many other treasures, a Shakespeare First Folio – the first collected edition of Shakespeare's plays – and a copy of Henry VIII's Great Bible of 1541.

On the Grand Staircase are a portrait of the Earl of Essex and a portrait of Lord and Lady Cobham and their family by Hans Eworth (1540–75).

Longleat is 4 miles south-west of Warminster, off the A362.

Longstanton *Cambs.*

CHURCH OF ALL SAINTS The monuments to the Hatton family in this beautiful 14th-century church are a reminder of how Sir Francis Drake's ship *Golden Hind* received her name.

The Hatton crest, which appears in the church both in stained-glass windows and in carved stone, has as its main feature a golden hind. Drake renamed the ship in which he sailed round the world in honour of his patron, Sir Christopher Hatton (1540–91), who was a favourite of Elizabeth and her Lord Chancellor.

Loseley House *Surrey*

Sir William More, built this superb Elizabethan mansion between 1561 and 1569. The house is set in a large park, famous today for its pedigree Jersey herds.

Much of the stone for the house was taken from Waverley Abbey, near Farnham, and the interior has some notable features. There are fine plaster ceilings, panelling from Henry VIII's Nonsuch Palace at Cheam, and an unusual chimney-piece carved from a block of local chalk.

Loseley is 3 miles south-west of Guildford.

Lyveden New Bield *Northants.*

One of the most idiosyncratic Elizabethan buildings in the country, Lyveden New Bield was designed by its 16th-century builder, Sir Thomas Tresham, as a statement of religious faith. Its ground plan is in the form of a symmetrical cross, and its exterior is decorated with friezes embodying shields and Latin phrases from the Vulgate version of the Scriptures.

Thomas Tresham, whose father had proclaimed Elizabeth's sister, Mary, queen at Northampton on July 18, 1553, was knighted by Elizabeth, and was her sheriff of Northamptonshire between 1573 and 1574. However, his prospects were blighted when, in 1580, he chose the traditional Catholic faith of his family.

Accused in 1581 of harbouring the Jesuit priest Edmund Campion, Tresham spent some years in prisons. In the intervals of freedom however, he built houses; Lyveden was his greatest achievement. 'Bield' is an old word for 'building'; Lyveden Old Building is an Elizabethan farmhouse. The New Bield was still unfinished when Sir Thomas died in 1605, and only its roofless shell remains today.

Lyveden lies in open countryside 4 miles south-west of Oundle, off the A427.

Mayfield *E. Sussex*

A feature of this attractive village is the Middle House Hotel, a good example of decorative half-timbering in southern England. The building is dated 1575. There are also the remains of a palace of the Archbishops of Canterbury.

Melford Hall *Suffolk*

'There was in Suffolk suche sumptuous feastinges and bankets as seldom in ani parte of the worlde there hath been seen afore.' Thus a contemporary chronicler records the visit of Queen Elizabeth to Melford Hall in 1578.

The Hall had been completed just in time for the royal visit. Its builder was Sir William Cordell, a lawyer who rose to be Speaker of the House of Commons and Master of the Rolls. With its pinnacles, cupolas, turrets and twisted chimneys, Melford is an exuberant example of a mid-16th-century mansion. The original ground plan was a hollow square, but later additions have given it a U shape.

The Hall is in the centre of the village of Long Melford, 3 miles north of Sudbury on the A134.

Montacute *Somerset*

One of the most beautiful country houses of Elizabethan times, Montacute has been little altered, except for one addition, since it was completed in 1601. Its builder was Sir Edward Phelips, who later became Master of the Rolls and Speaker of the House of Commons.

Montacute is certainly impressive, and its Long Gallery is, at 189 ft, the longest gallery of the period to survive. The house is supremely beautiful, with its glowing, honey-coloured stone.

In 1786 Phelips's descendant, another Edward Phelips, moved the entrance from the east to the west front and built a two-storey addition. He built it of stone taken from the façade of Clifton Maybank, a Dorset mansion of 1550 which was being demolished.

The interior contains heraldic stained glass of the Elizabethan period, magnificent panelling and plasterwork, and a collection of fine furniture and fabrics, including a tapestry woven in Tournai in about 1480.

Montacute is 4 miles west of Yeovil, on the south side of the A3088.

Nantwich *Cheshire*

In 1583 a great fire virtually razed this ancient market town. Elizabeth encouraged a countrywide collection to raise funds for rebuilding, herself contributing to it. An inscription on the Queen's Aid House in The Square commemorates the town's gratitude to Elizabeth:

'God grant our Ryal Queen
In England longe to Raign
For she hath put her helping
Hand to bild this towne again.'

Among other Elizabethan houses in Nantwich, Church's Mansion, in Hospital Street, is a well-preserved example built by a local merchant, Richard Churche, in 1577.

Oakwell Hall *W. Yorks.*

This moated stone mansion is an almost completely unspoilt example of the type of house local masons were commissioned to build for the new landed gentry of the Elizabethan age.

Henry Batt (c. 1505–72) and his son John Batt (1535–1607), who built the existing house in 1583, were small landowners who profited by the peace and prosperity of Elizabeth's reign to increase their wealth.

Through his trading activities Henry Batt made money and a reputation for dishonesty; it was said that he stole the bell of Birstall church, and embezzled the funds raised to build a school.

There is nothing grand about Oakwell; it is very much in the medieval tradition. The front is dominated by the window of the hall, beside which is a projecting porch.

Inside are Elizabethan panelling and plasterwork and an interesting collection of period furniture. This includes a 17th century diamond-back oak chair; a bed, dated 1590, carved with grotesque figures, in the Great Parlour Bedchamber; and another Tudor bed and a linenfold chest in the Little Parlour Chamber.

Oakwell Hall is just north-west of Birstall Smithies, off the A652.

Orton Waterville *Cambs.*

The church, which dates from the 13th century, has a fine Elizabethan carved pulpit. Manor Farm, a stone building dated 1571, retains its original, mullioned windows.

Oxburgh Hall *Norfolk*

Built in 1482 by Edmund Bedingfield, this fortified manor has been occupied by the Bedingfield family ever since. Sir Henry Bedingfield (1511–83) faithfully supported the cause of Queen Mary and was Governor of the Tower of London when Princess Elizabeth was imprisoned there. He was later her custodian at Woodstock where, in 1554, she was held under house arrest.

It is said that on Queen Elizabeth's accession to the throne Sir Henry presented himself at court to be told by the Queen: 'God forgive you that is past. That we doo: and if we have anie prisoner whom we would have hardlie and strictly kept, we will send him to you.' Certainly the Queen's forgiveness seemed to have been authentic, for she visited Oxburgh in 1578.

Oxburgh contains a unique collection of embroideries by Mary, Queen of Scots and Bess of Hardwick. Mary's embroideries – more than 100 panels of *gros point* and *petit point* on green velvet – were originally made as wall hangings and were later converted into bed hangings. They were made in 1570, when Mary was a prisoner in Tutbury Castle.

Oxburgh is at Oxborough, 7 miles south-west of Swaffham.

Oxford *Oxon.*

Elizabeth was as much concerned with the intellectual life of her kingdom as with its economic, political and social life, and she visited Oxford more than once. The ancient university city preserves several relics of the Queen, and has associations with some of her most famous subjects.

ASHMOLEAN MUSEUM Among the treasures of the museum, which is named after the 17th-century antiquary and astrologer Elias Ashmole, are Queen Elizabeth's buckskin riding boots and embroidered gloves. Elizabeth was noted as a horsewoman; and observers commented on a habit she had, when in pensive mood, of peeling off her gloves and drawing them on again.

BODLEIAN LIBRARY The original library was donated to the university by the youngest son of Henry IV, Duke Humfrey. When Henry VIII dissolved the monasteries in 1536–9 Duke Humfrey's collection was largely dispersed. But in 1598 Sir Thomas Bodley, one of Queen Elizabeth's most able diplomats, began to rebuild the collection, devoting the rest of his life to its restoration and expansion. The library is now one of the biggest in the world, containing more than 3 million volumes and thousands of manuscripts, among which are letters and exercise books in Elizabeth's hand.

CHURCH OF ST MICHAEL This church stood here at the time of Shakespeare's passing through the city on his journeys between Stratford-upon-Avon and London, and his attendance upon the Earl of Southampton when he received an MA degree in 1592.

CROWN TAVERN In 1937 Elizabethan wall-paintings were discovered in a room at this ancient inn, in Shakespeare's time known as the Crossed Keys. He would have known the inn and its characteristic murals.

Packwood House *Warks.*
Packwood lies in the heart of the Forest of Arden, which Shakespeare recalls in *As You Like It*. The core of the house was built between 1556 and 1560 by William Fetherston, a rich yeoman who contributed towards the preparations against the Spanish Armada in 1588. Over the centuries there have been many additions and alterations, but the house contains Elizabethan features.

The Great Hall, converted from a barn in the late 1920s, has a stone fireplace and plaster overmantel which came from an old wine-shop in Stratford-upon-Avon that had belonged to the Smith family, contemporaries of Shakespeare. The great window in the hall bears the arms of Elizabeth and of the Earls of Sussex and Suffolk. There is also an Armada fireback dated 1588.

In the parlour is a portrait of Philip II of Spain, Elizabeth's adversary, dated 1592. In the Long Gallery is a rarity – an Elizabethan 'Nonsuch' chest, inlaid with holly and bog oak.

Packwood is 11 miles south-east of Birmingham, near Hockley Heath.

Parham Park *W. Sussex*
In 1577 a two-year-old boy, Thomas Palmer, laid the foundation stone of the great new house that his grandfather, Sir Thomas Palmer, had begun to build on the estate granted to his family by Henry VIII in 1540.

Thomas grew up to sail with Drake to Cadiz. His mother, Eleanor Verney, was Queen Elizabeth's god-daughter, and the Queen may have visited Parham in 1593. In 1601 Thomas Palmer sold Parham to Sir Thomas Bysshopp.

Apart from Elizabethan furniture, carvings and interiors, the house contains portraits of some of the great personalities of the age. These include Elizabeth herself, in a dress with silk-worms and mulberry leaves embroidered on the sleeves; Robert Dudley, Earl of Leicester; Robert Devereux, Earl of Essex; and Lord Burghley.

Beyond the house stretch woodland and pleasure gardens with a lake, statuary, and a turf and brick maze.

Parham is 4 miles south-east of Pulborough, on the A283.

Penhurst *E. Sussex*
Penhurst is a piece of Elizabethan rural England that has survived into the 20th century. The small manor house, with its duck pond and farm buildings, stands by a medieval church in an unspoilt setting of meadows and trees.

The house was probably built by William Relfe, an iron-master with a forge at nearby Ashburnham.

Very few manorial groupings of such charm as that of Penhurst have survived.

Penhurst is 4 miles west of Battle, off the A269.

Penshurst Place *Kent*
In the medieval manor house of Penshurst Place was born in 1554 one of the most dazzling personalities of the Elizabethan age – Sir Philip Sidney, soldier, courtier and poet. The house has remained in the hands of the Sidney family and their descendants ever since, and contains relics both of Sir Philip and of the Queen he served.

The existence of a house at Penshurst is recorded in the Domesday Book. In the 14th century Sir John de Pulteney, a rich wool merchant, built the Great Hall which, 600 years later, still forms the south front. Two brothers of Henry V, the Dukes of Bedford and

Gloucester, added to Penshurst, and in 1552 Edward VI granted the house to his 'trustye and wellbeloved servant' Sir William Sidney, a hero of the English victory over the Scots at Flodden in 1513. He was succeeded by his son Sir Henry (1529–86), who was Queen Elizabeth's Lord Deputy of Ireland and Lord President of the Welsh Marches.

Sir Henry's first son, Philip, born at Penshurst on November 30, 1554, had an illustrious career in many fields. As a poet he wrote the masque *The Lady of the May* with which his uncle the Earl of Leicester entertained Queen Elizabeth at Wanstead in 1578. The 'Stella' of his sequence of sonnets *Astrophil and Stella* was Penelope Devereux, sister of the famous Earl of Essex.

Sidney was a man of action as well as a poet. In 1585 Elizabeth gave him a chance to see active service, appointing him Governor of Flushing in Holland. He was mortally wounded at the Battle of Zutphen in July 1586, as a result of quixotically refusing to wear his leg-armour. Sidney's death stirred the nation and inspired some 200 eulogies, the best known being that by his friend Edmund Spenser.

In the Great Hall at Penshurst is Sir Philip's helmet, carried at his funeral in 1587. The hall also contains the ancient trestle tables at which Henry VIII feasted when the house briefly belonged to the last Duke of Buckingham, and the State sword of the Earl of Leicester.

In the State Dining-Room are portraits of the Sidney family. In the Long Gallery are Queen Elizabeth's lead death mask and portraits of the Queen, Leicester, Sir Philip and Sir Henry Sidney.

The nearby village of Penshurst contains Tudor cottages, timbered and tile-hung, grouped around a courtyard named Leicester Square after the Elizabethan earl.

Penshurst Place is off the B2176. 5 miles south-west of Tonbridge.

Plymouth *Devon*

A focal point of Elizabethan seamanship lay in Plymouth. Into its great natural harbour Drake sailed in 1580, having completed the first circumnavigation of the world by an Englishman. Drake became Mayor of the town in 1582.

It was in Plymouth that the English fleet waited for the Armada in 1588; and it was from Plymouth in 1620 that the Pilgrim Fathers set sail in the *Mayflower* to build a new society in the New World. In an age of expansion, Plymouth was an expanding town, teeming and vibrant.

BARBICAN The narrow streets and thronged quays of this area were the heart of the old town, and there are many Elizabethan houses tucked away down alleys or hiding behind Georgian and 19th-century façades.

CITY MUSEUM (DRAKE CIRCUS) Local history collections are a feature of the museum; a prize exhibit in the silver collection is the Drake Cup, a silver-gilt cup and cover, together forming a globe which parts at the Equator. In 1992 it was on loan to Buckland Abbey.

ELIZABETHAN HOUSE (32 NEW STREET) The first written record of New Street was in 1584: 'Sperke's newe streate . . . paved, leading towards the new key.' 'Sperke' was John Sparke, a merchant, Mayor of Plymouth in 1583 and 1591. Between 1575 and 1600 the population of Plymouth doubled; the town was bursting at the seams.

No. 32 New Street is a typical example of the sort of houses Sparke built. The front is of moulded English oak, simply carved, between thick walls of local limestone. The interior, restored as a museum, has original features and a collection of furniture and artefacts of the period.

MERCHANT'S HOUSE (33 ST ANDREW'S STREET) The largest and finest 16th–17th-century house in Plymouth, the Merchant's House is now part of the City Museum. The first recorded owner was William Parker, who commanded the *Mary Rose* at the time of the Armada, sacked Puerto de Cavallos in 1597, and was certainly living in the house in 1608. Parker probably added the granite door frames and finely moulded timber partitions and window frames, though much of the building dates back to the early 1500s. The interior is rich in original panelling and plasterwork.

PLYMOUTH HOE Here Sir Francis Drake played his famous game of bowls before setting out to face the Spanish Armada in 1588.

Rotherfield Greys *Oxon.*

A graceful mansion and a Norman church in this quiet Oxfordshire village have associations with one of the most notable families of Elizabethan times.

GREY'S COURT Sir Francis Knollys, Elizabeth's Treasurer of the Household, was granted Grey's Court, the ancient seat of the de Grey family. The mellow brick-and-stone mansion is largely his work, though there have been 17th and 18th-century additions.

Sir Francis was one of Elizabeth's most trusted servants. His wife Catherine was a niece of Anne Boleyn, and therefore cousin to the Queen; his daughter Lettice was the wife of the Earl of Leicester, favourite of Elizabeth. Knollys was a Queen's commissioner at the trials of Mary, Queen of Scots, of Philip Howard, Earl of Arundel, and of Anthony Babington.

Sir Francis's son, Sir William Knollys, who inherited Grey's in

1596, is thought to have been the model for the pompous steward Malvolio in Shakespeare's *Twelfth Night*. Portraits of Sir Francis and Sir William, who was created Earl of Banbury in 1626, hang in the house.

CHURCH OF ST NICHOLAS The canopied marble and alabaster monument to Sir Francis Knollys and his wife was erected by William Knollys in 1605. It was repainted in its original colours in 1948.

Sir Francis lies in his Garter robes; Catherine Knollys lies beside him, and at her side is the figure of an infant girl. Round them kneel their seven daughters and seven sons. At Sir Francis's feet stands an elephant, part of the Knollys crest, and Catherine has a swan, emblem of the Carey family. The canopy is decorated with urns and cherubs and rests on six columns. On top, William Knollys and his wife kneel facing each other at a prayer desk.

Rotherfield Greys is 3 miles west of Henley-on-Thames.

Rycote Chapel *Oxon.*

As Queen, Elizabeth visited Sir Henry and Lady Norreys at their great house at Rycote six times. In 1745 the house was burned to the ground, but the chapel where the Queen worshipped still stands, together with a wing of the house.

Elizabeth knew Rycote in her youth. She stayed there on her way to Woodstock in 1554 when her host was Lord Williams of Thame. Williams's daughter Margery inherited the house in 1559, married Henry Norreys and became one of Elizabeth's closest friends and a lady-in-waiting.

In the autumn of 1592, Elizabeth and her court descended on Rycote, many of the lesser courtiers having to be accommodated in the stables.

The chapel is 15th century, built in Perpendicular style. There is a remarkable family pew, decorated with clouds and stars, which was built for the family. There is also a domed Royal pew built for Queen Elizabeth and later used by Charles I.

The famous yew tree in the churchyard is more than 26 ft in circumference.

Rycote Chapel is on the A329 near Thame, midway between the A418 and M40.

St Albans *Herts.*
CHURCH OF ST MICHAEL This ancient parish church contains a fine Elizabethan pulpit. Hexagonal in shape, and supported on a turned pillar, it is made in dark brown oak, richly carved. On the central panel of the backboard is a crowned Tudor rose.

Sir Francis Bacon, Lord Verulam and Viscount St Albans, is commemorated by a unique monument in the chancel. The alabaster statue, showing Bacon seated in a chair, was erected in 1626, soon after Bacon's death.

GORHAMBURY HOUSE In the gardens of this 18th-century house, built for the Earls of Verulam by the architect Sir Robert Taylor and completed in 1784, are the ruins of the Tudor mansion of Sir Nicholas Bacon (1509–79), Elizabeth's Lord Keeper of the Great Seal. Sir Nicholas was the father of Sir Francis Bacon, the statesman, essayist and philosopher.

The house contains portraits and books belonging to the Bacon family, whose fortunes were founded under Henry VIII and who flourished under Elizabeth.

Sherborne Castle *Dorset*
When Sir Walter Raleigh first set eyes on Sherborne Castle he fell from his horse. So, at least, it is claimed by Sir John Harington,

author of *An Apologie of Poetrie* and a godson of Queen Elizabeth.

According to Harington, Raleigh was on his way to Plymouth from London. From the high road Raleigh saw the battlements of the castle and the green meadows sloping down to the River Yeo. He was entranced. Flinging out a hand to draw the attention of his companions he startled his horse which reared and threw him. He looked on the castle, says Harington, 'as Ahab did upon Naboth's vineyard'. Within a few months Raleigh had persuaded Elizabeth to grant him a lease on Sherborne.

Released in 1592 from the Tower, where he had been imprisoned after incurring the Queen's displeasure by his secret marriage to Elizabeth Throckmorton, Raleigh took his bride to Sherborne and set about constructing a country retreat. At first he tried to convert the old castle into a comfortable home, demolishing the old curtain wall, but he soon abandoned this project. Instead he rebuilt the old Tudor hunting lodge near by.

The old castle was sacked in October 1645 during the Civil War and is now a picturesque ruin; but Raleigh's new 'Lodge' survives, with wings added. Over the centuries the lime plaster of the exterior walls has mellowed to a warm biscuit colour.

After Raleigh's execution in October 1618 the property passed to the Digby family, in whose hands it has remained to this day.

The Solarium, originally Sir Walter and Lady Raleigh's parlour, contains a fine chimney-piece, and the moulded ceiling in the Green Drawing-Room bears Raleigh's arms. One of the most interesting pictures in the Sherborne Castle collection is *The Procession of Queen Elizabeth I* by Robert Peake the

Elder. There is also a portrait of the Earl of Southampton, Shakespeare's patron.

Sherborne Castle is at Castleton, east of Sherborne.

Shipton Hall *Shropshire*
Broad gables and tall chimneys are the exterior distinguishing marks of this Elizabethan manor house, built by a local landowner, Thomas Lutwyche, in 1587. The front of the house is asymmetrical, with the porch set to one side and a curiously detached pediment 'floating' above the archway of the entrance. The house is built in the local Aymestry stone.

Though the interior furnishing is predominantly Georgian, there is much original timberwork. There is also a walled garden, with a medieval dovecote.

Shipton is 6 miles south-west of Much Wenlock, on the B4378.

Speke Hall *Merseyside*
A spectacular black-and-white half-timbered house, Speke was begun by Sir William Norris in 1490. Sir William's successors continued to enlarge and improve the house throughout the 16th century. Apart from the moat, which has disappeared, the house looks today almost exactly as it did at the end of Elizabeth's reign.

The Norrises were conservative in their taste, and ignored the Renaissance influence that was beginning to influence other Elizabethan builders. The result is a richness of patterns in the timberwork through a century of building.

The Great Hall contains a remarkable Elizabethan chimney-piece, and the plaster ceiling in the Great Parlour is particularly fine.

Speke Hall is three-quarters of a mile south-west of Liverpool airport, off the A561.

Stamford *Lincs.*

Stamford is an architectural cornucopia: there are scores of buildings listed as of historical or architectural importance within the boundaries of the original medieval walled town. Its Elizabethan associations are vivid; in 1564 Queen Elizabeth granted the Lordship and manor of Stamford to her trusted Lord Treasurer William Cecil, Lord Burghley.

BURGHLEY HOSPITAL AND ALMSHOUSES A Benedictine foundation of the 11th century, this hospital for the poor and elderly was greatly extended in the 16th century by Lord Burghley.

CHURCH OF ST MARTIN The chancel contains a grand monument to Lord Burghley, who died in 1598. On it he appears in armour and Garter robes.

See also BURGHLEY HOUSE.

Stirling Castle *Central*

Built on a rocky ridge, Stirling Castle dominates the Forth valley. For centuries it was the key to the military control of Scotland, commanding the gateway to the Highlands. In the Chapel Royal in 1543 Mary Stuart – then a nine-month-old baby – was crowned Queen of Scots.

Stonor Park *Oxon.*

In a room of the Tudor mansion at Stonor Park, the seat of the staunchly Catholic Stonor family, the Jesuit Edmund Campion secretly printed his anti-Protestant book *Decem Rationes.*

Campion, a distinguished scholar who had spoken before Elizabeth at Oxford in 1566 and enjoyed the patronage of the Earl of Leicester, was converted to Catholicism in France in 1571 and ordained a Jesuit priest in Rome in 1573. In 1580 he was sent to England to preach the Catholic cause.

On July 17, 1581 Campion was arrested at Lyford, Oxfordshire, and taken to London, to the Tower. With his arms bound, and his legs tied to his horse, he was led through the city to the boos and hisses of the mob. In his hat was stuck a paper on which was written: 'Campion, the seditious Jesuit.' Campion was hanged, drawn and quartered on December 1, 1581. He was made a saint in 1970.

Built in a grand setting in the Chiltern Hills, Stonor has a medieval core. For 800 years it has remained the property of the same family. The room in which Campion had his secret printing press can be seen, together with an exhibition dealing with the executed Jesuit's life and work.

Stonor is 5 miles north of Henley, off the B480.

Stratford-upon-Avon *Warks.*

This small market town in the heart of the English countryside was as early as 1624 a place of pilgrimage for admirers of William Shakespeare, whose plays had first been published in collected form in the First Folio in the previous year. Since then Stratford-upon-Avon, as the birthplace of England's greatest writer, has become one of the most treasured towns in the English-speaking world.

For all his success, his fame as an actor and playwright and his financial rewards from the theatre, Shakespeare remained deeply attached to his home town, visiting it constantly, investing in property, retiring and eventually dying there on April 23, 1616. Happily, much of the Stratford Shakespeare knew has been preserved.

ANNE HATHAWAY'S COTTAGE Shakespeare married Anne Hathaway in 1582. The marriage bond is dated November 28. This thatched cottage, dating in part from the 15th century, belonged to Anne's father, Richard Hathaway, a friend of Shakespeare's father. The cottage is at Shottery, about 2 miles from the centre of Stratford.

CHURCH OF THE HOLY TRINITY Here Shakespeare was baptised on April 26, 1564 – the original font has been preserved, though damaged – and buried in April 1616. On his gravestone are inscribed the famous lines:

'Good frend for Jesus sake forbeare,
To digg the dust encloased heare,
Bleste be ye man yt spares thes stones
And curst be he yt moves my bones.'

The monument by Gerard Johnson on the north wall of the chancel was erected by the Shakespeare family in 1623.

GUILD CHAPEL The room above the ancient Guildhall is the schoolroom where Shakespeare studied and acquired what his friend the poet Ben Jonson described as his 'small Latin, less Greek'.

HALL'S CROFT This beautifully preserved gabled house was the home of Shakespeare's elder daughter, Susanna, and her husband, Dr John Hall. The house contains treasures of 16th-century furniture and medical equipment.

MARY ARDEN'S HOUSE This Tudor farmhouse in the village of Wilmcote, 3 miles north-west of Stratford, was the home of Shakespeare's mother, Mary Arden.

NEW PLACE The mansion, formerly the property of Hugh Clopton, Stratford's great benefactor, was bought by Shakespeare in 1597. He at once set about restoring it. However, the building was demolished by a later owner and only the foundations remain. Next to the site is a re-creation of an Elizabethan knot garden.

Shakespeare's father, John, bought this half-timbered house for £40. Originally it was divided into two sections, one of them being used as a workshop for John Shakespeare's trade as a glovemaker and wool merchant. The interior is furnished with pieces of the period. The Birthplace Museum contains a large library and Shakespeare relics.

Temple Newsam House
W. Yorks.

Lord Darnley, who was to become the husband of Mary, Queen of Scots, was born at Temple Newsam House in 1545. The house is now a museum and art gallery, with several notable Elizabethan items.

The builder of the original house, Thomas, Lord Darcy, was beheaded in 1536 for his part in the Pilgrimage of Grace, a protest against the Dissolution of the Monasteries. Henry VIII gave the house to the Earl of Lennox, who had married the king's niece, Margaret Tudor, and it was there that their son Henry, Lord Darnley, was born. After Darnley's murder in 1567 Elizabeth confiscated the property; but James I, the son of Darnley and Mary, Queen of Scots, restored it to the Lennox family in 1603.

The house was rebuilt by the financier Sir Arthur Ingram who bought the estate in 1622.

Temple Newsam is 4 miles south-east of Leeds, off the A63.

Titchfield *Hants.*

CHURCH OF ST PETER At the Dissolution Henry VIII granted Titchfield Abbey to Sir Thomas Wriothesley (1505–50), later the 1st Earl of Southampton and Lord Chancellor. When Henry, the 2nd Earl, died in 1581 he made provision for a family monument to be raised in the South chapel.

One of the four carved alabaster figures on the side panels is the 3rd Earl of Southampton (1573–1624), Shakespeare's patron.

Traquair House *Borders*

Traquair has vivid associations with Mary, Queen of Scots. John Stuart, the second son of the 2nd Laird of Traquair, was a close friend of Mary who knighted him on her marriage to Lord Darnley in 1565. In the same year Sir John helped the queen escape from Holyrood to Dunbar after the murder of Rizzio. In August 1566 Sir John received Mary and Darnley at Traquair for a hunting expedition.

Many relics of the queen are displayed at Traquair. In the Museum Room are her rosary, crucifix and purse; the cradle in which she nursed her son, later James I of England; a silk quilt embroidered by her; and many letters bearing her signature. Above the Dining-Room door is an oak panel carved with Mary's cipher.

Traquair is south of Innerleithen, off the B709.

Trerice *Cornwall*

The Elizabethan manor house was completed by Sir John Arundell in 1573. The first Sir John Arundell (1485–1561), son of an ancient Cornish family, earned the favour of Henry VIII when in 1523 he captured a notorious Scottish pirate called Duncan Campbell, and was invited to deliver his prisoner personally to the Court. Nicknamed 'Jack of Tilbury', Arundell was Vice-Admiral of Cornwall under Edward VI, and he retained the office under Queen Mary.

The younger Sir John Arundell began building at Trerice in 1572. The entrance front is in the traditional E shape, but the elaborate gables on the east front are unique in the West Country.

The window of the Hall, which is mullioned and transomed, contains 576 panes of glass, many of them 16th century. The hall itself has a fireplace dated 1572, a minstrels' gallery, and a fine plaster ceiling. The Great Chamber has an even more elaborate ceiling, dated 1573.

Trerice is off the A3058, 3 miles south-east of Newquay.

Vyne, The *Hants.*

The Tudor manor house of brick and stone was built between 1500 and 1520 by Lord Sandys, a favourite of Henry VIII who made him a Groom of the Bedchamber in 1509, and later Lord Chamberlain. In 1535 Henry VIII visited the house with Elizabeth's mother, Anne Boleyn.

The third Lord Sandys entertained Queen Elizabeth at The Vyne in 1569. In 1601, when the Queen was staying at nearby Basing House, she lodged the French ambassador, the Duc de Biron, at The Vyne.

The Vyne is 4 miles north of Basingstoke.

Warwick *Warks.*

Henry VIII granted the first Royal Charter to 'The Burgesses of The Town of Warwick' in May 1545. Two years later John Dudley was created Earl of Warwick, but in 1553 he was executed for his part in the plot to put Lady Jane Grey on the throne. Elizabeth I restored the title to his son Ambrose, who died in 1590 and is buried in the Beauchamp Chapel in St Mary's Church. His brother Robert Dudley, Earl of Leicester, Elizabeth's favourite, lies opposite.

The affairs of Elizabethan Warwick are recorded in the 'Black Book' written by the Town Clerk, John Fisher. Fisher records the visit Elizabeth paid to Warwick in 1572. LORD LEYCESTER HOSPITAL The

Queen's favourite, Leicester, took over the 14th-century guildhall to found a hospital for veterans wounded in the Queen's wars. The façade of the Master's House is early Victorian, but the remainder of the building is original.

OKEN'S HOUSE Thomas Oken was one of Warwick's leading burgesses. His Elizabethan house is now a doll museum.

WARWICK CASTLE In the 16th century the medieval castle began to be converted from a stronghold into a mansion, and there were further extensions for a visit by Elizabeth. The castle was much added to in the late 17th century. A portrait of Queen Elizabeth by Stretes, on loan to Montacute in 1992, usually hangs over the sideboard in the Great Hall.

West Stow Hall *Suffolk*

In a room over the archway of Sir John Crofts's brick gate-house, built in the 1520s, is a rarity: a series of amusing Elizabethan wall-paintings on the theme of the Four Ages of Man. The first scene shows a young man hunting, with an inscription: *Thus do I all the day.* Next appear a young man and a young woman embracing, with the words: *Thus do I while I may.* Then there is a middle-aged man observing the lovers, with the inscription: *Thus did I when I might.* Finally there is an old man, bowed and bent, leaning on a stick, with the legend: *Good Lord, will this world last for ever.*

Sir John Crofts was Mary Tudor's Master of the Horse, and the gate-house bears her arms. The Hall itself (not open to the public) is essentially an Elizabethan mansion and, though much restored, has fine moulded ceiling beams.

West Stow is $7\frac{1}{2}$ miles north-west of Bury St Edmunds.

Wilderhope Manor *Shropshire*

Lying in a remote valley in Shropshire, Wilderhope (now a Youth Hostel) is one of the most unspoilt of Elizabethan houses. In the 19th century it became a farm-house.

Francis Smallman, of a Corvedale family, began building the house in 1584. He used the local Aymestry limestone, but the tall chimneystacks are of brick.

Inside, many of the original window frames survive but the chief feature is the plasterwork, which is abundant and elaborate. The ceiling of the parlour has a delicate pattern of intersecting star shapes; in the Hall the initials FS and ES (Francis Smallman and Ellen Smallman) are set round the rosette in the centre.

Wilderhope is $7\frac{1}{2}$ miles south-west of Much Wenlock, off the B4371.

Wilton House *Wilts.*

The original house at Wilton was Elizabethan, the home of Mary Herbert, Countess of Pembroke and one of the most cultivated women of the age. She was the sister of Sir Philip Sidney, the soldier-poet.

Mary Herbert's father, Sir Henry Sidney, was Lord President of the Welsh Marches, and she spent her childhood at Ludlow Castle with her brother Philip. In 1577 the Earl of Leicester arranged a marriage between Mary and Henry Herbert, the 2nd Earl of Pembroke.

It was at Wilton in the summer of 1580 that Sir Philip Sidney began his *Arcadia*, dedicated to Mary. Spenser, who described Mary as 'the ornament of womankind', dedicated his *Ruines of Time* to her.

Mary was herself a distinguished writer. In May 1590 she completed *A Discourse of Life and Death*, a translation of a French work by Du Plessis Mornay. Mary's praises were sung in scores of verses by the writers whom she supported, encouraged and entertained.

Mary died in September 1621 and was buried beside her husband in Salisbury Cathedral.

Something is left of Elizabethan Wilton in the central tower of the east front. The present house was built for the 4th Earl, influenced by Inigo Jones.

Wilton House is at Wilton, 3 miles west of Salisbury.

Woburn Abbey *Beds.*

Woburn was granted to John Russell by Henry VIII; in 1550 Russell was created 1st Earl of Bedford by Edward VI. The present house dates from the 17th and 18th centuries, but among its wonderful collection of art treasures is a famous portrait of Elizabeth I: the Armada Portrait.

Woburn is 9 miles north-west of Dunstable.

Wollaton Hall *Notts.*

One of the most splendid examples of Elizabethan architecture, Wollaton Hall was built for Sir Francis Willoughby by Robert Smythson between 1580 and 1588.

The extraordinary house Sir Francis built remains to impress succeeding generations. Its features include a soaring central tower-like hall and elaborate ornamentation, including Renaissance roundels and figures.

Wollaton is a departure from the normal E or H-shaped Elizabethan mansion. It is a square, two-storey building, with four corner pavilions as well as the central tower.

Inside, the main feature is the great central hall, which is over 50 ft high. The magnificent hammerbeam roof is carved and coloured to imitate stone.

Wollaton is $2\frac{1}{2}$ miles west of Nottingham. off the A609.

Acknowledgments

Artwork

The reconstructions on the cover and on pages *108–9*, *136–7*, *224–5* and *278–9* are by Ivan Lapper.

Photographs

In this list of people and organisations who kindly provided illustrations for *Elizabethan England*, the following abbreviations are used to indicate position on the page: *T* (top), *B* (bottom), *L* (left), *C* (centre), *R* (right). Work commissioned by Reader's Digest is shown in *italics*.

Page 8 Picturepoint, London **9** Bridgeman Art Library **10** Batsford **11** Reproduced by Gracious Permission of Her Majesty the Queen **12** Guildhall Library **14** BBC Hulton Picture Library **15** Public Record Office **16** National Portrait Gallery, London **18** *L* Picturepoint, London; *R* National Portrait Gallery, London **19** Pat Hodgson **20** By permission of the Governors of Christ's Hospital **21** Victoria & Albert Museum **22** National Portrait Gallery, London **23** National Portrait Gallery, London **24** Weidenfeld & Nicolson **25** BBC Hulton Picture Library **27** By courtesy of the Marquess of Salisbury **28** British Library Ms.Eger.2603 f 53 **29** *T* Vision International; *B* Ashmolean Museum **31** By courtesy of the Marquess of Salisbury **32** *TL* British Museum; *TR Penny Tweedie*; *BL* Public Record Office; *BR* National Museum of Antiquities, Scotland **33** *TL* Robert Harding Associates/Scottish National Portrait Gallery; *R* Scottish National Portrait Gallery; *CL* Tom Scott; *BL Anthony Howarth* **34/35** Bridgeman Art Library **36/37** Staatliche Kunstsammlungen, Kassel **38/39** Ashmolean Museum **39** Bridgeman Art Library **40** Bridgeman Art Library **42/43** E. T. Archive **44** E. T. Archive **45** Robert Harding Associates **46/47** Museum of London **47** Batsford **48/49** Picturepoint, London **50/51** Ashmolean Museum **50** Michael Holford **52/53** Weidenfeld & Nicolson **54** Weidenfeld & Nicolson **55** National Portrait Gallery, London **56** *L* National Portrait Gallery, London; *R* Batsford **57** National Portrait Gallery, London **58** *L* Turbeville 'Book of Hunting'; *R* By permission of His Grace the Duke of Buccleuch and Queensberry, K.T. **59** National Portrait Gallery, London **60** Richard Jemmett **61** Burrell Collection – Glasgow Museums and Art Galleries **62** *TR* Victoria & Albert Museum; *BL* Weidenfeld & Nicolson; *BR* Victoria & Albert Museum **63** *TL* Victoria & Albert Museum; *TR* Tate Gallery/Robert Harding Associates; *BL* National Trust; *BR Anthony Howarth* **64/65** National Portrait Gallery, London **67** John Freeman **68/69** Picturepoint, London **70** National Trust **71** E. T. Archive **72** BBC Hulton Picture Library **73** *T* Batsford; *B* Batsford/Bodleian Library **74** *L Drive Publications*; *R* BBC Hulton Picture Library **75** *Drive Publications* **77** Picturepoint, London **78** Museum of London **79** *L* Pat Hodgson; *R* Michael Holford **80/81** Robert Harding Associates **82** *T* Museum of London; *B* Pat Hodgson **83** Pat Hodgson **84** *Drive Publications* **85** *Philip Llewellin* **86** *TR* Bridgeman Art Library; *BL* National Trust; *BR* Bridgeman Art Library **87** *TL* Bridgeman Art Library; *TC* Museum of London; *TR* Bridgeman Art Library; *CL* George Rainbird Ltd/ Robert Harding Associates; *CR* Picturepoint, London; *BL* Museum of London; *BR* Museum of London **88/89** Weidenfeld & Nicolson/Guildhall Library **91** Weidenfeld & Nicolson **92** John Freeman **93** John Freeman **94/95** Museum of London **96** *T* Pat Hodgson; *B* Museum of London **97** Weidenfeld & Nicolson **98** *T* Mary Evans Picture Library; *B* Pat Hodgson **99** Bridgeman Art Library **100** By permission of His Grace the Duke of Buccleuch and Queensberry, K.T. **101** *T* Michael Holford; *B* Museum of London **102** Museum of London **103** BBC Hulton Picture Library **104** *T* Fotomas Index; *C* Fotomas Index; *B* BBC Hulton Picture Library **105** BBC Hulton Picture Library **110** Fotomas Index **111** Fotomas Index **112/113** Robert Harding Associates **114/115** Guildhall Library **115** Pat Hodgson **116** *T* Fotomas Index; *B* BBC Hulton Picture Library **117** *TL* Pat Hodgson; *TR* BBC Hulton Picture Library; *B* Batsford **118/119** Bridgeman Art Library **120/121** Bridgeman Art Library **122** National Trust **123** Nation Trust **124/125** Aspect **126** John Freeman **127** Bridgeman Art Library **128** E. T. Archive **129** *T* Fotomas Index *B* Pat Hodgson **130** *T* Pat Hodgson; *B* Batsford **131** Fotomas Index **132** John Freeman **133** British Library Ms.EG.1222 f.73 **138** Pat Hodgson **139** BBC Hulton Picture Library **140** *T* Pat Hodgson; *B* BBC Hulton Picture Library **141** BBC Hulton Picture Library **142** *TL* J. Whitaker/National Trust; *TR* British Museum; *BL* Fotomas Index; *BR* J. Whitaker/ National Trust **143** *T* Bodleian Library; *C* Fotomas Index; *B* National Trust **144/145** Bridgeman Art Library **147** Fotomas Index **148** Pat Hodgson **149** Fotomas Index **150** *John Bulmer* **151** British Library Ms.ROY 2a XVI f.98v **152** *T* BBC Hulton Picture Library; *B* Museum of London **153** Fotomas Index **154/155** Bridgeman Art Library **156** Edinburgh University Library **157** Fotomas Index **158** John Freeman **159** Robert Harding Associates/Rainbird **160** British Museum **161** *L* Pat Hodgson; *R* National Portrait Gallery, London **162** Batsford **163** British Library/Weidenfeld & Nicolson **164** *T* Fotomas Index; *B* Victoria & Albert Museum **165** BBC Hulton Picture Library **166** Reproduced by Gracious Permission of Her Majesty the Queen **167** John Freeman/Weidenfeld & Nicolson **168** Victoria & Albert Museum **169** Pat Hodgson **170** *L* Victoria & Albert Museum; *R* Angelo Hornak/Vision International **171** Victoria & Albert Museum/Robert Harding Associates **172** *T* British Museum; *B John Bulmer* **173** *TL* British Museum; *TC* Ulster Museum, Belfast, coins by R.A. Gardner; *C* British Museum, British Museum, British Museum, Museum of London, *B* Victoria & Albert Museum **174/175** Bridgeman Art Library **176** By permission of Lord Sackville/ Courtauld Institute **177** Fotomas Index **178** Picturepoint, London **179** Pat Hodgson **180** *T* BBC Hulton Picture Library; *B* Victoria & Albert Museum **181** Fotomas Index **182** Foxe's 'Book of Martyrs' **183** Picturepoint, London **184** National Portrait Gallery, London **185** National Portrait Gallery, London **186** Batsford **187** *T* Museum of London; *B* Country Life **188** British Library/Weidenfeld & Nicolson **189** BBC Hulton Picture Library **190** Society of Antiquaries **191** Fotomas Index **192** Fotomas Index **194** Pat Hodgson **195** Bridgeman Art Library **196** Pat Hodgson **197** *T* BBC Hulton Picture Library; *B* Fotomas Index **198** *T* Museum of London; *B* Robert Harding Associates **199** *TL* Picturepoint, London; *TR* Batsford; *C* BBC Hulton Picture Library; *B* BBC Hulton Picture Library **200/201** Bridgeman Art Library **203** British Library Ms Add 5415A f 15v 16r/Weidenfeld & Nicolson **204** National Maritime Museum, Greenwich **204/205** Michael Holford **206** City Museum & Art Gallery, Bristol/Robert Harding Associates **208** *Eileen Tweedie* **209** National Portrait Gallery, London, **210** Fotomas Index **211** British Library Ms Eg 2579/ Map/Weidenfeld & Nicolson **212** *Penny Tweedie* **214** *T* Victoria & Albert Museum; *B* Victoria & Albert Museum/ Map/Weidenfeld & Nicolson **215** National Portrait Gallery, London **216** National Maritime Museum, Greenwich/ Robert Harding Associates **217** British Museum **218** National Portrait Gallery, London **219** Robert H. and Margaret C. Power Collections **220** British Museum/ Weidenfeld & Nicolson **221** Victoria & Albert Museum **226** National Portrait Gallery, London **227** BBC Hulton Picture Library **228** British Museum **229** British Museum **230** *T* British Library/Weidenfeld & Nicolson; *B* Fotomas Index **231** Fotomas Index **232** *T* Bodleian Library; *B* British Museum **233** *T* British Museum/ Weidenfeld & Nicolson; *B* National Portrait Gallery, London **234** *T* BBC Hulton Picture Library; *B* By permission of the Master & Fellows, Magdelene College, Cambridge **235** *TR* Robert Harding Associates; *C* National Maritime Museum, Greenwich, National Maritime Museum, Greenwich; *B* Tiroler Landes Museum Ferdinandeum **236/237** Bibliotheque Nationale, Paris **239** Bridgeman Art Library **240** E.T. Archive **241** Pat Hodgson **242** Pat Hodgson **243** *T* Fotomas Index; *B* National Maritime Museum, Greenwich **244** Folger Shakespeare Library, Washington/Robert Harding Associates **245** *L* National Maritime Museum, Greenwich; *R* Fotomas Index **246** National Maritime Museum, Greenwich **247** Fotomas Index **248** *L* By permission of the Earl of Verulam/Robert Harding Associates; *R* Pat Hodgson **249** *T* Museum of London, Property of the Worshipful Company of Barbers; *B* Fotomas Index **250** Fotomas Index **251** National Maritime Museum, Greenwich **252** Bodleian Library **253** *T* Victoria & Albert Museum; *B* Bridgeman Art Library **254** British Museum/Weidenfeld & Nicolson **255** By permission of His Grace the Duke of Buccleuch and Queensberry K.T./Robert Harding Associates **256** BBC Hulton Picture Library **257** *T* Victoria & Albert Museum; *B* British Library **258** BBC Hulton Picture Library **259** Fotomas Index **261** Weidenfeld & Nicolson **262** *TR* British Tourist Authority; *CR* Museum of London; *BL* National Trust **263** *TL* Michael Holford; *TR* Jeremy Whitaker; *C* Michael Holford; *B* Michael Holford **264/265** British Library Ms Add 35324f 37v **267** By permission of Lord Methuen/Weidenfeld & Nicolson **268** *Drive Publications* **269** National Portrait Gallery, London **270** Weidenfeld & Nicolson/John Webb Photo **271** Batsford **272/273** Weidenfeld & Nicolson/British Museum **274** Fotomas Index **275** By permission of His Grace the Duke of Buccleuch and Queensberry K.T. **280** Royal Academy of Arts **281** By courtesy of the Marquess of Salisbury **282** *T* Museum of London; *B* Victoria & Albert Museum **283** BBC Hulton Picture Library **284/285** Michael Holford/British Museum **286** Robert Harding Associates/Hatfield House **287** British Museum **288/289** Robert Harding Associates/Hatfield House **290** A. F. Kersting **291** National Portrait Gallery, London.

The publishers also acknowledge their indebtedness to the following books and journals which were consulted for reference or as the source of quotations:

All the Queen's Men by Neville Williams (Weidenfeld & Nicolson); *Annals of Queen Elizabeth* by William Camden, ed. Wallace MacCaffery (University of Chicago); 'The Coronation of Queen Elizabeth I' by Neville Williams: *Quarterly Review* 597 (1953); *The Cult of Elizabeth* by Roy Strong (Thames & Hudson); *Elizabeth I* by Neville Williams (Weidenfeld & Nicolson); *Elizabeth I – A Study in Power and Intellect* by Paul Johnson (Weidenfeld & Nicolson); *Elizabeth, Queen of England* by Neville Williams (Weidenfeld & Nicolson); *Elizabeth R* by Roy Strong and Julia Trevelyan Oman (Secker & Warburg); *Elizabeth the Great* by Elizabeth Jenkins (Gollancz); *Elizabethan England* by A. H. Dodd (Batsford); *Elizabethan Government and Society* ed. Bindoff, Hurstfield & Williams (Athlone Press); *The Elizabethan Home* ed. M. St. Clare Byrne (Methuen); *The Elizabethan Renaissance: The Cultural Achievement* by A. L. Rowse (Macmillan); *The Elizabethan Renaissance: The Life of the Society* by A. L. Rowse (Macmillan); *The Elizabethans* by Allardyce Nicoll (Cambridge); *England and the Catholic Church under Queen Elizabeth* by A. O. Meyer (Routledge & Kegan Paul); *The England of Elizabeth* by A. L. Rowse (Macmillan); *Essays in Elizabethan History* by J. E. Neale (Cape); *The Expansion of Elizabethan England* by A. L. Rowse (Macmillan); *Palaces and Progresses of Elizabeth I* by Ian Dunlop (Cape); *Queen Elizabeth I* by J. E. Neale (Cape); *The Quest for Nonsuch* by J. Dent (Hutchinson); *Religion and the Decline of Magic* by Keith Thomas (Weidenfeld & Nicolson); *Robert, Earl of Essex: An Elizabethan Icarus* by Robert Lacey (Weidenfeld & Nicolson); *The Sea Dogs* by Neville Williams (Weidenfeld & Nicolson); *Sir Francis Drake* by George Thomson (Secker & Warburg); *Sir Walter Raleigh* by Robert Lacey (Weidenfeld & Nicolson); *Survey of London* by John Stow (J. M. Dent); *Tudor England* by S. T. Bindoff (Penguin).

40–048–3